E/2003/70/Rev.1
ST/ESA/283

DEPARTMENT OF ECONOMIC AND SOCIAL AFFAIRS

WORLD ECONOMIC AND SOCIAL SURVEY 2003

TRENDS AND POLICIES IN THE WORLD ECONOMY

UNITED NATIONS • NEW YORK, 2003

NOTE

Symbols of United Nations documents are composed of capital letters combined with figures.

E/2003/70/Rev.1
ST/ESA/283
ISBN 92-1-109143-8

PREFACE

In 2002, the world economy did not recover from its slowdown of the previous year, and exhibited another weak performance. Unemployment increased in many countries. International trade lacked dynamism. Capital flows to developing countries declined owing to the difficult economic and political environment that characterized much of the year and that persisted into early 2003. As part one of the World Economic and Social Survey 2003 shows, the world economy remains some distance away from achieving the fast and sustained economic growth needed to confront poverty and other challenges.

Part two of the Survey examines the effects on poverty of growth-enhancing economic policies. When Governments draw up fiscal and monetary policies, or seek to enhance trade and agricultural productivity, or, in the case of a number of countries, make the transition from a planned economy to the market, they should carefully assess the effects of these policies on the poor—especially in light of the commitment they have made to reduce, by the year 2015, the proportion of people living on less than a dollar a day and the proportion of those who suffer from hunger. The Survey argues that while long-term economic growth is a powerful force behind poverty reduction, it is necessary and possible to tailor policies in order to achieve even greater reductions.

The global target of the Millennium Development Goal for the eradication of poverty is bold but achievable. At the global level, many millions of people have been rescued from poverty, in particular because of progress in the world's most populous countries, China and India. However, the results there tend to obscure setbacks or stagnation elsewhere—for example, in many of the least developed countries, particularly in Africa, where the number of poor people is expected to rise. Governments therefore need to pursue the reforms that will ensure sustainable growth, and the international community must provide the assistance that can enable these policies to succeed.

Indeed, in a world where economies are increasingly more integrated, the importance of international cooperation cannot be overemphasized. The international community has forged consensus on development priorities and actions, as defined in the outcomes of the meetings in Doha, Monterrey, Mexico, and Johannesburg, South Africa, and has pledged to move forward on the basis of shared responsibilities and mutual commitments. This Survey is intended not just as a source of information and analysis, but also as a spur to action. I commend it to the widest possible audience.

KOFI A. ANNAN
Secretary-General

FOREWORD

After being delayed through increasing geopolitical tensions and other economic uncertainties, faster economic growth is expected to return to the world economy in the second half of 2003. Some signs have been already evident in the United States of America, a country that once again will be instrumental in launching the global recovery. Nonetheless, the sustainability of the recovery will depend upon how fast the positive impulses that originated in the United States are spread via trade and investment throughout the world and are picked up and maintained by the other economies. Part one of the **World Economic and Social Survey 2003** examines the factors that have shaped the recent economic performance of the global economy and analyses the forces that will likely determine its course in the near term.

The negative effects of the past boom in equity markets and capital spending continued to constrain economic activity in 2002 and early 2003, as overcapacity in several sectors discouraged new investment while growing unemployment constrained consumption. Increasing uncertainty brought about by geopolitical tensions and corporate governance failures compounded the problem. Sluggish global economic growth, with its accompanying weak trade and reduced capital flows, resulted in depressed commodity prices and fewer resources for developing countries. Growth suffered as a result, particularly in those developing countries that were also facing constraints on adopting counter-cyclical policies.

The invasion of Iraq took a heavy toll on human life and economic activity in the region. Another non-economic shock, a severe and highly contagious respiratory disease (severe acute respiratory syndrome (SARS)), clouded economic prospects in several countries in early 2003 but appears now to have been contained. Additionally, several positive factors remain in place to facilitate a recovery. Macroeconomic policy is supportive in several countries and interest rates continue to be low in many developed countries while cyclical inventory adjustment will also contribute to recovery.

It is likely, however, that the recovery's strength will not be as pronounced as in past cyclical upturns. The increase in longer-term unemployment, for instance, will continue to contain demand for some time. Furthermore, the depreciation of the United States dollar will moderate import demand by the United States, thus weakening a powerful stimulus to the world economy. Finally, this short-term economic outlook is surrounded by a number of uncertainties and risks, which are discussed further in part one of the *Survey*.

Part two of the *Survey* examines the relationships between recent economic policies and poverty reduction. The commitment by Member States to the achievement of the Millennium Development Goals has put poverty reduction at the top of the global agenda. Millennium Development Goal 1 is for a reduction in absolute poverty, but there is still widespread poverty throughout the developing countries and in some of the transition economies and still considerable pockets of poverty even in the richest of the developed countries. Thus, all groups of countries are trying to devise policies to eradicate poverty.

Sustained economic growth is an effective means to reduce poverty. Historical experience has shown that growth has always lifted a number of people out of poverty. Often the income distribution within a country has worsened while growth has accelerated, but it is unknown for the poor to lose ground in absolute (as compared with relative) terms during a period of long-term growth. As their incomes expand, the rich will always demand better goods and services from the poor and will have the ability to pay for them. The lifting of millions of human beings out of absolute poverty in China and India since their pro-growth and market-friendly reforms raised their growth rates has been one of the most significant and encouraging developments in the global economy at the beginning of the new millennium. It is to be hoped that their success will be emulated in other regions of the world where rapid growth has not yet been achieved.

The *Survey* looks at policies that countries adopt to promote growth—fiscal and monetary policies, trade and agricultural policies and the replacement of central planning by a market-based economy. It asks whether and how they can be attuned and, where necessary, complemented in order to achieve even greater reductions in poverty. The renewed national and international concern regarding poverty has led to the collection of much better data and to greater efforts to listen to the voices of the poor which will help policy makers in their task. Poverty Reduction Strategy Papers are now required for all World Bank and International Monetary Fund lending to low-income countries.

Chapter IV sets the stage for the subsequent discussion by examining in depth the growth-poverty nexus. While growth benefits the poor in income terms, periods of growth have not always seen improvements in other indicators of poverty, such as health and **educational achievements**. Moreover, in the short term, economic growth might affect some groups adversely. The analysis of a policy's effects on poverty cannot be unidimensional and confined to a simple headcount. It must address such matters as the time dimension and also the many different groups that can be affected, including women and vulnerable minorities, regions within a country, and urban and rural dwellers.

Chapter V looks at how monetary and fiscal policy, by achieving macroeconomic stability, assist in ensuring growth and poverty reduction. However, stability is particularly important, as periods of stop-go can be harmful to the poor who do not have the cushions to protect themselves during a downturn. For this reason, during economic expansion and prosperity, it would be wise for Governments to put in place those social protection schemes that will be needed if and when the economy falters. Many programmes, though, are designed to reach those in the formal sector, which leaves the informal sector unprotected and unattended after being hit by recession. Governments should, then, explore other forms of social assistance, based on grass-roots involvement, that reach the poor in the informal sector.

The effects of trade liberalization on the poor are examined in chapter VI. Trade reform is normally not undertaken with any specific intention of benefiting the poor. Rather, by expanding the choice of goods available to all consumers and increasing the competition between domestic and foreign suppliers, trade liberalization should benefit the poor by making their limited budgets stretch further. Trade liberalization can also spur economic dynamism and growth and, as growth reduces poverty, lead to a reduction in poverty. It is on the demand for labour that much concern is concentrated—concern that trade liberalization would displace the poor employed in domestic industries that cannot compete with imports, or that the need to attract foreign direct investment would induce countries to lower their labour standards. The *Survey* examines these possible negative effects of liberalization, and argues that, where necessary, these concerns can be addressed by specific policy interventions. They do not detract from the overall efficacy of trade and investment liberalization in helping everyone, including the poor.

Another area where liberalization has been pursued has been in agriculture, which is analysed in chapter VII. As with trade, the basic rationale of market liberalization is to make available to consumers a wider variety of goods at cheaper prices. This should benefit the poor as consumers of food. However, the rural poor are also producers of foodstuffs and this aspect must be taken into account in any programme of reform. In many cases, corrective measures will have to be taken as reforms are implemented. Market-based land reform, where a willing seller sells to a willing buyer, is another policy now being increasingly pursued. The chapter argues that this can lead to greater economic efficiency and more equitable patterns in rural growth.

The last chapter reviews the impact on poverty of the change from a centrally planned system to a market system. In the economies in transition, this could be brought about only through an initial recession—whose length and depth varied widely across countries—as industries that had been overmanned or otherwise not viable in a market economy were forced to shed labour or to close down. As social benefits were often provided by the place of work, those who lost their jobs were hit especially hard, through losing both their income and their social protection. What is now increasingly apparent in the transition economies is that, although the return to economic growth will lift out of poverty those whose situation was caused by their losing their jobs, there is still a large class of the chronically poor who will not benefit so easily from renewed growth. Carefully targeted interventions are necessary to address the causes of their poverty.

Part two of the *Survey*, then, presents a nuanced picture of the possibilities of reducing poverty. It balances the optimistic assessment that the Millennium Development Goal is achievable at the global level, with the realization that, unless strong measures are taken nationally and internationally, many countries will fail to reduce the number of the absolute poor and many regions and groups of people will not escape avoidable poverty. These strong measures do not imply an abandonment of those macroeconomic policies that have been seen to result in sustainable economic growth, but rather their refinement and the enactment of complementary policies to ensure that the resulting economic growth will bring about an even greater reduction in poverty.

Nitin Desai

Nitin Desai
Under-Secretary-General
for Economic and Social Affairs

CONTENTS

PART ONE. STATE OF THE WORLD ECONOMY

ANNEX

BOXES

Page

FIGURES

TABLES

Page

EXPLANATORY NOTES

The following symbols have been used in the tables throughout the report:

.. **Two dots** indicate that data are not available or are not separately reported.

— **A dash** indicates that the amount is nil or negligible.

- **A hyphen (-)** indicates that the item is not applicable.

- **A minus sign (-)** indicates deficit or decrease, except as indicated.

. **A full stop (.)** is used to indicate decimals.

/ **A slash (/)** between years indicates a crop year or financial year, for example, 1990/91.

- **Use of a hyphen (-)** between years, for example, 1990-1991, signifies the full period involved, including the beginning and end years.

Reference to "tons" indicates metric tons and to **"dollars" ($)** United States dollars, unless otherwise stated.

Annual rates of growth or change, unless otherwise stated, refer to annual compound rates.

In most cases, the growth rate forecasts for 2003 and 2004 are rounded to the nearest quarter of a percentage point.

Details and percentages in tables do not necessarily add to totals, because of rounding.

The following abbreviations have been used:

AGOA	African Growth and Opportunity Act (United States)
AIDS	acquired immunodeficiency syndrome
APEC	Asia-Pacific Economic Cooperation
ASEAN	Association of Southeast Asian Nations
bpd	barrels per day
bps	basis points
CAC	collective action clause
CACM	Central American Common Market
CAP	Common Agricultural Policy (EU)

CCFF	Compensatory and Contingency Financing Facility (IMF)
CDI	Commitment to Development Index
CEFTA	Central European Free Trade Agreement
CFA	Communauté financière africaine
CFF	Compensatory Financing Facility (IMF)
CIS	Commonwealth of Independent States
COMTRADE	United Nations External Trade Statistics Database
DAC	Development Assistance Committee (of OECD)
EAP	Enhanced Access Policy (IMF)
EBRD	European Bank for Reconstruction and Development
ECA	Economic Commission for Africa
ECB	European Central Bank
ECE	Economic Commission for Europe
ECLAC	Economic Commission for Latin America and the Caribbean
EFF	Extended Fund Facility (IMF)
EMBI+	Emerging Markets Bond Index Plus
EMU	European Economic and Monetary Union
EPZ	export processing zone
ESAF	Enhanced Structural Adjustment Facility (IMF)
ESCAP	Economic and Social Commission for Asia and the Pacific
EU	European Union
EURIBOR	Euro Interbank Offered Rate
FDI	foreign direct investment
f.o.b.	free on board
FTAA	Free Trade Area of the Americas
GATT	General Agreement on Tariffs and Trade
GDP	gross domestic product
GNI	gross national income
GNP	gross national product
GSP	Generalized System of Preferences
GSTP	Global System of Trade Preferences among Developing Countries
GWP	gross world product
HICP	Harmonized Index of Consumer Prices
HIPC	heavily indebted poor countries
HIV	human immunodeficiency virus
IADB	Inter-American Development Bank
IBRD	International Bank for Reconstruction and Development
ICO	International Coffee Organization

ICP	International Comparison Programme
ICT	information and communication technologies
ICTSD	International Centre for Trade and Sustainable Development
IDA	International Development Association
IEA	International Energy Agency
IFAD	International Fund for Agricultural Development
IFC	International Finance Corporation
IFI	international financial institution
IMF	International Monetary Fund
INTRASTAT	system of data collection for intra-EU trade
ITRO	International Tripartite Rubber Organisation
LIBOR	London Interbank Offered Rate
mbd	millions of barrels per day
MERCOSUR	Mercado Común del Sur (Southern Common Market)
NAFTA	North American Free Trade Agreement
NATO	North Atlantic Treaty Organization
NBER	National Bureau of Economic Research (Cambridge, Massachusetts)
NEPAD	New Partnership for Africa's Development
NIPA	National Income and Product Accounts
NPL	non-performing loan
NPV	net present value
ODA	official development assistance
OECD	Organisation for Economic Cooperation and Development
OPEC	Organization of the Petroleum Exporting Countries
pb	per barrel
ppp	purchasing power parity
PRGF	Poverty Reduction and Growth Facility (IMF)
Project LINK	international collaborative research group for econometric modelling, coordinated jointly by the Economic Monitoring and Assessment Unit of the United Nations Secretariat, and the University of Toronto
PRSP	Poverty Reduction Strategy Paper (IMF and World Bank)
R&D	research and development
RTA	regional trade agreement
SADC	Southern African Development Community
SAF	Structural Adjustment Facility (IMF)
SARS	severe acute respiratory syndrome
SDRs	special drawing rights (IMF)
SDT	special and differential treatment
SFF	Supplementary Financing Facility (IMF)
SITC	Standard International Trade Classification
SMEs	small and medium-sized enterprises
SRF	Supplemental Reserve Facility (IMF)
STF	Systemic Transformation Facility (IMF)
TRIPs	trade-related intellectual property rights
UNAIDS	Joint United Nations Programme on Human Immunodeficiency Virus/Acquired Immunodeficiency Syndrome (HIV/AIDS)
UNCTAD	United Nations Conference on Trade and Development
UN/DESA	Department of Economic and Social Affairs of the United Nations Secretariat
UNU	United Nations University
VAT	value-added tax
WIDER	World Institute for Development Economics Research

The designations employed and the presentation of the material in this publication do not imply the expression of any opinion whatsoever on the part of the United Nations Secretariat concerning the legal status of any country, territory, city or area or of its authorities, or concerning the delimitation of its frontiers or boundaries.

The term "country" as used in the text of this report also refers, as appropriate, to territories or areas.

For analytical purposes, the following country groupings and subgroupings have been used:[a]

Developed economies (developed market economies):

Europe, excluding the European transition economies
Canada and the United States of America
Japan, Australia and New Zealand.

Major developed economies (the Group of Seven):

Canada, France, Germany, Italy, Japan, United Kingdom of Great Britain and Northern Ireland, United States of America.

European Union:

Austria, Belgium, Denmark, Finland, France, Germany, Greece, Ireland, Italy, Luxembourg, Netherlands, Portugal, Spain, Sweden, United Kingdom of Great Britain and Northern Ireland.

Economies in transition:

Central and Eastern European transition economies (CEETEs, sometimes contracted to "Eastern Europe"):

Albania, Bulgaria, Czech Republic, Hungary, Poland, Romania, Slovakia and successor States of the Socialist Federal Republic of Yugoslavia, namely, Bosnia and Herzegovina, Croatia, Slovenia, the former Yugoslav Republic of Macedonia, Yugoslavia.[b]

Baltic States

Estonia, Latvia and Lithuania.

Commonwealth of Independent States (CIS)

Armenia, Azerbaijan, Belarus, Georgia, Kazakhstan, Kyrgyzstan, Republic of Moldova, Russian Federation, Tajikistan, Turkmenistan, Ukraine, Uzbekistan.

Developing economies:

Africa

Asia and the Pacific (excluding Japan, Australia, New Zealand and the member States of CIS in Asia)

Latin America and the Caribbean.

Subgroupings of Asia and the Pacific:

Western Asia plus Islamic Republic of Iran (commonly contracted to "Western Asia"):

Bahrain, Cyprus, Iran (Islamic Republic of), Iraq, Israel, Jordan, Kuwait, Lebanon, Oman, Qatar, Saudi Arabia, Syrian Arab Republic, Turkey, United Arab Emirates, Yemen.

a Names and composition of geographical areas follow those of "Standard country or area codes for statistical use" (ST/ESA/STAT/SER.M/49/Rev.3), with one exception, namely, Western Asia, which in the *Survey* includes the Islamic Republic of Iran (owing to the large role of the petroleum sector in its economy) and excludes the transition economies of the region. Also, "Eastern Europe", as used in this *Survey*, is a contraction of "Central and Eastern Europe"; thus the composition of the region designated by the term differs from that of the strictly geographical grouping.

b As of 4 February 2003, the official name of "Federal Republic of Yugoslavia" has been changed to "Serbia and Montenegro".

Eastern and Southern Asia:

All other developing economies in Asia and the Pacific (including China, unless listed separately). This group has in some cases been subdivided into:

China

South Asia: Bangladesh, India, Nepal, Pakistan, Sri Lanka

East Asia: all other developing economies in Asia and the Pacific.

Subgrouping of Africa:

Sub-Saharan Africa, excluding Nigeria and South Africa (commonly contracted to "sub-Saharan Africa"):

All of Africa except Algeria, Egypt, Libyan Arab Jamahiriya, Morocco, Nigeria, South Africa, Tunisia.

For particular analyses, developing countries have been subdivided into the following groups:

Net-creditor countries:

Brunei Darussalam, Kuwait, Libyan Arab Jamahiriya, Oman, Qatar, Saudi Arabia, Singapore, Taiwan Province of China, United Arab Emirates.

Net-debtor countries:

All other developing countries.

Fuel-exporting countries:

Algeria, Angola, Bahrain, Bolivia, Brunei Darussalam, Cameroon, Colombia, Congo, Ecuador, Egypt, Gabon, Indonesia, Iran (Islamic Republic of), Iraq, Kuwait, Libyan Arab Jamahiriya, Mexico, Nigeria, Oman, Qatar, Saudi Arabia, Syrian Arab Republic, Trinidad and Tobago, United Arab Emirates, Venezuela, Viet Nam.

Fuel-importing countries:

All other developing countries.

Least developed countries:

Afghanistan, Angola, Bangladesh, Benin, Bhutan, Burkina Faso, Burundi, Cambodia, Cape Verde, Central African Republic, Chad, Comoros, Democratic Republic of the Congo (formerly Zaire), Djibouti, Equatorial Guinea, Eritrea, Ethiopia, Gambia, Guinea, Guinea-Bissau, Haiti, Kiribati, Lao People's Democratic Republic, Lesotho, Liberia, Madagascar, Malawi, Maldives, Mali, Mauritania, Mozambique, Myanmar, Nepal, Niger, Rwanda, Samoa, Sao Tome and Principe, Senegal, Sierra Leone, Solomon Islands, Somalia, Sudan, Togo, Tuvalu, Uganda, United Republic of Tanzania, Vanuatu, Yemen, Zambia.

The designation of country groups in the text and the tables is intended solely for statistical or analytical convenience and does not necessarily express a judgement about the stage reached by a particular country or area in the development process.

STATE
OF THE
WORLD
ECONOMY

I THE WORLD ECONOMY IN 2003

The world economy has not yet recovered from its slowdown in 2001. Gross world product (GWP) increased by less than 2 per cent in 2002, marking a second consecutive year of growth substantially below potential. China and India, together with a number of economies in transition, were notable exceptions to the sub-par performance that characterized the majority of the world's economies. More generally, as in 2001, a substantial number of developing countries, as well as a few developed countries and economies in transition, experienced a decline in output per capita. Overall, the first few years of the new millennium have been a development disappointment for the majority of developing countries and an absolute setback for a number of them.

A global recovery is now forecast for the second half of 2003, with GWP expected to increase by 2 per cent for the year as a whole, accelerating to slightly above 3 per cent for 2004. The developed countries, most notably the United States of America, are expected to lead the recovery and to provide a stimulus to the rest of the world. However, world trade and international financial flows will continue to be sluggish by the standards of the 1990s, with exports growing by less than 4 per cent in 2003. Moreover, the stimulus provided by the United States will be reduced for many countries if the recent depreciation of the dollar against their currencies persists. Under these circumstances, few developing countries are expected to return to their desirable longer-term rates of growth before the end of 2004. The economies in transition, in contrast, have been relatively resilient in the face of this slowdown and are expected to remain so.

The world economy was beset by heightened geopolitical uncertainties in late 2002 and early 2003. Such factors continue to pose a downside risk to global economic growth, but this risk diminished substantially in the second quarter of 2003. A new non-economic shock—severe acute respiratory syndrome (SARS)—jolted economic activity in some countries in early 2003 but appears to have been largely contained. On the other hand, there remain some well-identified economic risks that could pose a threat to short-term global growth. The most important is linked to the nature of the inevitable adjustment of the United States external deficit, a process that appears to have started with the depreciation of the dollar. A second, related challenge is the possibility of deflation in a growing number of countries. In addressing these immediate threats, policy makers should not neglect the agenda that they have established to address longer-term global development issues.

DELAYED RECOVERY

It was expected that a recovery from the global economic slowdown of 2001 would begin in the United States in the second half of 2002 and gradually accelerate and spread throughout the world economy. There was a tentative recovery in 2002, but it quickly faded, largely because of the geopolitical uncertainties associated with the looming confrontation with Iraq.

The heightened geopolitical uncertainties and perceived risks that arose before the invasion of Iraq permeated the world economy through a number of channels. The fear that conflict might disrupt oil supplies raised the prices of oil far higher than warranted by economic fundamentals; higher oil prices were themselves a global economic shock that dampened aggregate demand and imposed additional price pressures in oil-importing countries. Global political tensions caused most equity markets to plummet, aggravating the global asset price deflation that had been in effect since 2000. In several countries, consumer and business confidence fell to their lowest levels in a decade. Business capital spending declined in many developed economies. Economically, the overall effect of the stand-off with Iraq was reduced activity in late 2002 and early 2003, with the setback being most pronounced in the developed countries (see table I.1). Instead of recovering as anticipated, growth in these countries in the first quarter of 2003 was generally lower than a year earlier.

With the exception of Western Asia, the developing countries and economies in transition were less directly affected by the geopolitical uncertainties surrounding the issue of Iraq. Nevertheless, indirectly, the delayed recovery in the developed countries itself had negative consequences. In some cases, most notably in Latin America, these were aggravated by domestic difficulties. To a greater extent, however, domestic economic circumstances in developing countries and particularly in the economies in transition served as a buffer against the weak external environment. China and India offered the most pronounced examples of this but most of the economies in transition also demonstrated an important degree of domestically led growth. To a lesser extent, sub-Saharan Africa displayed similar signs of resilience, although growth remained modest.

The invasion of Iraq took a heavy toll on human life and economic activity in the region. Nevertheless, the military action was briefer, less costly in human life, less extensive and less disruptive of global economic activity than had been feared, with the result that several of the earlier negative manifestations of the previous geopolitical uncertainty were quickly and measurably reduced. Oil prices retreated and are expected to fall further as global oil production recovers, with beneficial effects on global growth and on inflationary pressure in oil-importing countries. Equity prices rebounded in the post-invasion period, reflecting and contributing to increased optimism regarding economic prospects. There was also a post-conflict recovery in the indices of both consumer and business confidence. Most of the negative consequences of the earlier geopolitical uncertainties are expected to dissipate by the third quarter of 2003.

In addition, a number of the positive factors that were expected to prompt a recovery in 2002 remain in effect. The most important are the continuing stimulative effects of macroeconomic policy. Policy interest rates in the developed

Table I.1.
GROWTH OF WORLD OUTPUT AND TRADE, 1994-2004

Annual percentage change											
	1994	1995	1996	1997	1998	1999	2000	2001	2002[a]	2003[b]	2004[b]
World output[c]	3.1	2.8	3.2	3.5	2.2	2.9	4.0	1.2	1.8	2	3
of which:											
Developed economies	2.9	2.4	2.7	3.0	2.5	2.7	3.5	0.9	1.4	1¾	2½
North America	4.1	2.7	3.4	4.4	4.2	4.1	3.8	0.3	2.5	2½	4
Western Europe	2.7	2.3	1.6	2.5	2.8	2.7	3.3	1.5	1.0	1¼	2¼
Asia and Oceania[d]	1.3	2.0	3.5	1.9	-0.7	0.5	3.2	0.6	0.5	1	1
Economies in transition	-7.2	-0.6	-0.1	2.4	-0.8	3.4	6.7	4.4	3.8	4	4
Central and Eastern Europe	4.0	5.7	4.1	3.3	2.6	1.4	3.9	2.7	2.6	3¼	3¾
Baltic States	-4.7	2.2	4.2	8.4	5.8	-0.2	5.5	6.7	6.3	5½	5¾
Commonwealth of Independent States	-13.7	-5.1	-3.6	1.4	-4.0	5.5	9.3	5.7	4.7	4½	4¼
Developing economies	5.6	5.0	5.7	5.4	1.6	3.5	5.8	2.1	3.2	3½	5
Africa	2.5	2.7	5.2	3.0	3.0	2.9	3.1	3.3	2.9	3¼	4
Eastern and Southern Asia	8.4	8.1	7.3	6.0	0.5	6.3	7.1	3.7	5.7	5¼	6
Western Asia	-0.8	4.0	4.6	5.5	4.1	0.7	6.4	-1.2	2.0	1¼	3¾
Latin America and the Caribbean	5.3	1.4	3.7	5.2	2.0	0.4	3.9	0.3	-0.8	2	3¾
World trade	10.5	8.6	5.5	9.2	3.3	5.2	10.5	-0.9	1.8	4	7
Memorandum item:											
World output growth with PPP-based weights[e]	3.5	3.4	3.8	4.1	2.5	3.4	4.7	2.1	2.8	3	4

Source: Department of Economic and Social Affairs of the United Nations Secretariat (UN/DESA).

[a] Partly estimated.
[b] Forecasts, based in part on Project LINK, an international collaborative research group for econometric modelling, coordinated jointly by the Development Policy Analysis Division of the United Nations Secretariat, and the University of Toronto.
[c] Calculated as a weighted average of individual country growth rates of gross domestic product (GDP), where weights are based on GDP in 1995 prices and exchange rates.
[d] Japan, Australia and New Zealand.
[e] Employing an alternative scheme for weighting national growth rates of GDP, based on purchasing power parity (PPP) conversions of national currency GDP into international dollars (see introduction to annex: statistical tables).

countries continue to be low, with some limited room for further loosening in some cases. Most developed countries are also benefiting from fiscal stimuli, with further fiscal relaxation already promised in some countries. Coupled with the wealth effects of a surge in house prices in some developed countries, these two policy stimuli should reinvigorate consumer demand during 2003. Cyclical inventory replenishment will also provide a boost, possibly more substantial than previously anticipated because it has been delayed. Excess capacity in the information and communication technologies (ICT) sector, which was previously a major disincentive to investment, is also being reduced with the passage of time, particularly with the more rapid rate of obsolescence that now characterizes the sector. These underlying cyclical factors, reinforced by the positive developments since the end of the conflict in Iraq, augur well for a recovery in the second half of 2003.

At the same time, a number of factors will dampen the speed of the recovery. In particular, the extension of the period of below-average growth has aggravated some earlier weaknesses. For example, the further increase in unemployment, particularly, the increase in longer-term unemployment, is likely to constrain the growth of consumer demand. Similarly, the hostile international political environment had a particularly adverse effect on some specific sectors, notably international tourism and airlines, which had not recovered from the fallout of the terrorist attacks of 11 September 2001. Some of these sectors are not expected to recover fully for some time; meanwhile, their weakened positions, including bankruptcies, are likely to have negative effects on growth more generally. These negative factors are likely to reduce the acceleration in growth to levels below those usually seen in cyclical upturns.

Among the developed countries, the United States was the most adversely affected by the heightened geopolitical uncertainties and, correspondingly, is benefiting the most from the return to normalcy. As in 2002, therefore, the United States is expected to lead the global economic recovery. No other major economy appears to be in a position to assume this role in the near future. Japan, for example, continues to face difficulties in extricating itself from its slow growth path while Germany appears to have entered a recession in early 2003. Most countries are explicitly looking for improved growth in the United States to act as a catalyst in revitalizing their own economies.

Recovery in the United States is expected to materialize in the second half of 2003 and to provide a stimulus to growth elsewhere. The depreciation of the dollar in early 2003, if sustained, will reinforce this recovery in the United States but will reduce the extent of the stimulus that United States growth provides to the rest of the world. Nevertheless, there will be an acceleration in the growth of world trade, to the benefit of all countries. Many developing countries are also benefiting from improved, albeit still historically low, commodity prices and some have the advantage of lower interest rates in international capital markets.

A widespread recovery is necessary because, while they may launch a recovery, the present positive forces in the developed countries, particularly the United States, are unlikely to be sufficient on their own to sustain a recovery throughout 2004. Business investment has been particularly sluggish over the past two years and will need to revive in order to sustain the momentum. The decline in excess capacity should increase the demand for new capital, while improved equity prices and higher profits as a result of the revival of consumer demand should ease its financing. Although low interest rates have not stimulated business investment to date, they should facilitate increased investment if other conditions improve. However, there is also a need for a more positive international environment, comprising improved international trade and a revival of international capital flows, in order to induce increased business spending.

A better external environment will enable the economies in transition to build upon their recent domestic strength. In the developing countries, improving external demand in the second half of 2003 and 2004 is expected to buttress recovery in Latin America and to provide additional support to steady but limited growth in Africa. Partially because of the effect of SARS in the early part of the year, growth will moderate in Southern and Eastern Asia in 2003 but will rebound in 2004. Similarly, the situation in Iraq will cause a slowdown in Western Asia before the recovery forecast for 2004.

A LACKLUSTRE INTERNATIONAL ECONOMIC ENVIRONMENT

Particularly when contrasted with the 1990s, both world trade and capital flows currently lack dynamism, reflecting and contributing to the overall weakness in the world economy. Having declined in 2001, **world trade** increased by only 1.8 per cent in 2002 and is expected to grow by less than 4 per cent in 2003, with expansion of some 7 per cent forecast for 2004 (see table I.1). The non-economic shocks to the world economy were detrimental to world merchandise trade, but above all to trade in such services as travel and tourism. In addition to there being a lower rate of growth of trade than in the 1990s, the ratio of the growth of merchandise trade to the growth of output, having tended to increase from about 2 towards 3 as a result of globalization, has reverted to the lower figure.

Having risen for more than a year, **oil prices** reached a 12-year high in mid-February 2003, but fell following the invasion of Iraq, largely because the disruption to the oil supply from the region was expected to be less serious than previously feared. For 2002 as a whole, the average price was similar to that in 2001 (see table I.2), but is expected to decrease in 2003.

With the slow growth of the global economy and international trade, average **non-fuel commodity prices** continued their downward trend in 2002. Within the total, adverse weather conditions reduced the supply and increased the prices of a number of agricultural commodities. The brief strengthening of global growth early in 2002 had improved the prices of most minerals and metals before setbacks reversed the gains after mid-year. Prices regained upward

Table I.2.

INDICATORS OF THE INTERNATIONAL ECONOMIC ENVIRONMENT, 1998-2002

	1998	1999	2000	2001	2002
World prices					
Oil (price per barrel (dollars))[a]	12.7	17.8	28.3	24.4	25.0
Non-fuel commodities (1990 = 100; base year 1985)[b]	96.3	86.9	92.7	93.2	89.2
Manufactured export prices (1990 = 100)[c]	95	91	87	84	86
Trade-weighted exchange rate of US dollar (1997 = 100)[d]	116.5	116.9	119.7	126.1	127.2
Interest rate (US six-month LIBOR[e]) (percentage)[f]	5.6	5.5	6.7	3.7	1.9
Emerging market yield spread (percentage)[g]	11.5	8.2	7.6	7.3	7.7
International financial flows (billions of dollars)					
Net transfer of resources to developing countries	-33.7	-120.9	-179.3	-155.1	-192.5
Official development assistance	52.1	56.4	53.7	52.3	56.6
Foreign direct investment	128.0	133.0	125.6	145.3	110.0

[a] International Energy Agency, *Oil Market Report*.
[b] United Nations Conference on Trade and Development (UNCTAD), *Monthly Commodity Price Bulletin*.
[c] United Nations, *Monthly Bulletin of Statistics*.
[d] United States Federal Reserve.
[e] London Interbank Offered Rate.
[f] International Monetary Fund (IMF), World Economic Outlook Database, April 2003.
[g] J.P. Morgan Co. (Emerging Markets Bond Index Plus (EMBI+)).

momentum towards the end of 2002. With the global economic recovery gaining momentum and with the weakening of the dollar, most non-fuel commodity prices are expected to strengthen during 2003 as a whole and in 2004.

There was a substantial movement in the **exchange rates** among the major currencies in mid-2002 and in the first few months of 2003, most notably a decline in the value of the United States dollar against the euro and, to a lesser extent, other major currencies. If this depreciation of the dollar is sustained, it will have major implications for global economic prospects (see below).

Net official financial flows to developing countries remained substantial in 2002 but this was mostly because of large International Monetary Fund (IMF) loans to a few countries facing financial pressures. More encouragingly, official development assistance (ODA) increased in 2002, not only in absolute terms but also, marginally, as a proportion of the gross national income (GNI) of donor countries. There were also pledges during the year of future increases in ODA, hopefully marking a turnaround in the downward trend that has characterized recent years.

Private international financial flows continued to be lacklustre in 2002 and no major improvement is expected in the short term. Among the developed countries, the global economic slowdown and the bursting of the bubble in equity markets have created a lull in international financial transactions, notably large cross-border mergers and acquisitions between companies.

For developing countries, official and private capital outflows and payments abroad associated with earlier inflows not only exceeded the corresponding receipts for the sixth consecutive year in 2002 but did so by a record amount. This **net financial transfer** has exacerbated the negative effects for developing countries of the slow growth in the real sectors of the developed countries.

Foreign direct investment (FDI) flows to developing countries initially withstood the global economic slowdown of 2001, possibly because of the lag between investment decisions and implementation. In 2002, however, global economic conditions and the slowdown in privatizations resulted in a fall in FDI flows to developing countries, with the notable exception of China. A major resurgence in these flows seems unlikely in the short term. FDI flows to Eastern European economies, on the other hand, continue to be robust, prompted not only by cost considerations but also by the prospect of their entry into the European Union (EU); these flows are expected to be sustained.

Reflecting their largely pro-cyclical nature as well as the poor geopolitical climate, **other private capital flows** to developing countries continued to be weak in 2002 and were exceeded by outflows. For those developing countries that are able to participate in international capital markets, the cost of international borrowing has tended to fall as lower interest rates in the developed countries have been coupled with lower "spreads" for borrowing developing countries, particularly since the invasion of Iraq. Private financial flows to developing countries may increase as the global geopolitical environment improves and the world economy gains momentum. However, these same developments are likely to prompt a recovery in financial markets in developed countries, which may reduce the present incentive to channel funds to developing countries.

POLICY RESPONSES TO SLOW GROWTH

The extent of the initial economic slowdown, while severe, was reduced by the counter-cyclical policy measures, including those of an automatic nature, adopted by many countries. There were, however, variations in the extent to which countries were able or willing to adopt expansionary measures, particularly as the period of slow growth lengthened. The continued sluggishness suggests the need for more stimuli, but the policy framework in a large number of economies is constraining many authorities from adopting such measures.

The immediate reaction to the economic slowdown in 2000-2001 was substantial reductions in policy interest rates in developed countries. Although energy and, in some countries, housing prices rose in 2002, inflation was not seen as a major threat in the majority of developed countries and low interest rates were maintained in most countries throughout the year and into early 2003. Some central banks, notably the Federal Reserve of the United States (Fed), reduced interest rates further in this period, bringing them to unusually low levels in many cases. The inflation-targeting rule followed by the European Central Bank (ECB) until early 2003 gave it less room for manoeuvre and delayed its cuts in policy interest rates until March 2003. At the same time, it changed its inflation objective of 2 per cent from a ceiling to a target, allowing greater flexibility in its monetary policy. The possibility of deflation has encouraged a number of central banks to indicate that they would consider the possibility of further monetary easing if necessary. In several countries in Eastern Europe, interest rates were reduced in 2002, primarily to dampen any appreciation of the exchange rate so as to maintain competitiveness.

Most countries have had less scope for expansionary fiscal policies because the size of their fiscal deficits has made them subject to either a self-imposed budgetary rule or a possible adverse reaction from global financial markets or the international financial institutions. A major exception has been the United States where increased central government expenditures and reduced taxation in 2002 combined to produce a sizeable fiscal stimulus and a growing fiscal deficit. In Western Europe, fiscal policy was slightly expansionary in 2002, but France, Germany and Italy are under pressure to consolidate their budgetary positions in order to meet the 3 per cent deficit ceiling embodied in the Stability and Growth Pact. Although it has no such policy rule, the Government of Japan is already in a difficult financial position and any further sizeable fiscal stimulus would aggravate the risk of a further downgrade in its sovereign debt by international rating agencies, further damaging economic confidence.

Many developing countries and some economies in transition improved their fiscal positions in the 1990s but deficits remain a problem, aggravated since 2001 by reduced government receipts and, in some cases, increased expenditures to offset the economic slowdown. However, there is a broad dichotomy between developing countries with relatively sustainable macroeconomic positions and those with macroeconomic disequilibria and/or other, often external, constraints. China and most economies in East Asia have been able to use monetary and fiscal instruments in the appropriate counter-cyclical manner during the present period of slow growth. In contrast, most economies in Latin America and Africa have had to give priority to addressing their macroeconomic imbalances; this has usually required using their macroeconomic policy instruments in a restrictive, currently pro-cyclical manner, rather than as a means of offsetting the present sluggish conditions. This dichotomy is likely to continue in 2003 and will contribute to a continuation of the divergent growth outcomes, and hence widening income disparities, across regions and countries.

REGIONAL PERFORMANCE AND PROSPECTS

Because they have faster rates of population growth, developing countries need to grow faster than developed countries if they are to achieve a year-to-year improvement in the well-being of their average citizen. If they are to make meaningful progress towards reducing the number of people living in poverty, developing countries have to maintain a high growth rate continuously for an extended period of time. The current period of sub-par growth has compromised both these objectives.

Although growth in the developed countries has been generally deemed unsatisfactory, only four of these countries experienced a decrease in per capita income in 2002 (see table I.3). The economies in transition fared even better, with only two suffering such a setback. In the case of the developing countries, per capita output fell in 33 of the 95 countries monitored (compared with 37 in 2001). These 33 countries accounted for 8 per cent of the world population (compared with 10 per cent in 2001). In 2002, 16 developing countries, accounting for 46 per cent of the world population, achieved an increase in per capita output exceeding 3 per cent. However, most of the people in this group were accounted for by China and India. If these two countries are excluded, only about one fifth of the 2.5 billion people in the rest of the developing world were living in countries where the increase in GDP per capita exceeded 3 per cent. Of the 41 least developed countries for which data are available, 15 recorded a fall in per capita GDP in 2002. Only seven least developed countries, five less than in 2001, achieved growth in their per capita GDP exceeding 3 per cent more in 2002. These data suggest that, for most countries and people in the developing world, 2002 was another year in which there was little progress in reducing poverty

Developed countries: recovery derailed

The uncertainties associated with the possibility of conflict in Iraq constituted a major factor causing GDP growth in the **United States** to plummet from 5 per cent at the beginning of 2002 to 1.4 per cent in the fourth quarter. With the "war overhang" largely eliminated, the economic outlook has improved and growth is expected to accelerate as 2003 progresses. The household sector was weak during the pre-war period, but should strengthen: consumer confidence has recovered, interest rates are still at historic lows and the housing and residential construction markets remain strong. The depreciation of the dollar will provide a boost to exports and import-substituting activities in the medium term, when the recovery will depend more heavily on an upturn in business spending. Growth in **Canada** slowed as 2002 progressed, largely because of

Table I.3

FREQUENCY OF HIGH AND LOW GROWTH OF PER CAPITA OUTPUT, 2000-2002

	Number of countries monitored	Decline in GDP per capita			Growth of GDP per capita exceeding 3 per cent		
		2000	2001	2002[a]	2000	2001	2002[a]
		Number of countries					
World	145	25	41	39	69	45	40
of which							
Developed economies	24	1	3	4	14	2	3
Economies in transition	26	0	1	2	21	23	21
Developing countries	95	24	37	33	34	20	16
of which							
Africa	38	14	10	10	7	12	7
Eastern and Southern Asia	18	1	7	2	13	4	6
Western Asia	15	3	7	7	7	3	2
Latin America	24	6	13	14	7	1	1
Memorandum items:							
Least developed countries	41	16	12	15	9	12	7
Sub-Saharan Africa	31	13	9	9	5	10	7
	Share[b]	**Percentage of world population**					
Developed economies	16.6	0.0	4.8	0.1	3.6	0.2	0.3
Economies in transition	17.9	0.0	0.0	0.1	5.8	5.6	5.3
Developing countries	65.5	5.1	10.3	8.0	57.4	45.9	46.4
of which							
Africa	26.2	3.6	2.4	1.9	1.0	4.1	1.5
Eastern and Southern Asia	12.4	0.1	1.3	0.5	48.4	40.4	42.2
Western Asia	10.3	0.4	2.4	1.3	2.9	1.2	2.3
Latin America	16.6	1.0	4.3	4.3	5.1	0.2	0.4
Memorandum items:							
Least developed countries	28.3	2.6	2.1	2.1	4.2	4.4	2.2
Sub-Saharan Africa	21.4	3.1	2.3	1.8	0.7	3.5	1.5

Source: UN/DESA, including population estimates and projections from *World Population Prospects: The 2000 Revision*, vol. I, *Comprehensive Tables* and corrigendum (United Nations publication, Sales No. E.01.XIII.8 and Corr.1).

[a] Partly estimated.
[b] Percentage of total number of countries monitored.

weaker exports. Growth is forecast to fall in 2003, but exports and business investment are expected to lead a recovery in 2004.

The economy of **Japan** grew only 0.2 per cent in 2002, with strong exports being the major factor preventing the economy from falling into recession. The outlook remains sombre: housing investment is sluggish, public investment is expected to be reduced further and the prospects for household consumption are discouraging. With an anticipated replenishment of inventories and some recovery in corporate investment, growth is expected to improve but remain low in 2003 and 2004. However, growth remains highly dependent on exports and is therefore vulnerable with respect to the appreciation of the yen.

Following growth of only 1.0 per cent in 2002, **Western Europe** is expected to recover somewhat in 2003, with a further improvement in 2004. The extended period of below-trend growth has led to higher region-wide unemployment and to a number of States' approaching or exceeding the fiscal deficit ceiling of 3 per cent of GDP called for by the EU Stability and Growth Pact. Together with the appreciation of the euro, these factors will dampen the recovery, but consumption is expected to strengthen slowly and business investment is forecast to rebound.

In both **Australia** and **New Zealand**, strong domestic demand offset the weak external sector in 2002, with both economies growing by over 3½ per cent. High business profitability and low debt levels contributed to higher capital spending, while growth in employment and increases in real wages led to strong household spending. Growth in both economies is expected to decelerate, but will remain between 2½ and 3 per cent in 2003 and 2004.

Economies in transition: limited deceleration

Growth in **Central and Eastern Europe** was almost unchanged in 2002, but is expected to strengthen in 2003 and 2004. By the end of 2002, there were already some indications of strengthening industrial production in Central Europe. More generally, growth is expected to be supported by growing domestic demand, continuing FDI inflows and associated investment and by some further relocation of production from EU to the region.

The economies of the **Commonwealth of Independent States** (CIS) continue to be largely sheltered from global economic uncertainties, having recorded strong growth each year since 2000. Robust domestic demand in both the Russian Federation and Ukraine, and rising oil prices and corresponding hydrocarbon investment in the Caspian region, have been the primary causes of this expansion. In Central Asia, many economies continue to surge owing to large oil and gas investments, while smaller economies are benefiting from expansion in their mining and metals sectors. Growth for the region as a whole is projected to be 4½ per cent in 2003, moderating to 4¼ per cent in 2004.

The **Baltic countries** grew by 6.3 per cent in 2002 on the basis of strong domestic demand and their flexibility in responding to robust demand from CIS to offset decreased demand from EU. Growth is expected to moderate in 2003 and 2004, with domestic demand remaining the driving force.

Developing countries: continuing underachievement

Africa's GDP growth is forecast to improve modestly in 2003 and to continue accelerating in 2004. Exports are expected to increase as global economic growth picks up in the second half of 2003. Projected price increases for almost all categories of export commodities will additionally strengthen export revenues and support GDP growth in many countries.

Reduced Organization of the Petroleum Exporting Countries (OPEC) quotas and sluggish international demand dampened North Africa's performance in 2002, but these economies are expected to grow more vigorously in 2003.

Sub-Saharan Africa's growth in 2002 was driven largely by domestic factors: most countries benefited from increased agricultural output, lower inflation and significant growth in non-agricultural sectors. The impact of these positive forces is expected to continue in 2003 and 2004. At the same time, the outlook for some subregions remains clouded by the persistence of instability in a few countries.

East Asia's rebound from its sharp slowdown in 2001 started to ease in the second half of 2002. Sluggish external demand persisted in the first quarter of 2003 and expected growth for the year as a whole has been further reduced by the outbreak of SARS. If the epidemic is contained, growth is expected to improve in the second half of the year and into 2004. Import demand from the United States and continuing robust demand from China will support export growth, while broadly accommodative policies, lower oil prices and improving confidence will strengthen domestic demand and boost industrial production, particularly in export-oriented industries.

Growth in **China** accelerated in early 2003. Both domestic demand and the external sector expanded rapidly. Fixed investment in all sectors and regions has been leading domestic demand, although housing continues to expand rapidly. Both exports and imports grew by more than 15 per cent in 2002 and are forecast to increase by nearly 20 per cent in 2003. Despite some perennial challenges, such as large-scale unemployment, widening income gaps, and the fragility of the financial system, GDP growth is expected to remain high in 2003 and 2004.

South Asia's growth increased modestly in 2002 and the region's near-term prospects are positive. Growth is being supported by both domestic demand and exports. Exports in most countries were increasing in the first half of 2003 and are expected to increase further as external demand picks up in the second half of the year. Domestic demand is also expected to strengthen, supported by lower interest rates, rising exports and a better harvest as weather conditions normalize. Stronger growth will emerge by mid-2003 and the outlook for 2004 is for a further increase, with more balance across the region.

Following a decline in 2001, **Western Asia**'s economy grew modestly in 2002 as oil production declined in most oil-exporting countries and the uncertainties associated with the conflict between Israel and Palestine and the situation in Iraq resulted in declines in FDI, tourism revenues and consumer and investment confidence. The invasion of Iraq had negative economic effects on the country and the region. While the damage to oil infrastructure was limited, a return to former levels of oil production and exports may take several months. Regional prospects are expected to improve in 2004 as oilfield development and several petrochemicals projects come on-stream. The reconstruction of Iraq will provide additional stimuli to the region, although growth in the other oil-exporting countries will be modest. Oil-importing economies of the region are not expected to exhibit much dynamism.

After contracting in 2002, **Latin America** is making a limited recovery, although the weak international environment and domestic economic or political problems in a number of countries are a constraint. Growth in the region remains heavily dependent on the volume of foreign capital flows. Although FDI continues to be the major source of external finance, inflows are generally weak while portfolio flows have been volatile.

SHORT-TERM UNCERTAINTIES AND RISKS

The overriding task for policy makers in the short term must be to restore global economic growth to its long-term potential. Although the immediate economic outlook has become more positive than earlier in 2003 and a gradual global recovery is expected to take off in the second half of the year, the short-term outlook is fraught with a number of uncertainties and risks, the balance of which are on the downside.

First and foremost, although some **geopolitical uncertainties** have abated, they have not all evaporated. The invasion of Iraq removed the pre-war uncertainties but future political developments pertaining to Western Asia, as well as to some other regions, remain uncertain. There were further international terrorist acts perpetrated in the second quarter of 2003, suggesting that such activities are likely to continue in future. Experience shows that such acts can have large effects on confidence and hence on short-term growth.

Although **oil prices** have declined since the invasion of Iraq, they remain highly volatile and therefore present both upside and downside risks. In this case, the balance is likely to be on the upside since potential oversupply could cause prices in late 2003 and 2004 to fall further than expected, with beneficial effects on global growth.

SARS reduced growth in a number of Asian developing countries in the first half of 2003. While the outbreak appears to have been largely controlled, a widespread occurrence of this or a similarly devastating disease could adversely affect some regional economies or even the world economy as a whole.

The global recovery continues to depend heavily on having the United States act as a catalyst and driving force and it is therefore vulnerable to the uncertainties and risks faced by the United States economy. The major uncertainties that are unique to the United States economy are the nature and timing of the inevitable adjustment of its **external deficits**. This correction may have started with the fall in the value of the dollar in the first months of 2003, but the depreciation itself poses a number of risks for the global recovery (see box I.1).

A separate but related risk is that posed by the burgeoning **United States fiscal deficit**. While this does not pose any immediate threat (to the contrary, a further increase in government expenditures in 2003 is an appropriate countercyclical measure), difficulties are likely to arise in the medium term through crowding-out effects. These will include higher interest rates with adverse effects on consumption as well as investment expenditure.

Furthermore, other risks that apply in varying measure to the economies of many developed countries are—again because of its key role—particularly pertinent to the economy of the United States. There continues to be **overcapacity** in some industrial sectors, either globally or within particular countries. This tendency initially applied most notably to the ICT sector, where overcapacity has since been reduced. However, there is now overcapacity in a number of sectors that have been most acutely affected by the geopolitical developments of the past two years (such as airlines and travel) and a number of other industries (such as automobiles). Such excess capacity will have a dampening effect on the business investment that is necessary to sustain the recovery.

Equity markets are recovering from the negative effects of the Iraq situation and a further substantial or prolonged fall in prices, which was feared ear-

Box I.1

ECONOMIC IMPLICATIONS OF THE
DEPRECIATION OF THE UNITED
STATES DOLLAR

The value of the United States dollar has declined substantially since the beginning of 2003 relative to a broad range of other currencies, most precipitously against the euro. The trade-weighted index of the dollar vis-à-vis 10 other major currencies has dropped by almost 20 per cent from the peak of 2002 (see figure), although the index is still over 10 per cent higher than in the last trough of 1995. Relative to the euro, the dollar has declined some 30 per cent and is at its lowest level since the introduction of the euro in January 1999.[a]

a   If the deutsche mark is used as the proxy for the period prior to the introduction of the euro, the value of the dollar is about 20 per cent higher than the lows of 1995.

TRADE-WEIGHTED VALUE OF THE UNITED STATES DOLLAR

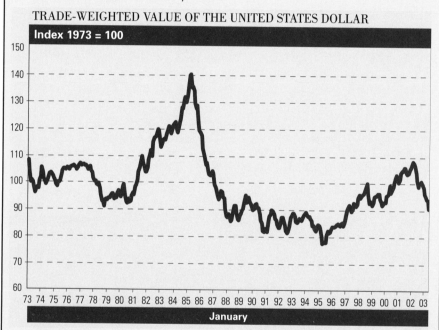

Index 1973 = 100

January

Source: Federal Reserve of the United States.

It has long been understood that movements in exchange rates can overshoot well beyond the range warranted by such economic fundamentals considered to be influential as differentials across countries in inflation rates, in the rates of return on financial assets and in GDP growth rates, and relative balance-of-payments positions among countries. Policy interventions and political stability are also important. In this context, the depreciation of the dollar can be seen as a reversal of its strength in the late 1990s in that a number of forces that favoured the United States currency at that time have now diminished, or even reversed.

Part of the retreat of the dollar around the beginning of 2003 was caused by the concern over the prospect of war in Iraq, but a dominant factor was the long-standing and increasingly heightened concern about the sustainability of the large trade deficit of the United States[b] Interest rate differentials among major countries may also be at play, as the Federal Reserve of the United States (Fed) has reduced interest rates more aggressively than most other economies have, particularly those in the euro area and the rest of the "dollar bloc"—Australia, Canada and New Zealand. In the late 1990s, when equity prices in the United States were appreciating at an unprecedented pace, giving rise to large capital inflows and driving the demand for the dollar, the role of interest rate differentials was overshadowed, but the influence of those differentials may have re-emerged after equity prices fell. Moreover, GDP

b   See *World Economic and Social Survey, 2001* (United Nations publication, Sales No. E.01.II.C.1), chap. I, subsect. entitled "Uncertainties and downside risks".

Box I.1 (continued)

c   As indicated by the baseline outlook, GDP growth for the United States is expected to recover at a rate much stronger than that of other major economies, in favour of the dollar.

d   Various econometric studies, including Project LINK, indicate that it will take about one year to pass about half of the depreciation of the dollar through to relative prices, and depreciation of the dollar by 10 per cent would lead to an increase of about 1 percentage point in the GDP of the United States in the second year.

e   This is due to the so-called "J-curve" effects. When the price elasticity of import demand is low, as is the case in the United States, the adjustment in the real demand for imports will be smaller than the increase in the relative price of imports, leading initially to an even higher bill for imports.

growth of the United States has slowed significantly, at least in the short run, reducing the growth differential relative to other economies. Furthermore, the "strong dollar" policy of the United States for the past decade seems to have been jettisoned, at least tacitly. In face of all these developments, the long-anticipated depreciation of the United States dollar is not surprising; nonetheless, the prospects for the dollar remain uncertain, as overshooting can occur in both directions.c

The weaker dollar has implications not only for the economy of the United States but for the economic growth of the rest of the world. In principle, the depreciation of the dollar is expected to benefit the United States economy, particularly the manufacturing and exporting sectors, which have been weak for the past two years. Most of the impact on the real economy is likely to be felt only gradually as the pass-through of the depreciation into the changes of relative prices will take time, and the response of real demand and supply to the price changes will take even longer.d The weaker dollar is reinforcing the monetary stimulus engendered by the low interest rates policy of the Fed, which is especially auspicious for exports and corporate profits—for the large United States transnational corporations in particular. The impact on the trade deficit will also not be tangible immediately—to the contrary, the deficit may continue to widen in the short run.e

On the other hand, the depreciation of the dollar is likely to have a negative impact on financial markets in the United States because it will result in losses for foreign investors who are holding dollar-denominated financial assets. This may lead to a further decline in capital inflows to the United States, and reduced demand for the dollar, begetting a further depreciation of the dollar. If such a vicious circle was formed, financial markets worldwide would be in jeopardy, and so would be adversely affected, to the detriment of economic growth.

The impact on economic growth in the rest of the world will be mixed. The depreciation has weakened import demand and thus the role of the United States as the global locomotive for the economic recovery in many other economies. Major developed economies, particularly those in the euro area, will face more downward pressure on their manufacturing and external sectors. Developing countries whose currencies are pegged to the dollar or have not appreciated much against the dollar, such as China and a few others, will benefit from the dollar depreciation, and their import demand from the United States will not be affected. The prices of many commodities are likely to rise because of the weaker dollar, boosting export revenues for many developing economies, but the real purchasing power of the revenue, or the terms of trade, for these economies may not improve. The weaker dollar will also provide some relief for developing countries with dollar-denominated debts, particularly those that are highly indebted.

The impact of the dollar depreciation on the rest of the world will also depend on the policy response of the economies. For example, with a stronger euro and hence less inflationary pressure, the European Central Bank (ECB) may become more flexible in reducing interest rates in the euro area, and this will stimulate domestic demand. At the same time, a number of developing countries, particularly those where interest rates have been maintained at high levels, now have more room to reduce rates, thereby making them more supportive of growth.

lier, now seems unlikely to materialize. However, a **housing bubble** is widely perceived to exist in a number of developed countries. Rising house prices have been an important element in sustaining strong consumer expenditure, as well as the housing and construction industry itself, in such countries. These rising prices, together with the experience of Japan, suggest that a bursting of the bubble could have sizeable negative effects on these economies.

Deflation has already had profound negative consequences for the Japanese economy; it has also touched a number of other Asian economies and is now viewed by some observers as a possibility in some of the major industrialized economies. The depreciation of the United States dollar reduces the possibility of deflation in the United States but makes it more likely in economies with appreciating currencies, notably the EU countries (particularly Germany). Some Asian economies have experienced brief periods of deflation without widespread detrimental effects but Japan's experience highlights the dangers of allowing deflation to become entrenched. Measures against deflation need—to an even greater extent than an anti-inflationary policy—to be pre-emptive and based on prospects rather than on current developments. Inevitably, such an approach embodies its own set of risks.

DELIVERING ON THE NEW DEVELOPMENT COMMITMENT

For any improvement in growth to be sustained over the medium term, it will be necessary to revitalize international cooperation for development in order to address some underlying challenges to growth in developing countries. Cooperative international development efforts can contribute to repairing the damage inflicted on multilateral cooperation during the past year, as well as constitute an important means of addressing the global inequality that contributes to the underlying geopolitical tensions.

Prior to the emergence of the geopolitical uncertainties that hampered global economic growth in late 2002 and early 2003, the international community had forged, through a sequence of global meetings, an international consensus on development priorities and actions. The Fourth Ministerial Conference of the World Trade Organization, held at Doha in November 2001, the International Conference on Financing for Development, held in Monterrey, Mexico, in March 2002, and the World Summit on Sustainable Development, held in Johannesburg, South Africa, in August-September 2002, collectively defined a new global partnership for development between developed and developing countries. The overriding objective of this partnership is to accelerate development through shared responsibilities and mutual commitment. In each case, the programmes for the implementation of this partnership give attention to both resources and policies.

During the past year, work has continued on the refinement and implementation of these programmes. An important dimension of this work has been an increasing need for coherence among policies and programmes. This is particularly apparent where policies are in direct contradiction, but more generally it requires ensuring not only that all policies and actions are development-friendly but that they are so to the fullest extent possible.

Securing progress on the trade agenda

Inevitably, progress in the implementation of the programmes drawn up at Doha, Monterrey and Johannesburg has been mixed, but it is discouraging that progress on the work programme with the shortest time frame and, in some ways, the largest short-term potential, namely, the "Doha Development Agenda", has been the most limited. Many of its deadlines for agreement on specific issues have already passed without having been met. Most such issues are of particular concern to developing countries, not only from the point of view of trade but because they relate to a priority developmental concern. Given the slow start, the successful completion of the Doha programme will require a high degree of political determination, including a willingness on the part of the developed countries to undertake the types of adjustment measures that developing countries have long been called upon to make in liberalizing their trade regimes.

The Doha work programme is ambitious both in its scope and in its time-horizon and yet it has been agreed that it should be a "single undertaking" where "nothing is agreed until everything is agreed". The Doha negotiations are too important to fail so the fact that progress to date has been limited makes the originally ambitious goal even more so. It is essential that meaningful progress be registered at the Fifth Ministerial Conference of the World Trade Organization, to be held in Cancún, Mexico, in September 2003, whose main task will be to undertake a mid-term review of progress in negotiations and other work under the Doha Development Agenda. This will require all Governments to take a more flexible approach to these negotiations and, above all, to see them not as trade negotiations but as part of the new partnership to foster development. They should also be seen in the context of the current need to accelerate global economic growth in the short term. To this end, Governments may wish to focus for the immediate future on a few issues of overriding development concern and, in so doing, to adopt a more open approach.

A priority issue is to enhance the World Trade Organization Declaration on the TRIPS agreement and public health (WT/MIN(01)/DEC/2) adopted at the Fourth Ministerial Conference on 14 November 2001.[1] The declaration has been an important development breakthrough because it authorizes a developing country to issue a licence to a domestic entity to produce a patent-protected pharmaceutical "predominantly for the supply of the domestic market" (article 31 (f) of the TRIPS agreement). However, countries without the necessary pharmaceutical manufacturing capacity are unable not only to take advantage of this provision but also to import from countries that have been granted such a licence. Such excluded countries are frequently the poorest, the most disease-afflicted and the most in need of low-cost drugs. Governments agreed to resolve this problem in the World Trade Organization but have failed to meet two self-imposed deadlines for doing so (although several developed countries have declared a moratorium on applying the existing restrictions until a solution is found). This problem relates directly to human well-being and so is at the very core of development. A prompt compromise solution, possibly involving a sequenced approach, would provide a much-needed boost to the Doha negotiations, as well as testify to the validity of the new partnership for devel-

[1]   For the Agreement on Trade-related Aspects of Intellectual Property Rights (TRIPS agreement), see *Legal Instruments Embodying the Results of the Uruguay Round of Multilateral Trade Negotiations, done at Marrakesh on 15 April 1994* (GATT secretariat publication, Sales No. GATT/1994-7), annex 1C.

opment not only between the developed and the developing countries but also between the public and the private sectors.

A second major concern is agricultural trade, in particular the subsidies and other support that developed countries provide to their agricultural sector. Developing countries have long been encouraged to eliminate subsidies in order to remove distortions in their economies and to improve their fiscal balances but the developed countries continue to maintain massive agricultural subsidies for, as well as high tariffs on, many agricultural products. Because of the central role of the agricultural sector in many developing countries, these measures are directly to the detriment of developing countries, offsetting or even undoing the benefits of other forms of cooperation with those same countries. They are therefore in direct contradiction to the principles of partnership and coherence that form the backbone of the new development compact. Developed countries should therefore begin to reduce agricultural subsidies without delay and make time-bound commitments to eliminating them without a quid pro quo in other Doha negotiations. A starting point would be the elimination of all export subsidies and the discontinuance of the "dumping" of agricultural products in developing countries; this would have an immediate salutary effect on the agriculture sector in developing countries—and hence on the livelihoods of millions, including many of the poorest.

The question of "special and differential treatment" for developing countries assumes particular significance in a round of negotiations that aims at making the global trading system more development-friendly. It is generally agreed that countries at lower levels of development should be subject to less stringent trading rules than more developed countries, but there is little agreement on how this principle should be made operational. As a result, the negotiations on special and differential treatment have also failed to meet a succession of deadlines.

The least developed countries constitute one group that is particularly deserving of special treatment. This is recognized in World Trade Organization negotiations, as well as in some bilateral and regional concessions. In particular, the EU "Everything but Arms" initiative allows duty-free access to all non-arms imports from least developed countries except so-called sensitive products—bananas, sugar and rice; duties on these products are to be eliminated by 2009. As a first step towards enhanced differential treatment for developing countries, all developed countries should adopt the "Everything but Arms" principle and such commitments should be bound within the World Trade Organization. In addition, some of the more advanced developing countries should apply the same principles to the less advantaged members of the group. Finally, every effort should be made to advance the date for the elimination of duties on sensitive products, even if this is done on a case-by-case basis.

Addressing external debt

The past few years have highlighted the fact that, more than 20 years after the debt crisis erupted in Latin America, many developing countries continue to face difficulties servicing their external debt. A long-term solution to this problem would be for developing countries to rely as far as possible on non-debt-creating flows. This already appears to be taking place with the reduced willingness of capital markets to lend to many developing countries. In the meantime, the magnitude of the Argentine crisis underscores the need for more effective international arrangements to deal with private sector debt crises associated with existing obligations. The ongoing discussions on means to avoid and resolve financial crises in middle-income countries should be continued.

It is also necessary to resolve the immediate difficulties of the heavily indebted poor countries (HIPCs). There are 15 HIPCs, such as those emerging from conflict situations, whose cases have not yet been considered and whose eligibility needs to be assessed as soon as conditions permit. Of those already reviewed, only 3 more of the 26 countries that had reached the "decision point" in the enhanced HIPC Initiative moved on to the "completion point" between April 2002 and April 2003, bringing the total to 8. Further measures need to be taken to ensure that all eligible countries reach the completion point as expeditiously as possible. For those that have already done so, the amount of relief that is required to achieve debt sustainability as originally envisaged has turned out to be higher than anticipated in several cases; this is often because growth and/or export earnings have been lower than expected, owing frequently to a fall in commodity prices. It is necessary to ensure that the HIPC programme reduces a country's debt to a level that remains sustainable even when it is adversely affected by events beyond its control. Most importantly, the quantity of debt relief provided is already being threatened by the insufficient funding for the HIPC Trust Fund and by the fact that not all creditors are providing relief. Renewed efforts are required to mobilize the resources necessary to implement the Initiative fully.

Reviving concessional financial flows

There was an encouraging increase in ODA in 2002 and there are commitments to further increases by a number of donors in the next few years. Reflecting the recognition that even these improvements would fall short of what is widely perceived to be required, a proposal was launched in 2003 by the United Kingdom of Great Britain and Northern Ireland for an international finance facility which would aim at doubling the flow of ODA in the next few years. Although a number of donors have had questions about the proposal, it reflects official donor recognition of the need for a substantial increase in ODA flows. There was also progress towards improving the effectiveness of aid flows by the members of the Development Assistance Committee (DAC) of the Organisation for Economic Cooperation and Development (OECD) through the simplification and harmonization of procedures.

These favourable developments were counteracted by an increased politicization of aid flows. There is a growing tendency in the donor community to concentrate assistance on recipient countries that comply with donors' current perceptions of "sound policies", including "good governance". It is a truism that sound policies and good governance foster development, but defining these terms is less straightforward. Conceptually, it is difficult to reconcile this approach with the widespread recognition that conditionality is ineffective, that "one size doesn't fit all" and that "ownership" is central to successful development. A modicum of modesty might be more appropriate in the light of the donor community's limited successes to date.

The global geopolitical situation is also having a bearing on aid flows. The United States, the largest donor, recorded a sudden and substantial increase in ODA flows in 2002, but this was largely a response to the terrorist attacks of 11 September 2001. It is anticipated that the reconstruction of Iraq will also result in a substantial increase in ODA flows over the next few years. The donor community has made several efforts over recent years to ensure that ODA is appropriately defined and measured, for example, by excluding high-income recipients. Inasmuch as ODA inevitably serves geopolitical purposes to some extent funds used for purely geopolitical or commercial objectives should be separately identified so as to ensure that they are not disbursed at the cost of providing development assistance to the many countries that need it to confront long-term development challenges.

II INTERNATIONAL TRADE AND FINANCE

International trade and capital flows were in the doldrums for much of 2002 and the early part of 2003. International trade lacked dynamism in the face of sluggish global growth and was beset by geopolitical uncertainties, staging only a mild recovery from the reversal it had suffered in 2002. Some acceleration is expected in the second half of 2003 and into 2004, when the growth of world trade in goods is expected to be about 7 per cent. One of the notable features of the past few years, however, has been the disruption to trade in services, particularly travel and tourism, caused by a sequence of non-economic shocks, from the terrorist attacks of 2001 to the outbreak of severe acute respiratory syndrome (SARS) in early 2003. Apart from the sectors themselves, small economies heavily dependent on these sectors were severely affected.

International capital flows were also slowed by the difficult economic and political environment. Banks continued to reduce their lending to developing countries, although a number of emerging markets made successful bond issuances in this period and some saw improvements in their international credit ratings. With the notable exception of China, flows of foreign direct investment (FDI) to developing countries also declined in 2002. A reflection of the financial difficulties facing a small number of developing countries was another year of substantial non-concessional net lending by the international financial institutions. More encouragingly, there was an increase in official concessional flows to developing countries in 2002. Seemingly reversing the downward trend of the past few years, official development assistance (ODA) increased, with pledges of further additions in the future. This, however, was the only bright spot because, in aggregate, there was a record net financial transfer out of developing countries in 2002.

On the policy front, progress was muted. Negligible progress was made in the trade negotiations launched in Doha in 2001, and early prospects in the run-up to the Fifth Ministerial Conference of the World Trade Organization, to be held in Cancún, Mexico, in September 2003, were discouraging. In addition to the increase in ODA flows and commitments, other follow-ups to the International Conference on Financing for Development held in Monterrey, Mexico, in March 2002 included continuing efforts to formulate means of preventing and resolving international financial crises. One major initiative in this area failed to find approval but the use (and market acceptance) of collective action clauses (CACs) in a number of bond issuances by developing countries in early 2003 was a more encouraging development.

INTERNATIONAL TRADE

After contracting in 2001, the volume of world merchandise trade grew by 1.8 per cent in 2002, the second weakest performance in two decades. In dollar terms, world trade expanded by 4 per cent, reflecting, in addition to increased volume, modest increases in the prices of commodities and manufactured products, as well as the depreciation of the United States dollar vis-à-vis other major currencies. World trade is expected to continue its recovery and grow by 4 per cent in 2003, still well below its performance in the 1990s (see table I.1). As the growth of the world economy accelerates in 2004, the increase in world trade is expected to reach 7 per cent.[1]

The changes in international trade were uneven during 2002. There was a strong recovery in the first half of the year, reflecting improved economic conditions in many countries and a revival in manufacturing (see figure III.2), which had suffered from the existence of large inventories and excess capacity, particularly in the information and communication technologies (ICT) sector. In the last quarter, new shocks to consumer and investor confidence emerged (see chap. I), demand slowed, industrial production lost momentum and the recovery of global trade decelerated. This weakness intensified in early 2003 as conflict with Iraq loomed (see figure II.1).

The uneven performance of trade was not only temporal but also regional. Over the past few years, the health of global trade has been determined largely by developments in the economy of the United States of America. More recently, new trends have emerged. One has been the renewed dynamism of trade in East Asia, notably in China, which has increased its share of international trade and has partially offset the softening of global demand in some countries. Similarly, the economies in transition have sustained robust import

[1] Figures reflect average of import and export growth.

Figure II.1.
WORLD TRADE: VALUE OF MONTHLY EXPORTS,
JANUARY 2001-FEBRUARY 2003[a]

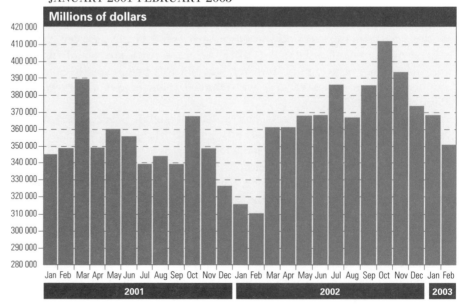

Sources: Asian Development Bank, International Monetary Fund and other international and national sources.

[a] Based on a sample of countries representing about 70 per cent of world trade.

growth, supported by domestic demand, FDI and favourable terms-of-trade developments.

In the United States, robust demand growth and the strong dollar had caused imports to grow at annual double-digit rates since the Asian crisis, prompting the country to be dubbed "buyer of last resort". This changed in 2001 when imports contracted. The year 2002 witnessed the return to past trends—despite the weaker dollar—and much of the growth in international trade in the year was attributable to the recovery of import demand from the United States. Nonetheless, according to preliminary estimates, United States import growth decelerated sharply in early 2003 (see figure II.2), reflecting the contraction in private investment, as well as in consumption expenditures on durable goods, in the first quarter of the year.

There was a decline in the volume of United States exports for the second consecutive year in 2002 owing to increased international competition, soft demand elsewhere and economic difficulties in some trading partners in Latin America. As a result, the United States trade deficit increased to $482 billion in 2002 (see table A.20) and is expected to continue to expand in 2003 and 2004. The depreciation of the United States dollar vis-à-vis other major currencies is expected to curb the trade deficit, but not in the short run.[2] Elsewhere in North America, Canada's trade stagnated in 2002 but is expected to recover in the second half of 2003. The growth of both exports and imports of the region is forecast to reach 7-8 per cent in 2004.

Import demand remained anaemic in Japan in 2002 (see figure II.2). A surge in the import bill for crude oil in the first quarter of 2003 was outweighed by a sharp decline in imports of other items, especially ICT-related components, which contributed to the deceleration of international trade during the period. On

[2]   The depreciation of the dollar against the euro will have limited trade effects for the United States, as the currencies of many of its trading partners in Asia and other developing regions either are pegged to the dollar or have not appreciated much against the dollar. Meanwhile, the "J-curve" effect—occurring when the price elasticity of import demand is less than unity—would mean a worsening of the trade deficit in the short run.

Figure II.2.
SELECTED DEVELOPED ECONOMIES: GROWTH OF IMPORTS OF GOODS AND SERVICES, SEASONALLY ADJUSTED, FIRST QUARTER 2001-FIRST QUARTER 2003

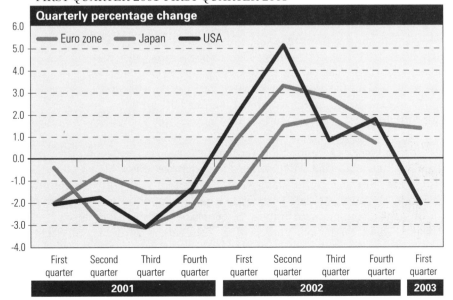

Sources: European Central Bank, Government of Japan/Economic and Social Research Institute, and United States Department of Commerce.

the other hand, strong Japanese export performance, due particularly to buoyant trade in Asia in 2002 and the integration of Japanese manufacturing with that in East Asia, was the major impetus preventing the economy from falling into a recession.[3] Shipments to other parts of Asia continued to boom in early 2003, while exports to the United States declined sharply and exports to the European Union (EU) remained weak. The growth of Japanese exports is expected to be about 3 per cent for 2003-2004 and the growth of imports is expected to be similar, with the annual trade surplus remaining at about $100 billion.

After a modest performance in 2001, imports by EU showed almost no real growth in 2002, as continued weak domestic demand countered any boost from currency appreciation. Almost no change in the volume of imports is expected in 2003 as domestic demand remains lacklustre, but growth of some 3½ per cent is forecast for 2004 as the effects of currency appreciation on prices feed through and domestic demand strengthens. Meanwhile, export volume growth decelerated further in the region in 2002 owing to slow world demand and the appreciating currency, which hurt competitiveness.[4] Continued dollar depreciation is expected and will place further pressure on European exporters who are expected to lose market share. Nevertheless, exports are expected to pick up over the course of 2003 and gain further momentum in 2004, as world demand revives.

Among the economies in transition, imports continued to grow in the Central and Eastern European region, owing to the growth of private consumption. In some countries, Bulgaria and Croatia in particular, strong import growth was associated with high rates of investment; in the Czech Republic, increased imports were due to recovery from the floods. Import growth is expected to remain strong in 2003, driven both by private and public consumption and by investment, FDI in particular.

Most economies in Central Europe exhibited modest rates of export growth in real terms owing to lower EU import demand and stronger currencies. In some cases, stronger exports to the Commonwealth of Independent States (CIS) and Central European Free Trade Agreement (CEFTA) countries compensated for stagnant exports to EU. The export performance of a number of countries in Southern and Eastern Europe (notably Bulgaria, Romania and Yugoslavia) improved because of increased intraregional trade and improved competitiveness brought about by FDI. Exports from other States of this sub-region remained weak owing to remaining constraints on industrial capacity. The prospects for the region's exports in 2003 are largely dependent on EU: an upturn in EU will encourage exports of intermediate products from Central and Eastern Europe. In addition, an impetus to the region's trade may be provided by growing import demand from the CIS economies, as well as a number of developing countries. Some bilateral trade agreements that took effect in the region in 2002 and 2003 will also have a favourable effect.

Imports by the Baltic and CIS countries, with the exception of Turkmenistan, also increased in 2002. Higher imports reflected strong consumer demand and investment in several countries as well as, in the case of the Russian Federation, the real appreciation of the ruble against the dollar and the euro, and, in the case of Estonia and Lithuania, the appreciation of their euro-pegged currencies against the dollar. Continued strong domestic demand in these countries will provide an impetus for import growth in 2003.

CIS countries also had a strong export performance in 2002. In most cases, merchandise export revenues increased substantially, by almost 50 per cent in dollar terms in the case of Armenia. Azerbaijan was the only country that reported a drop (6 per cent) in nominal exports. In the Russian Federation, the volume of exports increased by over 10 per cent in 2002, largely on account of increased oil exports. Oil exports cannot, however, increase much further, as capacity limits have been reached. The State-owned company that controls exports neither has plans for expansion nor is willing to relinquish control and allow private companies to build their own pipelines. The growth of Russian exports is therefore likely to decelerate in 2003. Geographically, Russian trade continues to shift away from the CIS countries: non-CIS countries accounted for 83 per cent of Russian foreign trade in 2002.

Among the developing regions, Africa's merchandise trade showed weak but resilient growth in both imports and exports in 2002. Imports grew moderately, reflecting a return to more normal patterns after sharp declines in 2001. Food imports accounted for large increases in import expenditures in drought-afflicted countries while higher oil prices increased the import bills of most net fuel importing countries. Imports are expected to grow moderately in 2003, reflecting similarly moderate growth of gross domestic product (GDP), increased demand for imported consumer goods and increased imports of capital goods for large-scale investment in infrastructure development and industrial projects in several countries. The spike in food imports in southern Africa should recede with the easing of the drought in most of the affected countries.

Meanwhile, in oil-exporting countries, export revenues in 2002 were driven by higher prices and increased demand for oil, supported by increased production in Angola, Equatorial Guinea and the Sudan. Non-fuel commodity exporting countries benefited from the modest improvement in prices and demand in 2002. Sharp increases in the prices of precious metals, such as gold and platinum, and an increase in the demand for diamonds, all as a result of the geopolitical uncertainties in the months leading up to the United States invasion of Iraq, benefited South Africa and other producers of minerals and metals in southern Africa. Export volumes are expected to increase only marginally in 2003.

East Asia was one of the few bright spots for trade in 2002. Imports increased in most economies in line with strong consumption and rising demand for intermediate inputs to export industries. Import growth in China reached 20 per cent in real terms in 2002 (see table A.13) and was over 50 per cent in nominal terms in the first quarter of 2003. This latter pace, however, was due partially to seasonal factors, such as the rush of importers to use remaining 2002 quotas and a significant increase in imports of petroleum, and will not be sustained throughout the year. For the region as a whole, import growth is expected to pick up in the second half of 2003 (in response to a strengthening of both domestic demand and exports) and to accelerate in 2004. In most economies, the reversal of the deterioration in their terms of trade (as oil prices weaken and the prices of manufacturing exports bottom out) will favour their trade balance, countering the increase in import volume.

Exports by Eastern and Southern Asia grew robustly in 2002, after the decline in 2001 (see table A.13). Export growth is likely to be moderate until mid-2003, dampened by the uncertainties associated with SARS and the continuing subdued recovery in major developed countries. Export growth is expected to pick up from the second half of 2003, boosted by strengthening demand in major developed countries and continuing robust imports by China. China, Hong Kong Special Administrative Region (SAR) of China and Malaysia, with their currencies pegged to the depreciated United States dollar, will begin to benefit from stronger competitiveness. In 2004, export growth will accelerate further in response to strengthening world trade but may not be as strong as in 2000 because demand in the developed countries will be weaker. A marked contribution from ICT exports is likely because, through the regional processing network, the demand for components quickens rapidly in response to rising global demand. However, given excess capacities, a full recovery in the world ICT cycle, particularly in the United States, is unlikely until late 2004.

Imports increased in most South Asian countries in 2002 and are expected to strengthen from mid-2003 in response to rising domestic demand and ongoing import liberalization, resulting in widening trade deficits. Exports recovered in most countries in 2002 but individual performances reflected differences in export structure, market access and security. Export growth is expected to strengthen in the second half of 2003, but competition and socio-political uncertainties are expected to continue to restrain export growth in Bangladesh, Nepal and Sri Lanka. These countries' narrow export base, notably their heavy dependence on garments, makes them vulnerable to intensifying competition in their major export markets, the United States[5] and EU. The diversification and upgrading of their export base are a major policy challenge for these countries.

Imports in most Western Asian oil-exporting countries virtually stagnated in 2002, reflecting weak domestic demand, while export volumes contracted owing to reduced oil output. Despite the rise in oil prices, export revenues were slightly lower than in 2001, although most countries recorded trade surpluses. Among the region's oil-importing countries, the value of Turkey's exports increased by over 13 per cent in 2002, while import costs soared almost 23 per cent, reflecting partly economic recovery and partly higher oil prices. As a result, the trade deficit widened. The region's external balance is expected to improve, but with divergent trends between oil-importing and oil-exporting countries. Growth in the region's export receipts is expected to be about 6 per cent in 2003, mainly reflecting increased oil production and higher oil prices. However, export earnings will decline in most oil-importing countries in 2003, as the Iraq war and the subsequent suspension of the oil-for-food programme reduced trade flows between Iraq and its trading partners in the first half of the year. At the same time, the region's import bill is expected to contract by about 2½ per cent, owing mostly to weak domestic demand but also to the adverse effects of the Iraq war on regional trade flows. Jordan, for example, used to import all its oil from Iraq on generous terms, half in grants and the remainder at a discount. Overall export prospects for 2004 are more favourable.

The most salient feature of Latin America's external sector in 2002 was the sharp adjustment in its current-account deficit, which was slashed by 70 per cent to about $15 billion (see table A.22), largely reflecting the reduced availability of external financing. The region's aggregate trade balance recorded a surplus in 2002. Imports were drastically curtailed in such countries as Argentina, Brazil and Venezuela, reflecting weak internal demand and adjustments in real exchange rates, whereas exports remained stagnant in both nom-

---

5   In addition, the United States allowed low-income Caribbean and sub-Saharan African countries free access to its market for their garment exports in 2000.

inal and real terms. The region is also facing increased competition in its major export markets. China, for instance, has recently overtaken Mexico as the second largest external supplier of the United States. Export volumes are expected to advance by about 2 per cent in 2003, reflecting the moderate recovery of international trade. Imports are expected to recover from 2002, supported by a limited improvement of domestic demand throughout the region. Import growth, however, is expected to remain below 1 per cent in real terms.

COMMODITY PRICES AND MARKETS

The prices of non-fuel commodities in 2002 continued the downward trend that had begun in 1995 and was interrupted only in 2000 (see table A.17). Oil prices, in contrast, recovered in 2002 but were highly volatile during the year. Some price increases are expected for non-fuel commodities in 2003. Nonetheless, such increases reflect largely the weakening of the United States dollar because excess supply, including large inventories in many commodity markets, continues to exert pressure on prices. With the end of the war in Iraq and the recovery of production, not only in Iraq but also in other countries that recently experienced disruptions, oil prices are expected to remain within the target price range of the Organization of the Petroleum Exporting Countries (OPEC) in 2003.

World oil market: recent developments and prospects

Oil prices recovered in 2002 owing to increased demand, low inventories and relatively low quotas for OPEC countries (totalling 21.7 million barrels per day (mbd)).[6] In contrast, oil output in the Russian Federation increased by over 9 per cent in 2002, reaching a record post-Soviet level of 7.62 mbd. Prior to the invasion of Iraq, oil prices rose to a 12-year high in mid-February 2003 (see figure II.3), reflecting mostly increased geopolitical tensions but also underlying market fundamentals. There was fear that conflict in Iraq could create severe oil shortages due to disruptions in supply and in transportation: prices were bid up accordingly. In addition to the war premium, there was tightness in world oil markets because of reduced production, rising global demand and resulting lower inventories. The strike in Venezuela, the third largest producer of OPEC, reduced the country's oil supply by some 2.7 mbd. In response to these developments, OPEC decided to increase its production quotas initially to 23.0 mbd with effect from 1 January 2003 and then, in an emergency meeting on 12 January 2003, to 24.5 mbd from 1 February 2003.

Nevertheless, pressure on prices continued to build as the inevitability of a war in Iraq became increasingly apparent, and oil prices reached $35 per barrel (pb) in early March 2003. World inventories continued to decline, as the Venezuelan strike had removed a total of some 100 million barrels from the global oil market. At the end of February 2003, total oil stocks of the Organisation for Economic Cooperation and Development (OECD) countries were at their lowest level since March 2000. In the United States—the world's largest oil consumer—stocks were at their lowest level since 1975, as cold weather boosted demand. Higher oil prices also contributed to the decline in

6   OPEC quotas refer to crude oil only and exclude Iraqi production.

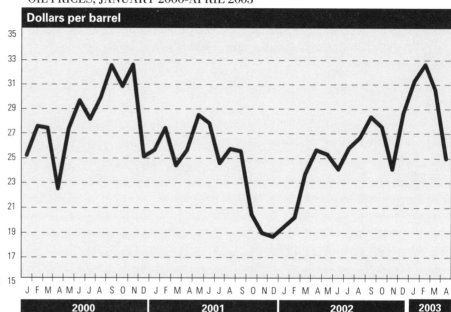

Figure II.3.
OIL PRICES, JANUARY 2000-APRIL 2003[a]

Source: International Energy Agency, *Oil Market Report.*

[a] Prices of Brent oil.

United States oil stocks, as many United States refiners withdrew oil from their own inventories. Other countries were affected as well. For instance, China's oil stockpile fell to only 14 days of oil imports—much lower than the international standard of 90 days.

At a meeting on 11 March 2003, OPEC decided to keep production quotas unchanged but expressed its commitment to compensating for any shortfall emanating from disruptions in the Iraqi supply. The Organization also called on other oil producers to help in containing the rise in prices and in supplying markets adequately. In the meantime, the strike in Venezuela ended and output was slowly recovering. As a result, world oil supply increased during the first quarter of 2003 (see figure II.4).

With the invasion of Iraq, some 3 mbd of oil were removed from the world market. Iraq's supply of about 2.3 mbd was lost owing to the war and the consequent suspension of the United Nations oil-for-food programme; Kuwaiti oil fields near the border with Iraq were also closed, removing a further 700,000 barrels per day from the market. World supply conditions deteriorated further when political unrest disrupted oil production in Nigeria. Surprisingly, oil prices fell to $26 pb during the first days of the war (see figure II.3).

Several factors were at play. First, the previous uncertainty about possible developments regarding Iraq was replaced by a perception in oil markets that the conflict would be short-lived and would involve minimal interruptions to oil supplies. In particular, more than 80 per cent of Iraqi oil production is located in the country's southern region and this was quickly controlled by American and British troops with minimal damage to the oil infrastructure. Second, some of Saudi Arabia's stockpile of 28 million barrels had already been drawn upon and was in transit and expected to reach developed countries

Figure II.4.
WORLD OIL SUPPLY AND DEMAND AND OPEC PRODUCTION, FIRST QUARTER 2000-FOURTH QUARTER 2003

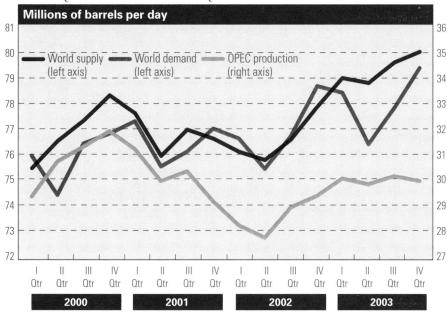

Sources: International Energy Agency, *Monthly Oil Market Report;* and Energy Information Administration, *Short-term Energy Outlook,* April 2003.

in May 2003. This led markets to believe that the anticipated oil shortage would fail to materialize. Third, government officials in major net oil importing countries and the International Energy Agency (IEA) had indicated that their respective strategic oil reserves could be released to offset any acute oil shortfall. Finally, OPEC countries had compensated for the loss of Iraqi and Venezuelan crude oil production with increased supplies. OPEC countries' production was estimated at 27.4 mbd, compared with their quota total of 24.5 mbd. Non-OPEC production also increased moderately. As a result, world oil supply was estimated at about 77.6 mbd in February 2003 and 80.3 mbd in March 2003; OPEC countries accounted for more than three fourths of this increase. Mounting fears of a possible oil glut in the global market prompted OPEC countries to decide at an emergency meeting on 24 April 2003 to reduce their production by 2 mbd to 25.4 mbd, effective 1 June 2003.

On the demand side, after increasing for most of 2002, world oil demand moderated slightly in the first quarter of 2003 (see figure II.4), despite unusually cold weather in the northern hemisphere, low Japanese nuclear power output and increased jet fuel consumption, mostly related to the military operations in Iraq. At the start of the second quarter of 2003, global oil demand slowed more substantially with the end of winter demand in the northern hemisphere, weak global economic growth and the onset of SARS; the last-mentioned factor reduced commercial air travel and hence jet fuel demand, particularly in Asia, a region that accounts for one third of incremental jet fuel demand.

World oil demand is expected to recover in the second-half of 2003. United States oil inventories in early May 2003 fell by 800,000 barrels to 287 million barrels, compared with the minimum of 270 million barrels required by United States refiners. Crude oil stockpiles also declined in other countries. The need to replenish world oil inventories will therefore support global demand. Jet fuel demand (accounting for 10 per cent of world oil demand) is likely to recover during the second half of 2003 as the adverse impact of SARS eases, but supply is also expected to increase with production in both Iraq and Venezuela returning to earlier levels. A modest excess supply is expected to keep oil prices at the lower band of the OPEC target price range of $22-$28 pb during the last quarter of 2003. For the year as a whole, oil prices are expected to average $28 pb, an increase of 12 per cent over 2002.

Non-fuel commodities: excess supplies and weak demand

Non-fuel commodity prices continued their downward trend in 2002, with the United Nations Conference on Trade and Development (UNCTAD) combined commodity price index falling by an additional 2 per cent (see table A.17). Over the past five years, the drop in the prices of the main tropical commodities (namely, coffee, cotton and sugar) has been severe, leading to increased poverty and vulnerability in a large number of countries. The fall in prices was due to various factors, such as the slowdown in global economic growth,[7] structural oversupplies (for example, in coffee) and market distortions (for example, in cotton and sugar).[8] Nonetheless, from October 2002 to March 2003, the prices of some commodities increased, mainly owing to increased geopolitical uncertainties and associated risks, but also to the weakening of the United States dollar. However, this price increase is likely to prove temporary and should not be taken as an indication of a general strengthening of market fundamentals.

For some commodities, the deterioration in consumer confidence, perceptions of a worsening economy and geopolitical factors affected decisions by a large number of economic actors from late 2002 to early 2003. For instance, there were instances of flight into "safe havens", such as gold, while turmoil in West Africa temporarily boosted prices in the cocoa sector. However, after the initial shocks, the situation in these markets is returning to normal, while the prices of a large number of other commodities remain depressed. Coffee prices, for example, continue to be subject to the pressures of the large surplus accumulated over the past four years. Similar observations apply to cocoa—where earlier supply problems could lead to the complete reshaping of an already fragile sector—and to sugar and cotton. In the two last-mentioned sectors, both Australia and Brazil are challenging the support regimes maintained in EU and the United States (see below).

Agricultural commodities

After two years of increase, prices of **food** products fell by 4 per cent in 2002 (see table A.17). However, the various items of this group showed diverging movements between 2001 and 2002, with a moderate deterioration for bananas and beef, but a fall of over 20 per cent in the case of sugar. In contrast, prices of such commodities as fishmeal and wheat rose by more than 20 and 15 per cent, respectively.

Several factors explain the decline in the price of sugar in the first part of 2002, including record production in Brazil and trade arrangements between EU and the African, Caribbean and Pacific (ACP) countries and between the

[7] The downturn, in particular in the automobile and telecommunication sectors, had a severe impact on the minerals and metals sectors.

[8] For more information on commodity market structures and characteristics, see United Nations Conference on Trade and Develoment (UNCTAD) and Cyclope, *World Commodity Survey 2003-2004* (Geneva, UNCTAD, June 2003).

Figure II.5.
NON-FUEL COMMODITY PRICES, 1994-2003
(Indices of dollar prices, 1985 = 100)

Source: UNCTAD, *Monthly Commodity Price Bulletin.*

United States and some other producing countries. The EU import quota for ACP countries was cut by 115,000 tons and the system of stock financing, which had been used under the Protocol 3 on ACP Sugar to the Partnership Agreement Between the Members of the African, Caribbean and Pacific Group of States, and the European Community and its Member States (Cotonou Agreement), was abolished, potentially increasing the supply of sugar in world markets. In addition, market distortions may be boosting production by insulating domestic producers from international market signals.

From October 2002 to March 2003, the price of sugar increased by 3.3 per cent, probably pointing to some increase in demand.[9] The growth of consumption in such markets as the Russian Federation and the other CIS countries will be a major factor influencing price developments in the medium term.

The prices of grains in general improved in 2002, mainly as a consequence of drought and other unfavourable weather conditions which reduced supply from major producing areas. According to the International Grains Council, the improvement in the crop outlook for all grains in developed countries for 2003 (particularly countries in North America, Australia and EU countries) "reintroduced a more bearish tone in the major markets"[10] and the price of wheat declined in the first half of the year.

After a strong decline in 1994, followed by continued slower erosion from 1996 to 2001, the price of rice increased 11 per cent in 2002. The major factors behind this upturn, which was sustained into the first quarter of 2003, included a decline in production and, in Thailand, domestic market interventions and higher taxes on transportation. Since Thai rice prices serve as an international benchmark, these decisions influence the market directly.

The price index for **tropical beverages** dropped by over 50 per cent from 1997 to 2001, but there was an 8.7 per cent increase in 2002 (see figure II.5). This was due mainly to higher cocoa prices, which were strongly influenced by the security problems in Côte d'Ivoire[11] during the last quarter of 2002, and rose by 63 per cent for the year as a whole. The increase in cocoa prices, however, subsequently lost momentum, mainly because there were no major supply disruptions in Côte d'Ivoire: high prices provided an incentive for producers to harvest the crop, despite security concerns.[12] The volume of cocoa reaching Ivoirian ports was close to normal, leading to an accumulation of stocks of more than 1.1 million tons. Combined with good crops in Ghana and Indonesia, the result was a sizeable production surplus. Looking ahead, countries such as Indonesia are increasing production, while others, such as Brazil, have found a new variety of cocoa plant resistant to witches' broom disease and have rehabilitated their plantations.

Although the world coffee price increased 4.7 per cent in 2002, prices remained depressed following the drop of two thirds between 1997 and 2001. This downward trend was due mainly to three factors: the rapid increase in production in the late 1990s from such emerging producing countries as Viet Nam; record Brazilian production; and the stagnation of consumption. In the last two quarters of 2002, there was a break in the downward price trend, chiefly resulting from speculation about a possible decline in Brazilian output, the efforts of some coffee-producing countries (for example, Brazil, Côte d'Ivoire and Viet Nam) to rationalize their production in order to adjust to the depressed market, International Coffee Organization (ICO) awareness-raising efforts and a new

---

[9] There has been a slight decrease in production in developed countries (with the exception of Australia), but sugar production in developing countries (for example, Thailand and Brazil) is still growing.

[10] See International Grains Council, Grain Market Report Summary (http://www.igc.org.uk/gmr/gmrsummary.htm).

[11] Côte d'Ivoire accounts for about 45 per cent of world production.

[12] Some cocoa was smuggled into Liberia and Guinea and also into Côte d'Ivoire from Ghana in January and February 2003 (source: ED&F Man, *Cocoa Market Report*, April 2003).

"Coffee Quality-Improvement Programme" which took off in October 2002. [13] Nonetheless, the market turned soft again in March 2003. Supply factors have continued to maintain pressure on the market; global availability (production plus stocks) is estimated to have been some 151 million bags in the crop year 2001/02, slightly higher than in 2000/01, and forecasts for 2002/03 are 157.5 million bags.

Tea prices did not experience any change in their trend, with an 8 per cent decrease from 1998 to 2002, due mainly to regular growth in supply and stagnating consumption, leading to the accumulation of a high level of stocks.

The prices of **vegetable oilseeds and oils** improved by over a quarter in 2002, after a 19 per cent fall from 1997 to 2001 (see figure II.5). This turnaround was confirmed in early 2003 with increases in prices for most vegetable oilseed and oil products, in particular cottonseed oil (13.6 per cent) and groundnut oil (8.9 per cent). Although each item in the group has its own dynamics, one of the factors influencing the market is the growing pace of imports in some countries, particularly China, where the growth of imports of soybean and palm oil exceeded expectations.

The price of **agricultural raw materials** fell by 6.7 per cent in 2002, owing mainly to slow world economic growth, leading to weak demand and high stocks. There had been a decline in both cotton price indices (A and B, corresponding to different qualities of cotton) of 10 per cent per year from 1995 to 2002, to which strong competition from synthetic fibres contributed. During the period October 2002-March 2003, cotton prices rose by nearly 4 per cent, mainly owing to the role of China, a major player in the raw cotton market and one that has just become a net importer.[14] Nonetheless, the price of cotton in international markets has been severely affected by subsidies to domestic production, for instance, in China and the United States. The case of the United States subsidies to upland cotton is currently under consideration in the World Trade Organization following a claim by Brazil that United States producers received domestic subsidies in excess of 100 per cent of crop value in 2001.[15]

In 2002, natural rubber prices rose by almost one third and were slightly higher in early 2003 as a consequence of strong demand growth, appreciating exchange rates in the main producing countries and supply/demand imbalances. Global rubber consumption is forecast to increase by 7 per cent in 2003.[16] Weather conditions and the creation of the International Tripartite Rubber Organisation (ITRO), which has the objectives of rationalizing and coordinating production, have also had some influence on rubber price developments.

Minerals and metals

The uncertainty about the outlook for the world economy affected **minerals and metals** prices in 2002 and early 2003. The situation was further aggravated by the volatility of financial and oil markets and declining confidence in the corporate sector in the wake of the accounting scandals in the United States. Moreover, developments in the minerals and metals sector are now driven mostly by supply-side factors, owing to excess capacity for most metals since the investment boom of the late 1990s. The most important factor on the demand side is the emergence of China as a key consumer and importer. This country is now seen as an important price-maker for such commodities as iron ore, aluminium and alumina[17] and copper.

[13] This is a voluntary programme aimed at removing low-quality coffee beans from the market.

[14] China's recent membership in the World Trade Organization is of great importance to the world cotton sector, since China has agreed to open an import quota of over 800,000 tons at a tariff rate of 1 per cent and plans to reduce cotton production and export subsidies.

[15] Brazil has listed a large number of laws and regulations that provide support to United States cotton producers and exporters, claiming that these violate at least six provisions in the World Trade Organization Agreement on Agriculture (see *Legal Instruments Embodying the Results of the Uruguay Round of Multilateral Trade Negotiations, done at Marrakesh on 15 April 1994* (GATT secretariat publication, Sales No. GATT/1994-7)) and five in the Agreement on Subsidies and Countervailing Measures (ibid. 1), as well as three rules of the General Agreement on Tariffs and Trade (GATT). (See International Centre for Trade and Sustainable Development (ICTSD), *Bridges Monthly Digest*, Year 7, No. 25, March 2003).

[16] See International Rubber Study Group, *Statistical Data* (http://www.rubberstudy.com/report.aspx).

[17] According to *Metal Bulletin*, No. 8767, 24 April 2003, "the strong alumina market shows little sign of waning as healthy buying interest from China holds the spot price firmly above $300 per tonne f.o.b. Australia".

Apart from a one-time recovery in 2000, the overall trend in the prices of minerals and metals has been negative since 1995 (see figure II.5). Prices decreased a further 1.8 per cent in 2002, although the declining trend was reversed for some mineral and metal products between October 2002 and March 2003. There were increases in prices in this period for nickel (4.6 per cent), tin (2.4 per cent), copper (1.8 per cent) and aluminium (1.3 per cent), even though the SARS outbreak in China put downward pressure on metal and mineral prices.[18] However, the increase in prices in United States dollars is largely offset by the depreciation of the dollar against other major currencies. Moreover, despite some cuts in production, high stock levels and gloomy demand prospects in several cases militate against a sustainable revival.

Iron ore production is estimated to have increased by about 10 per cent in 2002, following a fall in 2001. Strong demand from the steel industry in almost all countries caused the increase in production. Demand from China, where iron ore imports expanded by over 20 per cent, was a major factor and Chinese import demand is expected to grow at roughly the same rate in 2003. Iron ore supply contract negotiations set price increases at about 9 per cent for 2003.

The recent surge in nickel prices can be explained by continued demand growth of between 3 and 4 per cent per year and limited supply additions. The strong growth of Chinese demand (both directly and indirectly, in the nickel content of stainless steel imports) accounted for roughly half the total global growth in nickel demand in 2002. Underinvestment in new nickel capacity might limit production capacity and the market, which is at present finely balanced, might move into deficit over the next two years, giving a further boost to prices.

Despite robust demand, aluminium stocks reached a 15-year high in December 2002 and are still exercising a depressing influence on prices. China is a major factor in world aluminium supply and has shifted from being a net importer (120,000 tons in 2001) to being a net exporter (205,000 tons in 2002), a trend likely to continue in 2003-2005 with the entry into production of new smelting capacity in the country. These projects may add to the already high stocks and delay the recovery of the market further. Since the balance between supply and demand is considerably tighter in the case of alumina, the rapid expansion of Chinese aluminium production and consequent rapid growth in alumina imports (almost 37 per cent in 2002) has caused alumina spot prices to rise by 50 per cent.

The copper market moved from extensive surplus in 2001 to close to balance between supply and demand at the end of 2002.[19] This was due to the supply discipline introduced at the end of 2001, when producers accepted the necessity of reducing deliveries. Accordingly, despite sluggish demand growth, stocks held in the warehouses of the London Metal Exchange (LME) have stabilized, although at a high level. However, one of the leading world producers, CODELCO (Corporación Nacional del Cobre, Chile), is building a stock of 17,000-20,000 tons of copper per month, with the total stock planned to reach 200,000 tons at the beginning of 2004.

Both production and consumption of lead have been relatively stagnant over the past few years. Owing to the increasing use of secondary lead, coming mainly from used batteries and accounting for 62.2 per cent of total refined lead production in 2002, primary producers have been squeezed and close-

18   Platinum prices, for instance, were hit by the outbreak of SARS as demand by China plummeted (*Metal Bulletin*, No. 8769 of 1 May 2003).

19   According to the International Copper Study Group (ICSG), "the apparent refined copper surplus for the year 2002 has declined from December's estimate to 207,000 tonnes. Preliminary results for January 2003 show a surplus of 53,000 tonnes of refined copper compared with a surplus of 99,000 tonnes in January 2002" (ICSG press release of 9 April 2003).

downs have occurred at both the mine and smelter stages. Stocks grew steadily until mid-2002 and prices remained depressed. A slight upturn in prices in early 2003 was reversed in April. However, since stocks appear to be on a downward trend, prices may strengthen later in 2003.

Tin prices were low in 2002, owing to slow demand growth and high stocks. However, in mid-2002, stocks at LME began to fall as a result of reductions in Chinese production; and exports and prices began to recover. The downward trend in stocks continued in the first four months of 2003 and led to a recovery in prices. Future developments depend mainly on whether the limits on Chinese production remain in place, since consumption growth is relatively weak. Moreover, tin is particularly dependent on the electronics sector and could still suffer from the weakness in the ICT sector.

Mine production of zinc declined by 2 per cent in 2002, while refined metal production increased by 1 per cent. Consumption increased by 1.6 per cent, owing mainly to strong Asian, particularly Chinese, demand. Nevertheless, prices continued their downward trend as LME stocks increased. During the first months of 2003, however, both prices and stocks levelled out. Zinc mine output is expected to increase with the reopening of Outokumpu's Tara mine in Ireland (with an annual capacity of 165,000 tons) and with the potential opening of Anglo American's Skopion operations in Namibia (as well as potential increases in Australia, India, Peru and Sweden). It is therefore unlikely that any improvement in prices will be sustainable, particularly in the absence of measures to reduce capacity.

TRADE POLICY DEVELOPMENTS

Launched in November 2001, the Doha round of trade negotiations has been facing increasing challenges to its scheduled conclusion by 1 January 2005 as a single undertaking. Several negotiation deadlines were missed during 2002 and early 2003 and the lack of progress in certain key areas—particularly those of special interest to developing countries—has raised concerns whether the Fifth Ministerial Conference of the WTO in Cancún, Mexico, 10-14 September 2003, will be able to recover lost ground by resolving the wide range of outstanding and sensitive issues. A few areas of negotiations have advanced but, even in these, many pending issues remain.

In the case of services, there has been agreement on the modalities to give "credit" to countries that unilaterally liberalized this sector, often developing countries in the context of a structural adjustment programme with the World Bank or the International Monetary Fund (IMF). On the other hand, there has been resistance to the idea of emergency safeguards which many developing countries feel are necessary in view of their limited knowledge of the possible consequences for their economies of further liberalization of the service sector. As a result, only a few countries met the deadline of 31 March 2003 for specific offers of liberalization in services.

Developing countries have a particular interest in increasing market access in services through Mode 4 of services supply, that is to say, through the presence of natural persons in the importing market.[20] Total labour remittances are well above ODA flows[21] and represent a considerable source of foreign exchange for many developing countries. Greater international labour mobility

[20] The other three modes of service supply, as recognized by the General Agreement on Trade in Services (GATS), are cross-border trade, consumption abroad and commercial presence.

[21] Data include transition economies of Europe and Central Asia. See World Bank, *Global Development Finance, 2003* (Washington, D.C., World Bank, 2003).

could expand such flows and their contribution to development and poverty reduction. Currently, Mode 4 is limited to a narrow range of professionals, highly skilled individuals, high-level managers and business visitors and covers only temporary arrangements. It thus does not apply to the vast majority of immigrants from developing countries engaged in low-skilled activities or seeking permanent migration.

Negotiations on market access for non-agricultural goods have been progressing although negotiators did not meet the deadline of 31 May 2003 for an agreement on modalities. The United States proposed the elimination of all tariffs on industrial goods in two phases over a period of 10 years. This proposal would require substantial tariff cuts by developing countries, exposing their domestic manufacturing sector to external competition in a relatively short period of time. Additionally, the loss of revenue from trade taxes—though less significant than previously in many developing countries—would need to be addressed, since many low-income developing countries and small island economies continue to rely heavily on trade taxes as a source of government revenue.[22] EU also tabled a proposal: it included tariff compression with a flatter range of tariffs; elimination of peaks and high rates; deeper cuts for products that are of interest to developing countries (clothing, footwear and textiles); elimination of tariffs at and below 2 per cent; and unilateral tariff elimination for imports from least developed countries (in the spirit of the EU "Everything but Arms" initiative for these countries).

There has been limited progress in negotiations on implementation-related issues and concerns. Implementation issues are the incomplete, unrealized or post-dated elements from the Uruguay Round of multilateral trade negotiations and range from textiles to dispute settlement proceedings. Out of the 93 such points raised by the developing countries, 39 were the subject of immediate delivery by adoption of the Doha implementation decision,[23] but few of the remaining issues witnessed advances after Doha. Meanwhile, work on World Trade Organization rules (anti-dumping, subsidies and countervailing duties, and regional trade agreements (RTAs)) is nearing the end of its first phase, namely, the identification of issues to be addressed; and a significant number of proposals and comments have already been submitted. This negotiating group does not have any specific deadline before the Cancún meeting.

The deadline of 31 December 2002 (and its two subsequent extensions) established by the Declaration on the TRIPS Agreement and public health (WT/MIN (01)/DEC/2) by which to remove constraints faced by developing countries in making effective use of compulsory licensing was not met. The governments of some developing countries have dealt with domestic public-health crises, such as the acquired immunodeficiency syndrome (AIDS) pandemic, by granting licences to the domestic pharmaceutical industry, as provided for under the Declaration, to manufacture patented drugs, enabling them to supply the necessary treatment at zero or minimal cost. However, most developing countries, particularly least developed countries, lack such manufacturing capacity. This could be dealt with by importing the needed medicines at low cost from those developing countries that possess the manufacturing capacity but that are not allowed by World Trade Organization rules to export drugs produced under compulsory licensing arrangements. Disagreement emerged, as some developed countries wished to limit the right of compulsory

[22] The share of trade taxes in total government revenues was about 25 per cent in Africa in 1996-1999 but averaged 40 per cent in the Caribbean islands during the 1990s (IMF, "Developments in the Doha round and selected activities of interest to the Fund", 8 April 2003) http://www.imf.org/external/np/pdr/doha/2003/040803.htm.

[23] See Implementation related issues and concerns: decision of 14 November 2001 (http://www.wto.org/english/tratop_e/dda_e/implem_explained_e.htm).

licensing in third countries to a specific list of diseases, while developing countries argued for an open-ended list of diseases. Canada, Switzerland and the United States, however, have agreed not to challenge any developing-country members of the World Trade Organization (except those with a high income) that export drugs produced under compulsory licensing to a country in need until a permanent solution to the issue is found. The moratorium applies, however, only to human immunodeficiency virus (HIV)/AIDS, malaria, tuberculosis and other infectious diseases. EU has also declared a moratorium but with fewer restrictions on eligible diseases.

Negotiations on the strengthening of special and differential treatment (SDT) also failed to meet their extended deadline. SDT provisions give developing countries a series of privileges in implementing World Trade Organization rules and include measures to increase trade opportunities. Developing countries felt that such provisions needed revision, not only to enhance their efficiency but also to widen their scope. Such improvements could be achieved by making them mandatory, thus changing the language of certain best-endeavour provisions. Developed countries, however, do not want to amend existing texts or alter the existing balance of rights and duties.[24] Negotiators could not agree on a final report on a package of agreement-specific proposals and on the framework for continuing the negotiations, which was to be submitted to the General Council of the World Trade Organization. Members even failed to have a common understanding of their mandate and sought a clarification from the General Council.

Another major setback for developing countries, and for the progress of negotiations, was the failure of the Committee on Agriculture to agree on modalities for future commitments on trade in agriculture. Special provisions and subsidies by developed countries have created distortions in the trade of agricultural products and have prevented developing countries from exploiting their natural comparative advantages, constraining them in their pursuit of faster economic growth and development. The chairman of the Committee presented a first draft on modalities but the document—even after being revised—failed to gather support, as members remained deeply entrenched in their divergent positions. The United States and the Cairns Group of agricultural exporters are pushing for increased market access through significant reductions of tariffs and expansion of tariff rate quotas, while including the right of developing countries to safeguards under certain conditions.[25] Additionally, this group of countries, as well as many developing countries, supports a fast dismantling of trade-distorting domestic and export subsidies. EU members and other developed countries have supported a less aggressive schedule for the reduction of tariffs, domestic support and subsidies, with comparable burden-sharing among World Trade Organization members. EU is also proposing a special safeguard instrument for developing countries to ensure food security. A complicating factor in the negotiations is the erosion of preferences for ACP countries and least developed countries in the EU market. Other complicating factors include domestic policy developments in major countries. The United States adopted a major expansion of its farm support programme in 2002 (an additional $70 billion over a 10-year period), including increases in direct support payments to farmers and increased subsidies for grains and cotton producers; while some steps have been taken to reform the EU Common Agricultural Policy (CAP), the implications for the Doha negotiations are unclear.

[24] World Trade Organization, Special Session of the Committee on Trade and Development, report by the Chairman, Ambassador Ransford Smith (Jamaica), to the Trade Negotiations Committee (TN/CTD/8), 4 March 2003.

[25] Under the present system, only products that have been "tariffied", that is to say, only products that have lost protection through the reduction of quotas and/or other trade barriers, are subject to special agricultural safeguards. As most developing countries have few non-tariff barriers on agricultural products, the special agricultural safeguards are of limited use to them (International Centre for Trade and Sustainable Development, "Agriculture" (*Doha Round Briefing Series*, vol. 1, No. 2 (February 2003)).

Lack of progress in areas that are of special interest for developing countries may compromise the pace of negotiations in other areas. Several countries have argued that progress in negotiations on agriculture, in particular, is necessary to support negotiations elsewhere. Negotiations on "Singapore issues" (investment, competition policy, transparency in government procurement and trade facilitation), for instance, are to be launched in Cancún if there is an explicit consensus at the ministerial meetings on the modalities. There has been very little progress on these issues and agreement seems unlikely. Investment and competition policy remain the most controversial issues. Developing countries have resisted expanding the scope of trade negotiations into these areas and are concerned about agreeing on issues and standards that may be difficult and costly for them to implement and incompatible with their level of development.[26]

These major setbacks, as well as the slow progress in other areas, may leave an overwhelming number of issues to be agreed upon at Cancún. If that happens, there will be very little time for analysis and assessment during the negotiations themselves, particularly for developing countries, which have less technical capacity than developed countries. Besides the overcrowding of the agenda, a lack of political will could hamper negotiations. In their reports, several chairmen referred to the wide gaps among members as the main reason for the slow or non-existent progress in their respective negotiating groups. The Doha trade negotiations need to be given the political attention that Governments committed themselves to.

Bilateral and regional developments

Other developments indicate conflicting trends in multilateralism and global trade liberalization. Several free trade agreement (FTA) initiatives have been launched or concluded since early 2002. While further trade liberalization can entail benefits for the countries concerned, the proliferation of regional trade agreements (RTAs) may also create a complex web of competing and conflicting jurisdictions that could restrain, not promote, trade. The examples in the following paragraphs are illustrative. Additionally, it is not clear whether developing countries have enough resources to engage in simultaneous negotiations at the bilateral, regional and multilateral levels. Negotiations at the multilateral level, and thus developing-country gains, may suffer as a result.

Most of the new regional initiatives include a major developed country. For instance, the United States trade agenda for 2003 includes the negotiation of FTAs with the Southern African Customs Union (Botswana, Lesotho, Namibia, South Africa and Swaziland), the Central American Common Market (Costa Rica, El Salvador, Guatemala, Honduras and Nicaragua), Australia and Morocco. Moreover, the United States is a major force behind negotiations towards the establishment of a Free Trade Area of the Americas (FTAA) and has signalled future trade liberalization initiatives with the Association of Southeast Asian Nations (ASEAN) countries. EU is conducting FTA negotiations with the Southern Common Market (MERCOSUR) and moving forward with the implementation of the Euro-Mediterranean Free Trade Area by 2010. As of early 2003, EU had signed Association Agreements with 11 Mediterranean countries; Egypt, Jordan, Morocco and Tunisia concluded negotiations for a regional FTA in January 2003. In April 2003, EU held consultations to facilitate trade with ASEAN countries. Meanwhile developing coun-

[26] Razeen Sally, "Whither the WTO? a progress report on the Doha round", *Cato Institute Trade Policy Analysis*, No. 23, 3 March 2003.

tries have also been active in forging free trade alliances. India and China announced trade negotiations with the ASEAN nations, whereas MERCOSUR started negotiations with India.

Bilateral and regional negotiations may move faster than their multilateral counterparts because fewer actors are involved, but RTAs have not necessarily promoted the interests of developing countries. While trade liberalization on industrial goods has advanced further in RTAs, concessions in agriculture, for instance, have been limited. Most RTAs have failed to promote deeper liberalization in agriculture, as tariffs remain high despite preferential treatment.[27] Additionally, issues such as agricultural subsidies are often referred to World Trade Organization negotiations and not advanced in regional agreements.

A broad point is that developing countries' bargaining power may be weakened outside multilateral forums, where they can use their numbers to strengthen their positions, particularly in their negotiations with developed countries. In their quest for increased access to developed countries' markets, developing countries may agree to concessions in RTAs that they would not necessarily accept in a multilateral context when dealing as a group.[28] Issues that have not yet been fully discussed and agreed in a multilateral forum, such as competition policy, are frequently included in RTAs and often based on legal provisions in the United States. A similar approach exists in the EU Association Agreements with the Mediterranean developing countries, which include a series of provisions beyond trade liberalization that aim at making the partner's economic legislation similar to that of EU. Developed countries' economic policies were designed to respond to those countries' specific needs and goals and are compatible with their level of development. This does not imply, however, that they are suitable for developing countries facing different conditions and different constraints.

FINANCIAL FLOWS TO DEVELOPING COUNTRIES AND ECONOMIES IN TRANSITION

Developing countries made a net transfer of financial resources to other countries for a sixth consecutive year in 2002, as payments of foreign investment income and net financial outflows, including increases in holdings of foreign reserves, exceeded receipts of foreign investment income and net financial inflows from abroad (see table II.1). In dollars, this was the largest negative resource transfer ever by these countries. There was also a net outward transfer of financial resources from economies in transition in 2002.

A net inward transfer of financial resources can be an important supplement to gross domestic saving in financing domestic investment. Conversely, a net outward transfer of resources reduces the resources available for consumption or investment in the country. The large net outward transfer of financial resources from Latin America in 2002 was brought about by a sharp contraction of imports as crisis countries compressed consumption and investment in response to the withdrawal of capital flows by international investors. On the other hand, in Eastern and Southern Asia, the large net outward resource transfer grew further, but in an environment of strong growth of exports and imports underpinned by economic growth. Financial resource outflows from this region took the form of a net repayment of debt and the purchase of foreign assets,

[27] WTO secretariat, "Regional trade integration under transformation" (preliminary draft prepared for Seminar on Regionalism and the World Trade Organization), Geneva, 26 April 2002.

[28] For instance, the recent FTAs that the United States negotiated with Chile and Singapore place considerable restrictions on the use of capital controls ("US backs curbs on capital controls", *Financial Times*, 2 April 2003).

Table II.1.
NET TRANSFER OF FINANCIAL RESOURCES TO DEVELOPING
ECONOMIES AND ECONOMIES IN TRANSITION, 1994-2002

Billions of dollars									
	1994	1995	1996	1997	1998	1999	2000	2001	2002[a]
Developing economies	44.2	49.7	30.3	-2.7	-33.7	-120.9	-179.3	-155.1	-192.5
Africa	4.6	6.6	-4.4	-3.7	15.6	5.1	-18.8	-11.2	-9.0
Sub-Saharan (excluding Nigeria and South Africa)	6.7	8.2	10.5	7.9	13.2	9.7	5.0	9.0	9.5
Eastern and Southern Asia	5.1	25.6	22.4	-34.6	-130.1	-134.8	-110.4	-111.0	-141.5
Western Asia	15.2	18.8	11.2	11.4	36.1	-0.3	-48.3	-34.9	-13.2
Latin America	19.3	-1.3	1.1	24.2	44.7	9.1	-1.8	2.0	-28.8
Economies in transition	-2.2	10.0	20.0	30.2	33.7	4.5	-23.4	-9.7	-9.5
Memorandum item: Heavily indebted poor countries (HIPCs)	9.6	10.9	10.7	11.2	13.7	10.7	5.7	8.2	10.3

Source: UN/DESA, based on International Monetary Fund (IMF), *World Economic Outlook*, April 2003, and IMF, *Balance of Payments Statistics*.

[a] Preliminary estimate.

especially official reserves. The net inward transfer of resources to sub-Saharan Africa consisted of net private and official financial flows which helped to finance the trade deficit.

Focusing on the net capital flow component of the net transfer, developing countries received an estimated $75 billion in net capital inflows in 2002 (see table II.2). The only sources of net capital inflows in 2002 were FDI and official loans and grants, as financial markets and international banks continued to reduce their exposure to developing countries as a whole. Net capital flows to transition economies were almost unchanged in 2002, consisting of net inflows of FDI, portfolio credit and equity investment and official flows.

Private capital flows

International investors' confidence in developing and transition economies was unusually low in 2002 owing to the crisis in Argentina, uncertainty over the direction of policy in Brazil and other factors in Latin America and elsewhere. In early 2003, along with the weak global economic situation, investors were concerned about rising oil prices, war in Iraq and the threat of international terrorism. Nevertheless, the beginning of economic recovery in Argentina, the direction of the economic policies of the newly elected Government in Brazil and positive developments in economic policies and performance in Colombia and Peru strengthened investor sentiment. The consequent reduction in the yields on these countries' bonds reduced the average spread between the yield on bonds of Latin American countries and that of the risk-free benchmark, United States Treasury bonds (see figure II.6). Investment risk in Turkey was also perceived to have diminished after the election of a new Government in November 2002, although concerns soon emerged about the economic and political fallout of possible conflict in Iraq.

Table II.2.
NET FINANCIAL FLOWS TO DEVELOPING ECONOMIES AND ECONOMIES IN TRANSITION, 1992-2002

Billions of dollars	Average 1992-1996	1997	1998	1999	2000	2001	2002[a]
Developing economies							
Net private capital flows	149.1	96.6	38.9	66.2	18.2	17.9	51.8
Net direct investment	66.1	120.5	128.0	133.0	125.6	145.3	110.0
Net portfolio investment[b]	63.0	41.6	-3.7	39.0	9.7	-41.7	-40.0
Other net investment[c]	19.9	-65.5	-85.3	-105.8	-117.2	-85.8	-18.2
Net official flows	23.3	40.8	49.3	10.5	-0.7	25.6	22.9
Total net flows	172.4	137.4	88.2	76.7	17.5	43.5	74.7
Economies in transition							
Net private capital flows	19.8	-20.9	14.5	29.8	32.9	20.9	34.1
Net direct investment	8.2	15.5	20.8	23.8	23.4	25.2	29.2
Net portfolio investment[b]	10.5	6.9	5.4	2.4	2.4	3.2	3.4
Other net investment[c]	1.1	-43.3	-11.8	3.6	7.1	-7.4	1.5
Net official flows	-2.6	15.5	33.7	3.5	-3.1	13.2	2.9
Total net flows	17.2	-5.4	48.2	33.3	29.8	34.1	37.0

Source: International Monetary Fund, *World Economic Outlook Database*, April 2003.

a   Preliminary.
b   Including portfolio debt and equity investment.
c   Including short- and long-term bank lending, and possibly including some official flows owing to data limitations.

Figure II.6.
YIELD SPREADS ON EMERGING MARKET BONDS,
2 JANUARY 2002-30 APRIL 2003

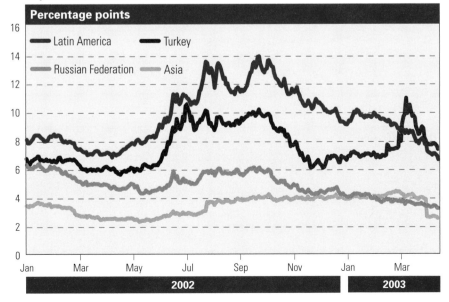

Source: J.P. Morgan Chase Co., New York.

Investors continued to discriminate among markets with different levels of risk in late 2002 and early 2003, as reflected in the differences in the bond spreads among emerging markets. Sovereign credit ratings were upgraded in 2002 for a number of countries, including Mexico, the Republic of Korea and the Russian Federation. Notably, the sovereign debt ratings of the Republic of Korea and Mexico were increased to "investment grade", making their bonds eligible for purchase by pension funds and other regulated institutional investors in developed countries. In Asia, prospects for continued robust export and economic growth underpinned a perception of relatively low risk, although concerns about the prospect of war in Iraq and a slower-than-expected global recovery, as well as elevated geopolitical tensions in the Korean peninsula and the feared spread of SARS in the region, contributed to increased uncertainties in early 2003. Continued strong economic growth and the external surplus of the Russian Federation resulted in a fall in the yield on Russian bonds to a low level in early 2003.

A number of "high-grade" emerging market bonds were issued in late 2002, followed by a strong rebound in the issuance of what the market characterizes as lower credit quality bonds. Such countries as Colombia, Peru and Turkey regained access to international financial markets. Brazilian corporate borrowers were able to access international credit, mainly to refinance maturing debt, but there was no issuance of Brazilian sovereign bonds until the end of April 2003. Other countries in Latin America and Asia were able to issue bonds at lower yield spreads, reflecting their high credit ratings.

All in all, however, private capital flows into emerging market bonds were depressed in 2002. Bond issuance by Latin American countries was less than half the volume in 2001. In contrast, bond issuance by countries of Asia was unchanged as robust economic growth and continued strengthening of financial systems made the region attractive to investors, especially against the backdrop of financial difficulties in Latin America. At the same time, the Russian Federation and a number of other economies in transition increased bond issuance. At the end of 2002 and beginning of 2003, declining risk and the relatively high yields of emerging market bonds in an environment of low interest rates in developed countries and depressed prices in global stock markets attracted increased investment flows. In addition, anticipation of the invasion of Iraq led some planned bond issuances to be advanced.

Developing and transition economies made net repayments to foreign banks in 2002, albeit in substantially lower amounts than in 2001. This resulted from decreased amortizations and a low level of new lending, continuing a trend that had begun a few years previously as international banks reduced their emerging market loan operations in favour of fee-based transactions. Also, local currency loans and bond markets have grown in some of these countries, in such regions as Western Asia and Eastern and Southern Asia, reducing demand for foreign currency borrowing. Most of the international private lending was to corporations considered low credit risks, for example, in Asian countries, Central and Eastern European countries (the Czech Republic, Hungary and Poland) and the Russian Federation. There was a large net repayment by Latin America of bank loans in 2002 and Turkey continued to make net repayments.

Although net FDI inflows to developing economies were less in 2002 than in 2001, they did total over $100 billion and were the only source of net private capital flow to these countries (see table II.2). Adverse global economic and political conditions and dampened investment activity of corporations, especially in mergers and acquisitions, slowed FDI, as did financial difficulties in some Latin American countries and reduced levels of privatization in a number of countries in Latin America and North Africa. The exception was an increase in FDI in China, with its desirability as a location for low-cost manufacturing reinforced by its accession to the World Trade Organization. FDI in transition economies also increased modestly in 2002.[29]

Prices in emerging stock markets declined by 8 per cent in dollar terms for 2002 as a whole, even after a recovery from lows in September.[30] Latin American markets suffered the largest decline; only the markets of the European transition economies made gains. The issuance of shares was subdued for a second year and remained concentrated in a few countries. Asia continued to dominate equity issuance, with China accounting for about one third of the total. Latin American issuance was very low, with little activity in the second half of the year. Russian energy and financial corporations dominated issuance by the economies in transition. In the first quarter of 2003, prices of emerging market equities as a whole continued to fall in tandem with the prices of equities in developed markets.

Official flows

Official financial flows to developing countries in 2002 were high for the second consecutive year (see table II.2), reflecting substantial multilateral lending. IMF was a net provider of $15 billion to the developing countries (down from $17.6 billion in 2001), as it continued to make large disbursements in support of economic programmes to countries in financial distress (see table A.23). The major disbursements were under standby facilities: $13 billion to Turkey, $6 billion to Brazil and $1.4 billion to Uruguay. The net repayment of funds to IMF by countries with economies in transition fell to $1.8 billion in 2002 from $4.1 billion in 2001, owing mainly to lower repurchases by the Russian Federation (see table A.24).

Argentina's difficulties in late 2002 in meeting scheduled debt-service payments on some loans to multilateral creditors were resolved in early 2003.[31] In January 2003, Argentina reached agreement with the IMF for a "rollover" loan, that is to say, funds to be used to service IMF debt maturing through August 2003. The agreement with IMF, together with Argentina's payment of arrears to the World Bank, paved the way for the release, also in January, of a sizeable World Bank sectoral loan. In the same month, Argentina also settled its arrears with the Inter-American Development Bank (IADB).

Resource commitments to developing and transition economies by the multilateral development institutions and programmes decreased from $46.5 billion in 2001 to almost $43.1 billion in 2002 (see table A.27), about the same amount in real terms as in most years since 1997. Non-concessional commitments in 2002 fell by 14 per cent in dollar terms, marked by the sharp decrease in commitments by the IADB owing to decreased lending to Argentina, fewer emergency loans, the slowdown in loan approvals for Brazil as its election results were awaited and a drop in overall investment activity in Latin America due to the recessionary conditions. Non-concessional resource commitments

[29] For a detailed discussion of FDI developments in developing and transition economies in 2002, see *World Economic Situation and Prospects, 2003* (United Nations publication, Sales No. E.03.II.C.2), chap. II, sects. entitled "Reduced FDI flows" and "International financial cooperation".

[30] Morgan Stanley Capital International, Emerging Markets Free Index (EMFI).

[31] See *World Economic Situation and Prospects, 2003* (United Nations publication, Sales No. E.03.II.C.2), p. 24.

from the International Bank for Reconstruction and Development (IBRD), which had provided, on average, more than 25 per cent of total non-concessional finance through the years, fell by 10 per cent as loans to several major borrowing countries, including Argentina and Turkey, were smaller in 2002 than in 2001. In contrast, commitments from the European Bank for Reconstruction and Development (EBRD) rose sharply on the strength of robust lending and investment in the Russian Federation and in countries in South-eastern Europe. About 60 per cent of EBRD commitments went to the financial sector and infrastructure. Concessional commitments rose by 6 per cent as a result of the strong increase in International Development Association (IDA) credit commitments following its refunding agreement. Commitments from the Development Fund for Africa fell 30 per cent in 2002 owing largely to the disruptions in its activities and delayed loan agreements caused by disturbances in Côte d'Ivoire.

Official development assistance

Official development assistance (ODA) may finally have begun to recover in 2002, rising 8.8 per cent to $57.0 billion from $52.3 billion in 2001 (see table II.3). When the effects of inflation and exchange-rate movements are taken into account, "real" ODA rose by 4.8 per cent. The ODA "effort" of Organisation for Economic Cooperation and Development/Development Assistance Committee (OECD/DAC) member countries as a group, measured as the ratio of ODA to donor gross national income (GNI), rose to 0.23 per cent from the record low of 0.22 per cent in each of the previous three years. Twelve of the 22 OECD/DAC member countries reported an increase in ODA in real terms. Nine countries reported an increase of more than 10 per cent. ODA from the United States, the largest donor, increased by 11.6 per cent in real terms in 2002, while that from Japan, the second largest donor, declined by 1.8 per cent. The increases by a number of donors, including Canada, EU, Norway, Switzerland and the United States, reflected commitments made in the context of the International Conference on Financing for Development in Monterrey, Mexico.[32] According to DAC estimates, fulfilling the Monterrey pledges to increase ODA will raise the volume by 31 per cent (about $16 billion) and the ODA/GNP ratio to 0.26 per cent by 2006.[33] However, the ratio would still fall far short of the 0.33 per cent consistently reached until 1992.

Denmark, Luxembourg, the Netherlands, Norway and Sweden are still the only countries to meet the United Nations ODA target of 0.7 per cent of GNP. Three countries, however, have declared dates to reach that target: Ireland by 2007, Belgium by 2010 and France by 2012. EU, as a group, is committed to raising its ODA-to-GNP average to 0.39 per cent by 2006; in 2002, EU member countries collectively increased their ODA by 2.8 per cent, in real terms, with an average ODA-to-GNP ratio of 0.34 per cent.

ODA would rise more dramatically if a proposal by the United Kingdom of Great Britain and Northern Ireland to establish an international finance facility (IFF) was enacted.[34] The IFF would bring forward ODA contributions by borrowing funds from the private market through bond issuance and servicing the borrowing with annual ODA outlays (15 years per bond issue). Other major donors did not immediately commit to the proposal and it is unclear whether the United Kingdom would use the approach unilaterally if other donors did not join.

[32] See report of the Secretary-General entitled "Follow-up efforts to the International Conference on Financing for Development" (A/57/319-E/2002/85), paras. 4-14.

[33] See OECD news release, "OECD DAC countries begin recovery in development aid: 5 % increase in 2002", Paris, 22 April 2003 (www.oecd.org/dac).

[34] See United Kingdom Treasury and Department for International Development, "International Finance Facility", January 2003.

Table II.3.
OFFICIAL DEVELOPMENT ASSISTANCE OF MEMBER COUNTRIES OF THE DEVELOPMENT ASSISTANCE COMMITTEE, 2002

	ODA (millions of dollars)	ODA/GNP (percentage)[a]	Real change 2001 to 2002[b] (percentage)
Australia	962	0.25	2.1
Austria	475	0.23	-16.5
Belgium	1 061	0.42	13.7
Canada	2 013	0.28	31.6
Denmark	632	0.96	-6.4
Finland	466	0.35	12.5
France	5 182	0.36	15.3
Germany	5 359	0.27	0.4
Greece	295	0.22	34.2
Ireland	397	0.41	25.4
Italy	2 313	0.20	31.5
Japan	9 220	0.23	-1.8
Luxembourg	143	0.78	-3.5
Netherlands	3 377	0.82	-2.2
New Zealand	124	0.23	0.5
Norway	1 714	0.89	13.8
Portugal	282	0.24	-4.6
Spain	1 608	0.25	-15.7
Sweden	1 754	0.74	-2.3
Switzerland	933	0.32	-5.6
United Kingdom	4 749	0.30	-3.5
United States	12 900	0.12	11.6
Total DAC	56 598	0.23	4.8
Average country effort (unweighted)	–	0.40	–
Memorandum items:			
EU countries combined	29 093	0.34	2.8
European Commission	6 502	–	1.2

Source: Organisation for Economic Cooperation and Development, news release, OECD On-line, Paris, 22 April 2003 (www.oecd.org/dac).

[a] Beginning in 2001, ODA/GNP ratios were reported by the DAC secretariat as a percentage of gross national income (GNI) instead of gross national product (GNP). The change has been only in terminology, introduced with the 1993 revision of the System of National Accounts, inasmuch as GNI is GNP as it would currently be measured.

[b] Taking account of both inflation and exchange-rate movements.

The Monterrey Consensus of the International Conference on Financing for Development recognized that, as a complement to additional ODA flows, there had to be an enhancement of the effectiveness of aid (para. 43).[35] In its communiqué of September 2002, the Joint Ministerial Committee of the Boards of Governors of the World Bank and the IMF on the Transfer of Real Resources to Developing Countries (Development Committee) expressed the commitment of its members to further action in streamlining aid policies, procedures and requirements.[36]

These issues were the focus of a high-level forum held in Rome in February 2003. The forum, convened by major aid donors and users, aimed at better harmonizing ODA procedures and reducing "red tape", building on the commit-

[35] See *Report of the International Conference on Financing for Development, Monterrey, Mexico, 18-22 March 2002* (United Nations publication, Sales No. E.02.11.A.7), chap. I, resolution 1, annex.

[36] See communiqué of the Joint Ministerial Committee of the Boards of Governors of the World Bank and the International Monetary Fund on the Transfer of Real Resources to Developing Countries (Development Committee), Washington, D.C., 28 September 2002 http://www.imf.org/external/np/cm/2003/041303.htm, para. 7.

37 See letter dated 18 March 2003 from the Permanent Representative of Italy to the United Nations addressed to the Secretary-General transmitting the Rome Declaration on Harmonization (A/57/763).

ments of the Monterrey Consensus.[37] The experiences reviewed in the forum highlighted the fact that although some countries had acquired sufficient capacity to evaluate their development needs, many had not yet reached this level of expertise. In addition to taking stock of the "good practice" work of DAC and the multilateral development banks and the work in progress in the United Nations Development Group, forum participants committed themselves to enhancing harmonization in a number of ways and to setting out a voluntary work programme to improve harmonization of development assistance at the country level. After roughly half a century of development cooperation and many attempts to reduce the administrative burden of ODA, this initiative could be a breakthrough.

The view that developing-country efforts, when combined with enhanced policy coherence among donor countries and higher levels of aid, lead to greater aid effectiveness was voiced also by Development Cooperation Ministers and Heads of Aid Agencies at the Annual High Level Meeting of DAC, held in Paris in April 2003. At that meeting, the participants discussed ways to further improve policies and strategies in order to achieve the Millennium Development Goals. They expressed support for better monitoring and reviewing of development outcomes. Aid agencies pledged to strengthen results-based management of aid and promised to support country-led development strategies. In a further boost to promoting policy coherence in development cooperation, it was noted that DAC had begun to work with the Economic Commission for Africa (ECA) on mutual reviews of development effectiveness.

38 See report of the High-level Panel on Financing for Development, transmitted in a letter dated 25 June 2001 from the Secretary-General to the President of the General Assembly (A/55/1000), recommendations of the Panel, sects. entitled "Estimates of need", "Further debt relief for highly endebted poor countries" and "More development aid needed".

Even the most effective and efficient delivery of the current volume of ODA will fall far short of what is needed to meet the Millennium Development Goals. The High-level Panel on Financing for Development estimated that ODA on the order of two times the current level, or roughly an additional $50 billion a year, was required to meet these Goals, and that a further increase on the order of $50 billion a year would be needed to reach the aid target of 0.7 per cent of GNI.[38] The challenges remain both to translate the increases in ODA associated with the International Conference on Financing for Development into outlays as quickly as possible and to raise commitments substantially.

Initiative for the Heavily Indebted Poor Countries (HIPCs)

The Monterrey Consensus stresses that the speedy, effective and full implementation of the Initiative to lighten the external debt burden of the Heavily Indebted Poor Countries (HIPCs) is critical if it is to strengthen the economic prospects and poverty reduction efforts of beneficiary countries. As of end-April 2003, only 8 of the 26 HIPCs that had reached the intermediate benchmark, the "decision point",[39] had proceeded to their "completion point". Moreover, some of the eight countries appear to have experienced worsening debt indicators, owing to lower world commodity prices and export receipts than had been assumed. "Topping up" debt relief at the completion point is possible if commodity prices have fallen since the projected need for relief was calculated, and such arrangements were made for Burkina Faso in early 2003. However, the length and complexity of the HIPC process and the repeated need to enhance it remain concerns.

39 Mali and Benin became the seventh and eighth countries to reach the completion point, on 7 March and 25 March 2003, respectively.

IMF and the World Bank attribute the delay in bringing more countries to their completion point to the complications that a number of countries have faced in implementing programmes to meet their fiscal targets and the difficulty that some countries have had in preparing Poverty Reduction Strategy Papers (PRSPs), which are prerequisites for receipt of irrevocable debt relief at the completion point under the HIPC Initiative.[40] In part, the domestic policy disappointments reflect the weak international economy of the past few years or, in some cases, domestic insecurity. However, they also raise questions whether expectations were too high about the benefits that would be derived in the near term from the policy reforms that the international community had sought from the HIPCs. Long-term debt sustainability in these countries requires not only some reduction in their debt stocks under the HIPC Initiative, but also domestic policies in support of more rapid and broad-based growth and a supportive international economic environment. In addition, the concept of debt sustainability may not have been sufficiently robust in the light of the performance of the international economy. This matter is being given further consideration by the Bretton Woods institutions.

Other factors have slowed the implementation of the HIPC programme. The Joint Ministerial Committee of the Boards of Governors of the World Bank and the International Monetary Fund on the Transfer of Real Resources to Developing Countries (Development Committee) and the International Monetary and Financial Committee of the Board of Governors have urged further Bank and Fund efforts to address such factors as HIPC-to-HIPC debt relief and creditor litigation issues.[41] Although the total costs of HIPC-to-HIPC debt relief are small (about 1 per cent of total costs of debt relief provided by all creditors to these countries), the amount may be significant to a creditor HIPC that is itself heavily in debt. This may explain, in part, why not all HIPC creditors have made commitments to deliver debt relief. In other cases, disputes over technical matters have resulted in delays in reaching full agreement on settlements between creditors and debtors. In cases where the creditor's financial constraints make the provision of debt relief more difficult, it has been recommended that a donor trust fund be established to improve creditor participation in debt-relief efforts.

Compounding these problems is the difficulty being faced by the international community in raising resources to fully fund the current framework of the HIPC Initiative. As at end-April 2003, paid-in contributions were $2.4 billion out of total pledges of $2.6 billion. Full funding of the HIPC Trust Fund is about to occur at a time when the adequacy of the total pledges can be questioned. Even when pledges are fully paid, the HIPC Trust Fund would lack the resources required to attain its objectives, especially in light of the fact that the economies of many HIPCs remain more fragile than expected and the international situation is not very supportive. The latter pertains, above all, to disappointing trade trends, but it also reflects the need of HIPCs to receive more of their capital inflows in the form of grants. A review of the HIPC Initiative by the World Bank's Operations Evaluation Department in providing an explanation for the slow progress of the programme, concluded that the objective of the HIPC Initiative had been to reduce debt to sustainable levels as part of a broader strategy to achieve debt sustainability. This is a less ambitious goal than assuring a permanent exit from debt rescheduling, which would be a more appropriate goal for these impoverished countries.[42]

[40] International Monetary Fund and International Development Association, "Heavily Indebted Poor Countries (HIPC) Initiative: status of implementation", 23 September 2002 (IMFC/Doc/6/02/4).

[41] HIPC relief for outstanding official bilateral claims of HIPC creditors on the 26 HIPC countries that have reached the decision point amounted to $143.3 million in 2001 in net present value (NPV) terms. The total is concentrated heavily on a few HIPC countries: Honduras to Nicaragua ($102.2 million NPV); Angola to several HIPC countries ($25.8 million); Côte d'Ivoire to Burkina Faso ($9.7 million); and the United Republic of Tanzania to Uganda ($3.4 million).

[42] See World Bank, Operations Evaluation Department, "The Heavily Indebted Poor Country (HIPC) Debt Initiative: an OED review", 20 February 2003.

CONTINUING REFORM OF THE INTERNATIONAL FINANCIAL ARCHITECTURE

Especially since the Asian financial crisis, the international community has made considerable efforts to help countries prevent financial crises and withstand potential shocks. It has also considered ways to speed up workouts from financial crises when they do occur. There have been considerable reforms of the international financial architecture, but much still needs to be done to achieve a more stable and development-friendly international financial system. This need was recognized in the Monterrey Consensus which noted the need for international efforts to reform the international financial architecture "to be sustained with greater transparency and the effective participation of developing countries and countries with economies in transition".[43]

43 See *Report of the International Conference on Financing for Development, ...,* para. 53.

Crisis prevention activities

Much attention was focused in the year under review on two major components of the global crisis-prevention strategy: multinational surveillance and the implementation and design of financial standards and codes.

Multilateral surveillance

Multilateral surveillance of national economic and financial policies, primarily by IMF, is a critical instrument of the international community for crisis prevention. The key objective is early identification of risks and vulnerabilities. Beyond the traditional macroeconomic policy areas, surveillance is now also focusing on improvement in the transparency of countries' policies, implementation of various standards and codes, and the provision of more specialized financial sector assessments. Increased attention is also being paid to improving the assessment of debt sustainability and vulnerability to financial crisis.

Most of the recent efforts have targeted developing and transition economies. In this regard, concerns have been raised about the increased burden of the various surveillance exercises on national authorities. It has also been argued that the growth of initiatives may dilute policy advice, undermining the main purpose of surveillance. With so many instruments being introduced, there may be less focus on those areas that can really enhance a country's crisis prevention capacities.

Accordingly, there is a growing view that further expansion of the scope of IMF surveillance should be avoided and that the existing surveillance framework needs to be consolidated. The surveillance framework for any particular country should demonstrate the relationships between the different policy areas and thereby facilitate a deeper analysis and discussion to inform policy formulation. Consolidating the framework also requires tailoring priorities within surveillance so that they accord with country needs and capacities; this requires selectivity among the wide range of issues that could potentially require attention. Sometimes, to ensure that advice has impact, it may be preferable to do less but to do it better.

One reason for the focus on developing and transition economies is that, in the age of liberalized financial markets and high international capital mobility, weakness in the financial infrastructure of a single developing or transition economy could set off a financial crisis, as in the case of Thailand in 1997. However, country-specific factors do not drive crises from country to country. Indeed, globalization has heightened the significance of factors that can spread financial distress, including the behaviour of international short-term investors.

In addition, there is a broadly held view that, because their macroeconomic policies can have a global impact, multilateral surveillance of major developed countries should be intensified. The economic policies of these countries significantly affect other economies and may be the source of systemic shocks and vulnerabilities. These countries have thus been repeatedly called upon to pay particular attention to the coherence of their policies with respect to global objectives and priorities.

It has been suggested that recent financial crises could be, at least in part, the by-products of the rapid credit expansion, asset price increases and overinvestment in the industrialized countries in the 1990s.[44] Institutional shortcomings in many emerging market countries contributed to the crises, but these excesses played an important role. Accordingly, improving governance, developing and implementing standards and codes and strengthening financial architecture in developing and transition economies are important, but their effectiveness depends on the global macroeconomic policy-setting. This, in turn, depends almost solely on the actions of the major industrialized countries.

It has therefore been suggested that IMF should give greater weight in its assessments of the major economies to the systemic impact of their macroeconomic development and policies. However, according to many observers, including IMF itself, industrialized countries have been much less receptive to Fund advice than other members, as they are unlikely to seek financing from the Fund, and therefore find it less necessary to take account of the views of the international community in the formulation of their policies.[45] As a result, this important segment of surveillance is weak.

International standards and codes and their implementation

A fundamental part of crisis prevention strategy is for countries to strengthen their financial and macroeconomic systems by following international standards and codes of best practice. As part of this process, the international community has sought to develop a single set of international rules and principles for crucial areas of domestic policy in the financial and monetary spheres. These rules and principles have been developed in a variety of forums, with different degrees of participation by developing countries and countries with economies in transition.

Because the financial sector is characterized by considerable interdependence and complementarity, the standards cover many issues, but they can be grouped in three main areas: transparency (official data and fiscal, monetary and financial policy decisions); regulation and supervision of the main types of financial intermediaries (banks, securities issuers and insurance companies); and market integrity of the corporate sector (corporate governance, accounting, auditing, insolvency, creditor rights and payment systems). To make the process of implementation manageable, the Bretton Woods institutions and the Financial Stability Forum (FSF), which brings together the ministries of

[44] William White, "International financial crisis: prevention, management and resolution", speech at a conference on "Economic governance: the role of markets and the State", Bern, 20 March 2003 (www.bis.org).

[45] International Monetary Fund, Policy Development and Review Department, "Enhancing the effectiveness of surveillance: operational responses, the agenda ahead, and next steps", 14 March 2003 http://www.imf.org/external/np/pdr/surv/2003/031403.htm, p. 9.

finance, central banks and main financial regulators of the major global markets, have selected 12 core standards out of more than 70 different standards that have been issued by various bodies.

While most of the standards have largely been developed, they are regularly reviewed and revised in the various standard-setting bodies. Over the past year, much of this activity has focused on the "market integrity" cluster of standards and codes, reflecting the need for enhanced corporate governance, accounting and auditing which was highlighted by the spate of large corporate failures associated with improper management behaviour in developed countries. The major development in the area of accounting has been the global move towards the adoption of principles-based internationally convergent accounting standards, as developed by the International Accounting Standards Board (IASB). On 11 September 2002, the EU regulation on international accounting standards (IAS) entered into force. It requires that, by 2007, all EU listed companies prepare their consolidated financial statements using the international accounting standards.[46] Meanwhile, in the United States, amid corporate scandals, the attitude to IAS is becoming more positive. In October 2002, the United States Financial Accounting Standards Board (FASB) and IASB issued a Memorandum of Understanding formalizing their commitment to the convergence of United States and international accounting standards and agreed on a project to achieve this convergence. The Boards expect to issue a joint draft to address those differences in the latter part of 2003.[47]

Along with the adoption of international accounting standards, the growing instances of accounting irregularities at major corporations have prompted international efforts to further improve accounting standards and close the existing gaps in the guidelines. Those include treatment of stock options, pension fund deficits and financial derivatives.

As for other parts of the market integrity segment, there is an ongoing effort to finalize the principles and guidelines on insolvency regimes and creditor rights by converging to a single standard set of principles based on the models developed by the World Bank and the United Nations Commission on International Trade Law (UNCITRAL). Also, in March 2003, the IMF Executive Board agreed to include the Recommendations for Securities Settlement Systems developed by the International Organization of Securities Commissions (IOSCO) and the Committee on Payment and Settlement Systems (CPSS) as another standard for member countries with substantial securities trading.

FSF has also taken up these issues. At its ninth meeting in March 2003, it endorsed the ongoing revision of the Principles of Corporate Governance of OECD.[48] It also affirmed the importance of ensuring strong auditor independence, called for development of sound international audit practice standards and welcomed work by the Securities and Exchange Commission of the United States and by international bodies to address possible conflicts of interest and issues relating to credit rating agencies. In addition, the Forum reviewed progress in addressing earlier concerns, including assessment of offshore financial centres.

Meanwhile, efforts to foster implementation of international standards, especially in developing and transition economies, face complications. In an ideal world, standards would represent global best practices and be equally

[46] Regulation No. 1606/2002 of the European Parliament and the Council of 19 July 2002 on the application of international accounting standards (http://europa.eu.int).

[47] FASB News Release, 29 October 2002 (www.fasb.org).

[48] See Financial Stability Forum (FSF), ninth meeting of FSF (Berlin, 24 and 25 March 2003) (www.fsforum.org).

applicable to all countries. However, countries differ in their historical and cultural characteristics. In practice, this calls for some degree of differentiation in the application of standards, even in countries that seem to have similar levels of financial development. For countries at an early stage of development, the low level of sophistication of the domestic financial system conditions the extent to which particular standards or best practices can be adopted. Requiring such countries to apply standards in their full complexity might unnecessarily delay the implementation process and even deter countries from starting it.

Moreover, the notion that "standards must always be standard" (in other words, best practices rather than minimum requirements or principles) essentially confines country-specific flexibility to decisions about sequencing and prioritization in implementation. It has been argued that international acceptance of the importance of sequencing and prioritization is not sufficient to resolve the "one size fits all" dilemma.[49] Indeed, it is not clear how sequencing and prioritization per se could make most standards and codes designed mainly for industrialized countries applicable in economies with different legal and institutional situations and at different stages of development.

There have thus been suggestions that standards and codes should not be based on single models, but rather should have some flexibility with which to reflect local cultures and economic policy frameworks. In particular, standards and codes in developing countries should not only safeguard financial stability but also contribute to the creation of a financial sector supportive of development. Consequently, there are doubts whether global standards are appropriate at all.[50] The development of models reflecting the realities of developing countries requires, first of all, increasing these countries' participation in their design, through either regional or subregional standard-setting bodies or representation in global standard-setting bodies, and including areas of interest to these countries in the work of such bodies.

In addition, recent experience suggests that the implementation of standards and codes has limits as a crisis prevention mechanism. Before its crisis, Argentina had received high marks for compliance. With hindsight, it can be seen that reports on standards and codes failed to capture the factors that made the country vulnerable to crisis. Reliance on standards and codes could be taken to excess, lead to complacency and divert attention from more pressing sources of vulnerability to crisis.

IMF and the World Bank play an important role in the implementation of the wide range of standards. They are using their consultation missions with member countries to carry out, on a voluntary basis, Financial Sector Assessment Programs (FSAPs) and Reports on the observance of Standards and Codes (ROSCs). As of end-2002, over 340 ROSCs had been prepared for 89 countries.[51] The coverage of ROSCs remained very uneven across regions. For instance, only 24 per cent of Asian countries had completed at least one ROSC, compared with 80 per cent of Central and Eastern European countries and 58 per cent of the member countries of the Commonwealth of Independent States (CIS).[52] In addition, no corporate governance, accounting, auditing or insolvency ROSC had been undertaken with any industrialized country, despite the recent problems in these areas.

Technical assistance to facilitate implementation of standards and codes has been inadequate. Only one quarter of developing countries and countries with

[49] Benu Schneider, "Issues in implementing standards and codes", paper presented at the ODI Conference on International Standards and Codes: The Developing Country Perspective, Overseas Development Institute (ODI), London, 21 June 2002, p. 9.

[50] For a discussion of this issue, see, for instance, Stephany Griffith-Jones and Ricardo Gottschalk, "Enhancing private capital flows to developing countries in the new international context", report on a Major Commonwealth Secretariat, World Bank and Commonwealth Business Council Conference, London, August 2002.

[51] Report of the Managing Director to the International Monetary and Financial Committee on the IMF's policy agenda (IMFC/Doc/7/03/9), International Monetary Fund, 11 April 2003 http://www.imf.org/external/np/omd/surv/2003/041103.htm, p. 10.

[52] "International standards: background paper on strengthening surveillance, domestic institutions and international markets", International Monetary Fund, 5 March 2003 http://www.imf.org/external/np/pdr/sac/2003/030503sl.pdf, p. 4.

53 "IMF Executive Board reviews international standards: strengthening surveillance, domestic institutions and international markets", Public Information Notice, No. 03/43, 3 April 2003.

54 "International standards: background paper…", p. 27.

55 See http://www.standardandpoors.com/Forum/RatingsAnalysis/

56 Fitch Ratings, "Standards and codes: their impact on sovereign ratings", 10 July 2002 (www.fitchibca.com).

57 For an overview of the Basel II proposal, see secretariat of BCBS, "The New Basel Capital Accord: an explanatory note", Bank for International Settlements, January 2001.

economies in transition that had completed ROSCs or FSAPs received follow-up technical assistance. In addition to the lack of country-specific flexibility, the resource constraint could be a problem in implementing standards and codes.

Resources are also needed for the assessment exercises themselves. The experience with FSAPs and ROSCs has demonstrated the costs of these programmes. In response, the Fund and the Bank are trying to make those programmes more efficient and effective through streamlining and prioritization.[53] This means bringing greater selectivity to the scope and pace of assessments, as well as better tailoring the assessments to individual country circumstances. Account will be taken in this regard of relative costs and benefits, as well as the authorities' priorities and capacity constraints, in scheduling future ROSCs.

From the beginning, it was thought that the implementation of international standards and codes would increase confidence of potential investors in emerging economies. This has been slow in coming, but there seems to be some evidence of progress in market response to the standards initiative. For instance, a survey of large, internationally active financial institutions found that 58 per cent of respondents used ROSCs in their financial decision-making, while another 25 per cent were aware of ROSCs, but did not use them frequently. The use of ROSCs is mostly concentrated in New York, and fairly limited in institutions based in Japan and Europe.[54] The rating agencies also find ROSCs useful. For instance, Standard and Poor's explicitly considers standards in assigning ratings.[55]

There are some indications that the observance of standards and codes may be associated with higher credit ratings. One study found that, following publication of a ROSC, a country was more likely to receive an upgrade in its sovereign credit rating (or to retain its rating) than to receive a downgrade.[56] However, it is understood that the implementation of standards and codes is a long-term strategy for confidence-building and it is too early to draw conclusions concerning investors' response to the standards initiative. The "pay-off", in terms of increased capital inflows as a consequence of complying with a large number of standards and codes, may also require a long-term perspective.

The New Basel Capital Accord

One of the most important regulatory developments since the 1997-1998 financial crisis has been the proposal by the Basel Committee on Banking Supervision (BCBS) regarding a new capital adequacy framework to replace the 1988 Basel Capital Accord (Basel I). Basel I was the first international standard for regulation by national authorities of the commercial banks that were active in international finance. It has since grown into a standard for bank regulation globally, but regulators in the major financial centres have found it increasingly unsatisfactory for their needs. The first draft of the proposed new accord (Basel II) was circulated in June 1999.[57] After almost five years of discussion and revision, BCBS is expected to finalize the New Capital Accord in the fourth quarter of 2003, with implementation to begin in late 2006.

Basel I is considered insufficiently sophisticated to address the expanded activities of complex banking institutions because of the lack of differentiation among the degrees of risk they face and thus the capital they should hold against unforeseen emergencies. Risk management and the determination of appropriate capital requirements have evolved since Basel I was designed.

Banks themselves have developed and adopted new techniques to improve their risk management and internal control measures. Basel II is supposed to create incentives to accelerate adoption of these new techniques by large banks and promote the future evolution of risk management by establishing a framework that is more risk-sensitive.

Unlike the 1988 Accord, the new framework begins by acknowledging that "one size does not fit all" and thus provides a spectrum of approaches, from simple to advanced, for the measurement of risk in determining capital levels. For the measurement of credit risk, two principal options have been proposed. The first is the standardized approach, generally for smaller and simpler banks, and the second is the internal ratings-based (IRB) approach, for larger and more complex banks, with two variants, "foundation" and "advanced".

The standardized approach is conceptually the same as the present accord, but is more risk-sensitive. Banks are required to differentiate their exposures through broad categories, such as loans to corporations, loans to sovereign borrowers and loans to banks. The loans in each category are multiplied by a category-specific "risk weighting" and the results aggregated. The required capital is then a specified fraction of this sum. However, under the new Accord, these broad categories will be divided into several subcategories with risk weights being assigned by reference to a rating provided by an external credit institution (such as a rating agency). For example, the existing Accord provides only one risk weight (100 per cent) for corporate lending, but the new Accord will provide four categories (20, 50, 100 and 150 per cent). Also, under the current system, claims on Governments denominated in foreign currency and claims on banks with maturity over one year are treated differently, depending on whether the borrowers are located within or outside the member countries of OECD. The latter group are subject to much higher capital charges. In the proposed modification, loans to similarly rated banks or sovereigns, whether located in OECD countries or not, would receive the same risk weight.

Under the IRB approach, banks will be allowed to use their internal estimates of borrower creditworthiness to assess credit risk, subject to strict methodological and disclosure standards. These estimates of a potential future loss amount will form the basis of minimum capital requirements. In other words, the banks' internal ratings systems are expected to accurately and consistently differentiate between degrees of risk. Under the IRB approach, the range of risk weights will be more diverse than in the standardized approach, resulting in greater risk-sensitivity.

To ensure that each bank has sound internal processes in place, a "second pillar", supervisory review, has been included in the draft framework. Supervisors will be expected to review banks' own assessments and their methodologies for arriving at the amount of capital they should hold relative to their risk. That pillar had not been deemed necessary when the original Accord was prepared. Another innovation is the "the third pillar", market discipline, which calls for more extensive public disclosure of risk management procedures and financial conditions of regulated entities. The expectation is that banks with superior risk management systems would be rewarded with higher stock market valuations and lower spreads on their borrowings than other banks.

Despite the effort and progress made by BCBS over the past five years, questions remain in both the developed and developing countries about aspects of the Basel II framework. The fact that the rules are enormous in number and complexity is one source of concern. Complex rules have been developed primarily for a relatively small number of large, complex internationally active banking organizations that are supposed to implement the IRB approach. For the majority of banks that are likely to implement the standardized approach, the new Accord adds little. Also, to accommodate concerns expressed by developing countries, BCBS has developed a simple version of the standardized approach of about 12 pages (compared with about 500 pages for the advanced IRB approach).

There are also doubts whether the transition to any form of Basel II makes sense for most banks. For instance, United States supervisory authorities intend to apply only the advanced IRB version of Basel II and will likely require only large United States banks to adopt it. All other banks will remain on the Basel I capital standard. United States supervisors believe that, for most banks, Basel I is adequate for the foreseeable future and that the costs of requiring most banks to shift to Basel II may far exceed the benefits.[58]

For the largest banks and their regulators, the complexity of the new Accord may become a problem. There is widespread concern that Basel II regulatory requirements for banks applying the IRB approach are not clear enough to be well understood by institutions that are expected to implement them, by their regulators, or by third parties.[59]

The prospect of different regulatory treatment for different types of banks has also raised concerns about the potential effect of Basel II on the competitive balance between large and small banks, as well as between banks and non-banks. It is expected that banks implementing the IRB approach will experience lower capital requirements in some lines of business. This may put smaller banks at a competitive disadvantage when competing against the large banks in these same product lines. For many large banks, the principal source of competition is non-banks. There is concern that the implementation of Basel II may exacerbate differences in regulatory requirements to the disadvantage of depository institutions.

Another concern is that a more risk-sensitive framework may increase the cost and reduce the supply of bank lending to certain categories of borrowers, notably small and medium-sized enterprises (SMEs). In response to these concerns, BCBS has set capital requirements for lending to SMEs below those for large corporations. The justification for this change was that the probability of default was less correlated among SMEs than among large firms. It has been suggested that a similar case can be made for developing countries because of the lower correlation of their risk with that of developed countries (as compared with the correlation among developed countries).[60]

Many observers find the most controversial aspect of the standardized approach to be the suggestion that assessments by credit rating agencies of developing countries be used to categorize borrowers. There has been very limited penetration of ratings in developing economies, especially at the firm level, and rating agencies have had a mixed record in these countries. Their sovereign risk assessments, it is argued, have tended to lag changes in market conditions, first encouraging excessive investment through overly optimistic ratings and then aggravating abrupt and huge capital outflows with negative assessments.

[58] Testimony by Mr. Roger W. Ferguson, Vice-Chairman of the Board of Governors of the United States Federal Reserve System, before the Subcommittee on Domestic and International Monetary Policy, Trade and Technology of the Committee on Financial Services of the United States House of Representatives, Washington, D.C., 27 February 2003.

[59] See, for instance, statement of John D. Hawke, Comptroller of the Currency, before the Subcommittee on Domestic and International Monetary Policy, Trade and Technology of the Committee on Financial Services of the United States House of Representatives, Washington, D.C., 27 February 2003.

[60] See, for instance, S. Griffith-Jones, M. Segoviano and S. Spratt, "Basel II and developing countries: diversification and portfolio effects", Institute of Development Studies, Sussex, United Kingdom, 2003 (www.ids.ac.uk/intfinance/).

There is also a view that increased risk-sensitivity due to the New Capital Accord may increase the "pro-cyclicality" of bank lending. The proponents of this view argue that, if capital requirements were more sensitive to risk, banks would cut lending even more in economic downturns (when measured risk tends to increase), thus aggravating the decline, and the opposite during a boom.

The financial sphere is inherently pro-cyclical and financial liberalization and innovation, including the proliferation of internal risk management systems in the chief transnational financial institutions, may have already reinforced pro-cyclicality in financial behaviour. Most risk measures are of short-term nature, and existing techniques of risk assessment are said not to pay sufficient attention to the movement of risk through the business cycle. Besides, many leading financial institutions use similar models to guide their behaviour. In this situation, what is sensible and rational for an individual market participant, acting in isolation may produce a devastating outcome for the market as a whole.[61]

The architects of Basel II are trying to moderate the gravity of the problem. They note that supervisory oversight and market discipline (pillars II and III) should reinforce the incentive for banks to maintain a cushion of capital above the minimum so as to have a margin of protection in downturns. They are also urging financial institutions to adopt risk management practices that take better account of the evolution of risk over time and that are not excessively vulnerable to short-term revisions.[62] The regulators' success in dealing with this problem within the context of Basel II remains a concern.

Approaches to crisis resolution

Notwithstanding the best efforts to strengthen crisis prevention, it is widely believed that financial crises will still occur. Those crises may range from short-term liquidity problems to problems of solvency, but they all entail significant economic shocks. The international community acknowledges that it needs a strong and comprehensive set of instruments to help countries resolve such financial difficulties.

The role of official financing

It is recognized that if a crisis is clearly identified as a problem of external liquidity rather than solvency, official financial support, possibly in large amounts, may help the country resolve its problem and that a clear framework is needed to guide official actions in such cases. Clearly stated principles of official intervention would help debtors and their creditors to formulate expectations and set the stage for greater accountability on the part of policy makers.

To heighten the degree of clarity and predictability about the official response to crises, IMF has developed a new framework for exceptional access to its resources in capital-account crisis.[63] IMF is prepared to provide larger loans than normally allowed if a country meets the following criteria: exceptionally large need; a debt burden that will be sustainable under reasonably conservative assumptions; good prospects of regaining access to private capital markets during the period of the IMF loan; and indications that the country's policies have a strong chance of succeeding.

[61] For a discussion of why and how market-sensitive risk management systems may raise volatility, see, for instance, Avinash Persaud, "Liquidity black holes: what are they and how are they generated", paper presented at a seminar on "Basel II: The Challenges for the G-24", IMF headquarters, Washington, D.C., 11 April 2003.

[62] See, for instance, Andrew Crockett, "Central banking, financial stability and Basel II", speech at the 38th South East Asian Central Banks (SEACEN) Governors Conference, Manila, 13 February 2003 (www.bis.org).

[63] See "IMF concludes discussion on access policy in the context of capital-account crisis; and review of access policies in the credit tranches and the Extended Fund Facility", Public Information Notice, No. 03/37, 21 March 2003.

64   For a discussion of the IMF analytical framework, see Christina Daseking, "Debt: how much is too much?", *Finance and Development*, December 2002, pp. 12-14.

Among those criteria, the central, and most controversial, is the judgement about debt sustainability. Knowledge of whether a country is facing a liquidity, as opposed to a solvency, crisis is crucial for deciding whether international liquidity support is desirable or not (in other words, there is no point in lending to an insolvent country since the debt outstanding already exceeds the maximum serviceable).

To better distinguish cases of illiquidity from cases of unsustainability, IMF developed a new standardized analytical framework for debt sustainability assessments, which was published in June 2002.[64] The framework covers both fiscal and external debt sustainability and centres on the medium-term projections for a country's economy. In addition to baseline projections for public and external debt, the framework incorporates a set of sensitivity tests to simulate the debt dynamics under alternative assumptions about key variables (including economic growth, interest rates and the exchange rate).

The framework may be useful not only for making decisions on exceptional access to official financing, but also in debt workouts for insolvent countries. An indicator of debt sustainability is needed in restructuring the debt of such countries so as to guide debtors and creditors in their discussions on how much debt reduction is required in order to reach a manageable pattern of repayments over time. Such a framework may also be useful for crisis prevention, as it could better identify when debt levels had moved towards dangerous levels so as to enable action to be taken to avoid a crisis.

Nevertheless, past experience has shown that, in many external financial crises, it is not known initially whether solvency is at issue or not. It is not easy, even theoretically, much less operationally, to distinguish clearly between solvency and liquidity difficulties. For instance, with a loss of confidence in a country's situation, the international financial market may demand very high interest rates, which could make the debt unsustainable; but with lower interest rates that were believed to be consistent with the underlying economic fundamentals, there would be no solvency crisis. In this case, the international community might seek to calm the market and reduce interest rates by providing substantial financing. Alternatively, the market could be forced to face the implications of its own judgement that the country's debt is unsustainable and, in the absence of up-front official financing, begin negotiations on debt restructuring as soon as possible. In addition to difficulties in identifying purely "technical" aspects of the crisis, there will always be political considerations and associated pressures.

Given the difficulty in identifying ex ante the origins of almost any crisis, as well as the myriad political and social factors, it is doubtful whether simple and mechanical calculations, formulas, thresholds or ratios alone would be very helpful. Ultimately, the key test will be the judgements that are made in individual cases. In order to be credible, those judgements should be as consistent as possible in providing signals to markets concerning when the international community's support will be forthcoming and when it will not.

Along with developing a clearer framework in respect of when to use official resources, IMF has sought to improve the design of its loan facilities to better support countries in capital-account crisis. Most of the Fund's facilities were designed in a period of low capital mobility to deal with slowly evolving current-account crises. However, the traditional strategy of enforcing policy conditionality by disbursing money in tranches over time may not be fully appropriate for dealing with modern capital-account crises which move much faster and may generate large swings in capital flows.

In response to these new realities, IMF in 1997 established the Supplemental Reserve Facility (SRF). SRF can provide larger and more front-loaded financing to countries hit by a capital-account crisis. In March 2003, the IMF Executive Board decided to lengthen the maturity of drawings from the SRF by one year, as experience had shown that the duration of countries' balance-of-payments needs might be longer than originally expected. At the same time, it decided to retain quota-based limits on access to the SRF (300 per cent of quota). It has been argued, however, that exceptional access norms should not be linked to country quotas and that it is necessary to examine other approaches.[65]

According to many observers, SRF has not gone far enough and there is a need to supplement this strategy with the possibility of the provision of a large amount of funding quickly, based on ex ante judgements and preconditions.[66] This was the intention of the Contingent Credit Line (CCL), introduced by the Fund in 1999. Besides providing external liquidity with a high degree of automaticity to pre-qualified countries during an emergency, it was expected to have a preventive function, that is to say, by providing an agreed credit line in advance, it could help discourage a sudden withdrawal of external credit. However, as of May 2003, no member country had availed itself of the facility. The key problem is that potential users are concerned that application for the facility, not to mention drawing from it, would be viewed as a sign of weakness by the international financial market, thereby reducing, rather than strengthening, confidence in the country. The scheduled expiration of the facility is November 2003 and there appears to be insufficient support to extend it.

In May 2002, the World Bank introduced a structural adjustment counterpart to the CCL, the Deferred Drawdown Option (DDO), to protect core structural programmes if a country faces reduced access to international financial markets. A DDO gives borrowers a credit line on which they can draw for up to three years, provided that overall programme implementation and the macroeconomic framework remain adequate. Several countries have already established DDO facilities, as they consider that this instrument, unlike the CCL, does not have the negative signalling effect.

Sovereign debt restructuring

In addition to clear policy on handling liquidity crises, it is necessary to have an agreed international strategy for resolving solvency crises. In such crises, the level of debt has to be reduced. Intense work in the past year has focused on cases in which the primary insolvent debtor is the government. One aim of this work has been to provide incentives to sovereign debtors and their private sector creditors to quickly begin constructive negotiations on restructuring unsustainable debt. However, along with incentives, there should be a process that is a clear and known in advance. Debtors and creditors should also have confidence that it can produce an orderly and effective resolution of unsustainable debt situations without undue delay. The lack of such a process is considered to be one of the major gaps in the international financial architecture.

[65] See, for instance, International Monetary and Financial Committee, statement by Aleksei L. Kudrin, Deputy Prime Minister and Minister of Finance of the Russian Federation, Washington, D.C., 12 April 2003 http://www.imf.org/external/spring/2003/imfc/state/eng/rus.htm, p. 6.

[66] See, for instance, Thomas D. Willet, "Why is there so much disagreement about the IMF and reform of the international financial architecture?", paper prepared for the IMF seminar on current developments in monetary and financial law, August 2002 http://www.imf.org/external/np/leg/sem/2002/cdmfl/eng/willet.pdf, pp.19-20.

One of the approaches explored recently, the "contractual" approach, which focuses on one instrument for sovereign lending, namely, bonds, would add new clauses to each sovereign bond contract specifying how to carry out restructuring of the bond issue in a crisis situation. The Group of 7, the Group of 10 and the International Monetary and Financial Committee have endorsed this approach. Also, the Group of 24 has indicated its preference for approaches to restructuring that are voluntary, country-specific and market-friendly, and the contractual approach is deemed to be so.[67]

[67] Communiqué of the Group of 24, Washington, D.C., 11 April 2003, pp. 3-4.

Central to this approach are collective action clauses (CACs), which would prevent a small minority of bondholders from sabotaging the bond's restructuring. These clauses would specify what majority would be needed to approve a change in the financial terms of the bond. In addition, representation clauses (specifying how debtors and creditors would come together in the event of restructuring), initiation clauses (describing how the sovereign debtor would initiate the process) and commitments to keep bondholders informed on the proposed treatment of other creditors would be included.[68] Furthermore, the borrowing Government and the bondholders would pledge to follow a code of conduct for both crisis prevention and crisis resolution, which broadly stipulated the respective roles that key parties would be expected to play during times of crisis. There are various proposals for the content of the code, including one from private sector organizations.[69]

[68] See John B. Taylor, Under Secretary of the Treasury for International Affairs, "Using clauses to reform the process for sovereign debt workouts: progress and next steps", remarks at the Emerging Markets Traders Association (EMTA) Annual Meeting, New York, 5 December 2002.

[69] See "Sovereign debt restructuring", discussion draft of a joint statement by EMTA, the Institute of International Finance, the International Primary Market Association, the International Securities Market Association, the Securities Industry Association and the Bond Market Association, 6 December 2002 (available at www.emta.org).

The concept of CACs is not new: they are incorporated in sovereign bonds governed by the laws of the United Kingdom and Japan. About 30 per cent of the total outstanding volume of emerging market sovereign bonds already include CACs. There is no evidence that these bonds trade at a discount to bonds without this feature and thus it may be said that they have market acceptance. Nevertheless, most bonds are subject to New York State law, under which *all* bondholders must agree to any amendment of payment terms. The proposal is thus to extend CACs to bonds issued under New York law, as well as to modify the CACs in other bond issuances.

The contractual approach, however, has several shortcomings. One is that, even if bond contracts were written so as to bring the holders of all outstanding bonds together to vote on a bond restructuring (referred to as aggregation across debt contracts of the same class), it would remain to coordinate relief given by bondholders with that of other classes of creditors ("comparable treatment") so as to reach an adequate overall relief package. Proponents of CACs responded to this criticism by advocating the inclusion of the same clauses in all private loan contracts (bonds, bank loans, trade credits etc.)[70] and the formation of a voluntary forum to organize the negotiations and resolve disputes in individual cases, entailing the introduction of a major aspect of the statutory approach described below, but as a voluntary device.[71] Another weakness is that, if the clauses were included only in new issues, it would take many years before all outstanding sovereign bonds of any country had these clauses.

[70] R. Glen Hubbard, Chair, United States Council of Economic Advisors, "Enhancing sovereign debt restructuring", remarks at the Conference on the IMF Sovereign Debt Proposal, American Enterprise Institute, Washington, D.C., 7 October 2002.

[71] See "Sovereign debt restructuring", loc. cit., p. 8.

To make the use of such clauses more common, EU member States have pledged to include them in their own government bonds issued under foreign jurisdictions. Before that decision, among the developed countries, only Canada and the United Kingdom had CACs in their foreign currency bond and note contracts. Meanwhile, both the Governments in the working group of the Group of 10 and private creditor associations have been drafting sets of model clauses.

These efforts are already bringing results. The first countries to include a CAC in a New York law-governed bond were Lebanon (2000), Qatar (2000) and Egypt (2001). However, Mexico was the first large emerging market issuer that publicly announced the inclusion of such clauses in the bond issuance. In late February 2003, Mexico included a version of a CAC in a new $1 billion issue of bonds governed by New York law. The Mexican issue will allow creditors holding 75 per cent of the bonds to modify the payments terms. There was no evidence of a premium priced into the new bond because of the CAC.[72] This may help emerging market issuers to embrace this practice more broadly. Following Mexico's lead, Brazil, South Africa and Uruguay decided to include CACs in bond issues governed by New York law.

To address criticisms of the contractual approach, IMF proposed in November 2001 establishing a new international statutory framework for debt workouts, to be called the sovereign debt restructuring mechanism (SDRM). While the framework was revised several times in response to public reaction, its core objective remained, namely, to enable a debtor in crisis and a qualified majority of its creditors to make a restructuring agreement binding on all creditors in all the covered classes of debt through a formal international process.[73] Although a number of countries expressed interest in developing the proposal, it did not find broad enough support to move from proposal to implementation.

Under the proposal, after the activation of the SDRM by the debtor, all covered creditors would be formed into separate classes for the purpose of voting on a proposed debt restructuring. The sovereign would then formally propose the component draft agreements to each class, which would vote on them. The overall debt agreement would be considered adopted when approved by the stipulated supermajority (for example, 75 per cent) of the outstanding principal of registered claims in each class. New lending during the restructuring process would have repayment priority over defaulted claims, so as to facilitate essential credit flows to the debtor Government during the crisis period from some private as well as official sources.

A new international legal mechanism, the sovereign debt dispute resolution forum (SDDRF), was proposed to oversee the formation of the classes, validate the claims of individual creditors, and resolve disputes on the allocation of individual creditors to the classes and voting process. The SDRM would be established through amendment of the IMF Articles of Agreement, which would bind all IMF member States, even those that had not endorsed the amendment per se.

Many issues in the design of SDRM have been controversial, for example, that concerning the scope of the debt that would be covered. There were also concerns that the adoption of the SDRM through an amendment of the IMF Articles of Agreement would put the mechanism too close to IMF, which is itself a creditor, as well as the body responsible for negotiating an adjustment programme with the Government. For this reason, there have been proposals to create the SDRM or something similar under a standalone treaty, since there was nothing in the operation of the mechanism itself that needed to directly involve IMF.

Many emerging market countries fear that the SDRM might not only raise their borrowing costs and impede market access, but also entail a loss of sovereignty, especially if bound by an IMF amendment for which they did not

72 International Monetary Fund, *Global Financial Stability Report: Market Developments and Issues* (Washington, D.C., March 2003), p. 58.

73 For the latest version of the IMF proposal, see "Report of the Managing Director to the International Monetary and Financial Committee on a statutory sovereign debt restructuring mechanism", IMF, 8 April 2003 http://www.imf.org/external/np/omd/surv/2003/040803.htm.

vote. In their turn, many private sector creditors worry that, by overriding existing bond contracts, the SDRM would curtail the legal rights of bondholders. In early 2003, the United States, which had previously been open to developing the SDRM proposal, signalled that it was neither necessary nor feasible to continue working on the SDRM.[74] It appears that further work on the SDRM will not go forward at this time.

There remains a concern whether the contractual approach, which by design is not comprehensive, will suffice. Mechanisms that incorporate or build on the contractual approach should continue to be investigated, as should issues of how to ensure the overall adequacy of negotiated debt relief from the point of view of the debtor country and its people, how to bring about comparability of treatment of creditors, how to ensure full participation of all creditors in each creditor class, and how to resolve debt crises more expeditiously. Non-treaty approaches, which could include other potential international legal instruments, as well as voluntary mechanisms, should also continue to be explored, especially as interim measures that could help foster adequate and fair debt resolution and demonstrate the value of the comprehensive approach.

[74]   See Meeting of the International Monetary and Financial Committee, "Statement by Secretary John W. Snow, United States Treasury", International Monetary Fund, Washington, D.C., 12 April 2003 http://www.imf.org/external/spring/2003/imfc/state/eng/usa.htm, p. 2.

III THE CURRENT SITUATION IN THE WORLD'S ECONOMIES

There was some recovery in growth in most countries during 2002, but the momentum weakened towards the end of the year and into early 2003. Growth is expected to accelerate as 2003 progresses but, in most countries, the average for the year will be only a modest improvement over 2002. With the recovery continuing, growth is expected to move closer to its long-term potential in most countries in 2004.

The anticipated recovery in the developed market economies in 2002 was delayed, in large measure by various fears associated with the situation in Iraq. A recovery is now forecast for the second half of 2003, with the United States of America expected to lead and be the driving force. The recovery in Western Europe and Japan is projected to be less robust and will be dampened further by the additional appreciation of their currencies vis-à-vis the dollar which took place in the first half of 2003.

The economies in transition continue to be the fastest growing of the three major country groupings, although they have gradually decelerated from their high point of 2000. Most members of the Commonwealth of Independent States (CIS) and the Baltic countries now appear to be on a long-term path towards recovery from the setbacks endured in the 1990s. Growth in the countries of Central and Eastern Europe slowed in 2001 and 2002, but exceeds that of their Western neighbours. Their forthcoming accession to the European Union (EU) should accelerate convergence.

The developing countries as a group are making a sluggish recovery from their slowdown in 2001, the more so if the strong performances of China and India are excluded. In Latin America, there was a fall in output in 2002 after a very weak performance in 2001. The opposite applied in West Asia, but the rise in the output of the group was mainly due to the recovery of Turkey from the crisis of 2001, while many other economies in the group suffered from the heightened geopolitical conflicts in the region. Each of these two regions has achieved an increase in per capita output in only one of the past four years and the prospects for 2003 suggest only a modest gain. Growth in Africa fell below 3 per cent in 2002 and only a minimal improvement is expected in 2003. The reappearance of conflict in parts of sub-Saharan Africa has already adversely affected growth in the concerned areas and, unless very quickly contained, will damage medium- and longer-term development prospects more widely. In contrast with all other regions, Eastern and Southern Asia rebounded strongly in 2002. Some deceleration in early 2003 is forecast to be reversed as the year progresses so that the region is likely to maintain, with some margin, its position as the most economically dynamic in the world.

DEVELOPED ECONOMIES

Growth prospects in the developed countries were dealt a blow by the many uncertainties associated with, as well as the real economic effects of, the war in Iraq. Growth slowed significantly during the second half of 2002, particularly in the fourth quarter, bringing to an end a promising resurgence of activity in the first half of the year. Consumer confidence plummeted and industrial production stalled in the three major economies (see figures III.1 and III.2). Growth in these countries as a group has been below 1.5 per cent for the past two years and is expected to be only marginally stronger in 2003, with some acceleration in 2004. One of the most damaging aspects of the renewed downturn is that the period of below-potential growth has been extended. This may have longer-term consequences, particularly in labour markets, where short-term unemployment may become more long-term in nature. Policy options have also been affected.

To counteract this negative shock, policy has generally been active. Monetary policy has brought short-term interest rates down to record lows in most countries. Fiscal policy has been generally expansionary, with the strongest fiscal impulse in the United States. However, the prolonged period of slow growth will have used up much of the ammunition for further stimulus if activity does not pick up.

Another consequence of the long period of slow growth is the developed countries' greater vulnerability to external shocks than would have been the case given stronger growth dynamics. The depreciation of the United States dollar, which has gathered considerable momentum since the end of 2002, may have important consequences. It is expected to shift growth dynamics within the region, boosting the United States but dampening both Western Europe and (albeit less so) Japan.

North America: recovery under way

The prospects for economic growth in North America are improving, although both Canada and the United States finished the first quarter of 2003 on a subdued note. The war in Iraq, and the heightened uncertainties prior to the war, derailed an already anaemic economic recovery in the United States; in Canada, robust domestic demand, which had offset external weakness for the previous two years, moderated substantially. While some weaknesses may linger, a gradual rebound is expected in the second half of 2003, to be strengthened further in 2004 (see table A.2), though it will be subject to a number of downside risks and uncertainties.

The impact of the geopolitical uncertainties on the economy of the United States was manifest as early as the fourth quarter of 2002, when annual growth of gross domestic product (GDP) plummeted to 1.4 per cent from 5 per cent at the beginning of the year (see table III.1). Rising energy prices and declining confidence (triggered by geopolitical uncertainties) aggravated the post-bubble consolidation in an economy still recovering from the terrorist attacks of 11 September 2001 and domestic financial scandals. The economy deteriorated further in the first quarter of 2003: consumer confidence had dropped to its lowest level since 1993 (see figure III.1); payroll employment continued to fall; consumer spending, which had been the main support for the economy,

Figure III.1.
CONSUMER CONFIDENCE IN THE MAJOR ECONOMIES, 1998-2003[a]

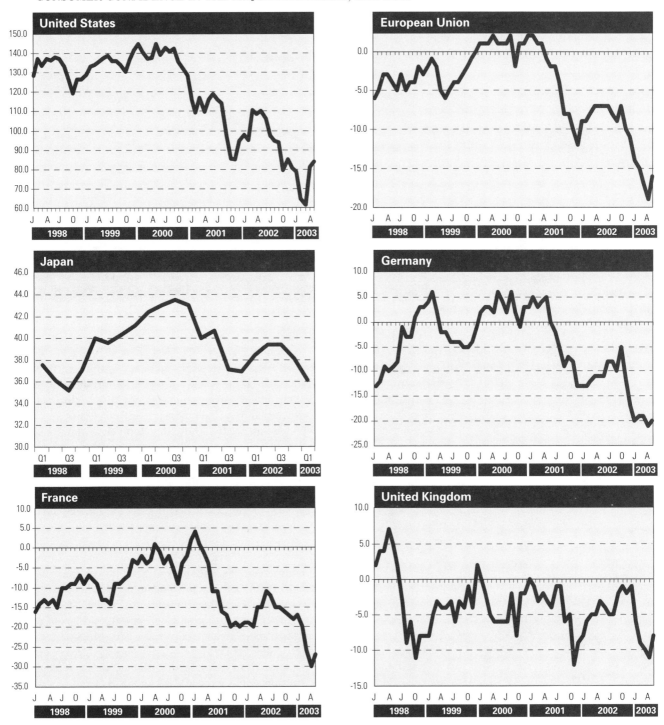

Sources: United States: The Conference Board; Japan: Economic and Social Research Institute; all European Union countries: *European Economy*, Business and Consumer Surveys.

[a] For United States, measure is an index (1985 = 100); for Japan, measure is a composite index (percentage); for European Union, measure shows percentage of respondents to survey who expect an improvement minus percentage of those who expect a deterioration.

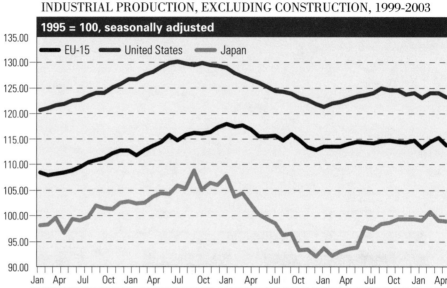

Figure III.2.
INDUSTRIAL PRODUCTION, EXCLUDING CONSTRUCTION, 1999-2003

1995 = 100, seasonally adjusted

EU-15   United States   Japan

Source: OECD, Main Economic Indicators.

[1] Activity indices, compiled by the Institute for Supply Management (ISM), in both the manufacturing and services sectors plunged below levels typically associated with economic contraction.

started to weaken; retail sales declined; industrial production turned down (see figure III.2); and there was even weakness indicated in the services sector.[1]

With the end of the war in Iraq, and aided by its quick resolution, the "war premium" receded to a large degree: petroleum prices have dropped to within a normal range, stock markets have recovered notably, yield spreads on corporate borrowings have narrowed, and various measures of consumer and business confidence have rebounded markedly. These developments, along with the stimulatory monetary and fiscal policies either already in place or expected, constitute the harbinger of an economic recovery in the second half of 2003.

Household spending remains the key to a timely recovery in North America, particularly in the United States. Conspicuously resilient during the economic downturn of the past few years, to the extent that it prevented the economy of the United States from falling into an otherwise deeper recession, household spending has slowed markedly since late 2002, dropping from an average growth of about 4 to about 1 per cent. War jitters, high oil prices, diminishing wage gains, declining employment, and inclement winter weather all contributed to the slowdown. Nevertheless, factors that bolstered the household sector over the past two years persist: interest rates are still at historic lows and there is, as yet, no sign of a collapse in the housing market; and house prices have appreciated substantially in the past few years, offsetting part of the wealth losses from the equity markets. With consumer confidence recovering, household consumption is expected to regain some strength in the second half of 2003. However, consumption is not expected to regain its pace of the late 1990s, as households are likely to have to rehabilitate their overstretched balance sheets and raise savings rates.

While sustained consumption spending is important, it is business spending that will be crucial for the strength of the recovery. Business capital spending contracted significantly in both economies during the 2000-2001 downturn,

Table III.1.
MAJOR INDUSTRIALIZED COUNTRIES: QUARTERLY INDICATORS, 2001-2002

	2001 quarter				2002 quarter			
	I	II	III	IV	I	II	III	IV
Growth of gross domestic product[a] (percentage change in seasonally adjusted data from preceding quarter)								
Canada	0.6	0.3	-0.5	2.9	5.8	3.8	2.7	1.6
France	2.3	-0.3	1.7	-1.0	2.9	2.0	1.3	-0.2
Germany	2.4	-0.1	-0.8	-1.2	1.2	0.8	1.1	-0.1
Italy	2.7	0.0	0.8	-0.8	0.8	0.9	1.1	1.7
Japan	1.5	-4.8	-4.3	-1.8	0.0	5.2	3.1	1.9
United Kingdom	3.1	1.0	1.7	1.7	0.3	2.4	4.4	1.7
United States	-0.6	-1.6	-0.3	2.7	5.0	1.3	4.0	1.4
Major developed economies	0.9	-1.8	-1.0	0.6	2.7	2.4	3.0	1.2
Euro zone	2.4	0.0	0.8	-0.8	1.6	1.6	1.2	0.4
Unemployment rate[b] (percentage of total labour force)								
Canada	6.9	7.0	7.2	7.7	7.8	7.6	7.6	7.6
France	8.6	8.5	8.5	8.5	8.6	8.7	8.8	8.9
Germany	7.8	7.8	7.8	7.9	8.0	8.1	8.3	8.4
Italy	9.7	9.5	9.4	9.2	9.1	9.0	9.0	8.9
Japan	4.8	4.9	5.1	5.5	5.3	5.4	5.4	5.4
United Kingdom	5.0	4.9	4.1	5.1	5.1	5.1	5.2	5.0
United States	4.2	4.5	4.8	5.6	5.6	5.9	5.8	5.9
Major developed economies	5.6	5.8	5.9	6.4	6.4	6.5	6.5	6.5
Euro zone	8.4	8.3	8.0	8.0	8.1	8.2	8.3	8.5
Change in consumer prices[c] (percentage change from preceding quarter)								
Canada	0.9	6.9	0.3	-3.5	2.7	6.1	4.3	2.1
France	-0.1	5.3	0.4	0.3	2.7	3.2	0.9	1.8
Germany	4.3	4.1	0.6	-1.7	4.5	0.8	0.6	-0.4
Italy	3.4	3.5	1.4	1.3	3.5	3.0	1.9	2.7
Japan	-1.2	-0.3	-1.1	-1.5	-2.8	1.8	-0.7	-0.4
United Kingdom	-0.5	5.1	0.2	-0.5	0.2	5.1	1.4	3.6
United States	3.9	4.2	0.5	-1.1	1.4	4.4	1.7	1.3
Major developed economies	2.0	3.2	0.1	-1.1	0.9	3.2	1.0	0.9
Euro zone	1.5	6.1	0.4	1.1	2.9	4.0	0.4	2.2

Source: UN/DESA, based on data of IMF, *International Financial Statistics;* Organisation for Economic Cooperation and Development (OECD); and national authorities.

[a] Expressed at annual rate (total is weighted average with weights being annual GDP valued at 1995 prices and exchange rates).
[b] Seasonally adjusted data as standardized by OECD.
[c] Expressed at annual rate.

when the information and communication technologies (ICT) investment bubble of the 1990s burst, and there was a protracted decline in equity markets. There was gradual recovery in corporate equipment investment in part of 2002, but the upturn was curbed by the revelation of corporate accounting chicaneries and by geopolitical uncertainties. In the outlook, a recovery in business spending is expected in late 2003 and into 2004, particularly for equipment and software, which are expected to grow at double-digit rates. Recovering corporate profits, strengthening equity prices and the end of the protracted consolidation in the ICT sector will provide the foundation for the growth in capital spending. Available data in the second quarter of 2003 indicate an appreciable improvement in all three areas. For example, the earnings of many firms in the United States, particularly those in manufacturing, have shown tangible growth since late 2002, after significant declines for two years. At the same time, demand for ICT sector products has been reviving, although overcapacity remains and needs more time to be absorbed.[2] While some ICT investments from earlier years will continue to drive changes in business organization and behaviour, generating further productivity gains, a large proportion of businesses have yet to introduce state-of-the-art ICT solutions but are expected to do so. Continued innovation and diffusion of ICT are expected to remain the main driving force for the economic growth.

Furthermore, the broadening of the recovery, and hence its sustainability, will eventually depend on an improvement in the labour market, with increased business activity translating into stronger employment growth; this, in turn, would reinvigorate consumer activity. The unemployment rate in the United States has stalled at about 5.8 per cent for the past year, up from the lows of 4 per cent before the downturn (see figure III.3). The situation in the labour market may, however, be even worse than that reflected by the unemployment rate:

[2] The financial bubbles in ICT equity prices evaporated and many ICT companies that could not live up to prior inflated expectations went bankrupt. However, the benefits brought by the ICT revolution for both consumers and businesses are real and lasting. At the macrolevel, the gains can be seen in the sustained rise in productivity in the United States over the past few years. At the microlevel, the evidence has been more salient and, in some cases, has even exceeded earlier expectations that were considered to be exuberant. For example, e-commerce between businesses in the United States stands at more than $2 trillion annually, a figure much higher than what was boldly projected in 1999. For details, see "The e-biz surprise", *Business Week*, 12 May 2003.

Figure III.3.
UNEMPLOYMENT RATES IN THE EU-15, JAPAN
AND THE UNITED STATES, 1999-2003

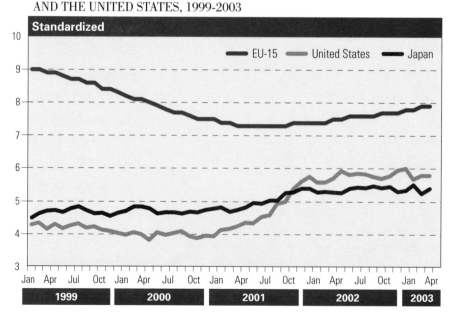

Source: OECD, Main Economic Indicators.

there was a net loss of a half-million jobs between the fourth quarter of 2002 and the first quarter of 2003, and some unemployed may have dropped out of the waiting queue. An increase in hiring always lags the recovery in output during a cyclical upturn; given low capacity utilization and rising productivity, a measurable improvement in the labour market is not expected in the United States until 2004. By contrast, employment in Canada registered robust growth during 2002, softening only at the beginning of 2003.

The net contribution of the external sector to growth in the United States has been negative for many years, and it was also insignificant for Canada in 2002. This situation will likely continue in the near term. International trade in both economies dwindled over the past two years. Exports of the United States, in volume terms, declined for two consecutive years, while imports recovered by only 3.7 per cent in 2002 from a drop in the previous year. Canada's trade stagnated in 2002. Trade is expected to recover in the second half of 2003, as world demand strengthens, and the growth of both exports and imports of the region is forecast to reach about 7-8 per cent in 2004 (see table A.13). The depreciation of the United State dollar is expected to provide some boost to net exports in the United States over the medium term. At the same time, the appreciation of the Canadian dollar against the United States dollar has already had some adverse impact on Canada's exports, and hence its growth.

The inflation outlook for the region remains benign. Inflation in the United States rose to an annual rate of about 3 per cent in the first quarter of 2003, mainly because of the surge in oil prices. Inflation in Canada in 2002 and early 2003 has been just above the target of 2 per cent of the Central Bank of Canada (CBC). With the prices of oil having retreated, and with the large slack in the economy, particularly in the United States, inflation rates are expected to decline. Deflation is a possibility, but an unlikely one.

Monetary policy is expected to remain accommodative in the United States. The Federal Reserve of the United States (Fed) is expected to keep interest rates at their current level, the lowest in four decades, until the fourth quarter of 2003, tightening gradually thereafter. The Central Bank of Canada is expected to tighten further during 2003.

Fiscal policy in the United States will continue to be stimulatory, with federal spending growing by 10 per cent in 2003, offsetting the drag of restrictive budget stances by many State and local governments. The most recent package consists of $359 billion in tax cuts. The budget deficit for the United States is expected to reach $330 billion in 2003 and $400 billion in 2004. In contrast, the fiscal stance in Canada is expected to be neutral to slightly stimulatory, and the government budget will remain in small surplus, or at least balanced, during 2003-2004.

The foregoing baseline outlook is subject to a number of uncertainties and downside risks. The major military operation in Iraq has ended, but not all of the geopolitical uncertainties have dissipated. On the economic front, the large and growing trade and fiscal deficits in the United States, along with their implications for exchange rates, portend risks, not only for the stability of the domestic economy but also for the world economy and global financial markets. In the medium term, the crowding-out effects of increased military spending may dampen potential growth.

Developed Asia and the Pacific: subdued growth in Japan and vigour elsewhere

After another year of stagnation in 2002, when GDP grew by 0.3 per cent, the economy of Japan remains fragile; GDP is expected to grow by under 1 per cent in both 2003 and 2004. Despite an improvement in some economic indicators at the beginning of 2003, economic fundamentals continue to be weak. The lingering danger of a deflationary spiral persists as asset prices continue to decline, aggravating severe problems in the banking sector and in the real economy.

Strong support from net exports in the past year kept the economy from falling into a recession. The growth of exports is expected to be about 3 per cent for 2003-2004, while the growth of imports is expected to occur at a similar pace (see table A.13).

A noticeable improvement by the end of the first quarter of 2003 was the stabilization of business sentiment, and, correspondingly, a rise in business projections for capital spending, supported by a recovery in corporate profits and an anticipated replenishment of inventories. Business investment is expected to grow by about 2 per cent in 2003, recovering from a decline of 3 per cent in 2002. Housing investment, however, remains sluggish, and public investment is expected to decline further.

The prospects for household consumption remain lacklustre, as there are no signs of improvement in the labour market or household income. While the number of new job offers is increasing gradually, most recent business surveys indicate that firms of all sizes continue to reduce personnel expenses: wages continue to decrease and the number of long-term employees is declining. The unemployment rate, particularly the number of involuntarily unemployed, remains at a historically high level (see figure III.3).

Despite a rise in the prices of imports at the beginning of 2003—mainly because of the surge in the price of oil—broad price indices continue to fall, though at a slower pace. Meanwhile, equity prices dropped to their lowest level in 20 years and real estate prices, both commercial and residential, continued a decade-long slide. Deflation is expected to continue in 2003 and 2004.

The government fiscal position continues to deteriorate. Official budget projections suggest that a revenue gap of about 40 trillion yen would have to be met by new bond issuances in fiscal year 2004 and annual new issuances could reach 45 trillion yen in the next few years. With current debt levels and the issuance of new government bonds, a sizeable fiscal stimulus is unlikely, as it would imperil the Government's financial position and increase the risk of a further downgrading in sovereign debt by international rating agencies.

During the war in Iraq, the Bank of Japan (BoJ) injected more liquidity into the economy with the aim of stabilizing financial markets. The outstanding current-account balance of the Bank, the official target of monetary policy, retreated after the war, but has remained at a high level. The overnight call rate continues to be virtually zero; nevertheless, a large gap between the growth of the monetary base and that of the broad measure of money supply persists, reflecting the dysfunction of the commercial banking system and the inefficacy of monetary easing in boosting real economic activity. Constrained by mounting non-performing loans (NPLs), lending from commercial banks continues to decrease, insensitive to the low interest rates and the high growth in the monetary base. Despite the adoption of various institutional measures, efforts to dispose of NPLs have shown only marginal progress, with growth of new NPLs occurring faster than disposal of old ones.

The prospects for the growth of the Japanese economy remain highly dependent on exports and thus highly vulnerable to external shocks: the outbreak of severe acute respiratory syndrome (SARS) in a number of developing Asian economies, for example, is threatening the growth of exports, and the depreciation of the United States dollar against other major currencies, including the yen, is also inauspicious for Japanese exports.

A sharp contrast can be found in the economies of Australia and New Zealand, in which strong, even overheated, domestic demand has overcome the weakness in the external sector. GDP growth in these two economies is, however, expected to moderate in 2003 and 2004, although it will still be above 3 per cent.

The business sector has been in better shape in Australia than in most other developed economies. High profitability and low debt levels in the corporate sector have contributed to robust capital spending and growth in employment. The unemployment rate declined significantly in 2002, reaching a record low of about 6 per cent, although the momentum has softened since late 2002. Strong employment growth and increases in real wages have in turn boosted household income, leading to strong household spending.

In New Zealand, a surge in immigration, with the population growing by 2 per cent in 2002, together with a conspicuous rise in incomes of farmers in the past couple of years, has added significant stimulus to consumer demand.

The housing sector has been particularly buoyant in both of these economies, contributing to their strength through both strong construction activity and the rising prices of houses, the wealth effects of which helped sustain consumer spending. Developments in the housing cycle, in terms of both construction and pricing, will be a crucial factor for the outlook in the near term. There have been signs of a moderation in the housing sector in Australia, with approvals for the construction of private houses declining for a few months while, in New Zealand, the driving force for housing, namely, net immigration flows, may also have peaked. Policy makers have been increasingly concerned about the rapid rise in house prices over the past few years and the possibility of a large downward adjustment.

While Australia offset, through enhanced linkages to developing countries in Asia, some of the adverse impulses from major developed economies, New Zealand benefited over the past couple of years from a rise in the prices of its export products. Some positive factors, however, have turned less favourable, or waned gradually: the currencies of both economies have appreciated against the United States dollar, with the New Zealand dollar rising by more than 20 per cent, and the central banks in both economies raised interest rates during 2002, reversing part of the earlier easing. The combination of currency appreciation and the rise in policy interest rates implies a substantial tightening in monetary conditions in these economies. In April 2003, the Reserve Bank of New Zealand, noting the slowing economy, reduced interest rates by 25 basis points.

Economic strength has moderated more noticeably in Australia than in New Zealand. Drought has been the main cause, estimated to have reduced the production of a number of crops by about 60 per cent, but there are also imbalances facing Australia: the unsustainable boom in the housing sector, the large current-account deficit, and the low, recently negative household saving rates. In New Zealand, a rise in the inflation rate in the non-tradable sector to about 4 per cent indicates an overstretched utilization of capacity and resources.

Western Europe: upturn faces negative headwinds

The outlook for growth in Western Europe has deteriorated substantially. In the euro zone, growth in the final quarter of 2002 was only 0.4 per cent, well below the average for the major developed economies (see table III.1), with five countries in the region, including France and Germany, having contracted. Preliminary estimates for the first quarter of 2003 suggest that there was no growth in the euro zone as a whole, that Germany may have been and the Netherlands was in recession, and that other countries in the region faired little better.

Much of the current weakness can be traced to the effects of the run-up to the war in Iraq, with higher oil prices and depressed confidence. Consumer confidence declined dramatically in the months prior to and including the war, and the rebound in confidence in the post war period has been more muted than in the United States (see figure III.1). This led to further delays in spending decisions and should be seen against the backdrop of a long period of slow growth, starting in 2001, that had stemmed from previous negative world shocks and continuing structural problems plaguing some of the major economies in the region. The delay is evident in industrial production, which has displayed little upward movement since mid-2002 (see figure III.2). This protracted period of growth below potential has led to an increase in unemployment across the region and further slippage in government budget positions. The former has negatively impacted consumer confidence, raising savings rates, while the latter has put pressure on Governments to consolidate budgets. This delay has also raised the risks of renewed downturn. An acceleration of activity in the second half of 2003 is envisaged, but the effects of the delay are expected to weaken the upturn, with growth in the EU-15 expected to register only 1.3 per cent in 2003 (compared with 0.9 per cent in 2002) and the forecast for growth in 2004 to be 2.4 per cent (see table A.2).

The weaker outlook is exhibited in both domestic and foreign demand components, but the weakness in domestic demand is the most troubling. In the euro zone, for example, final domestic demand, in 2002, contributed only 0.4 percentage points to growth, while net exports contributed 0.5 percentage points. However, the strength of the latter was due more to import weakness, reflecting the weak domestic demand, than to export strength.[3] Export growth registered only 1 per cent in 2002, stalling completely in the final quarter of the year. The weak recovery profile for external demand, together with the appreciation of the euro since the end of 2002 and its effect on competitiveness, is expected to dampen the rebound in exports, with growth of only 3 per cent in 2003, and 6.5 per cent in 2004 (see table A.13).

Consumption expenditure held up over the course of 2002 and was the main impetus to growth, but was still running at its slowest pace since the early 1990s. Real disposable income was constrained by persistently high inflation and increasing unemployment. The latter had the added effect of increasing uncertainty over future employment prospects which, when combined with the heightened uncertainty arising from the war in Iraq, led consumers to increase their savings rates. Wealth was depressed by lower equity prices, offset in some coun-

[3] In Austria, Germany, Portugal, and Switzerland, final domestic demand detracted from growth in 2002 (see *OECD Economic Outlook*, spring 2003, pp. 55-56).

tries by rising house prices—the United Kingdom of Great Britain and Northern Ireland saw particularly strong rises, but in Germany the housing sector has remained depressed. Consumption is expected to strengthen in 2003 and 2004 as inflation falls and uncertainty recedes. Government consumption was the other main support to growth in 2002, but at the expense of generally deteriorating budget positions. Given fiscal constraints in many countries, such expenditure is not expected to be a major contributor to growth in 2003 and 2004.

Investment expenditure was a serious drag on growth in 2002. Some rebound is expected in 2003 and 2004 but its strength will be limited. Profits have been hit by poor demand, particularly from the export sector, and by increased costs, mainly from higher oil prices. With the falling dollar, profits of European companies with United States subsidiaries are also being squeezed. Despite low interest rates, weak corporate balance sheets, due to both depressed equity values and high levels of debt, kept the cost of financing for firms relatively high, while financial difficulties in the banking sector of some countries may have reduced lending. Added to this, the heightened uncertainty stemming from the war in Iraq led many businesses to delay outlays. The removal of this uncertainty, together with continued progress in the rebuilding of corporate balance sheets, should provide some impetus to capital spending, but the outlook remains weak owing to expected continued poor export performance.

Inflation remained above 2 per cent in 2002, but is expected to decelerate throughout the remainder of 2003 and into 2004. The price of oil, and poor weather and animal diseases, were the main impulses, some of which passed through into wage growth in excess of productivity gains. There is also some question whether the introduction of euro notes and coins led to a surge in inflation at the beginning of 2002.[4] Core inflation reached 2.5 per cent in mid-2002, but then moderated, falling below 2 per cent in the first three months of 2003 (see figure III.4). Weak demand, the significant appreciation of the euro, and the unwinding of the spike in oil prices all point to a gradual diminution of

[4] The popular perception has been that there was a significant impact. However, this may have been due to the price rises' being concentrated in particular and highly visible sectors, such as restaurants, food, hotels and other services. The overall impact is still likely to have been small (see European Central Bank, *Annual Report, 2002* (Frankfurt am Main, 2003), pp. 40-41).

Figure III.4.
EURO ZONE: SELECTED PRICE INDICES, JANUARY 1999-APRIL 2003

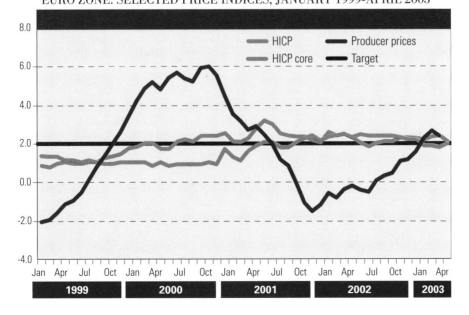

Source: OECD, Main Economic Indicators.

inflationary pressures (see table A.8). However, the dispersion of rates of inflation across the region remains wide, even among the largest economies of the region. The inflation differential of Germany vis-à-vis Italy and Spain was 2 percentage points in April 2003, and it was nearly 1 percentage point vis-à-vis France.

Unemployment has increased significantly since the beginning of 2002, climbing in the EU-15 from a low of 7.4 per cent in December 2001 to 7.9 per cent in March 2003 (see figure III.3), with a yearly average of 7.6 per cent in 2002. Continued below-trend growth in the first half of 2003 is expected to lead to a further increase to 8.0 per cent in 2003, before levelling off in 2004 (see table A.7). This pattern of rising unemployment was spread widely across the region. Since the end of 2001, the largest absolute increases have occurred in Belgium, Germany, the Netherlands, Portugal and Spain, all of which experienced a rise of 1 percentage point or more in the unemployment rate. Sizeable increases were also registered in Austria, France, Ireland, Luxembourg, Denmark and Norway. Only in Finland, Italy and the United Kingdom has unemployment remained stable. Compared with previous slowdowns, however, labour-market performance has so far been encouraging, reflecting in part the effects of structural change in some countries.[5] However, it is too soon to know whether this is a sign of greater labour-market flexibility or of firms' having chosen to hoard labour, owing to the high costs of hiring and firing, as they wait for more evidence of future prospects.

Macroeconomic policies in the second quarter of 2003 were stimulative, but not tremendously so. The European Central Bank (ECB) lowered its policy rate, the minimum bid rate, to 2.5 per cent in early March 2003 and then to 2.0 per cent in June, a cumulative 75 basis points (bps) since the beginning of 2003. These moves were prompted by continued evidence of economic weakness, the downside risks that mounted over the situation in Iraq, the appreciation of the euro against the United States dollar (which serves to tighten monetary conditions) and the behaviour of core inflation, which fell below the 2 per cent upper bound of the Bank's inflation target in the first three months of 2003. The movement in oil prices represented a strong positive impulse for inflation earlier in the year, muted by the appreciation of the currency, but subsequently became an element of downward pressure on inflation. Towards the end of the second quarter, short-term interest rates, both nominal and real, were at their lowest level since the beginning of the European Economic and Monetary Union (EMU). However, the degree of stimulus is lessened to some extent by the appreciation of the euro. In addition, as mentioned, inflation differentials vary widely across the region, so that real interest rates are still high in countries with low inflation. Germany, with the lowest rate of inflation in the euro zone, has the highest real interest rate. Given the long time lag for monetary policy to achieve its maximum impact, there should be a substantial boost to activity between mid-2003 and mid-2004. In making the forecasts of growth, it was assumed there would be no further easing and that policy would gradually return to a more neutral stance as growth strengthened and downside risks diminished.

Fiscal policy was moderately supportive of growth in 2002 owing both to the workings of automatic stabilizers and to some additional expansionary measures. However, this led to an increase in fiscal deficits across the region, which in some cases came into conflict with the 3 per cent maximum deficit allowed under the terms of the Stability and Growth Pact. Consequently, poli-

[5]   During the recession of the early 1990s, unemployment rose by 2.5 percentage points.

cy in 2003 and 2004 is expected to be, at best, broadly neutral, with some countries involved in fiscal consolidation programmes.

The fiscal deficit for the EU-15 deteriorated in 2002, for the second consecutive year, increasing by a full percentage point to 1.9 per cent of GDP. Further deterioration is expected in 2003, before some improvement in 2004. Most of the deterioration was due to the economic downturn, with higher expenditure on unemployment benefits and lower tax receipts. There were also some expenditure overruns, particularly in health-care spending, while receipts were lower than expected owing in part to tax cuts implemented in previous years and to the sharp fall in asset prices. However, discretionary policy also played a role.[6]

The free play of automatic stabilizers led to difficulties in countries that had not already attained medium-term balance in their fiscal positions or that continued to maintain large debt positions. At the end of 2002 and the beginning of 2003, excessive deficit procedures were initiated by the European Commission against Portugal and Germany, and an early warning recommendation was issued to France. In Italy, there are dangers that the deficit will breach the bound in 2004. So far, only Germany and Portugal have put into place programmes for consolidation, but there is pressure on France and Italy to consolidate. Debt is also a constraining factor. Belgium, Greece and Italy have debt-to-GDP ratios greater than 100 per cent, while Austria, France, Germany and Portugal either are close to or have exceeded the 60 per cent reference value. On the other hand, countries that have achieved budget balance and sustainable debt positions in the recent past have had room to allow the full play of their fiscal stabilizers. For example, the United Kingdom has embarked on a public investment programme that will lead to higher deficits in 2003 and 2004, but it currently enjoys a low debt-to-GDP ratio.

The euro continued its appreciation against the United States dollar in the first two quarters of 2003, the exchange rate increasing to $1.19 per euro in May, from $1.05 per euro in January. The appreciation against the yen was less dramatic, owing in part to currency market interventions by Japanese authorities to reduce the yen's appreciation against the dollar. In trade-weighted terms, the euro appreciated by nearly 14 per cent between its low in February 2002 and April 2003. This, however, has been more a matter of dollar weakness rather than euro strength, and can be attributed to a combination of long-standing structural issues and the uncertainties surrounding the war. The United States dollar has long been considered overvalued, from both purchasing power parity (PPP) and current-account deficit perspectives, but superior perceived returns in the United States relative to the rest of the world outweighed these considerations. However, with both the euro zone and the United States experiencing weak growth and their respective equity markets performing poorly, concern over the United States current account and its financing requirements has gained more attention. Interest rate differentials have also become an important factor favouring the euro, as monetary policy has been far more active in the United States than in the euro zone. Added to this, the currency movements experienced during the Iraqi conflict suggest that the United States dollar has lost much of its allure as a safe haven currency.

The forecast assumes, however, that not all of these gains are permanent, but rather that the euro will retrench somewhat against the dollar in the second half of the year. Some of the appreciation in the first half of 2003 can be ascribed to the overshooting that currency markets are often prone to—a phenomenon

[6] The European Commission estimates that, in the euro zone, 0.3 per cent of the deterioration in the overall deficit could be attributed to more relaxed budgetary stances, as measured by the change in the cyclically adjusted primary balance. By this measure, the majority of countries pursued looser policy in 2002 (see *European Economy*, No. 2/2003 (Luxembourg, European Commission, 2003), p. 37).

which has been exacerbated by foreign exchange markets' singular focus on the dollar's fall. In addition, interest rate differentials are expected to narrow in the second half of the year. Finally, relative growth rates are expected to regain their significance inasmuch as expansion in the United States in the second half of the year is forecast to be more robust than in the euro zone. Overall, it is expected that the euro will appreciate significantly in 2003 compared with 2002, with further, but more moderate, appreciation assumed in 2004 as current-account financing problems continue to play a prominent role.

The largest risk surrounding the current outlook is a further and rapid appreciation of the euro. This risk is compounded by the fact that, so far, most of the correction of the United States dollar has been against the euro, despite the fact that the United States current-account imbalances vis-à-vis other regions in the world are more pronounced. Further appreciation would add to the loss of competitivity for European exports and represent a major deflationary shock to the European region, particularly to those countries most dependent on exports. A second and related risk is that the upturn could be further delayed or even turn into a downturn. In early 2003, Germany was in recession and some other countries in the region were experiencing extremely slow growth. The unemployment situation is another area of concern. If the relatively mild deterioration in unemployment results from labour-hoarding by firms rather than structural improvements in the labour market, there is a risk that the unemployment situation could deteriorate further. Finally, the implementation continues to be in doubt of the many different reforms in labour-market regulations, pension systems and health care that have long been under consideration and that have made the region vulnerable to external shocks. These reforms need to be initiated as soon as possible as part of the effort both to revive growth in the short term and to enhance growth over the medium term.

ECONOMIES IN TRANSITION

There was a further slowdown in growth in the economies in transition in 2002. All three subgroups of countries played a contributing role but the deceleration was greatest in the rapidly growing CIS and least in Central and Eastern Europe. Growth in the latter region is forecast to improve with a recovery in Western Europe in 2003 and 2004, whereas a further modest consolidation of growth towards a more sustainable long-term rate is expected for other economies in transition during this period. For the Baltic countries and those of Central and Eastern Europe, the present overriding challenge is that of joining EU, including meeting all its economic benchmarks. For the CIS countries, there is a continuing need for wide-ranging reforms; moreover, a number of them also face long-term development challenges and need international support akin to that provided to developing countries.

Central and Eastern Europe: withstanding the global slowdown

Economic growth in Central and Eastern Europe decelerated from 2.7 per cent in 2001 to about 2.5 per cent in 2002, but is expected to strengthen to about 3 per cent in 2003. While a larger decline in response to the slowdown in EU could have been expected, higher rates of growth, and especially investment, are needed for these economies to converge to the average EU per capita GDP levels in a short period of time. Foreign direct investment (FDI) flows into the region and modernization of the economies continued in 2002, but investment rates in Central Europe remained modest.

The deceleration in 2002 was largely a consequence of weak export performance. From almost double-digit rates in 2001, growth of external trade dropped to about 3 per cent as a result of weak business confidence, weak import demand in EU and, to a large extent, currency appreciation. Strong currencies undermined exports to EU and, in the case of Hungary, encouraged some foreign investors to consider relocating their production facilities to Asia. In response, monetary policy in the region was focused on weakening the currencies so as to restore export competitiveness. While the small, export-oriented economies of Central Europe tried to cope with the lacklustre demand in EU, the largest, Poland, suffered a second year of economic stagnation.

By the end of 2002, there was a strengthening in industrial production in export-oriented sectors in Central Europe, although high inventories raised concern. In early 2003, stronger exports to EU were registered in Central Europe, with the exception of Hungary, reflecting the success of actions aimed at weakening the exchange rate.

With exports subdued, growth in the economies of Central and Eastern Europe (with the exception of Poland) was supported by strong domestic demand; both private and public consumption in the region grew by about 4 per cent. Expansionary fiscal policies, triggered by parliamentary elections throughout the region in 2002, played a role, as did rising household incomes, stronger currencies and lower interest rates. A repetition of such a scenario in 2003 is unlikely, however, since monetary and fiscal authorities in the region have become more concerned about meeting the criteria for entry into the euro zone. While neither changes in the fiscal system nor austerity measures are anticipated at this stage, a strong fiscal expansion is not expected in 2003. This will undermine the recent dependence of these strongly export-oriented economies on domestic demand as a primary source of growth. Growth, however, will continue to be supported by continuing FDI flows and associated investment and possibly by some further relocation of production from EU to the region.

The economic situation in Central Europe remains mixed. The Czech Republic is recovering from the floods in 2002, which caused damage to a number of industrial areas and affected the tourism industry. The economy of Poland is improving and, following two consecutive years of growth at about 1 per cent, is expected to expand at 2½ per cent in 2003. The financial condition of the private sector is improving and investment is expected to recover, following two years of decline. Export performance was good towards the end of 2002, in part because the currency was not as strong as those of other Central and Eastern European countries. In Hungary, exports declined at the beginning of 2003, but private consumption and public consumption are expected to be buoyant and to act as the main engine of growth. In contrast, Slovakia registered record sales in the automotive industry at the beginning of 2003. Private consumption in the country is also strong and will support growth.

The economies of both Bulgaria and Romania grew at above 4 per cent in 2002 and South-eastern Europe will become the fastest growing subregion in 2003. Growth in Bulgaria was supported mostly by strong government consumption and good export performance. In Romania, although public consumption remained weak, an increase in FDI resulted in a high rate of investment. In both countries, economic policy is focused on fiscal consolidation and privatization, as called for in standby agreements with the International Monetary Fund (IMF). Growth was also strong in Croatia, supported by public spending on infrastructure projects and by growing consumer credit. The current standby agreement with IMF, however, limits the budget deficit and public debt and, following policy tightening, growth is expected to decelerate in 2003.

The economic situation in other countries of the subregion has been more difficult. Industrial output in Albania was disrupted by energy shortages in the first half of 2002. The economy of Serbia and Montenegro expanded by 3 per cent in 2002, mostly owing to the services sector. Growth of 4 per cent is expected in 2003, although political uncertainty may impede macroeconomic stabilization and discourage much-needed foreign investment. The country needs to upgrade its economy and infrastructure, as well as harmonize the monetary, taxation and tariff systems of Serbia with those of Montenegro. Cooperation with IMF continues, with emphasis on fiscal stability and privatization. The economy of the former Yugoslav Republic of Macedonia, which became a member of the World Trade Organization in April 2003, is still feeling the effects of the 2001 crisis; its growth of 0.3 per cent in 2002 was achieved owing to the increase in services, since both industrial and agricultural output declined. The prospects of future growth are contingent on political stability and improved business confidence, as well as foreign investment flows.

Inflation in the region decelerated in 2002 (see table III.2) and hit record lows for the entire transition period in the Czech Republic, Poland and Slovakia; there was even deflation in the Czech Republic at the beginning of 2003. That this occurred despite high real wage growth (which outpaced productivity growth in the Czech Republic, Hungary and Slovakia), strong private consumption, a series of interest rates cuts (followed by domestic credit growth), and higher oil prices was owing to the fact that these pressures were outweighed by the strong currencies and low inflation in EU, low food prices, frozen administered prices in Slovakia and economic stagnation in Poland.

Inflation targets for 2002 were undershot in a number of countries, even in Poland despite a mid-year downward revision of the target in that country. Stronger inflation was registered late in 2002 in Hungary, where the Central Bank abandoned its inflation-targeting policy in favour of targeting the exchange rate. Similar action is also possible in the Czech Republic. Inflation was above the regional average in Romania, owing to lax monetary policy and an increase in energy prices, and in Serbia and Montenegro, owing to price liberalization.

Inflation in the region is expected to decelerate further in 2003, with the exception of Slovakia, where administered prices, including prices of energy, are to be liberalized in 2003. Strong portfolio capital inflows and price liberalization are the main inflationary forces in the region.

Benefiting from low inflation and low interest rates in the developed countries, the Central Banks of the Czech Republic, Hungary and Poland relaxed monetary policy at the beginning of 2003. This continued the trend started in 2002 and was aimed at weakening the exchange rates and also, in the case of the Czech Republic, at fighting deflation. Interest rates in the Czech Republic

Table III.2.
ECONOMIES IN TRANSITION: QUARTERLY INDICATORS, 2001-2002

Percentage[a]	2001 quarter				2002 quarter			
	I	II	III	IV	I	II	III	IV
	Rate of growth of gross domestic product							
Belarus	2.4	5.4	5.3	5.4	3.7	5.6	4.2	5.4
Czech Republic	3.5	3.4	3.0	2.5	2.6	2.1	1.7	1.5
Hungary	5.7	5.5	3.9	5.1	3.2	7.0	6.7	5.9
Kazakhstan	11.7	13.3	14.8	14.0	10.5	8.1	9.6	9.8
Poland	2.2	0.9	0.8	0.2	0.4	0.8	1.6	2.1
Romania	4.3	5.1	5.7	5.3	3.1	5.7	4.7	4.8
Russian Federation	4.8	5.3	5.8	4.3	3.7	4.1	4.3	4.7
Ukraine	8.2	11.3	11.3	9.0	4.1	4.7	4.3	6.1
	Change in consumer prices							
Belarus	83.3	70.6	55.0	46.3	47.2	44.6	43.1	37.4
Czech Republic	4.2	5.1	5.4	4.3	3.8	2.3	0.8	0.6
Hungary	10.4	10.6	8.7	7.2	6.3	5.6	4.8	5.0
Kazakhstan	9.1	9.7	8.3	7.0	5.7	5.5	6.4	6.4
Poland	6.8	6.6	4.8	3.8	3.5	2.0	1.1	0.8
Romania	40.1	36.9	31.8	30.5	26.8	24.2	21.3	18.5
Russian Federation	22.3	24.5	21.1	18.9	18.0	15.8	15.1	15.1
Ukraine	19.4	14.5	8.9	6.1	3.7	0.8	-0.9	-0.5

Sources: UN/DESA and ECE.

a   Percentage change from the corresponding period of the preceding year.

were reduced to below the euro zone rates, since the currency experienced upward pressure not only from speculative capital inflows, but also from foreign assistance associated with the recovery from the floods. Interest rates in Poland were drastically reduced in 2002 and 2003 in order to revive the economy. Even in Bulgaria, which is under a currency board arrangement, domestic credit is growing, reflecting easing monetary conditions. Further relaxation in 2003 is possible, as well as increased focus on the exchange rate rather than on inflation.

Structural fiscal deficits remain a problem for the region, but significant changes are not expected in the short term. Most Governments are focused on economic growth rather than on fiscal consolidation. For example, the Czech Republic approved additional spending on flood recovery and revitalization of the banking system in 2002. In Hungary, tax revenues declined sharply in 2002, while expenditures remained at the planned level, leading to a marked increase in the deficit. Bank restructuring costs increased the deficit in Slovakia, while a fall in custom duties hit the budget in the former Yugoslav Republic of Macedonia.

Privatization revenue is often used to finance budget deficits in the region, delaying structural fiscal changes. Some Governments have already decided not to implement any fiscal changes before 2004, and the decision to call early elections in Poland in 2004 will make any structural changes unlikely. The accession to EU will impose additional fiscal costs, associated with improvements in infrastructure and environmental policy, on all prospective members. Payments to the EU budget will be substantial, and many EU-assisted programmes are funded only on condition of co-financing from the recipient country's budget. EU has promised to compensate any "net loss" to new members for the first three years following the accession, but it is not clear how quickly this will materialize.

Lower interest rates alone were not sufficient to generate an upturn in investment in Central Europe in 2002. Investment even fell in Poland, owing to the poor financial condition of the corporate sector and weak business confidence. There was also a decline in investment in Slovakia. On the other hand, in Bulgaria investment grew at about 9 per cent, as bank lending to the private sector increased and many newly privatized firms upgraded their facilities. Strong investment was also registered in Romania, following privatization and increased FDI flows.

The employment situation in the region remains difficult owing to the ongoing privatization and restructuring of enterprises. The low mobility of the population and the underdeveloped housing market are additional impediments to raising employment. The situation in rural areas is especially difficult. As in previous years, unemployment is highest in Bulgaria, Poland, Slovakia and most of the former Yugoslav States. Government programmes to deal with the issue have produced limited results so far.

With the exception of Slovenia, the current accounts of the economies of Central and Eastern Europe remain in deficit owing to the strong domestic demand in the region and falling exports, as well as low tourism receipts in 2002, when floods affected most of the region. The strong currency adversely affected the services balance and stimulated retail sales of foreign brands. Profit repatriation was another source of deficit, although low interest rates in the developed countries reduced debt-servicing costs. Since imports of technology, including for greenfield investment, will continue throughout the region and spending on flood recovery needs will continue to require imports in the Czech Republic, no significant improvement in current-account balances is expected in the near future. Most deficits have been covered by FDI in the past, although the recent drop in foreign investment in Hungary may raise concern. In Serbia and Montenegro, inflows of FDI are insufficient to cover the current-account gap and foreign assistance is therefore crucial.

The process of EU enlargement continues as planned, after most of the obstacles, largely associated with the Common Agricultural Policy and EU regional aid, were removed at the EU Copenhagen summit at the end of 2002. Prospective members were offered more generous assistance following their admission to EU than originally planned. Most of the proposed assistance, however, is to be co-financed by the new member States themselves and this may complicate the implementation of some projects. New members are expected to join the Union on 1 May 2004.

The Baltic countries: the world's fastest growing region

The Baltic countries were the world's fastest growing region in 2002, with an increase of 6.3 per cent in GDP. Buoyant domestic demand and strong import demand in CIS offset weakened import demand from EU. The revival in domestic demand was broad-based with investment expanding at a double-digit rate and private consumption boosted by higher real wages, credit expansion and declining unemployment. Three years of sustained strong economic growth finally resulted in an improvement in the employment situation in the region. The unemployment rate fell in Estonia and Lithuania, the latter recording a drop of over 1 percentage point in 2002 to 11.3 per cent of the workforce.

Growth in industrial output slowed somewhat in 2002. The strongest deceleration was in Lithuania, reflecting a continuing decline in oil refining, owing to disruptions in deliveries of oil to the Mazeikiai refinery. This problem eased, however, in the fourth quarter, when supplies of oil from the Russian Federation increased as the change of ownership[7] started bearing fruit. This should enhance the stability of Lithuania's industrial output and export revenue.

In 2003, growth in the region will continue to be driven by domestic demand and is expected to stabilize at about 5¼ per cent. The largest deceleration is expected in Latvia owing to a sharp drop in transit trade through the port of Ventspils, which has been the most affected by the Russian Federation's opening of a new oil terminal in the Gulf of Finland. The Russian company Transneft has announced that it will not resume shipments through Ventspils until the end of the second quarter of 2003. It is likely that a 50 per cent stake in Ventspils Nafta will be sold to Transneft in order to secure steady shipments.

Exports from Latvia and Lithuania increased by 12 and 10 per cent respectively in 2002 as import demand from EU recovered slightly and the countries continued to redirect some of their exports to CIS. Estonia, on the other hand, experienced a 2 per cent fall in exports, as a result of a sharp contraction in foreign sales of mobile telephones and related components in the first half of 2002. Prospects for Estonian exports in 2003 are more encouraging, as the growth in import demand in Sweden and Finland, Estonia's main trading partners, is expected to outperform that in the rest of EU.

Reflecting export performance, the current-account deficit increased substantially in Estonia in 2002, reaching 12.5 per cent of GDP, but decreased in Latvia and remained about the same in Lithuania. A reduction in the region's current-account deficit is contingent on EU economic recovery's generating increased demand for Baltic exports. High deficits in these countries are manageable, however, because of substantial FDI inflows. FDI inflows more than doubled in Latvia and increased by almost 60 per cent in Lithuania in 2002, but fell by 45 per cent in Estonia (which had previously attracted the largest amount of FDI per capita).

The Baltic economies have transformed themselves into fully functioning small open economies and maintain a strong record of reform and sound policies. All three countries signed the accession treaty at the EU summit in Athens on 16 April 2003 and are due to join EU on 1 May 2004 subject to their referendums on membership. Lithuania has already held its referendum and 90 per cent voted in favour of joining EU. Referendums in Estonia and Latvia are scheduled to be held in September 2003.

7 The Russian company Yukos acquired a majority stake in the Mazeikiai refinery.

Fiscal and monetary policies in all three countries are influenced by the Maastricht criteria. Maintaining a currency board or close equivalent reduces the scope of monetary policy and makes prudent fiscal policy particularly important. All three countries maintained a tight fiscal stance in 2002. Estonia reported a fiscal surplus while Latvia and Lithuania had deficits of 2.6 and 1.2 per cent of GDP respectively. Fiscal deficits will widen in 2003. The 2003 budgets reflect a loosening of fiscal policy to accommodate increased expenditures related to the costs of membership in the North Atlantic Treaty Organization (NATO) and preparations for EU membership. Even Estonia, whose law requires its budgets to be balanced, except in extraordinary circumstances, approved a 2003 draft budget that was the first with a deficit since 1991. However, all three Governments have indicated that they will ensure that budget deficits are kept below the Maastricht criterion of 3 per cent of GDP.

Average inflation in the region declined to about 1.6 per cent in 2002. The main reason for the fall was a drop in food prices and lower import prices due to the appreciation against the dollar of the euro-pegged currencies in Estonia and Lithuania. Inflation is expected to inch up in 2003, reaching an average rate of about 2.5 per cent. The moderate upward pressure will result from the slight loosening of fiscal policies and continued strong domestic demand.

Commonwealth of Independent States (CIS): sustaining robust growth

Following two years of strong performance, the CIS economy expanded at a lower pace of 4.7 per cent in 2002. The region had little exposure to the global slowdown and benefited from higher oil prices. All countries in the group, with the exception of Kyrgyzstan, recorded rates of growth of over 4 per cent. Robust domestic demand in the Russian Federation and Ukraine and, to a lesser extent, in other CIS countries, backed by rising real incomes,[8] lower interest rates and a continuing oil-related investment boom in the Caspian region, will sustain growth at a similar rate in 2003.

The recent deceleration mostly reflected a slowdown in the Russian Federation and Ukraine. The Russian economy grew by 4.3 per cent in 2002, mostly on the basis of recovering private consumption and strong energy exports. The volume of crude oil exports rose by 14 per cent and oil products by almost 20 per cent in 2002. Growth in 2003 will continue to be driven by these two factors. Investment, which had a poor performance in 2002, is also likely to pick up in 2003 if oil prices continue to be high. Investment reportedly grew by close to 10 per cent in the first two months of 2003, partly owing to an investment of almost $7 billion in the oil sector by a foreign corporation. Oil output in the Russian Federation increased by 9.1 per cent in 2002, reaching a record post-Soviet level of 7.62 million barrels per day (bpd). Exports of oil cannot, however, be increased without building additional pipelines, as the export capacity limit has been reached. The system is controlled by a State-owned company, but the State does not have plans for sufficient expansion, nor is it willing to give up control and allow private companies to build their own pipelines.

In Ukraine, growing private consumption did not fully offset the impact of lower external demand, mostly from the Russian Federation. Lower prices of steel and the proliferation of trade barriers also resulted in a slump in metallurgy production in the first half of 2002. However, steel production started recovering towards the end of 2002, reflecting mostly the reorientation of exports to

8   Real wages and real incomes in the Russian Federation rose 17 per cent and 9 per cent respectively in 2002.

markets in West Asia and other CIS countries. In Ukraine, as in the Russian Federation, a return to the high rates of growth recorded in 2000 and 2001 is unlikely without further restructuring and a substantial increase in investment to address supply bottlenecks, which continue to constrain output growth.

The boom in Azerbaijan and Kazakhstan will continue in 2003, thanks to continuing FDI flows related to large-scale oil and gas projects and rising oil exports. The construction of the Baku-Tbilisi-Ceyhan (BTC) pipeline, which officially started in September 2002, will benefit Georgia as well. Growth in Turkmenistan, another hydrocarbon exporter, will slow from its high rates because the country has reached its export capacity limits. However, the country's export capacity will increase substantially, reducing its dependence on such traditional markets as the Russian Federation and Ukraine, if an alternative pipeline from Turkmenistan through Afghanistan to Pakistan is built. This massive project has been revived with the end of the war in Afghanistan and now seems feasible.

Many other smaller economies of the region enjoyed continued strong growth. Armenia grew by almost 13 per cent in 2002, reflecting continuing recovery in the industrial sector, mostly in precious metals and stone processing, as well as booming construction. The country's exports increased by almost 50 per cent, while investment rose 43 per cent. In line with ongoing restructuring and improving efficiency in the industrial sector, strong growth is likely to continue in 2003, albeit at a lower rate. Reflecting continued industrial expansion,[9] Tajikistan recorded 9.1 per cent growth in 2002. In the case of the Republic of Moldova, strengthening domestic demand raised growth to 7.2 per cent. Growth in these economies is likely to decelerate somewhat in 2003.

Kyrgyzstan was the only CIS country whose economy did not grow in 2002. Its GDP contracted by 0.5 per cent owing to a sharp drop in production of gold in the Kumtor gold mine,[10] caused by a switch to mining lower-grade ore and an accident in July. Growth will recover in 2003, provided gold production is restored to full capacity.

The Russian Federation remains the regional engine of growth, but the links are weakening as Russian trade continues to shift away from the CIS countries. Also, mutual investment is increasing very slowly. For example, the Russian Federation is only the fifth largest source of foreign investment in Ukraine. These economic factors, together with some political considerations, led the four largest CIS countries—the Russian Federation, Ukraine, Kazakhstan and Belarus—to sign a joint statement in February 2003, on forming a single economic space. It remains to be seen what is envisaged.

Despite robust growth in these countries, employment-generation is still lagging owing to productivity improvements. In most CIS countries, unemployment remains high and any changes are difficult to follow owing to the unreliability of official data. Unemployment in the Russian Federation declined in 2002 but began to rise in September and had reached about 9 per cent of the workforce by January 2003.

The external position remained uneven across the CIS region in 2002. The Russian Federation and Ukraine reported current-account surpluses of 9.1 per cent and 6.4 per cent of GDP respectively. For the Russian Federation, this nevertheless represented a deterioration compared with 2001, reflecting a decline in exports in the first half of 2002 and an almost 10 per cent growth in imports due to strong domestic demand and continued real appreciation of the rouble against

9 The aluminium sector accounts for up to 60 per cent of industrial output.

10 Gold production accounts for 40 per cent of the country's industrial production, 90 per cent of which is provided by the Kumtor mine.

Box III.1

CIS-7 INITIATIVE TO PROMOTE
POVERTY REDUCTION, GROWTH
AND DEBT SUSTAINABILITY IN
THE LOW-INCOME COUNTRIES OF
THE COMMONWEALTH OF
INDEPENDENT STATES

a   It varies from US$ 158 in Tajikistan to US$ 652 in
     Azerbaijan, compared with $1,720 in the Russian
     Federation (see International Monetary Fund and
     World Bank, "Poverty reduction, growth and debt
     sustainability in low-income CIS countries", 4
     February 2002 (http://www.imf.org/external/np/
     eu2/2002/edebt/eng).

The CIS-7 Initiative to Promote Poverty Reduction, Growth and Debt Sustainability in the Low-income Countries of the Commonwealth of Independent States was launched in April 2002 by the Asian Development Bank, the European Bank for Reconstruction and Development (EBRD), the International Monetary Fund (IMF) and the World Bank. The CIS-7 Initiative aims to accelerate economic growth and poverty reduction in seven low-income CIS countries—Armenia, Azerbaijan, Georgia, Kyrgyzstan, the Republic of Moldova, Tajikistan and Uzbekistan—while maintaining fiscal and external debt sustainability.

Transition from a centrally planned to a market economy in these poorer former Soviet republics has been more difficult than in other transition countries. Real GDP for the group as a whole fell by 55 per cent between 1990 and 2000 (compared with an average of 23 per cent for all transition countries) and poverty increased to high levels (see chap. VIII below). GDP per capita fell by more than half during that period in every country.[a] In the Republic of Moldova and Tajikistan, more than 80 per cent of the population were below the national poverty line in 1999, compared with 13 per cent and 59 per cent respectively in 1988. Many of the CIS-7 countries are labouring under a large external debt, all of which has been accumulated since the beginning of the transition. In Kyrgyzstan, the Republic of Moldova and Tajikistan, the ratios of external debt to GDP exceed 100 per cent.

The countries included in the CIS-7 Initiative have committed themselves to strengthened reform programmes, fiscal consolidation and macroeconomic stability. The international community, in turn, has pledged to provide these countries with greater market access and financial assistance. Actions under the CIS-7 Initiative are intertwined with other activities of the international community and therefore difficult to identify separately. Nevertheless, the CIS-7 Initiative has provided a useful umbrella for enhanced cooperation by the participating international financial institutions and has provided the CIS-7 countries with increased visibility in the eyes of the donor community.

One of the key objectives of the CIS-7 Initiative is to enhance donor assistance and coordination, including debt relief where needed. Georgia and Kyrgyzstan have already rescheduled their debts with Paris Club creditors and Armenia has concluded a debt-equity swap agreement with the Russian Federation. A high-level conference held in Lucerne, Switzerland, in January 2003, recommended that more grant financing should be provided by both the International Development Association (IDA) and bilateral donors.

The CIS-7 Initiative stresses the importance of the CIS-7 countries' taking greater ownership of their reform programmes, particularly through nationally developed Poverty Reduction Strategy Papers (PRSPs). A third Forum on Poverty Reduction Strategies for the CIS-7 countries, held in Almaty in December 2002, provided the CIS-7 countries with advice on how to address policy issues related to the PRSP process, emphasizing that PRSPs needed to become fully integrated into the Governments' normal operations, including national budgets.

An important objective of the CIS-7 Initiative is to build capacity in the CIS-7 countries to design and implement reforms in such areas as poverty reduction, rural development, public financial management, private sector development, labour-market development, infrastructure and social policies. Discussions on these subjects were initiated during the conference in Lucerne and will be followed up with in-depth technical seminars and workshops in the CIS-7 countries, as well as with targeted partnerships that will help to raise donor support for the financing of specific programmes.

Strengthening public expenditure management has been another focus of the CIS-7 Initiative. The thrust of the technical and financial assistance from the World Bank is to help ensure that public resource use reflects scarcity and PRSP priorities. Public expenditure reforms to improve governance and reduce corruption are a key focus in adjustment loans under preparation by the World Bank in Armenia and Kyrgyzstan. An added challenge in the resource-rich countries is prudent management of natural resource wealth. The

Box III.1 (continued)

establishment of a legal and administrative framework for an oil fund in Azerbaijan is an example of work in this area.

Policy and expenditure reforms in education, health and social protection are supported by technical assistance, analytical and advisory services and lending from the World Bank and the Asian Development Bank. Tax policy and administration, including customs reforms in each of the CIS-7 countries, have received technical assistance from IMF and the World Bank.

Energy sector reforms remain an urgent task in all CIS-7 countries which, following the break-up of the former Soviet Union, suffered massive terms-of-trade shocks because of the increase in their energy import prices to world levels. The Asian Development Bank, EBRD and the International Finance Corporation (IFC) are involved in power sector projects in many of these countries, frequently focusing on improving regional cooperation in power transmission.

Improving the investment climate for small and medium-sized enterprises (SMEs) is another priority. The IFC Private Enterprise Partnership was set up to provide SMEs with technical assistance and to work with the Governments on improving the legislative framework for SMEs. Initially, the Partnership focused on Armenia, Kyrgyzstan and Uzbekistan, but recently the programme was expanded to include Georgia and Tajikistan.

Each of the international financial institutions has been involved in extensive assistance to the financial sector. The Asian Development Bank, IMF and the World Bank provided support in such areas as bank restructuring, accounting, and payments system reform, as well as corporate governance reforms. The Asian Development Bank, EBRD and IFC have also supported private financial institutions through loans and technical assistance to commercial banks.

The CIS-7 Initiative also aims to promote greater regional cooperation in trade, transport, water, energy, and the environment, as well as in such key social areas, as the fight against human immunodeficiency virus/acquired immunodeficiency syndrome (HIV/AIDS) and tuberculosis. In particular, resolving the regional trade disputes created by the political tensions over Nagorny Karabakh, and in Georgian-Russian relations, as well as addressing the general lack of commitment to trade liberalization in Uzbekistan, remains a high priority for ensuring economic growth in the region.

Achieving prosperity in these small and relatively isolated economies also depends critically on improved trade access and transport links to the rest of the world. A number of initiatives are under way to facilitate trade in the region. The Asian Development Bank and the World Bank are conducting regional transportation facilitation projects in the Caucasus and Central Asia, focusing on regional road and rail transportation networks.

Despite fiscal consolidation, the challenge remains for oil-exporting countries to minimize the dependence of national income on the prices of oil. Following the example of Azerbaijan and Kazakhstan, the Russian Federation has decided to introduce a fiscal stabilization fund and the Government is planning to pass the necessary legislation by the end of 2003.

In line with the current disinflationary trend, most of the central banks in the region lowered their interest rates in 2002. Average inflation in the region declined to 14.4 per cent in 2002 compared with 18.5 in 2002, mostly owing to the fall in food prices, lower oil prices in the first quarter of the year, and relatively tight monetary policies in most countries. In several countries, inflation dropped to very low levels. Ukraine, for example, recorded less than 1 per cent inflation in 2002. However, inflation is still stubbornly high in Belarus, the Russian Federation and Uzbekistan. Inflation in the Russian Federation in 2002 was 15.1 per cent, despite the Russian Central Bank's target of 10–12 per cent inflation. If the Bank had continued to target the real exchange rate in order to protect domestic producers, inflation would likely have continued to exceed the official target. In early 2003, however, the Bank announced that it would allow 4-6 per cent real exchange-rate appreciation in order to curb inflation: this would lead to a decrease of 1–1.5 percentage points in the average inflation in the region in 2003. As a first step in this direction, the rouble strengthened 5 per cent against the dollar in real terms in the first quarter of 2003.

the United States dollar. However, exports started growing towards the end of the year and increased by about 6 per cent for the year as a whole. With the higher prices of oil, no substantial narrowing of the current-account surplus is expected in 2003. Ukraine is also likely to maintain a current-account surplus in 2003 although it will be reduced owing to gradual real appreciation of the currency and rising import demand. All the other CIS countries recorded current-account deficits or only marginal surpluses in 2002. According to the available data, the highest current-account deficit was recorded in Azerbaijan (8.4 per cent of GDP in the first 9 months of 2002), reflecting a sharp rise in investment in the oil sector. This deficit, however, was entirely covered by FDI inflows.

A continuation of reforms will be key to sustained economic growth in the CIS countries. The pace of Russian reforms slowed in 2002 after the successes of 2001. A noteworthy development in 2002 was the passage by the Duma of legislation to break up the State electricity monopoly, Unified Energy Systems. There has also been some progress in the reform of the banking system and the Duma has been discussing the Law on Deposit Insurance. The ongoing tax reform will, according to the government programme, concentrate on shifting the tax burden from the manufacturing sector to energy and other primary producers. Reforms are not likely to accelerate in 2003 because there are parliamentary and presidential elections in 2003 and 2004 respectively and the pending reforms include such socially sensitive issues as the deregulation of natural monopoly tariffs, as well as social security and the pension system.

Progress with reform in Ukraine will remain slow, particularly in the light of continuing political instability, which could intensify in the run-up to the 2004 presidential election. In February 2003, the National Bank of Ukraine announced a series of measures to liberalize the currency market and to increase safeguards against capital flight. A priority is to adopt a new tax code; if achieved by mid-2003, this would allow the next budget to be formulated on the basis of the new tax system.

A great deal of structural reform is still needed in other CIS countries. In oil-rich countries such as Azerbaijan and Kazakhstan, the lack of restructuring is hampering the expansion of the non-oil sector.

The CIS countries have achieved substantial fiscal consolidation over the past several years, to a large extent because of fiscal reforms and, in the case of the oil-producing countries, helped by higher prices of oil. In 2002, however, there was some deterioration of fiscal positions. In the Russian Federation, for example, the fiscal surplus decreased from 2.4 per cent of GDP in 2001 to 1.4 per cent of GDP in 2002. Fiscal loosening is expected in 2003 because of pre-election spending and a continued decline in revenues from custom duties and profit taxes, in the latter case because the tax rate was cut from 35 to 24 per cent at the beginning of 2002. The decline is reflected in the 2003 budget, which has been drafted with a 0.6 per cent surplus (compared with the 1.6 per cent surplus planned for 2002). In Ukraine, despite moderate fiscal loosening expected in 2003, the fiscal position will remain sound. It is expected to benefit from the passage of a new tax code which, as indicated above, it is hoped that parliament will approve by mid-2003.

Persistent fiscal deficits continue to be a problem for some of the highly indebted CIS countries, like Kyrgyzstan, the Republic of Moldova, Tajikistan, Armenia and Georgia, and debt servicing remains a major strain on their finances. These countries need more debt relief in order to achieve sustainability. Recognizing this, IMF, the World Bank, the Asian Development Bank and the European Bank for Reconstruction and Development (EBRD) have launched the so-called CIS-7 Initiative to Promote Poverty Reduction, Growth and Debt Sustainability in the Low-income Countries of the Commonwealth of Independent States[11] (see box III.1).

[11] CIS-7 comprises Armenia, Azerbaijan, Georgia, Kyrgyzstan, the Republic of Moldova, Tajikistan and Uzbekistan.

DEVELOPING ECONOMIES

Developing countries grew by 3.2 per cent in 2002. Faced with depressed external demand, limited and costly financial inflows, uncertainties that affected investor and consumer confidence worldwide and, in many instances, policy constraints that precluded the use of counter-cyclical domestic policies, this performance was below potential but an improvement over 2001, when growth had been only 2.1 per cent. Not all regions were able to participate in this mild recovery: GDP contracted in Latin America and growth decelerated in Africa. The enhanced performance was largely in Eastern and Southern Asia and, to some extent, Western Asia. In the latter, however, faster growth was mostly attributable to the recovery in Turkey.

With the further delay until the second half of 2003 of the economic recovery in major developed economies, weak trade flows and the persistence of financial and policy constraints, growth in developing countries will accelerate only slightly to 3½ per cent in 2003. This improved performance, however, masks shortcomings at the regional level: Latin America will record only modest growth, due mostly to the recovery in Argentina; Western Asia will decelerate owing to the impact of the war in Iraq, the continuation of the conflict between Israel and the Palestinian people and a slowdown in Turkey; and Africa will continue to grow at only about 3 per cent, while East Asia, confronted with the negative impact of SARS and the tentative recovery in world trade, will decelerate. The only bright spots in the outlook are South Asia, where growth is expected to reach 5¾ per cent in 2003, and China, which will continue its strong performance (see table A.4). Reflecting improved external conditions and a recovery in domestic demand in many economies, growth in 2004 is expected to accelerate in all regions, reaching 5 per cent.

Africa: the challenge of poverty reduction

Africa's overall GDP growth in 2003 is expected to reach 3¼ per cent, a slight increase from the 2.9 per cent recorded in 2002. Growth is projected to continue accelerating to 4 per cent in 2004.

For the first time in many years, in 2002 sub-Saharan Africa grew faster—albeit only slightly faster—than North Africa, as the large economies of the latter subregion were constrained by low Organization of the Petroleum Exporting Countries (OPEC) quotas and/or decreased external demand. Despite reduced growth in Nigeria, and only a marginal increase in growth in South Africa, more than 20 countries—almost all sub-Saharan—grew in excess of 3 per cent (see table I.3). However, this relatively faster subregional growth did not embody an increase in per capita GDP in all cases. Healthy performance generally reflected a variety of favourable domestic elements: most States benefited from increased agricultural output, which, given the dominance of this sector in many of them, led to higher rural incomes, lower inflation and significant growth in non-agricultural sectors, such as agro-based industries and distributive trades.

Only four countries—Côte d'Ivoire, Madagascar, Malawi and Zimbabwe—suffered contraction. Other than in Malawi, which endured a severe drought, contraction was a result of conflict, protracted in Côte d'Ivoire and Zimbabwe, and the continued consequences of earlier instability in Madagascar.

Increased mining output of both base metals (mainly copper) and precious metals (gold and platinum) and diamonds, together with slightly improved prices in international markets, contributed to growth in Botswana, the Democratic Republic of the Congo, Namibia, South Africa, the United Republic of Tanzania, Zambia and Zimbabwe. In Namibia, Zambia, Zimbabwe, and some of the other countries affected by drought, growth in minerals and metals output prevented steep declines in GDP growth.

Increased manufacturing output for exports to the United States under the preferential treatment provided by the African Growth and Opportunity Act (AGOA) contributed to an improvement in overall growth performance in Kenya, Lesotho, Mauritius, Madagascar and South Africa. Uganda's high rates of economic growth have been partly attributed to private capital inflows into a range of economic activities that support that country's export diversification strategy.

Towards the end of 2002, the external environment became less supportive of growth in the region as the EU economies decelerated and uncertainties mounted. The difficulty was exacerbated by decreased prices for almost all of Africa's food commodity exports—with the exception of cocoa—and the depreciation of the United States dollar against the euro. African commodities are sold in dollars, but the majority of imports are priced in euros, which means that the continent was increasingly hurt as the dollar declined. These difficulties persisted in the first half of 2003.

The impending combat in Iraq further hampered tourism in North Africa and increased political instability in many States in which citizens expressed violent disapproval of the war. States such as Egypt were severely impacted, facing losses in tourism earnings and currency value, which, combined with the consequences of its designation as being in a war zone, constrained growth during the final months of the year. The other major test for the continent arose out of the increasingly intractable crisis in Côte d'Ivoire, which began to have a region-wide impact. With the mass repatriation of its foreign workers, Côte d'Ivoire lost the backbone of its cocoa economy, and the region lost remittance flows, the locus of substantial FDI, and a prime engine of growth. The contagion effects of this crisis have been considerable; especially affected have been the landlocked countries of Burkina Faso, Mali and the Niger, whose economies have had to absorb not just reduced remittances and increased unemployment, but also substantially higher trans-shipment costs. Continued tensions in the Democratic Republic of the Congo, and between Ethiopia and Eritrea, as well as in Zimbabwe, also depressed end-of-year growth in other parts of the continent.

Nigeria, the largest economy in West Africa, was impacted both by global and by internal tensions. The key internal uncertainty related to the April 2003 presidential and legislative elections, campaigning for which began in early 2002. As is common in elections, there was a marked increase in fiscal spending by the incumbent Government (see box III.2), a strategy allowed by the

A key dimension of the broad process of political and economic reform in Africa since the beginning of the 1990s has been the trend towards the use of elections as the primary means of selecting Governments. Though a small number of elections had been held on the continent prior to the 1990s, it was only in that decade that elections became almost universal throughout Africa (see figure). Elections are not isolated events, but are part of a holistic process of democratic transition and governance. Regardless of national history or economic standing, elections—and broader aspects of democracy—began to be promoted in every corner of the continent. The unprecedented speed and pervasiveness of this change were brought about by a confluence of external and internal influences. External pressures, catalysed in part by the demise of the Soviet Union, included the growing international focus on individual rights, the communications revolution, and the resolve of donors and trading partners that their economic engagement should increasingly be linked with political reforms in partner countries.[a] These pressures, buttressed by domestic forces for democratization, with activists being ennobled by the "democratic contagion" from other States, were aided both by the new ideological climate and by the growing worldwide acceptance of the ballot as the most legitimate means to support or change leadership. The result of these myriad forces has been the continent-wide promotion of elections and wider political liberties, with most African States explicitly embracing greater democracy at the national level, as well as in such regional undertakings as the African Union and the New Partnership for Africa's Development (document A/57/304, annex).

The increasing use of elections in Africa augurs well for the future of the people on the continent. The human rights benefits of elections and democratization are evident. Free and fair elections, when accompanied by supporting institutions to ensure that the proper checks and balances are in place to prevent misuse of economic and political power by incumbents (such as an independent election commission, an independent judiciary and independent media), provide citizens with voice, redress and power to shape their surroundings and their futures. Additionally, by bringing a diversity of issues to the fore, elections can be a powerful tool for furthering and solidifying economic change and

Box III.2

ELECTIONS AND ECONOMIC STABILITY IN AFRICA

[a]   In regard to aid, donors announced and implemented new political and economic conditions that would be attached to the allocation of assistance and continued support. For instance, donors suspended aid to Equatorial Guinea, Kenya, Malawi and Zaire in the early 1990s to foster political and economic reform and resumed aid to Kenya and Malawi at the end of 1993 after multi-party elections were organized and economic reforms implemented. Concerning trade, the United States African Growth and Opportunity Act (AGOA) and the Partnership Agreement between the Members of the African, Caribbean and Pacific Group of States and the European Community and its Member States (Cotonou Agreement) are examples of the political/economic linkages required by partners. Eligibility for AGOA is predicated not only on applicant States' making positive market reforms, but also on their establishing reforms oriented towards enhanced human rights, as well as "rule of law and political pluralism". The Cotonou Agreement has a similar clause aimed at ensuring that beneficiaries of the trade agreement "encourag[e] the promotion of participatory methods...".

FIVE DECADES OF AFRICAN ELECTIONS

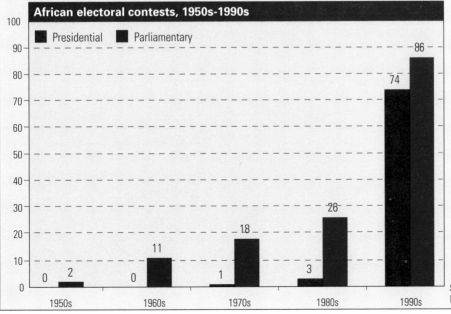

African electoral contests, 1950s-1990s

■ Presidential   ■ Parliamentary

	1950s	1960s	1970s	1980s	1990s
Presidential	0	0	1	3	74
Parliamentary	2	11	18	26	86

Source: International Institute for Democracy and Electoral Assistance (International IDEA).

Box III.2 (continued)

helping to ensure that reforms enjoy wide support. Even though democratization can make imposing such reforms more difficult—by opening up the space for dissent—the evidence in Africa suggests that successful economic reforms and political liberalization are not mutually exclusive.

However, in some instances, the introduction of elections in African countries has been the source of political and economic instability. Election-related economic instability takes a number of forms. In some countries, the formation of political parties along ethnic or religious lines has exacerbated existing cleavages, while in other cases, disputes over the legitimacy of candidates have led to hostility, actions against certain groups in the population, and economic disarray. Further, in a number of countries, balloting has involved intimidation and, in several cases, the outcome has been controversial often owing to disputes regarding vote-counting. Such friction has often reduced national unity, and interrupted domestic and regional commerce, and has sometimes sparked violence, all with negative effects on economic activity.

Election-related economic instability has also occurred in the absence of political violence. In the era of globalization, any tensions surrounding elections, particularly if they involve the potential for economic dislocation, can raise uncertainty in the international community about a country's economic prospects. Though private investors appreciate the predictability and the respect for the rule of law that is usually associated with elections and other democratic practices, in a number of countries uncertainties leading up to an election—due to the possibility of violence or of abrupt policy changes prior to, or in the wake of, the contest—have had negative impacts on both exchange rates and portfolio and FDI flows. Secondly, as in many countries, including developed countries, election campaigns in African countries have often been associated with fiscal indiscipline. Such indiscipline has involved not only an overexpansion in the public sector prior to a vote, but also a shift in fiscal expenditures from long-term investment to the provision of short-term goods and services intended to bolster the popularity of the incumbent. Though such election-induced spending is common in many States, in countries where the mobilization of public resources is challenging, as is the case for most African States, the long-term cost of such a reallocation of resources can be high and may delay, or even derail, hard-won programmes of economic reform.

Finally, even if elections are held without such instability, campaigns held amid social discord, and seen to involve intimidation or other non-democratic features, may be deemed by the international community as not "free and fair". Such a designation entails a further economic risk, as it may result in the isolation of the State from bilateral donors and international financial institutions.

Almost 30 national-level elections (presidential and parliamentary elections, as well as 1 national referendum) are scheduled to take place in Africa during 2002-2003, continuing the rapid pace of democratization on the continent. Though there are increasing numbers of countries in Africa that have held free and fair electoral contests with only minor economic disturbances, on the basis of experience to date it must be expected that some of the impending contests will involve a degree of economic disruption. It thus remains a challenge for domestic policy makers and the international community to identify the national risks associated with electoral contests and to adopt countermeasures to mitigate the sources of conflict and instability. One clear requirement is to establish robust and flexible economic and political institutions designed to withstand the stresses of elections, without sacrificing continued democratization and economic development. Such institutions would strengthen and render more sustainable the social, economic and political reforms under way in many of Africa's emerging democracies.

repudiation of its IMF agreement in early 2002. As a result, Nigeria weathered macroeconomic instability throughout the year, with double-digit inflation and an unstable exchange rate, which depreciated by as much as 11 per cent during the year. The oil sector, which accounts for almost all of the country's foreign exchange earnings, was also the catalyst for two crises that impaired the economy. Continued, and often violent, disagreements between the littoral oil States and the federal Government as to the equitable distribution of oil earnings interrupted production from some fields.

South Africa, the largest economy in sub-Saharan Africa, witnessed a return to growth in private sector employment for the first time in over six years, in the third quarter of 2002. Reduction of high levels of unemployment nevertheless remains one of the key policy challenges of the South African authorities. The economy showed remarkable resiliency by growing 3 per cent in 2002. Growth was underscored by increased agricultural output and increased output in gold and platinum mining in a year when international prices for those two commodities had strengthened from recent lows, while export growth also improved.

Average inflation rates in Africa increased slightly in 2002 (see table A.10) and reached 9 per cent on average during the year, an outcome that masks continuing difficulties in maintaining low price growth in Ghana, Madagascar, Malawi, Mozambique, Namibia, Nigeria, South Africa and Zambia, all of which recorded double-digit inflation during the year. In South Africa, policy makers expressed renewed commitment to an inflation-targeting policy despite an inflation outcome that had exceeded the upper limits of the target set for 2002, even after revisions in the calculation of the consumer price index. By early 2003, inflationary pressures began to ease with the strengthening of the rand (due, in part to the depreciation of the dollar) and lower food and imported oil prices. In Zimbabwe, inflation increased sharply to triple-digit levels owing to severe shortages of food and other essential commodities and the steep depreciation of the currency. Other economies, notably Botswana, the United Republic of Tanzania and many Communauté financière africaine (CFA) countries, managed to reduce inflation, in many cases as a result of tight monetary and fiscal policies and increased domestic food supplies. Inflation in the Democratic Republic of the Congo, most notably, fell from 360 per cent in the previous year to 16 per cent in 2002.

North African States are expected to grow more vigorously in 2003. The oil States of Algeria and the Libyan Arab Jamahiriya, in response to higher OPEC quotas and momentary price spikes, should achieve higher growth, while Morocco and Tunisia are expected to continue their recovery from terrorist attacks. Though continent-wide growth will improve slightly, and African inflation will decline, the outlook for many African States remains clouded by events in the Middle East and continued instability in many subregions. The Iraq crisis, and the continuation of tensions between Israel and the Palestinian people, will also reduce Egypt's growth, while increasing its inflation rate.

Meanwhile, the predicament of Côte d'Ivoire will depress growth potential throughout West Africa, aggravating the economic fallout of election-related violence—and the disruption of oil production—in Nigeria. Additional instability visited this subregion during the first quarter of 2003, with a coup in the Central African Republic, increased fighting and political volatility in the Mano River region. Growing regional enmity in West and Central Africa means that, even if stability returns, the post-conflict scenario is troubling, with the frayed relations between many States in the subregion suggesting that trade flows could be reduced even after the conflict subsides, setting back efforts at further regional integration.

Some private investments into Africa will be impacted by the insecurity prevailing in certain areas; however, substantial financial flows into the hydrocarbon sector are projected to continue unabated in 2003. Additionally, large-scale manufacturing and infrastructure development projects by South African firms will provide an additional stimulus to economic activity in several countries.[12]

Other exogenous factors, such as the tentative recovery of major developed countries and the risks associated with it, make the immediate economic future of Africa uncertain. However, exports should increase if global economic growth picks up in the second half of 2003. Projected price increases for almost all categories of export commodities will additionally strengthen export revenues and GDP growth in many countries.

Global and subregional uncertainty may also affect official financial flows to the continent. Though African States continue to benefit from the Heavily Indebted Poor Countries (HIPC) Initiative (see chap. II), the aftermath of the war in Iraq and the continued rebuilding of Afghanistan may create competing demands for attention by the international community. That Africa's needs may be eclipsed by seemingly more pressing issues elsewhere could prevent faster progress by the region towards the achievement of the Millennium Development Goals (see document A/56/326, annex). Owing to a slow start in the early 1990s, many countries are now faced with the challenge of generating higher rates of sustainable annual GDP growth to satisfy the regional and global objectives of significant poverty reduction and other indicators of development.

Several countries face the risk of falling short of these poverty reduction targets because economic activities that account for high rates of growth are concentrated in some parts of those countries while other areas remain impoverished. This is most evident in Uganda where, despite its overall fast rates of growth, some areas remain immersed in continuing instability and armed conflict, thereby preventing the reconstruction and rehabilitation of infrastructure vital for economic development. In Angola, Nigeria, the Sudan and other oil States, economic growth is largely driven by oil production while the other sectors of the economy stay undeveloped. Similarly, most areas in Mozambique derive little benefit from recent large-scale industrial projects that have underpinned that country's rapid economic growth in recent years because the vast majority of these projects are located in the Maputo Corridor—in the country's far south—reflecting the preferences of foreign investors. Thus, high GDP growth rates mask the uneven patterns of development in each of those countries.

Even with improved macroeconomic management in most countries, there is widespread acknowledgement of a need for further economic reforms. As identified by stakeholders in the countries themselves, international financial institutions and donor countries, necessary reforms encompass a wide range of requirements related to addressing the need for good governance, the rooting out of corruption and mismanagement in the public sector and the implementation of required legal and regulatory frameworks in order to gain the confidence of domestic and foreign investors. These are considered vital preconditions for accelerating growth so as to achieve the required poverty reduction and social development targets.

[12]   These projects include the expansion of the Mozal aluminium smelter in Mozambique; the construction of a gas export pipeline from Mozambique to South Africa; the Bujagali Dam project for electricity-generation in Uganda; and the Inga Dam project to supply electricity from the Democratic Republic of the Congo to South Africa through transmission facilities in Angola and Namibia.

East Asia: dealing with shocks

Economic growth in East Asia accelerated to 5.8 per cent in 2002, a marked improvement over the region's performance in 2001. As the year progressed, adverse external conditions, including increased uncertainties due to a possible war in Iraq and the terrorist attacks in the region, imposed a toll on growth. The region's economies started to decelerate, with the exception of China, which continued to grow strongly (see table III.3). The persistence of weak external conditions in the first half of 2003, the outbreak of SARS and tensions related to the nuclear issue in the Democratic People's Republic of Korea, implies slower growth for the region—forecast to be 5 per cent for 2003 as a whole but strengthening to 6¼ per cent in 2004 (see table A.4).

An upturn in both exports and domestic demand supported the region's recovery in the first half of 2002. Export recovery started in the ICT sector in response to restocking in the United States and spread into the other sectors of the economy. In the latter part of 2002, surging imports from China offset negative global trends in the other economies in the region. Domestic demand, in turn, was supported by accommodative policies and rising exports. The main thrust of the region's recovery came from buoyant private consumption and increased public spending. In a number of economies, such as the Republic of Korea and Thailand, increased credit to households further boosted private consumption. Meanwhile, Indonesia, Malaysia and Thailand benefited from improved commodity prices while increased labour remittances contributed to higher incomes and consumption in the Philippines. The recovery, however, was modest in Hong Kong SAR, Singapore and Taiwan Province of China where high unemployment, weak asset prices and low confidence depressed private consumption. Private investment, with the exception of China, the Republic of Korea and Thailand, remained weak in most economies owing to excess capacity and the continuing relocation of facilities to China and other low-cost economies.

As the rest of East Asia decelerated owing to sluggish external demand, higher oil prices and other factors that dampened market sentiment and domestic demand, growth surged in China and the economy recorded a balanced and strong performance, which had not been seen since the Asian crisis. Private investment led domestic demand owing to policy stimuli and increased foreign capital inflows. Fixed investment growth remained robust in the first quarter of 2003, when it surged by nearly 23 per cent. In comparison, household spending has been growing more slowly, particularly in the rural areas, although an upturn was observed at the beginning of 2003. GDP growth accelerated to 9.9 per cent in the first quarter of 2003. Nonetheless, this fast pace of growth is unlikely to be sustained in the short run as the economy deals with the impact of SARS.

Reflecting improved economic performance in 2002, the unemployment rate fell somewhat in a number of economies, including the Republic of Korea and Thailand, but it remains above the pre-1997 level in most of them. Unemployment rose in Hong Kong SAR, Singapore and Taiwan Province of China owing not only to their cyclical weaknesses but also to the ongoing rebalancing in trade and industrial structures within the region. Urban unemployment also increased in China, where the official rate reached 4 per cent in 2002 owing to fast labour-force growth, restructuring of State enterprises and

Table III.3.
MAJOR DEVELOPING COUNTRIES: QUARTERLY INDICATORS, 2001-2002

	2001 quarter				2002 quarter			
	I	II	III	IV	I	II	III	IV
	Rate of growth of gross domestic product[a]							
Argentina	-2.0	-0.2	-4.9	-10.5	-16.3	-13.5	-9.8	-3.6
Brazil	4.3	2.1	0.5	-0.8	-0.8	1.0	2.5	3.4
Chile	3.2	4.1	2.9	2.0	1.3	1.7	2.4	3.2
China	8.1	7.7	7.1	6.7	7.6	8.0	8.1	8.1
Colombia	1.6	1.7	0.9	1.4	0.5	2.3	1.9	2.0
Ecuador	7.8	4.7	4.7	3.3	1.5	3.7	4.2	4.2
Hong Kong SAR[b]	2.3	1.6	-0.3	-0.9	-0.5	0.8	3.3	5.0
India	1.5	4.4	5.1	6.3	6.4	6.0	5.8	2.6
Indonesia	4.8	3.8	3.1	1.6	2.4	4.4	4.9	3.4
Israel	1.2	0.6	-3.9	-3.2	-2.9	-2.2	-0.6	0.2
Korea, Republic of	4.3	3.0	2.1	3.5	6.2	6.6	5.8	6.8
Malaysia	3.0	0.4	-0.9	-0.5	1.3	4.1	5.8	5.5
Mexico	2.0	0.1	-1.5	-1.6	-2.2	2.0	1.8	1.9
Philippines	2.9	3.0	3.0	3.9	3.7	4.8	3.8	5.8
Singapore	5.0	-0.5	-5.4	-6.6	-1.5	3.8	3.8	3.0
South Africa	2.3	2.6	1.8	3.2	3.0	3.8	2.9	2.4
Taiwan Province of China	0.6	-3.3	-4.4	-1.6	1.2	4.0	4.8	3.2
Thailand	1.6	1.9	1.8	2.5	3.9	5.1	5.8	6.1
Turkey	-1.0	-9.8	-7.5	-10.3	2.1	8.9	7.9	11.4
Venezuela	4.0	3.1	3.3	0.9	-3.8	-9.1	-5.6	-16.7
	Unemployment rate[c]							
Argentina[d]	..	16.4	..	18.3	..	21.5	..	17.8
Brazil	6.0	6.6	6.2	6.2	7.7	8.3	8.2	7.4
Chile	8.8	9.7	10.1	7.9	8.8	9.5	9.7	9.6
Colombia	18.9	16.7	16.6	15.4	17.5	16.3	16.5	15.7
Hong Kong SAR[b]	4.3	4.5	5.0	5.9	6.6	7.3	7.8	7.3
Indonesia	8.1	..	8.1	..	8.1	..	9.1	..
Israel	8.6	8.8	9.6	10.3	10.6	10.3	10.3	10.1
Korea, Republic of	4.8	3.5	3.3	3.2	3.6	2.9	2.7	2.8
Malaysia	4.0	3.7	3.3	3.7	3.7	3.8	3.2	3.2
Mexico	2.4	2.4	2.4	2.5	2.8	2.6	2.9	2.5
Philippines	11.3	13.3	10.1	9.8	10.3	13.9	11.2	10.2
Singapore	2.0	3.4	3.0	4.9	3.7	5.2	3.8	3.0
Taiwan Province of China	3.7	4.2	5.1	5.3	5.1	5.0	5.3	5.2
Thailand	4.8	3.5	2.6	2.4	3.2	2.9	1.8	1.8
Turkey	8.6	6.9	8.0	10.6	11.8	9.6	9.9	11.4
Uruguay	14.9	16.0	15.4	14.9	14.8	15.6	19.0	18.6
Venezuela	14.2	13.3	13.4	12.1	15.5	15.8	16.5	..

Table III.3 (continued)

	2001 quarter				2002 quarter			
	I	II	III	IV	I	II	III	IV
	Change in consumer prices[a]							
Argentina	-1.4	-0.1	-1.1	-1.6	4.2	23.3	36.0	40.3
Brazil	6.2	7.1	6.6	7.5	7.6	7.8	7.6	10.6
Chile	4.0	3.6	3.6	3.0	2.4	2.2	2.4	2.9
China	1.4	0.5	-1.0	-1.0	-0.6	-1.1	-0.8	-0.5
Colombia	8.1	7.9	8.0	7.8	6.6	5.9	6.0	6.8
Ecuador	67.6	39.6	28.9	24.1	14.7	13.2	12.4	9.9
Hong Kong SAR[b]	-2.0	-1.4	-1.1	-2.0	-2.6	-3.1	-3.4	-3.0
India	2.9	2.7	4.7	4.4	5.1	4.5	4.0	4.0
Indonesia	9.3	11.1	12.8	12.6	14.5	12.6	10.4	10.3
Israel	-5.7	-5.2	-4.4	-4.5	3.8	5.7	6.5	6.7
Korea, Republic of	4.1	5.2	4.1	3.0	2.6	2.7	2.5	3.3
Malaysia	1.5	1.6	1.4	1.2	1.4	1.9	2.1	1.8
Mexico	7.5	6.9	6.0	5.2	4.7	4.8	5.2	5.3
Philippines	6.8	6.6	6.4	4.7	3.6	3.4	2.8	2.6
Singapore	1.7	1.7	0.8	-0.2	-0.8	-0.4	-0.4	0.1
South Africa	6.4	5.1	4.1	3.8	5.9	9.0	12.6	14.7
Taiwan Province of China	0.6	0.1	0.0	-0.6	-0.1	0.0	-0.2	-0.5
Thailand	1.4	2.5	1.7	1.1	0.6	0.2	0.3	1.4
Turkey	35.6	52.3	58.6	67.5	70.3	47.0	39.5	31.6
Venezuela	12.6	12.4	12.7	12.4	14.6	18.9	24.8	30.6

Sources: IMF, *International Financial Statistics*; and national authorities.

a Percentage change from the corresponding quarter of the previous year
b Special Administrative Region of China.
c Reflecting national definitions and coverage that are not comparable across economies.
d Data are reported in May and October each year.

continuing pressure from the surplus rural labour force. Unemployment will remain a concern for Chinese policy makers over the medium turn, while it is expected to slowly decline in most other East Asian economies as growth picks up late in 2003 and employment policy measures take effect.

Inflation remained low in 2002 in most economies except Indonesia, which was still struggling with double-digit inflation during the year. In the outlook, inflation is expected to remain benign (see table A.10). China, Hong Kong SAR, Singapore and Taiwan Province of China experienced deflation in 2002 owing to several cyclical and structural factors, including weak demand, slack in the economy, intense price competition, and low import prices for manufactured goods. In China and Taiwan Province of China, tariff reduction in the context of their accession to the World Trade Organization was also a factor, while in Hong Kong SAR, a depressed real estate market compounded the problem. In China, however, general price indices rose for three months consecutively in the first quarter of 2003, indicating a turning point with respect to a protracted deflationary situation. Consumer prices are expected to rise in China in 2003.

Monetary policy remained accommodative in 2002 to support growth. Benign inflation, interest rate cuts in the United States and adequate foreign reserves facilitated the easing monetary policy, which is unlikely to be changed until late 2003. In most economies, interest rates are at historically low levels. Given uncertainties related to SARS and the subdued recovery, countries are expected to keep their policies flexible for a while. Most economies still have some room for further monetary easing. If external uncertainties fade and growth picks up in late 2003, however, countries are likely to begin to shift their policy to a less expansionary stance and to raise interest rates gradually. From then on, their interest rates will also be under upward pressure from rising international interest rates. In China, monetary policy will likely focus on liberalizing the controls on interest rates so as to increase the efficiency of the financial system and to improve the effect of monetary policy on the real economy.

Fiscal policy in most economies also remained broadly accommodative in 2002. Only Indonesia, the largest public debtor in the region, made significant progress in reducing its public deficit and debt under the IMF programme. In the near term, given its heavy public debt burden, Indonesia, as well as the Philippines, will continue to be under pressure to tighten fiscal policy. Hong Kong SAR and Taiwan Province of China will also be pressed to restore fiscal balance. Fiscal policy in most other economies is expected to focus on growth and remain flexible. In China, the budget for 2003 suggests a smaller stimulatory policy stance, and the amount of additional bond issuance for public investment in 2003 is slightly lower than in previous years. Nonetheless, the public deficit, which rose to 3 per cent of GDP in 2002, is expected to continue to widen. In the Republic of Korea, the budget for 2003 aimed at fiscal balance, with a modest spending increase to be financed by increased tax receipts but, in view of slowing growth, an additional fiscal stimulus is possible. Malaysia, given its high government deficit, armed as well for fiscal consolidation in 2003, but it also may inject an additional fiscal stimulus if growth falters. Despite the urge for fiscal consolidation, countries may have to take proactive measures to offset the negative impacts from exogenous shocks, such as SARS. If, however, growth strengthens in late 2003, policy will be tightened, reflecting these countries' concern about medium-term fiscal viability and longer-run potential growth.

The region's growth in the balance of 2003 will hinge crucially on the containment of SARS. If the disease is quickly controlled, growth will pick up from the second half of 2003. Reduced uncertainty and improved market sentiment, combined with lower oil prices, will lead to stronger domestic demand and exports. The strengthening demand in developed countries and continuing robust imports from China, in line with its strong domestic demand and trade liberalization, will boost exports. Domestic demand in the region will be strengthened in line with the reversal of adverse factors, broadly accommodative policies, stronger exports and improving market sentiment. ICT exports, which are important for a durable industrial recovery, remain fragile, but are likely to gain strength as world trade picks up, especially in view of the lower level of inventories and rising demand for inputs through the expanding processing network in the ICT sector. Nonetheless, owing to excess capacity and moderate expansion in global demand, a full recovery in the ICT sector is unlikely until late 2004.

In 2004, growth is expected to quicken but to be below that in 2000, as momentum will be tempered by the expected policy tightening and moderating external demand. Political tensions in the run-up to the elections in a number of countries in 2004 and, in the Republic of Korea, those tensions associated with the nuclear issue in the Democratic People's Republic of Korea, will also hamper the acceleration. In Hong Kong SAR, Singapore and Taiwan Province of China, outsourcing and retrenchment will continue to weigh on their employment and domestic demand.

South Asia: moving towards a more balanced growth

The growth performance of South Asian economies has been uneven, mainly reflecting different climatic and security conditions. The region's GDP growth reached 4.8 per cent in 2002, slightly higher than in 2001 (see table A.4). The modest increase in the region's growth in 2002 was largely due to the economic rebound in Pakistan and Sri Lanka. Bangladesh and India maintained about the same moderate pace as in 2001. The sharp downturn that had begun in Nepal in 2001 continued into 2002, as the country suffered its worst setback in two decades.

The region's near-term prospects are positive. Real GDP growth is expected to pick up in mid-2003, supported by both domestic demand and exports, and reach 5¾ per cent for the year as a whole. The outlook for 2004 is also favourable, as economic growth, forecast at 6 per cent, will be more balanced across the region, although its strength will be subject to structural factors, including fiscal constraints.

Rising exports and an improving economic environment supported domestic demand in Pakistan and Sri Lanka in 2002, while in Nepal, the security problem continued to depress domestic demand and tourism revenues. In India, after an improvement in the first half, private consumption eased in late 2002 owing to the autumn crop failure, slowing overall growth (see table III.3). In Bangladesh, weak agricultural production and socio-political uncertainties restrained domestic demand. In some countries, fiscal considerations constrained public spending on development projects. Sectorally, the recovery in Pakistan was largely led by services, the textile industry and livestock production. In Sri Lanka, the agricultural and trading sectors benefited from improved weather and the ceasefire in the country's long civil war, while the industrial sector grew marginally from a low base. Moderation of growth in India was due to a significant fall in the aforementioned autumn harvest as a result of the worst summer drought in more than a decade. On the other hand, the Indian industrial and service sectors exhibited a robust performance. Similarly, a healthy performance by the industrial and service sectors offset a weak agricultural outcome in Bangladesh. In contrast, the Nepalese economy remained severely weak owing to the heightened Maoist insurgency and an irregular monsoon.

Monetary policy in the region remained accommodative in 2002. Owing to the region's relatively stable inflation (see table A.10) and the need to support growth, most countries cut key interest rates gradually and tried to promote business lending. The soft monetary policy is expected to continue for a while, but the scope for monetary easing will remain constrained by the need to finance the large fiscal deficits most countries have. Despite these difficulties, fiscal policy has remained expansionary in the region, except in Bangladesh and Sri Lanka. Public deficits in 2002 were larger than anticipated in most countries (except Pakistan), owing to revenue shortfalls caused by the cyclical slowdown and structural factors, such as inefficient tax collection and the narrowness of the tax base. Although the budgets for fiscal year 2002/03 continued to stress fiscal consolidation, political resistance, increased spending on security and on the farm sector, and the need to support growth will continue to hamper strict implementation. In India, the budget for 2003/04 included stimulative measures, such as tax cuts and other incentives, and increased spending on infrastructure. Nevertheless, concerns about their fiscal positions will continue to limit the scope for fiscal stimuli in most countries.

During early 2003, growth in the region was moderate and mixed but is expected to strengthen in the near term. Pakistan and Sri Lanka continued to recover. However, in Bangladesh and India, growth decelerated owing to the lagged effects of unfavourable agricultural production. In Sri Lanka, the suspension of peace talks in April increased uncertainties about the country's outlook. Meanwhile, there have been some signs of a turnaround in Nepal since the formal ceasefire in late February 2003, though security issues continued to restrain the recovery. In contrast with East Asia, the impact of SARS on the region has been negligible. Several countries have intensified their domestic economic reforms and external liberalization to create a more conducive environment for growth. Success in fiscal consolidation and other reforms will also be crucial for medium-term fiscal viability and for securing a sustainable high-growth path.

From mid-2003, growth is expected to pick up in most countries as both exports and domestic demand strengthen. Exports should increase in line with rising external demand. Domestic demand will be supported by low interest rates, rising exports and, in a number of countries, a better harvest and improved security conditions. Sectoral performance is expected to be more balanced, particularly in Bangladesh and India, once normal weather returns. Industrial output is forecast to continue its upward trend, boosted by more stable oil prices and rising exports and domestic demand. Stronger primary activities will support the service sector in most countries. In Nepal, on the other hand, the upward momentum in most sectors will be modest for a while.

In 2004, growth is expected to accelerate further, supported by improvements in both the external and domestic sectors. Nonetheless, structural impediments, including fiscal imbalances, inadequate infrastructure, governance problems and, in a number of countries, a narrow export base and political uncertainties, will continue to constrain growth in the region.

Western Asia: caught between war and volatile oil prices

Largely owing to Turkey's strong recovery, GDP grew by 2.0 per cent in Western Asia in 2002, after a contraction of about 1.2 per cent in 2001.[13] Except for Turkey, the largest economy in the region and itself recovering from the severe recession of 2001, and a few other economies, economic performance in the region in 2002 was poor as the conflict between Israel and the Palestinian people caused growth in Israel to contract and the Palestinian economy to collapse, while oil production declined in most oil-exporting countries in response to reduced OPEC quotas. FDI declined, tourism rev-

[13] Excluding Turkey, the rate of GDP growth in the region actually decelerated further to 0.5 per cent in 2002 from 0.8 per cent in 2001.

enues plummeted and consumer and investor confidence declined owing to soaring uncertainties associated with the geopolitical climate that prevailed in the region throughout 2002.

Economic difficulties persisted in early 2003 as the invasion of Iraq imposed a severe toll on the Iraqi economy and on its main trading partners in the region, notably Jordan and the Syrian Arab Republic, as well as on other neighbouring economies where uncertainties and increased regional risks affected market sentiment and disturbed trade and capital flows, as well as tourism. Despite increased oil production in the major fuel-exporting countries, GDP growth is expected to decelerate to 1¼ per cent in 2003, as Turkey is unlikely to be able to sustain its fast pace of growth and Iraq is coping with the aftermath of the war. The outlook for 2004 is more favourable. GDP growth is forecast at 3¾ per cent as reconstruction in Iraq advances, oilfield development and several petrochemicals projects come on-stream, and market sentiment towards the region improves.

Most countries performed poorly in 2002. Oil production declined in most oil-exporting countries in the region, responding to a lower OPEC ceiling that was kept unchanged throughout 2002. The non-oil sector suffered from weak domestic and external demand; and the economies of both Iraq and Kuwait contracted in 2002.

In March-May 2003, Iraq was confronted with war which compounded the difficulties facing a country that had already been crippled by the 1991 Gulf war and international sanctions.[14] While damage to oil infrastructure was neg-ligible and most oil wells and oil production facilities were preserved, much of the Iraqi physical infrastructure was damaged or destroyed. Vandalism and looting have occurred, while law and security have not been restored. Iraqi oil production and exports were suspended and their recovery to pre-war levels may take some time.

Financing the reconstruction is yet another challenge facing the country. Excluding humanitarian needs and industrial rehabilitation, the cost of repair-ing part of Iraq's physical infrastructure—oil export facilities and power plants—has been estimated at about $25 billion. Oil revenues amount to some $12 billion annually which is insufficient to finance all of Iraq's reconstruction needs. In addition, Iraq's total external debt has been estimated at $383 billion, of which $199 billion is compensation from the first Gulf war, $127 billion is foreign bilateral debt (including $47 billion of accrued interest) and $57 billion is owed on pending contracts, inter alia, for energy and communication deals. Heavy debt-service payments remain a major obstacle for the country's eco-nomic rehabilitation.

Increased tension and the pre-war climate took their toll on the economic performance of the oil-importing countries of the region. The economic reces-sion in Israel deepened in 2002 (see table III.3). Most economic sectors con-tracted in 2002: manufacturing output and exports plummeted, tourism activi-ty declined and agricultural production decreased. Only construction output increased, responding to lower mortgage interest rates and the rising uncer-tainty in financial markets which encouraged investments in the real estate market. Imports also declined, and real wages slumped, leading to a sharp reduction in private consumption. Private investment deteriorated, but public consumption rose mainly owing to defence spending.

14 Iraqi GDP in 2002 was about 85 per cent of its 1990 level and the share of the economy in the region fell from 19 per cent in 1990 to 12 per cent in 2002.

Conversely, the Turkish economy recovered strongly in 2002. The robust growth was mainly due to a sharp rise in stock-building following substantial depletion in 2001. Public consumption and investment expanded moderately. External demand also contributed to the 2002 economic recovery. Meanwhile, private consumption, accounting for nearly two thirds of GDP, remained weak, reflecting deteriorating consumer sentiment, high unemployment and reduced credit. On the supply front, the recovery was broad-based across sectors. Agricultural output expanded in 2002. Despite weak domestic demand, industrial production rebounded, mostly driven by export-led manufacturing industries.

The employment situation continued to deteriorate in the region. Unemployment increased in both Turkey and Israel (see table III.3), while youth unemployment remains a serious problem in most fuel-exporting countries.

All oil-exporting countries framed their 2002 budgets under conservative assumptions with regard to both oil production and prices. With limited alternatives to increasing non-oil revenue, most countries opted for the continuation of fiscal consolidation in 2002. As in the past, reducing current spending (mostly wages and salaries, but also subsidies) remains politically sensitive. Capital expenditures on development projects were reduced. Fiscal deficits were projected to rise in most countries but, with higher oil prices during the year, fiscal deficits were much smaller than anticipated. In the outlook, most oil-exporting countries will adopt a more relaxed fiscal stance thanks to higher oil revenues and also owing to the need to lift their economies out of stagnation and, in some cases, recession.

Fiscal imbalances deteriorated in the larger oil-importing countries in 2002. In Israel, the fiscal deficit target was changed from 1.8 per cent of GDP to 3.9 per cent of GDP in 2002. The new budget target, however, was not attained, as tax receipts plummeted owing to continued economic recession and increased government spending. The 2003 budget calls for a drastic reduction in government expenditure and a rise in tax revenue of about 3.6 per cent in real terms. However, the first four months of the year have indicated that tax revenue continues to fall and defence-related spending to increase. With economic growth expected to remain weak this year, a sharper deviation from fiscal targeting is likely.

Turkey's fiscal policy was expansionary in 2002. Government spending rose, mainly owing to increased non-personnel outlays (mainly for the security forces), transfers payments to State enterprises, and social security. Moreover, debt-service payments soared, responding to rising interest rates, while fiscal revenues declined, reflecting weaker tax collection and tax rebates. As a result, the consolidated public sector primary surplus declined to about 4 per cent of GDP in 2002, below the official target of about 6.5 per cent—the minimum requirement for debt sustainability. The consolidated fiscal deficit has been estimated at about 13 per cent of GDP in 2002, higher than the official target of about 9.6 per cent.

Although relatively high, inflation remained stable in the region (see table A.10). Turkey made further advances in inflation control while Israel overshot its inflation target owing to the depreciation of its currency and higher oil prices. The Bank of Israel reversed its monetary easing in June 2002 by raising the interest rates by 4.5 percentage points to 9.1 per cent. As a result, the currency stabilized and inflationary expectations were slightly reduced. In a number of oil exporters, however, inflation—albeit still low—has been increasing recently in response to increased costs of imported goods, mainly because of the depreciation of the United States dollar against major trading currencies. Continued subsidies on basic goods and services will contain the rise in consumer prices.

Monetary policy in most oil-exporting countries remained unchanged in 2002 with the currency pegs against the United States dollar comfortably supported by abundant foreign reserves and assets. This implies that interest rates in these countries followed those in the United States and will continue to do so. Monetary authorities are expected to keep a positive interest rate differential vis-à-vis United States interest rates to avoid pressures on their domestic currencies.

Latin America and the Caribbean: slowly emerging from recession

The economy of Latin America and the Caribbean is in a serious predicament, with GDP having grown at very modest rates since 2000 (see table A.4). GDP contracted by 0.7 per cent in 2002, marking the worst overall performance in more than a decade and a new decline in the region's income per capita. Twenty years after the emergence of the debt crisis, over 10 years after the "lost decade", and after several years of reform effort, Latin American found itself once again immersed in external payments difficulties, with renewed debt crises either taking place or being barely avoided. A moderate recovery is expected for 2003, but it largely reflects Argentina's improved performance after a prolonged and painful recession. Other countries in the region will continue to exhibit modest growth but should benefit from the anticipated recovery of industrial activity during the second half of the year in the major developed countries—notably the United States—and more stable financial and currency markets. GDP growth is expected to reach 2 per cent in 2003, further strengthening to 3¾ per cent in 2004.[15]

Economic conditions in 2002 in Latin America were marked by a lacklustre external environment, which affected countries to varying degrees. Compared with such cases as Argentina and Venezuela, greater flexibility and consistency of the macroeconomic policy framework proved a key factor in absorbing external shocks in such countries as Brazil, Chile and Mexico, despite their diverse external vulnerabilities. Several trends were notable in 2002: much weaker external demand than expected; a significant contraction of capital inflows and tightening of financing conditions which were reflected in volatile and widening sovereign debt spreads and depreciating currencies; and low world prices for the region's major commodity exports. A sharp adjustment took place in the region's current-account deficit, which was slashed by 70 per cent to $14.5 billion. Efforts at stabilizing the current-account will likely persist in 2003. In Brazil, for instance, the current-account deficit fell to 1.7 per cent of GDP in 2002 from 4.6 per cent the year before and is expected to reach 1.1 per cent of GDP in 2003.

Notwithstanding the above, signs of a mild recovery of the economic activity became apparent in 2002. A turnaround in industrial production was evident as early as the second quarter of 2002 in Argentina and Brazil, a pattern of recovery that held up throughout 2002, with particular strength in the case of Argentina (see figure III.5). This evolution reflected the substantial adjustment of real exchange rates that has taken place in both countries and the resulting import-substitution processes, along with strong export growth in the case of

[15] Excluding Argentina, Latin America's GDP growth reached 1.2 per cent in 2001 and 1 per cent in 2002 and is forecast at 1.5 per cent in 2003.

Figure III.5.

LATIN AMERICA, SELECTED COUNTRIES: INDUSTRIAL PRODUCTION INDEX, SEASONALLY ADJUSTED, JANUARY 2001-FEBRUARY 2003

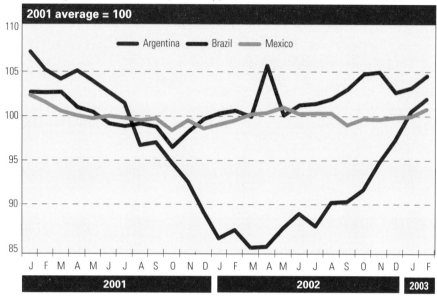

Sources: Instituto Nacional de Estadística y Censos (INDEC), Instituto Brasileiro de Geografia e Estatística (IBGE) and Banco de Mexico

Brazil. External financing conditions throughout the region have also improved remarkably since the last quarter of 2002, laying a more conducive basis for growth in 2003.

The crises in Argentina and Venezuela and their impacts elsewhere in the region heavily influenced overall regional growth in 2002. In Argentina, the collapse of the convertibility regime at the end of 2001 gave way to a sharp devaluation of the peso, a near collapse of the banking system and general disruption. GDP contracted almost 11 per cent in 2002, while poverty and extreme poverty levels soared.[16] Largely through financial linkages, the crisis spread to Uruguay, which also contracted in 2002. Clear signs of financial stabilization and improving confidence in Argentina were nevertheless apparent in the second half of 2002. Growth of 4 per cent is expected for 2003; however, pending progress in structural reforms, particularly in the banking and fiscal policy areas, will limit the strength of the recovery going into 2004. Both Paraguay (also negatively affected by the Argentine crisis) and Uruguay will remain in recession in 2003 as the Argentine recovery works its way through to these economies.

Venezuela contracted by almost 9 per cent in 2002 owing to a crisis in the oil sector which spilled over into the non-oil economy at the beginning of the year, the collapse of its crawling peg exchange regime, and renewed economic and political instability at the end of 2002. Having floated its currency in early 2002, Venezuela introduced exchange controls in February 2003 to prevent capital flight. Latin American countries continue to experiment with different exchange-rate regimes. These include official dollarization, as in the cases of Ecuador and El Salvador, where it has not been sufficient to place these economies on a sustainable growth path. In Ecuador, for instance, fiscal and financial indicators deteriorated in 2002 and the discouraging performance of the external sector reflected a loss in competitiveness owing to real exchange-rate appreciation, in the third year after dollarization had been adopted (see box III.3).

[16] See *World Economic Situation and Prospects, 2003* (United Nations publication, Sales No. E.03.II.C.2), box 3.1, entitled "Poverty in Argentina today".

Box III.3

ECUADOR AND EL SALVADOR: A
TALE OF TWO DOLLARIZATIONS

Both Ecuador and El Salvador have formally "dollarized" their economies. The two economies had presented different "initial conditions" and perceived dollarization as a means to accomplish different objectives. El Salvador adopted it as a growth-inducing mechanism, whereas Ecuador perceived it as a stabilization tool.

Ecuador experienced a severe crisis in the late 1990s with widening macro-economic imbalances (see table), increasing unemployment, the collapse of the exchange rate, a partial default on its external debt, a freeze on domestic bank deposits, and widespread bank failures.[a] In order to arrest the downturn spiral, official dollarization was announced in January 2000 and, after a brief period of intense political instability, the corresponding legislation was approved by the Congress in March 2000.

El Salvador, on the other hand, adopted dollarization under less dramatic circumstances. The exchange rate had functioned as the anchor of the country's stabilization programme and had been fixed to the dollar since 1994. While inflation declined (a freeze in official minimum wages since 1998 having contributed to this decline), real interest rates remained high and economic growth stalled after the initial spur brought about by the end of the civil war. The Government perceived dollarization as a means to reduce interest rates and to facilitate El Salvador's integration into the global economy by reducing transaction costs and eliminating the currency risk. Dollarization became official in November 2000.

Dollarization in Ecuador helped restore confidence and stopped the economic deterioration, at least initially. The banking system retained deposits once the freeze ended. The fact that interest rates fell drastically, even becoming negative in real terms, helped borrowers to honour their debt obligations, thus improving banks' portfolios. Nonetheless, banks remained fragile as the restructuring of larger loans suffered delays, and the country's largest bank failed in 2001. Credit has remained constrained. Interest rates also declined in El Salvador, in part owing to the elimination of currency risk and in part owing to the lower interest rates in the United States. However, credit has not increased in support of additional private investment and consumption as expected. Growth has thus remained subdued and largely sustained by reconstruction efforts after a severe earthquake in early 2001. Dollarization appears to have addressed one symptom (high interest rates), but has not dealt with the problems themselves (depressed domestic conditions, underdeveloped financial markets, a fragile portfolio etc.).

Unemployment stabilized and started to decline in Ecuador (see table), owing not only to the recovery of the economy but also to the increased migration of the labour force, particularly to the United States. At $1.4 billion in 2001, annual labour remittances are a major source of dollar earnings and attest to labour mobility—although largely informal and illegal—between Ecuador and the United States. This is also the case for El Salvador, which had the equivalent of 28 per cent of its population living in the United States in 2001.[b]

Inflation accelerated in Ecuador owing to the severe devaluation that had been suffered by the sucre immediately before dollarization. Moreover, certain key administered prices required adjustments. This implied some correction in wages as well. Annual inflation declined to 9.2 per cent in March 2003,

[a] On events leading to dollarization, see Paul Beckerman and Andrés Solimano, eds., *Crisis and Dollarization in Ecuador: Stability, Growth, and Social Equity* (Washington, D.C., World Bank, 2002); and Alfredo Calcagno and others, "Dollarization in Ecuador: a parallel with the Argentine 'convertibility' system" (paper presented at the Seminar on Monetary and Financial Integration, Kalamazoo College, Kalamazoo, Michigan, May 2001). For a discussion on the costs and benefits of dollarization vis-à-vis hard peg regimes, see *World Economic and Social Survey, 2000* (United Nations publication, Sales No. E.00.II.C.1), box III.4, entitled "Rethinking exchange-rate regimes in Latin America". See also footnote f.

[b] El Salvador's population was estimated at 6.3 million in 2001 and about 1.8 million Salvadorans lived in the United States in early 2001 (see *The New York Times*, 3 March 2001, p. A7; and Banco Central de Reserva de El Salvador, "Indicadores economicos anuales" (http://www.bcr.gob.sv/boletin.htm)).

Box III.3 (continued)

c   See ECLAC, *Estudio Económico de América Latina y el Caribe, 2000-2001* (United Nations publication, Sales No. S.01.II.G.2), p. 184.

d   Owing to the need to isolate public revenues from the vagaries of oil markets so that fiscal policy could be used counter-cyclically, an oil stabilization fund was created, where tax revenues generated by the new oil pipeline will be deposited. Nonetheless, the fact that Ecuador has pledged to fully compensate any shortfall in programmed oil revenues with expenditure cuts indicates that there will be some transition problems until the fund is fully operational. Moreover, only 20 per cent of such revenues can be used for contingencies. With most of the eventual oil windfall already earmarked to retire external debt, the stabilization fund's revenue smoothing function is severely curtailed.

e   Seigniorage is the net revenue accruing to the Government from issuing currency. In the case of Ecuador, annual average revenue from seigniorage has been estimated at 1.5 per cent of GDP during the period 1990-1998 (*Ecuador: Selected Issues and Statistical Annex*, IMF Staff Country Report, No. 00/125 (Washington, D.C., IMF, October 2000)). It is a significant source of revenue for a country constantly struggling to maintain fiscal sustainability.

still above world levels. The inflation differential implied an appreciation of the real effective exchange rate (see table A.12), which, in absence of required reforms, compromised the competitiveness of the economy, particularly in non-traditional sectors, and constrained diversification efforts. In El Salvador, annual inflation remained relatively low (see table) but since dollarization did not correct for the appreciation of the currency that had taken place under the fixed exchange-rate regime, there was some loss in competitiveness.[c] While Ecuador has lost the initial competitive advantage given by the sharp depreciation of its currency, El Salvador adopted dollarization at an appreciated exchange rate. As a result, both economies will need to bring inflation below world levels in order to regain competitiveness. This could require a fall in domestic prices, including wages or, in the absence of price flexibility, more rapid productivity growth than in the economies of trading partners.

Both economies continue to have external imbalances. In Ecuador, a trade deficit re-emerged in 2001 and 2002 as exports decelerated, whereas imports surged, in part owing to the recovery in private consumption and the strong appreciation of the currency. Imports of consumer goods increased, in dollar terms, by 73 per cent in 2001 and by 28 per cent in 2002. Imports also grew because of the capital goods required for a new oil pipeline. While the pipeline will double Ecuador's oil export capacity, it will also increase the country's dependency on oil and keep it vulnerable to the instability of oil markets. The latter may imply increased volatility of GDP growth and complicate the management of an economy with a reduced set of policy instruments and binding constraints.[d]

In El Salvador, terms-of-trade shocks and depressed external demand contributed to the persistence of large trade deficits. Traditional exports (such as coffee) have been affected by global excess capacity and lower prices while the in-bond industry—the country's major net exporter—is largely dependent on the United States economic cycle. It is also dependent on maintaining its international competitiveness, both to attract new investors to the processing zones and to retain those that are already operating in the country, particularly in view of the growing competition from lower-cost producers elsewhere. It is not clear how the new currency regime can contribute to increasing FDI or boosting exports.

External support helped Ecuador's stabilization. The country secured loans from the international financial institutions and was able to reduce its external debt through a restructuring with private creditors, which resulted in a lower debt burden. Oil prices recovered in 2000 and, together with expenditure compression and enhanced tax collection, contributed to the improvement of the fiscal position, despite the loss of seigniorage.[e] Later on, fiscal discipline eroded as public sector wages rose. Spreads on external debt soared owing to increased default risk and uncertainties due to the forthcoming presidential election. By the end of 2002, Ecuador was again facing the possibility of incurring payments arrears. The new Administration negotiated a stand-by agreement with IMF—the country's second since dollarization started. It

Box III.3 (continued)

included renewed fiscal austerity, including an increasingly large primary surplus, and a series of structural reforms.

Public finances are also a source of vulnerability in El Salvador. In early 2001, the country suffered a severe earthquake and expenditures increased. A reform of the public pension system entailed further costs while dollarization led to additional expenditures for the budget. Despite consolidation efforts, the public deficit has remained, leading to an increase in the country's external indebtedness (see table). The Government's policy of replacing the domestic debt (shorter maturities) with external debt (longer maturities) also contributed to increasing external indebtedness. Nonetheless, indebtedness (while still low in El Salvador) is an option that needs to be used with caution because it can rapidly become unsustainable, as amply demonstrated in Latin America.

These countries' fiscal performance demonstrates that the elimination of a central bank's function as lender of last resort per se cannot guarantee fiscal discipline. Additionally, the removal of currency risk and the reduction of transaction costs are not sufficient to attract larger inflows of FDI or increased exports. The appreciation of the effective exchange rate affects competitiveness, intensifies external imbalances and undermines diversification efforts. Experience so far reinforces the lesson that exchange-rate policies need to be complemented by appropriate fiscal and structural policies.[f] This is an important lesson for other economies considering embarking on official dollarization.

f   See *World Economic and Social Survey, 2000 ...*, box III.4, entitled "Rethinking exchange-rate regimes in Latin America".

ECUADOR AND EL SALVADOR, SELECTED INDICATORS, 1998-2002

	Ecuador					El Salvador				
	1998	1999	2000	2001	2002	1998	1999	2000	2001	2002
GDP annual rate of growth (percentage)	2.1	-6.3	2.8	5.1	3.3	3.8	3.4	2.1	1.9	2.3
Urban unemployment (percentage)	11.5	14.4	14.1	10.4	8.7	7.6	6.9	6.5	7	7.1
Consumer price index (annual percentage rate of change, December to December)	43.4	60.7	91	22.4	9.4	4.2	-1	4.3	1.4	2.8
Exchange rate (sucres/colones per dollar)	5 447	11 787	24 988	25 000	25 000	8.755	8.755	8.755	8.750	8.750
Percentage of GDP										
Non-financial public sector balance	-5.7	-4.7	1.7	0.7	0.7	-2.7	-3.1	-3.9	-4.1	-3.7
Current-account balance *of which,*	-9.0	5.5	5.8	-3.2	-7.0	-0.8	-1.9	-3.3	-1.3	-1.7
Merchandise trade balance	-4.4	9.3	8.8	-1.9	-4.5	-10.9	-10.9	-13.2	-13.9	-13.3
External debt	83.2	118.9	99.7	80.1	..	22.1	22.4	21.5	22.9	27.9

Sources: *Banco Central del Ecuador, Central Reserve Bank of El Salvador* and Economic Commission for Latin America and the Caribbean (ECLAC).

Colombia, a large supplier of manufactures to Venezuela, felt the impact of its dwindling activity, as well as the disruption of external payments, all of which added to the volatility on its external front. Growth remained weak in Bolivia as well, making Peru the only Andean country that had an acceptable growth performance in 2002 (see table A.4).

In Brazil, concerns over macroeconomic management by the Government that took office in October 2002 resulted in volatility in the value of the currency, mirroring the increases in spreads over sovereign bonds.[17] The new Government provided early assurances on its commitment to achieving sound macroeconomic management, not least by tightening its monetary and fiscal stances. Sluggish internal demand constrained growth in 2002 in spite of the dynamic external sector. The stabilization of the currency and other financial indicators since the last quarter of 2002, along with signs of moderating inflation, point to a possible monetary easing during the second half of 2003 which would lay the basis for gradually improving economic conditions.

Mexico, Central America and the Caribbean, which are heavily dependent on import demand from the United States, especially for manufacturing exports, were particularly affected by sluggish external demand in 2002. Mexico's performance reflected both the weakness of the external sector and its negative impact on private investment. However, this was offset by a mild recovery in domestic consumption from the contraction registered in 2001. Meanwhile, the Caribbean island States suffered from limited tourist inflows.

Economic conditions in 2002 and in early 2003 have been reflected in poor advances in job creation throughout the region. In Argentina, the unemployment rate remains high, at about 18 per cent according to the latest official figures. High unemployment and underemployment continue to represent a drag on the recovery of domestic demand in many countries in the region, a case in point being Colombia. In Mexico, employment losses in the manufacturing export sector, linked to stagnant external demand during 2001 and 2002, are yet to be reversed. On the other hand, significant advances in job creation have been apparent in Chile since the last quarter of 2002, a development that is expected to provide greater momentum for growth in 2003.

Inflation rates deteriorated in a number of countries (see table A.10), particularly during the second half of 2002 and the beginning of 2003, overshooting targets in such countries as Brazil, Colombia and Mexico. Spikes in inflation rates have been largely a supply-side phenomenon, reflecting in many cases a pass-through effect from depreciated currencies into the prices of tradable goods, particularly food, as well as upward revisions of energy prices due to higher oil prices. A case in point is Argentina, where a sharp realignment of the relative prices of tradable goods took place in 2002 following the devaluation. In Ecuador, inflation was still above 9 per cent at the end of 2002, reflecting continued price inertia from the 1999 crisis that had preceded dollarization, as well as strong public sector wage increases in 2002 (see box III.3). Hikes in Government-controlled prices have also contributed to higher inflation in Brazil and Mexico. Inflation is expected to gradually moderate in 2003, as currency markets stabilize. Disinflation will be key to preserving the real exchange-rate adjustment that took place in 2002 in countries like Brazil and Argentina.

Fiscal policies in Latin America in 2002 and early 2003 were framed by weak tax revenue growth and tightening financing conditions. Constrained by

[17] Between December 2001 and October 2002, the real lost 38 per cent of its value against the United States dollar, while the spread on sovereign bonds jumped from 843 basis points (bps) in January 2002 to 2,039 bps in October 2002.

large public debts and a difficult external environment, Governments generally maintained restrictive fiscal stances, even in a context of sluggish activity, with the exception of Chile. In Brazil, the primary surplus reached 3.9 per cent of GDP in 2002 and, at the beginning of 2003, the Government announced an increased target of 4.25 per cent for the year as a whole, whereas Argentina was well on course to meet primary surplus targets at the beginning of 2003. Compromised fiscal situations met the new Governments of Colombia and Ecuador, and extraordinary measures were implemented in both cases. Throughout the region, fiscal reforms remain high in the policy agenda, and many countries are currently implementing IMF-monitored economic programmes. Demonstrations against fiscal austerity measures in Bolivia in February 2003 resulted in several deaths and were a clear reminder of the challenges confronting fiscal reform and consolidation in times of crisis.

Rising inflationary expectations have prompted policy makers to tighten monetary stances in the region's two largest economies, Brazil and Mexico, since the third quarter of 2002: the SELIC rate rose by 850 bps in Brazil between September 2002 and May 2003.[18] Conversely, monetary conditions remained relatively lax and interest rates low in such countries as Chile, Peru and Colombia. In Colombia, however, the Central Bank moved in the first quarter of 2003 to prevent the peso's depreciation from feeding into inflationary expectations. Countries that maintained a relatively relaxed policy stance, however, have not witnessed a significant growth of bank credit, largely as a result of both lacklustre demand and cautious bank lending policies.

[18] SELIC is the acronym for Sistema Especial de Liquidação e Custódia (Special System for Settlement and Custody).

PART TWO | ECONOMIC
POLICY AND
POVERTY

OVERVIEW

The United Nations Millennium Declaration,[1] adopted by all 189 States Members of the United Nations on 8 September 2000, presents a set of commitments aimed at improving the well-being of humanity in the twenty-first century. The development goals set out in the Millennium Declaration focus on poverty eradication through broad-based sustainable development. The Millennium Development Goals include the objective of halving, between 1990 and 2015, the proportion of the world's population that lives on one dollar per day or less (a measure of extreme poverty) and the proportion that suffers from hunger.

Poverty is intrinsically a difficult problem to analyse because it touches on many aspects of the human condition, ranging from the economic and social to the environmental, political and cultural. Reflecting its multifaceted aspects, poverty is variously defined and manifested in terms of income, consumption, deprivation of access to health and educational resources, vulnerability, voicelessness and powerlessness.[2] Even those who live in poverty have no easy way to describe the deprivation and hardship they experience. However, their voicelessness is being addressed. Part of the World Bank's efforts to understand and reduce poverty has involved gathering and publishing the views, experiences and aspirations of the poor.[3]

Understanding the causes of poverty, the interactions among those causes and the consequences of poverty for human lives is essential for formulating and implementing policies to achieve the poverty reduction goals established in the Millennium Declaration. Measuring the extent of poverty at the national and global levels in turn enables Governments and the international community to assess the impacts of policy actions. It is within this context that the Millennium Development Goals were formulated to include various poverty indicators to monitor progress towards the targets and to evaluate national and international actions.

The goal of reducing poverty by half by the year 2015 has prompted policy makers to increase the attention given to policies and measures that are targeted directly at achieving this goal. At the same time, it is necessary to also examine earlier policies aimed at achieving this same goal, possibly through different channels, as well as policies and measures with other, possibly related, goals, that are expected to have a bearing on poverty, even if they are not specifically directed at poverty reduction per se. Part two of the present *Survey* examines a number of areas in which policies are expected to have a beneficial effect on poverty over the medium or longer term, even if poverty reduction is not those policies' primary short-term goal.

[1] See General Assembly resolution 55/2 of 8 September 2000. See also the report of the Secretary General entitled "Implementation of the United Nations Millennium Declaration" (A/57/270 and Corr.1), particularly the annex, entitled "Millennium development goals".

[2] *Report on the World Social Situation, 2003* (United Nations publication, forthcoming) discusses the aspects of social vulnerability, voicelessness and powerlessness and examines several policies aimed at removing economic, social and cultural barriers that contribute to the vulnerability of the poor.

[3] Part of the work undertaken for the World Bank *World Development Report, 2000/2001: Attacking Poverty* (New York, Oxford University Press, 2001) consisted in systematically seeking the views of more than 60,000 men and women living in poverty in 60 countries. These were published in three volumes: *Voices of the Poor: Can Anyone Hear Us?* (New York, Oxford University Press, 2000), *Voices of the Poor: Crying Out for Change* (New York, Oxford University Press, 2000) and *Voices of the Poor: From Many Lands* (New York, Oxford University Press, 2002).

In particular, Part two of this *Survey* examines the impact of economic policy in a number of areas on the material dimensions of poverty, such as income, consumption, employment and productivity, in the developing countries and economies in transition. The policies examined are monetary and fiscal policies (chap. V), trade policies (chap. VI), agricultural reforms (chap. VII) and the policies arising in the move from a planned to a market economy (chap. VIII). These policies are not specifically designed to combat poverty; their aim is rather to enhance the overall productivity of the economy and thus to reduce poverty in the long term. For example, macroeconomic and trade policies are considered to have a beneficial impact on poverty largely through economic growth: appropriate policies in these areas are expected to stimulate economic growth and growth, in turn, is expected to reduce poverty.[4] Agricultural reforms affect the incidence of poverty through increased efficiencies in agricultural production and distribution and more equitable patterns of rural development. Through various channels, these different policies affect the incidence of poverty, not just in the long term but also in the short and medium terms.

The primary importance given to poverty reduction by the international community is reflected in the fact that all World Bank and International Monetary Fund (IMF) lending to low-income countries requires the preparation of national Poverty Reduction Strategy Papers (PRSPs). These Papers not only focus on the consequences of macroeconomic policies for poverty reduction, but also include poverty-targeted microeconomic policies aimed at bringing employment and education to the poor in order to help them escape longer-term poverty, and such measures as income subsidies and food aid to help them overcome their present difficulties. This reflects the consideration that help should be provided to those who are poor but likely to find employment in the near future, as well as additional help to those who will remain poor without an improvement in their chances of obtaining employment. This distinction between transitory and chronic poverty is crucial, but is often disguised by the overall headcount figures for the poor, which do not distinguish between those who remained poor for longer than, say, a year, and those who had been poor at the time of the headcount but escaped poverty soon thereafter. This is of relevance to both the developing countries and the economies in transition. In the latter, Governments have combined macrolevel policies designed to ensure long-term employment-generating growth—and therefore the emergence from poverty of those who were plunged into it by the loss of employment during the transitional recession—with policies targeted at tackling chronic poverty (see chap. VIII).

There remains the question what is the impact on poverty of the economic policies available to Governments and the whole movement to liberalize economic activity. An examination of these different economic policies shows that, while they are effective instruments in reducing the incidence of poverty in the long term, they need to be complemented by micropolicies so as to achieve the greatest impact in reducing poverty in the short-to-medium term. A second consideration is that economic policies affect different groups of a society to varying degrees and, at least in the short and medium terms, some groups may be harmed if appropriate action is not taken. In particular, although trade liberalization nurtures the development of activities in which a country has a comparative advantage, it could lead to the longer-term decline—and even to

[4] For a criticism of the assumed connection among good policies, growth and poverty reduction, see the Special Contribution (Poverty, globalization and growth: perspectives on some of the statistical links) by Joseph E. Stiglitz in United Nations Development Programme, *Human Development Report, 2003* (New York, Oxford University Press, 2003), p. 80.

the disappearance—of other activities without such an advantage. Similarly, while market-based agricultural reforms encourage the more efficient use of available resources in the public and private domains, a State-sponsored financing scheme would need to be put in place to ensure that the poorest of the poor who have no access to credit do not lose but actually benefit. An immediate implication of these two considerations is that several complementary policies must be pursued, simultaneously or sequentially.

It is difficult, however, to demonstrate the linkages among these policies and their combined impact on poverty. Part two aims to address these questions. One of the lessons that emerges is that increased discussion is required at the domestic and international levels on prioritizing policies, on the trade-offs among complementary policies, and on the correct sequencing. For example, the experience of some countries with economies in transition during the 1990s shows that economic policies need to be implemented with an awareness of the likely effects on poverty, that is to say, there needs to be a combination of complementary policies that provide a buffer against their possible adverse impacts and that target those most likely to fall into chronic poverty.

To clarify the links among economic policies and poverty and with a view to setting the framework for evaluating the policies examined in Part two, chapter IV argues that the impact of policies on poverty should be assessed from different aspects. Assessing the impacts of a policy on the evolution of poverty critically depends on (a) which aspect(s) of poverty—including income and/or non-income dimensions—the policy maker chooses to focus on; (b) the level of aggregation used—for example, national or subnational, urban or rural, tradable or non-tradable sectors, female or male; and (c) the time-horizon—short- or long-run—over which the impact of the policy is to be assessed.

Chapter IV examines growth-poverty relationships and demonstrates, based on cross-country evidence and case studies, the importance of using all three aspects in establishing a framework for evaluating policy. Economic growth and the reduction of income poverty usually go hand in hand, but increases in average income levels are not necessarily associated with improvements in health status and educational attainment, which constitute an important dimension of chronic poverty. When only the income dimension of poverty is considered, economic growth is generally found to be beneficial for the poor. This finding, however, is based upon an average of many countries' experiences; and the same degree of improvement in economic growth may affect the incidence of poverty in different countries differently, depending on the initial economic and social conditions and the sources of growth (for example, export-driven growth as opposed to increases in agricultural production for domestic consumption). Economic growth may thus affect some groups of people adversely, particularly in relative terms. Moreover, because even long-term growth is rarely steady but often consists of short-run fluctuations, during an economic downturn, poor people—who have few assets to smooth out consumption over such fluctuations—are more likely to be impoverished even further, compared with the non-poor.

Chapter V analyses the impacts of monetary and fiscal policies on poverty, in both the short and the long run. Special attention is given to these relationships during times of economic crisis, when the poor constitute the group that is most adversely affected. The experiences of East Asia and Latin America during the past 10 years are examined in order to elucidate some of the possible effects, especially on poverty, of periods of stop-and-go in macroeconomic policy. The importance of maintaining macroeconomic stability during times of growth, in order to have a greater degree of freedom to manoeuvre during crises and to be able to protect the poor, is emphasized. The focus is on the urban poor since they have been identified as more vulnerable in times of economic crises than the rural poor. The analysis concludes that macroeconomic policies alone are not sufficient to address the problems of the poor: complementary measures are necessary.

The analysis emphasizes that preventing or reducing economic shocks is essential, particularly in the context of poverty, since the protection of the poor is rarely a priority in the macroeconomic responses to crises when they do occur. Therefore, preventive measures should be put in place within a social protection scheme even before a crisis erupts, and curative measures must be undertaken when a crisis occurs, with the degree of intensiveness depending on need. Access to health, education and nutrition is usually better in urban areas than in rural areas, but since many of the poor are in the informal sector, such programmes are more likely to reach the middle- and higher-income families in the formal sector. Thus, in addition to formal social programmes, other forms of social assistance based on grass-roots involvement are necessary in order to reach all of the poor, especially those in the informal sector.

Chapter VI demonstrates how trade liberalization is conducive to poverty reduction because of its long-run effects on growth and focuses on the effect of short- and medium-term adjustment on the incidence of poverty. The chapter analyses various channels through which trade liberalization affects poverty. These include changes in prices and in the availability of goods and services, impacts on labour markets, changes in the incentives for investment and the transfer of technology, effects on government tax revenues, and changes in income distribution. Overall, trade liberalization is beneficial to the poor, although it should often be complemented by other policies. There is little evidence of a "race to the bottom" as countries lower standards to attract foreign investment. However, there do remain major impediments to the poorest countries' taking full advantage of trade's income-generating potential, particularly the protectionist and subsidizing policies of the developed countries.

Chapter VII addresses selected market-based policies intended to increase agricultural productivity. It identifies the impact of such policies on the achievement of more equitable patterns of rural development, particularly in sub-Saharan Africa. The chapter demonstrates that liberalization of staple food markets is especially important for the rural poor, who often generate the bulk of their income from producing staple foods. Particular attention should thus be paid to the role of food marketing reform in rural economic growth. The chapter also analyses how land redistribution policies can promote greater economic efficiency and more equitable patterns in rural growth.

The chapter shows that market-based policies, although not primarily aimed at reducing rural poverty, can still have an indirect positive impact on poverty alleviation. Greater emphasis on market-based approaches, aimed at improving the efficiency and cost-effectiveness of agricultural production and marketing, has produced mixed results in terms of rural poverty alleviation. The major challenge for the future is thus to implement corrective measures to deal with problems that occur as reforms are being implemented while maintaining the improvements in efficiency, reductions in marketing costs and fiscal savings that have resulted from market-based approaches to reform.

Chapter VIII deals with the effects on poverty of the economic dimensions of a unique shock: the end of the centrally planned system first in Eastern Europe and then over the Soviet Union, which broke up into independent States. It was widely believed that, after the collapse, the market system would be created within a short time and would lead to much higher standards of living than had been enjoyed before.

For the countries that will enter the European Union in 2004, this prediction has proved broadly correct, although after a longer time than many had expected. Poverty rose in the first years of transition, but has now fallen. However, especially among the members of the Commonwealth of Independent States, the collapse of central planning has given rise to a dramatic rise in poverty, to widening income inequalities and to chronic poverty. Various groups of the population—the unemployed, ethnic minorities, single mothers, those living in previously closed military towns—were hit particularly badly by the transition. Moreover, no longer can mass poverty be viewed as a transitory phenomenon, as was the case in much of Eastern Europe—it must now be regarded as chronic. These States had to confront, at a time of diminished government resources, the challenge of constructing social safety nets that target the most needy. This task should be easier now that their economic revival is under way, but it still requires action on many fronts, as the form of chronic poverty from which they suffer is not likely to be removed by economic revival alone.

The experience of the transition economies highlights dramatically the main conclusion of Part two of the *Survey*, namely, that there is no inherent contradiction between poverty reduction and the pursuit of optimum economic policies, including those in the macroeconomic sphere, and liberalization in trade and agriculture, for these policies should result in faster economic growth which will serve to reduce poverty. Growth will make possible the enactment of those microlevel policies that can address the needs of the poor. However, the enactment of macroeconomic policies should also be infused with an awareness of the likely effects on poverty, and, where necessary, complementary policies should be pursued to ensure that they result in even greater gains in terms of poverty reduction.[5]

[5] For a discussion on how to achieve an equity-enhancing growth strategy and an analysis of the priorities of social policies in an integrated approach to growth, see the Report of the Executive Committee on Economic and Social Affairs of the United Nations entitled "Social dimensions of macroeconomic policy", New York, 22 June 2001 (ECESA/4).

IV GROWTH AND POVERTY: A FRAMEWORK FOR EVALUATING POLICY

It deserves to be remarked, perhaps, that it is in the progressive state, while the society is advancing to the further acquisition, rather than when it has acquired its full complement of riches, that the condition of the labouring poor, of the great body of the people, seems to be the happiest and the most comfortable. It is hard in the stationary, and miserable in the declining state. The progressive state is in reality the cheerful and the hearty state to all the different orders of the society. The stationary is dull: the declining melancholy.

Adam Smith, *An Inquiry into the Nature and the Causes of the Wealth of Nations* **Edwin Cannon, ed. (New York Modern Library, 1937), p. 81.**

Concerns for poverty have been expressed for many years at the national and international levels, even if its priority in the political agenda has not always been high. The World Summit for Social Development, held in Copenhagen in 1995, produced new initiatives for the eradication of poverty and, subsequently, all countries in the United Nations endorsed, for the first time, in the United Nations Millennium Declaration (see General Assembly resolution 55/2 of 8 September 2000) the commitment to halve the proportion of people living in extreme poverty by 2015. Combating poverty has become a priority in the agenda for the international community and every organization of the United Nations system.

The number of people in the world whose income is less than one dollar per day, measured at purchasing power parity (PPP), was estimated in 1999 to be about 1.2 billion, the most recent available figure (see figure IV.1).[1] This number constitutes about 23 per cent of the total population of developing and transition economies, an improvement from 30 per cent in 1990. During the period 1990-1999, only Eastern and Southern Asia had reduced the proportion of the population living on one dollar or less per day. The rest of the developing world increased the proportions of that population, though the increments were marginal in Latin America and the Caribbean and the Middle East and North Africa. The proportion of people living in extreme poverty in sub-Saharan Africa increased from 47.4 per cent in 1990 to 49.0 per cent in 1999 and, owing to high population growth, the number of people below the poverty line increased from 241 million to 315 million during the same period. The proportion of people living in extreme poverty in the economies in transition also increased because of

---

[1] Strictly speaking, this estimate is based on consumption/expenditure, not on income. Because it is now common to refer to this PPP per day figure as income, the present chapter follows the common usage. For details of the estimation method, see Shaohua Chen and Martin Ravallion, *How did the World's Poorest Fare in the 1990s?*, World Bank Policy Research Working Paper, No. 2409 (Washington, D.C., World Bank, August 2000).

Figure IV.1.
NUMBER OF PEOPLE LIVING IN EXTREME POVERTY IN
DEVELOPING COUNTRIES, BY REGION, 1990 AND 1999[a]

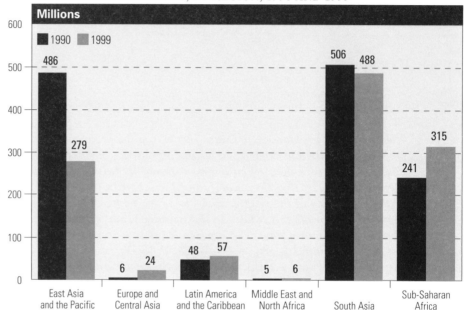

Source: UN/DESA, based on World Bank, *Global Economic Prospects and the Developing Countries, 2003* (Washington, D.C., World Bank, 2002), p. 30.

Note: People living in extreme poverty, as defined, live on less than one dollar per day.

[a] Regions are defined by the World Bank. The country data necessary to compute these aggregates according to the country grouping used elsewhere in the *Survey* are not available.

difficulties associated with their economic transformation. The pace of poverty reduction experienced in the world as a whole during the 1990s was fast enough to achieve the target of halving the proportion of people living in extreme poverty by 2015,[2] but this success came largely from significant advances in Asia—particularly in China and, to a lesser extent, India.

The poor are found in all population groups—among the young and the old, among the employed and the unemployed, and among women and men. They live in the slums of central cities and areas of rural blight. Pockets of the poor are found in developed countries and eradicating their relative poverty is a major policy issue. Poverty in developed countries, however, is different from extreme poverty in developing countries, particularly the least developed countries, where the national poverty income threshold is often set at the equivalent of one or two dollars per day. At this level of income, the risks of death through hunger and the vulnerability to disease are far greater than those faced by people regarded as poor in the developed countries. The aim of alleviating mass extreme poverty in developing countries thus has priority in the global agenda.

Understanding the causes of poverty and the interactions among them is essential for formulating and implementing economic policies that affect poverty. Measuring the extent of poverty at the national and global levels and setting measurable targets, in turn, enable Governments and the international community to assess the impacts of policy actions. It is in this context that the international community has established the Millennium Development Goals to measure progress and to evaluate national and international actions.

Various economic, social and cultural policies have been formulated and undertaken to reduce poverty, explicitly or implicitly.[3] Policies that target poor people explicitly include income subsidy programmes, food aid schemes and

[2] Report of the Secretary General entitled "Implementation of the United Nations Millennium Declaration" (A/57/270 and corr. 1), 31 July 2002, para. 40. The average annual rate of poverty reduction during the period was 2.7 per cent and if this rate prevails over the period of 1990–2015, the proportion of population living in poverty will be 15.1 per cent of the total population of developing countries, about 51 per cent of the 1990s level.

[3] Report on the World Social Situation, 2003 (United Nations publication, forthcoming) examines several social and cultural policies that help reduce social vulnerability, a source of poverty.

actions to provide employment and education. Because of the directedness of these policies, measuring their impacts on the people targeted and their effectiveness in relation to their intended goals is straightforward, at least in theory. However, many other policies do not place poverty reduction as their direct goal, even though their implementation may help eliminate poverty as part of the effort to improve the well-being of all. Macroeconomic policies, including structural adjustment programmes and trade policies, agricultural reforms, industrial policies, and national development plans are examples of such policies. They aim at strengthening or stabilizing activities within an economy, a sector or an industry in order to achieve sustained growth of the economy and, by doing so, improving the welfare of the population, including that of the poor. Their overall impacts on poverty are significant, and may sometimes surpass those of the direct policies because of the economy-wide effects that some of them have.

One distinction between the recent trends in policy-making and those formulated up until the mid-1980s (such as national development plans) lies in the current recognition of the roles that markets can play in economic development. Policy makers now formulate economic policies that nurture the development of markets and incorporate the working of existing markets in policy design. For example, instead of fixing the market interest rate at a predetermined level with little consideration of market conditions, more countries now adopt so-called inflation-targeting to stabilize the economy, with the monetary authorities communicating with the public through the money market so as to achieve the target.[4] Many countries have liberalized the external sector of their economies, instead of protecting certain industries with import tariffs and distorted foreign exchange rates. Prices of staple foods, water and electricity often used to be directly set by the Governments in many developing and transition economies, but these prices are now increasingly determined by market conditions, although in many cases some safeguard arrangements are still in place.

The linkages between each of these "market-friendly" policies and the incidence of poverty are complex because their effects on poverty are not direct: there are many channels through which each policy can affect poverty. In order to clarify the nature of the web of indirect links between policy and poverty and to set a framework for evaluating the policies examined in the following chapters of the present *Survey*, the present chapter argues that policies should be assessed from three different perspectives: that of the definition of poverty, that of the social and geographical level of aggregation of poverty, and that of the time-horizon.

As recognized in the Millennium Development Goals, poverty touches many aspects of the human condition, including the economic, social, environmental, political and cultural. As a reflection of its multifaceted aspects, poverty is defined in various ways. Which definition of poverty to adopt is not an issue of right or wrong: it depends on the objective of the policy, or the priority that policy makers set. For example, if the objective of a macroeconomic policy is to stabilize economic conditions, its effects on poverty should be judged in terms of income, consumption, employment or wages, but not in terms of health status or access to water. If, on the other hand, the goal of a health policy is to improve the general health status of women, that policy should be evaluated in terms of the health indicators of the women targeted, not in terms of the incomes that they earn.

4 See *World Economic and Social Survey, 2000* (United Nations publication, Sales No. E.00.II.C.1), box I.1.

The level of aggregation matters particularly when discussing the effectiveness of policy on individuals or on a certain group of people categorized by socio-economic or geographical attributes. A nationwide unemployment compensation scheme is an important tool with which to supplement income declines associated with job losses in the formal sector, but it is of little use to workers in the informal sector or those who are chronically impoverished because of the lack of productive employment. The effectiveness of such a scheme should not be judged on the basis of the number of poor people remaining in the informal sector.

Assessment of the impacts of a policy on poverty also critically depends on the time-horizon that policy assessors—policy makers, experts or civil society—choose to apply. While policies aimed at increasing the average level of educational attainment are conducive to reducing poverty over a long period of time, no one should expect to observe a measurable impact of such policies on poverty within a year or two.

The two extremes of a wide policy spectrum—anti-globalization groups and naive market liberalization groups—often oversimplify, in their own ways, the linkages between policy and poverty in order to justify their respective claims. This chapter argues that such oversimplifications do not capture the essence of the linkages and, in many instances, mislead policy debates; and that assessing growth-poverty relationships depends, instead, on the choice of the definition of poverty, the level of poverty aggregation and the time-horizon. Analysing the relationship between growth and poverty highlights several important issues that become critical when assessing the impacts on poverty incidence of the policies mentioned above.

RELATIONSHIPS BETWEEN DEVELOPMENT, POLICY AND POVERTY

Over the centuries, the world has witnessed many events and changes that have harmed people's lives and livelihoods. Man-made disasters, such as wars, civil strife and political instabilities associated with regime changes, have had adverse impacts on innumerable lives. Natural disasters, such as floods, droughts, earthquakes and volcanic eruptions, have affected them as well. Even in politically stable times, economic and political reforms, changes in the external environment, such as the oil shocks of the 1970s and 1980s and the currency and financial crises in the 1980s and 1990s, and serious epidemics, such as bubonic plague (the Black Death) which killed one quarter of Europe's population in the fourteenth century and human immunodeficiency virus/acquired immunodeficiency syndrome (HIV/AIDS), have all devastated not only human lives but many nations' economic vitality. In many cases, the poor have been affected most severely by these events and changes, owing to a lack of resources with which to address the situation.

At the World Summit for Social Development, held in Copenhagen in March 1995, the States Members of the United Nations recognized that poverty occurs in all countries—mass poverty in many developing countries, pockets of poverty amid wealth in developed countries, loss of livelihoods as a result of economic recession, and sudden poverty as a result of disaster or conflict. Member

States pledged to make the conquest of poverty, among other things, an overriding objective of sustainable development.[5]

The Programme of Action of the World Summit for Social Development recognizes that poverty has various causes, including structural and transitional ones, and that "poverty is a complex multidimensional problem with origins in both the national and international domains".[6] Poverty encompasses not only material deprivation (in terms of income, consumption and assets), but also poor health and inadequate education (human capital), vulnerability to adverse shocks, and a sense of voicelessness and powerlessness (lack of participation) in a society or State.[7] These facets are intertwined and often create a vicious circle: poor people's limited access to opportunities of earning adequate incomes reflects low levels of education and poor health, and their inadequate educational and health status, together with the lack of physical and political infrastructure, often results in the limited participation of the poor in national and local politics. Furthermore, low incomes, together with initial poor health, expose the poor to a higher risk of diseases, making it more difficult for them to participate fully in productive activities.

It is often misleading to focus on only one dimension of poverty because poverty manifests itself in various ways: even when one poverty-related indicator improves, others may worsen. For example, at various times in the 1990s, Ethiopia and Uganda showed improvement in all four aspects of well-being—poverty headcount, net primary school enrolment rates, child nutrition and mortality rates of children under age 5—and Ghana and Mauritania experienced similar trends (see table IV.1). Four other African countries, however, had mixed outcomes. While the poverty headcount increased slightly in

[5] Documents related to the World Summit for Social Development are available at http://www.un.org/esa/socdev/wssd/indec.htm. See, in particular, the Programme Action of the World Summit for Social Development (*Report of the World Summit for Social Development, Copenhagen, 6-12 March 1995* (United Nations publication, Sales No. E.96.IV.8), chap. I, resolution 1, annex II), chap. II entitled "Eradication of poverty".

[6] Programme of Action of the World Summit for Social Development, para. 23.

[7] For discussions on the nature of poverty, see World Bank, *World Development Report 2000/2001: Attacking Poverty* (Washington, D.C., World Bank, 2001), chap. 1. For a vision of poverty coming from the poor themselves, see World Bank, *Voices of the Poor: Can Anyone Hear Us?* (New York, Oxford University Press, 2000); *Voices of the Poor: Crying out for Change* (New York, Oxford University Press, 2002); and *Voices of the Poor: From Many Lands* (New York, Oxford University Press, 2002).

Table IV.1.
EVOLUTION OF STANDARD POVERTY MEASURES IN SELECTED SUB-SAHARAN COUNTRIES

Country and period	Poverty headcount[a]		Net primary school enrolment rate		Child malnutrition[b]		Child mortality (per thousand)	
	Initial level	Percentage change	Initial level	Change in percentage points	Initial level	Change in percentage points	Intial level	Change
Ethiopia (1994-1997)	39	**-26**[c]	19	**6**	66	**-11**	190	**-15**
Ghana (1992-1998)	51	**-24**	70	**12**	26	0	119	**-15**
Madagascar (1993-1999)	70	1	48	**16**	50	**-1**	170	**-21**
Mauritania (1987-1995)	58	**-40**	28	**13**	48	**-25**	..	..
Nigeria (1992-1996)	46	56	94	**4**	38	..	136	11
Uganda (1992-1997)	56	**-21**	68	**18**	43	**-4**	165	**-3**
Zambia (1993-1998)	74	**-3**	73	-7	40	3	194	**-5**
Zimbabwe (1991-1996)	26	35	83	**3**	30	**-7**	77	31

Source: UN/DESA, based on Luc Christiensen, Lionel Demery and Stefano Paternostro, "Growth, distribution poverty in Africa: messages from the 1990s" World Bank, March 2002, tables 1 and 6.

Note: Bold face type indicates improvement.

a   Consumption measured as regionally deflated real household expenditure per adult equivalent. Poverty lines are calculated according to the cost-of-basic-needs approach, which includes non-food needs (except Zimbabwe). Poverty line for Mauritania is based on a United States one-dollar-per-day equivalent.

b   Referring to children under age 5 whose height for their age is less than minus two standard deviations from the median for the international reference population ages 0 to 59 months.

c   Rural poverty only.

Madagascar, the other variables showed improvement. Nigeria and Zimbabwe experienced significant increases in the number of poor people and child mortality rates, but larger proportions of children attended school. In Zambia, on the other hand, the share of the population living below the poverty line and child mortality rates declined slightly, but a lower proportion of children attended school and the incidence of child malnutrition increased.

While the well-being of the poor in Ethiopia, Ghana, Mauritania and Uganda clearly improved on average during the periods specified—albeit from a very low level—it is not obvious how the changes in the poverty situation in the other countries can be summarized. Such complexity tends to make for extensive debate about the relationship among economic, social, political and other human development-related factors as causes and consequences of poverty.[8] Moreover, hard evidence is difficult to come by to support or refute arguments, because of the costs and technical difficulties associated with data collection. In the end, the complexity of the poverty issues and the lack of hard evidence "can overwhelm adequate understanding".[9] This situation poses a problem for policy makers, particularly when they design a policy that aims to improve the living standards of the poor and when they evaluate the outcome of this policy. A policy inevitably induces changes in economic, social and other variables in complicated ways; without adequate understanding, it is difficult, if not impossible, for policy makers to design and implement an appropriate policy with feasible targets.

Selecting a few poverty variables—depending on the policy goal established and on data availability—helps improve analytical capability and allows policy makers to examine more closely the relationship between poverty and policy actions. Given the current stock of knowledge about the relationships among poverty, development and policy, policy makers and experts in the field will gain practical insight, however incomplete, by focusing on a narrower range of manifestations of poverty, at the expense of a more in-depth description of the multifaceted experiences of the poor.[10]

Focusing on one or a few indicators that gauge material aspects of poverty (income, consumption and productivity) has additional advantages. One reason for this focus is the limited availability of internationally comparable data for analysing the impact of policy changes on consumption or income over time. Such data are indispensable because tracing the impacts of policy on poverty is inevitably required to track changes in poverty indicators over time (the so-called poverty dynamics). Second, there are well-established statistical definitions of the indicators related to the material dimensions of poverty, which is not the case for the sense of being powerless and voiceless, for example. Third, some indicators related to the material dimension of poverty are generally more responsive to economic policy changes than are such social variables as health, education and literacy rates. These indicators, particularly income and consumption, involve fewer measurement problems and are observed frequently enough to allow for the detection of the relationships between them and the changing socio-political environment, including policy changes. Fourth, and perhaps most importantly, the multidimensional definition of poverty tends to lead to a complex but static view of poverty—that is to say, a snapshot at one point in time—in which the focus of the anti-poverty strategy is on *what* people lack.[11] The narrower material definition of poverty, in contrast, makes more

[8] One way to evaluate the status of the poor is to construct a "poverty index", which assigns weights to various poverty-related variables and sums them up to create a single number. However, the question remains what variables should be included and what weight should be attached to each variable.

[9] United Nations Conference on Trade and Development (UNCTAD), *The Least Developed Countries Report, 2002: Escaping the Poverty Trap* (United Nations publication, Sales No. E.02.II.D.13), p. 40.

[10] The theoretical links between growth, poverty reduction and social indicators are discussed in Lance Taylor, Santosh Mehrotra and Enrique Delamonica, "The links between economic growth, poverty reduction, and social development: theory and policy", in *Development with a Human Face: Experiences in Social Achievement and Economic Growth*, Santosh Mehrotra and Richard Jolly, eds. (New York, Oxford University Press, 1998).

[11] See *the Least Developed Countries Report, 2002* ..., part two, chap. 1.

tractable the relationship between policy changes and poverty dynamics and allows policy makers to focus on *why* people lack certain things.[12] Furthermore, this approach allows policy makers to distinguish chronic poverty from transient poverty (that is to say, those stuck in poverty over a long period in contrast with those who can be expected to escape from poverty after a short period), each requiring for its reduction, in many cases, its own unique set of policy prescriptions.

The following sections in this chapter focus on the relationship between economic variables, especially growth, and poverty indicators, and examine the impact of economic policies on those variables and indicators, with a view to drawing implications and proposing guidelines for poverty reduction in the context of a macroeconomic framework.

AVERAGE RELATIONSHIPS BETWEEN GROWTH AND POVERTY

History suggests that sustained economic growth over "the very long run" is the critical factor for reducing or even to eliminating extreme poverty.[13] Without sustained growth over the centuries, Western Europe, where until the mid-eighteenth century most social scientists were resigned to accepting the phenomenon of poverty as an inescapable fact of life,[14] could not have achieved the high living standards that the region enjoys at present. This is true for developed countries in other regions as well. While the developed countries experienced wars, economic depressions, social unrest and other setbacks during the course of their development, they undertook countermeasures to rectify these situations and maintained long-term sustained growth that has led to their current developed status.

In the current debate on policy and poverty, however, the issue is how national authorities in developing and transition economies, assisted by the international community, can enable the poor to escape from poverty as quickly and effectively as possible, in order to reach the Millennium Development Goals by 2015. The importance of sustained economic growth over the very long term in eliminating poverty is recognized, but policy makers need to identify, beyond the economic and social policies adopted by the now-developed countries over the course of their development, a new set of policies that allow economic growth to reduce the incidence of poverty more positively.

One of the major policy debates on poverty has centred on the relationship between poverty and macroeconomic policies—policies that aim at stabilizing, sustaining or enhancing economic growth. The main questions raised have been the following: Do macroeconomic reforms based on free-market discipline have positive impacts on the poor? Is liberalization of trade and finance beneficial for poor people and poor countries, or does it only further enrich already rich people and wealthy countries? Is economic growth in general pro-poor and, if not, what types of growth are pro-poor?[15] More generally, has globalization of the world economy in recent years had a positive impact on people in developing countries, particularly the poor?

These questions seem to assume that various linkages—direct or indirect—between poverty and globalization, poverty and economic growth, and poverty

[12] Furthermore, as discussed later in this chapter, focusing on the dynamics of poverty narrowly defined sheds light on the issue of short- versus long-term impacts of a policy change, which has created disagreement on economic policy among policy makers, experts and non-governmental organizations. See Ravi Kanbur, "Economic policy, distribution and poverty: the nature of disagreements", *World Development*, vol. 29, No. 6 (June 2001), pp. 1083–1094.

[13] While no clear definition of it has emerged, the very long run refers generally to periods longer than a century. For an example of such an analysis, see Charles I. Jones, *Was an Industrial Revolution Inevitable?: Economic Growth over the Very Long Run*, National Bureau of Economic Research Working Paper Series, No. 7375 (Cambridge, Massachusetts, October 1999).

[14] *World Development Report, 2000/2001...*, chap. 3.

[15] The term "pro-poor growth" is now frequently used in policy debates, but there is no consensus as to its meaning. See Howard White and Edward Anderson, "Growth versus distribution: does the pattern of growth matter?", *Development Policy Review*, vol. 19, No. 3 (September 2001), pp. 267–289.

and economic reforms exist over reasonably short periods of time. As argued previously, however, poverty has various causes and manifestations and thus does not display any straightforward relationship with global or macroeconomic phenomena. It is argued below that, while some relationship showing statistical regularity exists between growth and income or consumption poverty over the medium-to-long term across many developing and transition countries, the impacts of growth on poverty depend on the different socio-economic conditions in different countries, including the degree of initial income inequality. The assessment of impacts of growth on poverty also depends critically on the level of aggregation (national, regional, sectoral or individual) and the time-horizon chosen (short- versus long-run), which give rise to different pictures of poverty dynamics, often leading to different policy implications.

General relationship between growth and poverty in the long run

16 World Bank, *Global Economic Prospects and the Developing Countries: Making Trade Work for the World's Poor* (Washington, D.C., World Bank, 2002), table1.8.

The World Bank estimates that 19 per cent of the world population lived on less than $1 per day and 46 per cent on less than $2 dollar per day in 1999.[16] The incidence of such poverty, however, exhibited a large variation among countries. The relationship between per capita income and poverty incidence, suggests some general tendencies related to income and poverty levels (see figure IV.2). First, on average, the higher the per capita income, the lower the incidence of poverty—which is not a surprising. Second, while poorer countries tend to have a higher incidence of poverty, the incidence varies widely among countries with similar annual per capita incomes. For example, among countries with per capita income less than $1,000 a year, the share of the population living on less than $1 per day varies between less than 20 and more than 70 per cent.[17] This variation reflects the degree of income inequality of the countries: for two countries with similar average income levels, the one with a higher income inequality tends to have a higher poverty rate.

17 UNCTAD defines "generalized poverty" as a condition in which a major part of the population lives at or below income levels sufficient to meet their basic needs, and in which the available resources in the economy are barely sufficient to cater for the basic needs of the population on a sustainable basis. See *the Least Developed Countries, 2002* ...

The relationships between poverty and average income and the differences in the incidence of poverty among countries with similar per capita income level are subjects of much research. However, the large differences in the incidence of poverty between richer and poorer countries point to the importance of achieving sustained growth, and the wide variation in poverty incidence (and income inequality) among countries with similar income levels suggests the need to improve income equality as a means to reduce poverty.

The consensus, however, stops at this point, and debates arise on the issue of the evolution of poverty and economic growth, defined as a rise in the average living standard of a country, that is to say, in income per capita. While a redistribution of income at any point of time could reduce poverty in the short run, the long-run relationship between income distribution within a country and growth is the subject of considerable interest and debate (see box IV.1). Over long period of time, growth, an increase in inequality and a reduction of poverty have occurred in tandem. More recently, the debate has extended to the relationship between poverty reduction and the globalization of the world economy, which is presumed to affect, in one way or another, growth and living standards in the country. The issues in their simplest form are whether or not sustained economic growth is good for the poor, and whether globalization of the world economy has a positive or negative impact on the poor, possibly via its effects on the growth of the national economy.

Figure IV.2.
PER CAPITA INCOME AND EXTREME POVERTY IN THE 1990s[a]

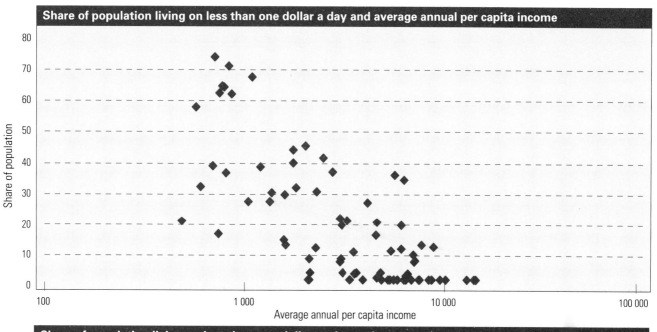

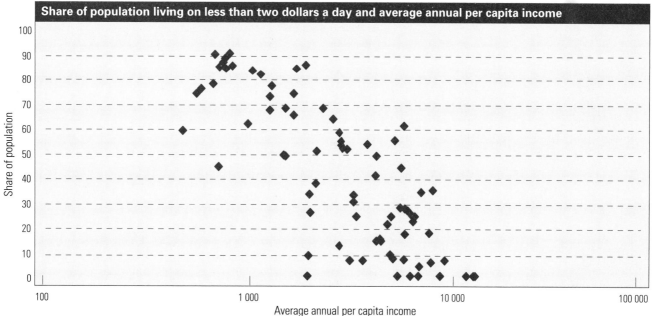

Sources: UN/DESA, based on World Bank, *2002 World Development Indicators, CD-ROM* (Washington, D.C., World Bank, 2002); and World Bank, *World Development Report, 2002: Building Institutions for Markets* (Washington, D.C., World Bank, 2002), table 2.

[a] Data covering 78 developing and transition economies. Share of population living on less than one or two dollars a day referring to various years in the 1990s and the average annual per capita income is to average per capita GDP (purchasing power parity-based 1995 US dollars) during 1995-1998.

Box IV.1

EQUALITY, GROWTH AND
POVERTY: ARE THERE
TRADE-OFFS?

a   See Simon Kuznets, "Economic growth and
    income inequality", *American Economic Review*,
    vol. 46, No. 1 (March 1955), pp. 1-28.

b   Ibid., p. 11.

c   For an analysis of the wealth generating possibili-
    ties of the capitalist system, see *World Economic
    and Social Survey, 2002* (United Nations publica-
    tion, Sales No. E.02.II.C.1), pp. 162-163; and
    William Baumol, *The Free Market Innovation
    Machine: Analyzing the Growth Miracle of
    Capitalism* (Princeton, New Jersey, and Oxford,
    United Kingdom, Princeton University Press, 2002).

The connection between the income distribution that results from growth and economic progress has been at the forefront of much recent economic analysis. The most important hypothesis put forward in this area was that of Simon Kuznets.[a] He argued that the income distribution within a country was likely to change over time with its progress in changing from a poor agricultural society to a rich industrial society. The average per capita income of the rural population is usually lower than that of the urban population, whereas income distribution within the urban population is more unequal. In the urban population, savings are concentrated in the upper-income groups and the cumulative effects of such savings would be the concentration of an increasing proportion of income yielding assets in the upper-income groups. Thus, as the weight of the urban sector increases in the economy with industrialization, the country's overall income distribution will tend to deteriorate until such time as the urban sector dominates. After that time, the income distribution will tend to stabilize because of three factors—the slower growth in the population of the wealthier classes, the exploitation of the opportunities for wealth-creation offered by technology undertaken by those whose property assets are not in established industries, and the shift of workers away from lower-income to higher-income industries—which are all indicative of the "dynamism of a growing and free economic society".[b] In addition, progressive direct taxes and government benefits would tend to equalize post-tax incomes. As posited by Kuznets, this pattern of income equality that first worsens and then improves with growth is a long-run phenomenon: for example, Kuznets saw the phase in which income inequality widened as have taken place between 1780 and 1850 in England (the first country to industrialize), from 1840 (and especially from 1870 onward) in the United States of America, and from the 1840s to the 1890s in Germany. Narrowing income inequality is thought to have taken place eventually—beginning in around 1875 in England and after 1918 in Germany and the United States.

Figures for the world economy after the free enterprise system—what has been described as the "innovation machine"—first started to produce increases in productivity and new inventions at a rate unlike any previously seen in world history shed light on this long-run phenomenon in an interesting manner (see table 1).[c] These figures take into account the difference in incomes within countries and not just the differences between the mean incomes of each country. Whether measured by the Gini or Theil coefficients, both of which increase as inequality increases, income distribution in the world deteriorated substantially between 1820 and 1950, halting between 1910 and 1929. After 1950, the pattern became less clear, with the Gini coefficient having stabilized between 1980 and 1992.

For the purpose of this analysis, the world was divided into country groupings: (a) Africa, (b) Asia, (c) Japan, the Republic of Korea and Taiwan Province of China, (d) Eastern Europe (including the Russian Federation and Turkey) and (e) Western Europe, Australia, Canada, New Zealand and the United States. How much of the inequality of income was due to inequality within country groups or between country groups was then calculated. In 1820, because mean incomes in all parts of the world were considered to have been broadly similar before the Industrial Revolution caused Western Europe to pull sharply ahead, only 12 per cent of total inequality was due to differences in income levels between the country groupings. As the Revolution progressed and embraced more countries in Europe and North America, this proportion increased to reach nearly 40 per cent before the First World War, to 47 per cent in 1929 and to nearly 60 per cent in 1950. After 1950, the situation stabilized as more countries—first Japan, the Republic of Korea and Taiwan Province of China and later China, India, Indonesia and other Asian countries—achieved rapid growth and saw their mean incomes rise. This period of rapid growth in Asia followed the end of direct or indirect control by the European powers, during which period growth, and particularly industrial growth, was often held back by policies designed to help those powers.

The period of rising income inequality at the world level, and in particular of rising differences between the country groupings, had seen a massive reduction in extreme poverty (measured as consumption per capita of one dollar per day in 1985 purchasing power parity (PPP)), from 84 per cent of the world's population in 1820 to 66 per cent in 1910 and to 55 per cent in

Box IV.1 (continued)

Table 1.
POVERTY AND INCOME INEQUALITY AT THE GLOBAL LEVEL, 1820-1992

	1820	1850	1870	1890	1910	1929	1950	1960	1970	1980	1992
Gini coefficient	0.500	0.532	0.560	0.588	0.610	0.616	0.640	0.635	0.650	0.657	0.657
Theil index	0.522	0.598	0.672	0.745	0.797	0.777	0.805	0.776	0.808	0.829	0.855
Inequality within country groups	0.462	0.470	0.484	0.495	0.498	0.412	0.313	0.318	0.315	0.330	0.342
Inequality between country groups	0.061	0.128	0.188	0.250	0.299	0.365	0.482	0.458	0.492	0.499	0.513
Inequality between country groups as a percentage of total inequality	11.7	21.4	28.0	33.6	37.5	47.0	59.9	59.0	60.9	60.2	60.0
Mean world income PPP dollars, 1990	658.7	735.7	890.0	1 113.8	1 459.9	1 817.1	2 145.5	2 798.6	3 773.8	4 544	4 962
Extreme poverty (percentage of world population)	83.9	81.5	75.4	71.7	65.6	56.3	54.8	44.0	35.6	31.5	23.7
Mean life expectancy (years)	26.5	..	..	29.9	32.8	38.5	50.1	..	59.4	..	61.1

Source: François Bourguignon and Christian Morrisson "Inequality among world citizens: 1820-1992", *American Economic Review*, vol. 92, No. 4 (September 2002), pp. 731-732, table 1, and p. 734, table 2.

1950. This continued, with 24 per cent of the world's population, according to these calculations, having been in extreme poverty in 1992. Over the same period, mean life expectancy rose sharply, from 26 years in 1820, to 50 years in 1950 and to over 60 years in 1992.

At the global level, then, the pattern of rising inequality, especially between countries, rising incomes and declining poverty would appear to have held good. The overall figures show that global income distribution, which plots the number of people or proportion of world population against the income they receive, has shifted to the right over time, indicating a rise in incomes. In addition, particularly since 1970, the two peaks in the distribution, with one for the poor at between the $1 and $2 per day poverty lines and the other for the rich at about $9,000 a year, have levelled out, indicating the rise of the middle class at a global level.

Yet, over the period 1970-1992, the situation in different regions shifted dramatically. According to one study, the number of the poor (measured by the $2 per day poverty line) in Asia decreased sharply, largely as a result of the success of China and India in achieving sustained growth (see table 2). In China, income inequality increased over the period, with, as the Kuznets hypothesis would have predicted, the urban sector progressing faster than the rural sector. However, in India, there was little change in the income distribution, while in Indonesia, income inequality declined as the economy grew. In Latin America, the "lost decade" of the 1980s had reversed the gains in poverty reduction achieved in the 1970s, and in the 1990s the situation started to improve so that the numbers of the poor became lower than in 1970. In Africa, though, the situation deteriorated throughout the period. In Nigeria, the largest country, those living on less than $2 a day rose from 45 per cent of the population in 1970 to 70 per cent in 1998. However, as the income distribution shifted to the left as the economy declined, with private consumption per capita having declined by 4.1 per cent per year between 1980 and 1998, the upper tail of the distribution shifted to the right, indicating that the richest Nigerians had become better off as the average Nigerian became worse off. This situation was not uncommon in Africa.

Box IV.1 (continued)

This is not the phenomenon that the Kuznets hypothesis had set out to explain, as his analysis was based upon what happens during economic growth rather than during decline. Although the African experience was comparable with that in some of the transition economies where income distribution worsened as the economy declined (see chap. VIII), the effects of the shocks that pushed the transition economies into recession have now been overcome in that economic growth has resumed. The present income distribution in many African countries can be seen as the end result of the interplay of many of the different factors—such as poor governance, the misdirection of mineral rents and the lack of attention paid to the rural sector, especially the rural poor—that accounted for much of Africa's disappointing economic performance in the last decades.

Whether rapid progress is possible with such an unequal distribution as now obtains is a crucial question whose answer depends upon political and social as well as economic factors. Sustained growth will be achieved only if the fruits of any advance are shared more fairly, particularly among the poor, than were the losses during the decline, when an ever-expanding share of a declining income was appropriated by the richest members of society. In any event, with large numbers of the world's population, especially in Asia, continuing to make rapid progress, and with Africa's population continuing to grow rapidly—even after the effects of human immunodeficiency virus/acquired immunodeficiency syndrome (HIV/AIDS) and other diseases - unless the absolute decline in Africa's economic growth is halted and reversed, the distribution of income in the world will become more unequal. Rather than signal considerably faster progress in some parts of the world than in others, as was broadly the picture from 1820 to 1950, a rise in world income inequality will indicate the effects of an absolute decline in one part amid often rapid expansion in other parts.

Table 2.
PEOPLE LIVING WITH AN INCOME LEVEL OF LESS THAN TWO DOLLARS PER DAY,
ASIA, LATIN AMERICA AND AFRICA, 1970-1998

Millions

	1970	1980	1990	1998	Total population in 1998
Asia (excluding Japan)	1 130.8	1 112.6	814.9	480.3	2 958
China	608.7	554.1	405.0	231.8	1 239
India	321.1	373.1	275.0	140.5	980
Indonesia	81.6	53.0	17.6	6.7	204
Pakistan	30.1	37.3	30.3	30.8	132
Bangladesh	39.3	55.6	54.1	42.8	126
Latin America	60.4	36.3	59.5	51.1	485
Brazil	29.8	18.7	24.3	21.4	166
Mexico	10.2	4.8	3.7	1.8	96
Colombia	5.7	4.6	6.0	7.0	41
Africa	141.2	193.0	270.9	368.4	579
Nigeria	24.2	37.6	60.7	84.4	121
Ethiopia	23.7	30.2	42.4	50.3	61
Congo	20.3	27.0	37.4	48.2	48
South Africa	4.5	4.7	6.4	7.7	41
United Republic of Tanzania	11.2	14.7	21.7	28.7	32
Kenya	8.5	10.3	14.9	18.5	29

Source: Xavier Sala-i-Martin, *The World Distribution of Income (Estimated from Individual Country Distributions)*, National Bureau of Economic Research Working Paper, No. 8933 (Cambridge, Massachusetts, May 2002), tables 5-7 (available at www.nber.org/papers/w8933).

Note: These figures may differ from those from other sources that use different methodologies for their compilation.

It is important to distinguish logical considerations from empirical findings. The logical answer to the question concerning the growth-poverty relationship is rather straightforward if no consideration is paid to the differences in socio-economic conditions of countries that are observed in the real world. The economic growth of a nation—an increase in its production or per capita income—is neither a necessary, nor a sufficient condition for poverty reduction: there is no logical linkage running from sustained growth to poverty reduction. Growth is not necessary for poverty reduction because poverty can be reduced by redistributing incomes among all members of the country in the absence of economic growth. Growth is not sufficient for poverty reduction because economic growth does not necessarily have any distributional aspects: sustained growth may make the rich richer with no trickle-down effects to the poor at all. While logically possible, however, this is unlikely, as the rich will increasingly demand more and better goods and services, and will be in a position to pay more for them. In short, there is bound to be some trickle down, although this could be very limited. The impacts of growth or globalization of the world economy on the poor thus cannot be judged a priori because of this lack of a firm and consistent logical linkage between growth or globalization and poverty.

Actual observations of market-based economies seem to suggest, however, a correlation between growth and poverty, contrary to the preceding logical conjecture. The observed relation is a result of the political and socio-economic environment in these economies—a factor that the logical considerations completely ignore—which limits the range of observable combinations. For example, while an income-redistribution policy that eliminates extreme poverty may be politically feasible for high-income countries, where the fiscal transfers (such as taxes and subsidies) required to eliminate extreme poverty are small relative to national income, it is not feasible for low-income developing countries. In the latter group of countries, eliminating poverty would require massive fiscal transfers relative to their national incomes. There are likely to be severe political difficulties to implementing such a policy and the measures might themselves undermine growth prospects. On the other hand, economic growth that benefits the rich disproportionally for a long time cannot be pursued, because of the increasing dissatisfaction of the majority of the population with the unfair distribution of incomes and consequent likelihood of political instability or social unrest. A continued high degree of income inequality may also adversely affect the work incentives of the non-rich.

Studies of the growth-poverty relationship have given rise to disagreements with regard to the measurement of income poverty, the compatibility of cross-country and inter-temporal data and the methods of analysis employed (see box IV.2). Even where consensus is reached, the data often give no clear conclusions, or are not very informative. The rest of this section therefore focuses primarily on the points of common understanding among experts about the relationship between growth and poverty, in order to create a framework for the subsequent review of policy issues.

One point of consensus is that growth is generally beneficial for the poor, albeit not without exceptions. Growth has been found beneficial for the poor when growth-poverty experiences in various countries are "averaged out" and each growth period is sustained over a reasonably long period, typically five years or more. Countries' experiences differ widely around the average, howev-

Box IV.2

DRAWING THE POVERTY LINE

[a]   Strictly speaking, the line is drawn at $1.08 per day in 1993 international purchasing power parity prices. See Shaohua Chen and Martin Ravallion, *How did the World's Poorest Fare in the 1990s?*, World Bank Policy Research Working Paper, No. 2409 (Washington, D.C., World Bank, August 2000).

[b]   For more technical aspects of the following arguments, see Angus Deaton, "Data for monitoring the poverty MDG", mimeo, Research Program in Development Studies, Princeton University, January 2003.

[c]   Another concern is connected with the unit of analysis (individual versus family), and is more technical in nature. See Deaton, loc. cit.

[d]   A. B. Atkinson, "Poverty", in *The New Palgrave: A Dictionary of Economics*, John Eatwell, Murray Milgate and Peter Newman, eds. (London, MacMillan, 1987), p. 931. See also Food and Agriculture Organization of the United Nations (FAO), *World Agriculture: Towards 2015/2030: An FAO Perspective* (London, Earthscan Publications, 2003), p. 214, box 8.1.

[e]   Deaton, loc. cit.

[f]   Ibid.

[g]   Some evidence is found in Christophe Muller, "Prices and living standards: evidence for Rwanda", *Journal of Development Economics*, vol. 68, No. 1 (June 2002), pp. 187-203.

[h]   See Jeffrey G. Williamson, *Winners and Losers over two Centuries of Globalization*, National Bureau of Economic Research Working Paper Series, No. 9161 (Cambridge, Massachusetts, September 2002).

The Millennium Development Goals for poverty reduction use an international absolute poverty line of one dollar per day in purchasing power parity.[a] The simplicity of the one dollar-per-day standard has been successful in promoting the concept of extreme poverty and has provided a useful reference mark for policy discussions. However, this line arouses controversy among experts with different professional points of view and experience.[b]

The one dollar-per-day line has been criticized on at least three grounds, namely, (a) the use of a single indicator as an international benchmark, (b) the calculation of purchasing power parity (PPP) conversion rates and, (c) the design of the household surveys used, and the sole reliance on them.[c]

With respect to (a), according to *some* researchers, the conception of poverty should refer to *minimum rights to resources,* and constitute a measure of the opportunities open to people to participate in the community's style of living with a salient set of elementary capabilities. The minimum resources (and thus income) required to participate in the community's lifestyle would depend on the community in which the individual/family resides, because lifestyles vary among countries. National poverty lines in many countries are constructed in a way that is consistent with this concept. "The notion of a fixed absolute poverty standard, applicable to all societies and at all times is therefore a chimera."[d] The international poverty line of one dollar-per-day is, on the other hand, based on the *standard-of-living approach* and is assumed to correspond to a specified level of consumption. It is designed to measure the number of very poor, most of whom live in the poorest countries, but not the community-dependent poverty in the rest of the world. It corresponds approximately to the national poverty lines of many low-income developing countries.[e]

With regard to (b) the purchasing power parity (PPP) conversion rate is a price index that is applied to convert the cost, measured in local currency, of a typical basket of goods that the average person consumes in a country to the cost in United States dollars. Besides the general problems associated with any index numbers,[f] there is a question about the relevance of the baskets of consumption used to calculate PPP rates. It is conceivable, and even likely, that the typical basket of goods consumed by the poor and the prices they pay are different from those relevant to the average person in the same country.[g] Furthermore, since some agricultural goods are available only in a particular local area and take a large share of local people's expenditure, it is difficult to find a relevant comparative price at the global level. In those cases, the cost of the basket relevant for poor people will not be accurately converted into dollars.[h] While these are important considerations, the current capacities of statistical offices in many countries do not allow for such detailed analysis.

As for (c), national household surveys are, in many cases, the source for constructing consumption or income distributions and estimating extreme poverty, but their designs are not standardized across countries and over time. Some experts use average consumption or personal income based on National Income

Box IV.2 (continued)

and Product Accounts (NIPA) to calculate poverty estimates because the conceptual framework of the NIPA is more standardized across countries and over time.[i] However, the NIPA framework does not necessarily produce more accurate information on consumption or income. Inasmuch as the NIPA framework demands much wider coverage of economic activities and more detailed estimation procedures, the chances are greater that the "residuals", that is to say, items that are unaccounted for by direct estimates, will become large and biased.

Another concern is how well a survey represents the population of a nation. It is often costly to travel to remote rural areas where the proportion of the extremely poor tends to be high, and in urban areas it is difficult to count and sample the homeless, or "street people". Moreover, rich people often refuse to participate in surveys or answer questionnaires dishonestly, because they fear that, based on answers they give, the tax authorities may discover their untaxed "informal" activities. While NIPA-based estimates are free from such problems, at least in concept, their estimates of consumption or income include items that do not represent actual expenditure of private persons, such as consumption by for- and non-profit organizations, imputed charges for financial intermediation (so as to remove double-counting) and imputed income from owner-occupied housing.[j]

Owing to the differences in design and methodology between household surveys and the NIPA framework, estimates of average consumption or personal income sometimes differ significantly. With NIPA-based numbers, estimated average consumption tends to be higher when economic growth is high, making poverty estimates lower than otherwise. When growth is stagnant, estimated consumption is lower and poverty higher. For example, using the NIPA method, the United Nations Conference on Trade and Development (UNCTAD) reports that the number of people in poverty in the least developed countries in Asia is found to be less than the number estimated by the World Bank, which is based on household surveys;[k] but UNCTAD also estimates that extreme poverty is much more widespread in sub-Saharan Africa than estimates by the Bank would indicate, owing to low growth in the region. Some researchers even claim, based on NIPA methods, that the Millennium Development Goals on poverty reduction has already been met, largely because of high growth in some developing regions outside sub-Saharan Africa.[l] These authors note, however, that, irrespective of their estimation procedures, mass poverty in sub-Saharan Africa should continue to be a major concern.

The construction and use of the one dollar-per-day poverty line entail several issues that are difficult to resolve. Resolving them would require actions by Governments, international organizations and experts to standardize household surveys across countries and over time and to improve the capabilities of national statistical authorities in developing countries.[m] Meanwhile, survey- and NIPA-based estimates should be considered complementary, rather than competing, sources of information.

[i]   Examples include: UNCTAD, *The Least Developed Countries Report, 2002: Escaping the Poverty Trap* (United Nations publication, Sales No.E.02.II. D.13), part two; and Xavier Sala-i-Martin, *The Disturbing Rise of Global Income Inequality*, National Bureau of Economic Research Working Paper Series, No. 8904 (Cambridge, Massachusetts, April 2002).

[j]   Average income or consumption and the distribution of either are also sensitive to the timing of visits of survey teams, particularly in agrarian communities, and the recall period.

[k]   See the Least Developed Countries Report, 2002, ...

[l]   See Sala-i-Martin, op. cit.; and Robert J. Barro, "The UN is dead wrong on poverty and inequality", *Business Week*, 6 May 2002, p. 24. Their poverty estimates are based on GDP. Their method takes into account government expenditure, such as health and education expenditure, that contributes to the living standard of the poor.

[m]   The United Nations has initiated a project on the efficient design and implementation of household surveys in developing and transition countries. See United Nations Statistics Division, "An analysis of operating characteristics of household surveys in developing and transition countries: survey costs, design effects and non-sampling errors" (ESA/STAT/AC.85), 3 September 2002, draft submitted to an Expert Group Meeting, New York, 2-11 October 2002.

er, and shorter-run fluctuations in the growth and poverty relationship do not fit neatly within the long-run relationship. Furthermore, the extent to which growth is good for the poor depends on the definition of income poverty chosen, even when the same data set is used (see box IV.3). Overall, while economic growth tends to benefit the poor, this assertion must be understood relative to the analytical framework (including the time-horizon) and definitions used. These subjects are among the sources of disagreements among policy makers, researchers and civil society about economic policy aimed at poverty reduction.

At the regional level for the period 1990-1999, there was negative correlation between growth and extreme poverty—higher growth was associated with a lower poverty rate—but the responses of extreme poverty to growth varied among the regions (see figure IV.3). For example, each 1 percentage point

---

Box IV.3

GROWTH AND RELATIVE POVERTY

[a] Nationally defined poverty used in figure IV.3 is such an example.

[b] The elasticity of average incomes in the bottom quintile with respect to overall average income is found to be unity, or very close to unity (see David Dollar and Aart Kraay, "Growth *is* good for the poor", Development Research Group, World Bank (March 2000)). It should be noted that this is equivalent to saying that the share of the lowest quintile is uncorrelated with GDP per capita. See Martin Ravallion, "Growth, inequality and poverty: looking beyond averages", *World Development*, vol. 29, No. 11 (November 2001), pp. 1803-1815.

[c] This does not mean that growth raises the income of the poor by the same absolute amount as that by which it raises the income of the average income-earner. The continued inequality of income distribution makes the average gains to the poor smaller than the average gains to the non-poor.

[d] See, for example, T.N. Srinivasan and Jagdish Bhagwati, "Outward-orientation and development: are revisionists right?", September 1999, mimeo; and Steven N. Durlauf, "Manifesto for a growth econometrics", *Journal of Econometrics*, vol. 100, No. 3 (January 2001), pp. 65-69.

Poverty is defined in absolute terms in the Millennium Development Goals. Once poverty is defined in relative terms (as encompassing, first example, the lowest quintile of the income distribution), however, a different growth-poverty relationship emerges, creating multiple but sometimes conflicting visions of the nature of growth's impact on poverty.

The conceptual difference between the absolute and relative definitions of poverty is closely related to the difference between the standard-of-living and minimum resources approaches to defining poverty (see box IV.2). According to the former approach, an individual needs to attain a specific level of consumption and (thus to spend a certain amount of money), no matter where that person resides. This is one reason that levels of absolute poverty are often based on the consumption basket. The latter approach, on the other hand, emphasizes the importance, when identifying poverty, of the community to which the individual belongs. For example, the needs of an individual who lives in a least developed country with respect to participating in the local lifestyle are recognized to be different from the needs of an individual who lives in a developed country. In many instances, relatively poor people are defined either as individuals or households whose incomes (which are taken to represent the opportunities for participation in the community) are at or below a certain percentage of the national average income,[a] or as those who belong to the lowest bracket of income distribution. In order to enjoy a certain level of the local lifestyle, an individual living in a developed country needs to consume more varieties of goods and services in, possibly, larger quantities than an individual in a least developed country.

If the poor are defined as the people in the lowest bracket of a country's income distribution—typically the lowest income quintile (20 per cent) of the size distribution of income— *and* if the growth periods are at least five years long, cross-country regression analysis suggests that the poor benefit from economic growth and suffer from economic decline as much as the average income-earners do;[b] that is to say, when the national average per capita income rises (or falls), the average income of the poorest quintile rises (or falls) by the same proportion.[c]

While the cross-country-regression approach to analysing the growth-poverty relationship has been criticized on technical grounds,[d] similar results have been obtained by a different approach, based on observations of fluctuations in economic growth and income inequality and the correlation between the two. Because countries' income distributions over time have been observed to be more stable than economic fluctua-

increase in per capita income was associated with a 1.2 percentage point decline in extreme poverty in East Asia, including China, but with only a 0.7 percentage point growth, but in a negative direction in South Asia. Europe and Central Asia saw the largest response in poverty to economic growth, but in a negative direction: each 1 percentage point decline in GDP led to a 5.9 percentage point increase in poverty incidence. Such a sharp increase in the poverty rate in response to economic contraction suggests that the collapse of the centrally planned economic system has affected the welfare of the population not only through economic decline, but also through the deterioration of social conditions, because of reductions in social expenditures by Governments.[18] Latin America and the Caribbean and the Middle East and North Africa experienced positive, albeit meagre, growth in per-capita GDP during the 1990s, but

[18] United Nations, *World Economic and Social Survey, 2001* (United Nations publication, Sales No. E.01.II.C.1), chap. VI.

Box IV.3 (continued)

tions over the business cycle, it is empirically impossible to claim that the non-poor alone benefited disproportionally and that the poor did not benefit. If this were the case, the income distribution would have worsened to an extent are not compatible with any historical records.[e]

Through its impressive growth between 1990 and 1999, China reduced absolute poverty significantly, both in the number and in the proportion of the poor. However, the percentage share in the country's total income of the lowest quintile declined from 7 only to 5.9 per cent.[f] Burkina Faso, on the other hand, saw the poverty rate rise from 44.5 per cent in 1994 to 45.3 per cent in 1998 despite strong growth during that period, but the share in total income of the lowest quintile was almost unchanged, increasing from 4.4 to 4.5 per cent.[g] These cases demonstrate that the income shares of the poor change very little, even when the economy shows strong growth, and that different poverty definitions give rise to different perspectives on the impacts of growth on poverty.

Overall, both approaches have shown that growth is distribution-neutral when the poor are defined as the group at the bottom of a country's income distribution. Based on both types of analysis, the share of the lowest quintile in a country's total income is not affected much by economic growth, thus making gains from growth proportional to the existing incomes of the poor and non-poor. For example, if the average income of the richest quintile is 10 times higher than that of the poorest quintile, the absolute income gain to the richest is 10 times higher than the gain to poorest, thus leaving the income distribution unaltered. Thus, a political question is whether or not policy makers and the general public, including non-governmental organizations, should accept such growth as "pro-poor", on the grounds that it benefits everyone, including the poor, inasmuch as the same growth can be labelled "anti-poor", on the basis that it widens the absolute income gap between the poor and the rest of the population. An advantage of defining poverty based on an absolute level is that distributional considerations between the poor and the non-poor are not at issue; as long as the poor escape from one dollar-per-day poverty, or some other agreed poverty level in absolute terms, growth can be called pro-poor.

The choice of the definition of poverty depends on the purpose of the analysis or the policy objective. There is no universally accepted concept of poverty that can be applied to every conceivable situation in every country. Nevertheless, the one dollar-per-day poverty benchmark is useful for evaluating how economic and social development affects extreme poverty in the poorer countries (see box IV.2).

[e] This is the argument employed and calibrated in Danny Quah, "Some simple arithmetic on how income inequality and economic growth matter", London School of Economics, Economics Department (July 2001), and "One third of the world's growth and inequality", London School of Economics, Economics Department (April 2002).

[f] Based on World Bank, *2002 World Development Indicators, CD-ROM* (Washington, D.C., 2002), table 2.8; and "Deininger and Squire data set: a new data set measuring income inequality", available at http://www.worldbank.org/research/growth/dddeisqu.htm.

[g] Based on Hippolyte Fofack, Célestin Monga and Hasan Tuluy, "Household welfare and poverty dynamics in Burkina Faso: empirical evidence from household surveys", mimeo, World Bank, 2001, table 2 and annex 1.

Figure IV.3.
GROWTH AND THE EVOLUTION OF EXTREME POVERTY, 1990-1999

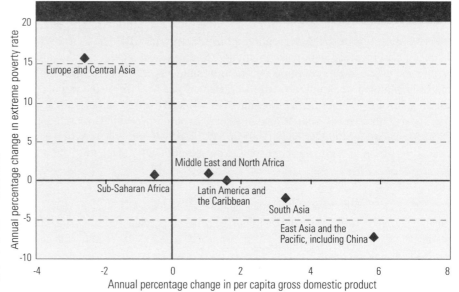

Source: UN/DESA, based on World Bank, *2002 World Development Indicators, CD-ROM* (Washington, D.C., World Bank, 2002); and World Bank, *2003 World Development Indicators* (Washington, D.C., World Bank, 2003), table 1c.

Note: Regional groupings are according to World Bank definitions, which are differerent from those adopted by the *Survey*. For the World Bank grouping, see World Bank, *World Development Report, 2002: Building Institutions for Markets* (Washington, D.C., World Bank, 2002), p. 241.

the incidence of extreme poverty increased slightly. In sub-Saharan Africa, where per capita GDP fell during the same decade, a 1 percentage point decline of per capita GDP was associated with a 0.8 percentage point increase in the proportion of people living in extreme poverty, a figure comparable with the one for South Asia in terms of the response of poverty change to economic growth/contraction.

Degrees of inequality in income distribution and the depth of extreme poverty are two important related factors that affect poverty incidence in relation to economic growth, as far as available statistics at the regional level show. Where the income distribution is highly unequal (as typically indicated by a higher Gini coefficient[19]), the poor receive, with other things being equal, little additional income from economic expansion, making it more difficult for them to escape from poverty. Higher income inequality in Latin America and sub-Saharan Africa (compared with East Asia) is a factor in the slowing down of poverty reduction in those regions.[20] In general, the growth-poverty relationship at the regional level (as well as at the national level) is sensitive to a region's degree of income inequality, which is considered to be a current snapshot of the economic, social, political and cultural processes inherited from the past. While it is beyond the scope of the present *Survey* to analyse the processes that have led to the current income inequalities in various regions, it should be noted that such processes are pervasive and that the way in which policies affect the incidence of poverty depends on the interactions between the processes and the policies chosen.

Where the depth of extreme poverty—typically expressed by the poverty gap ratio[21]—is high, very rapid economic growth is required to lift a large number of people out of poverty. The high degree of extreme poverty in sub-Saharan Africa means that particularly rapid economic growth is required to reduce poverty but weak links between the formal and subsistence sectors in the region

[19] Intuitively speaking, the Gini coefficient indicates the average gain expected by an individual from the option of being someone else with a higher income in a population, divided by average income. For example, if average income is $1,000 a year and the Gini coefficient is 0.6, then the expected gain from being someone else with a higher income is $600, a substantial gain. See Nanak C. Kakwani, *Income Inequality and Poverty: Methods of Estimation and Policy Applications* (New York, Oxford University Press, 1980), chap. 5.

[20] Douglas Smith, "International evidence on how income inequality and credit market imperfections affect private saving rates", *Journal of Development Economics*, vol. 64, No. 1 (February 2001), pp. 103-127, estimates that Gini coefficients of Latin America, sub-Saharan Africa, East Asia and developed countries are 0.472, 0.468, 0.427 and 0.322, respectively, based on a sample of countries.

[21] The poverty gap ratio is defined by the product of the proportion of people who live below the poverty line and the difference between the poverty line and the average income of the population living under the poverty line, expressed as a percentage of the poverty line. If, for example, 50 per cent of the population live below the one-dollar-per-day line and the average income of these people is 40 per cent below the poverty line (that is to say, 60 cent a day), then the ratio is 20 per cent.

impede the channelling into the latter of the gains from growth in the former. On the other hand, low poverty gap ratios in Central and Eastern Europe and Central Asia should make it possible for the region to reduce extreme poverty rapidly, once the countries of this region achieve sustained growth.[22]

LOOKING BEHIND THE REGIONAL AVERAGE

The above analysis, which shows the critical role of growth for poverty reduction, at least in the medium-to-long run, overlooks some important aspects of poverty evolution over time. One is the variation of individual countries' experiences around the average in their region, and the other is the mobility of individuals in and out of poverty, which leads to short-run fluctuations in the incidence of poverty incidence.

Deviation from averages

The above findings were based on regional experiences—the "average" experience of the countries in a region as a whole—and relatively long growth periods. As is often the case in statistical analyses, however, only a few countries fit the average figure, while many deviate from it considerably. Regional averages smooth out these deviations and may hide factors that systematically affect countries' performance.

Data on recent episodes of growth and changes in poverty incidence in 28 developing and transition economies[23], show a negative correlation between growth and poverty evolution, suggesting that growth tends to reduce poverty (see figure IV.4). However, there is wide variation. Many countries succeeded

[22] The same low response of poverty incidence to growth when income inequality is wide or when the depth of extreme poverty is high, is found at the country level. See Anne Epaulard, *Macroeconomic Performance and Poverty Reduction*, IMF Working Paper, No. WO/03/72 (Washington, D.C., April, 2003).

[23] Sample comprises countries for which at least two observations of poverty incidence over time are available.

Figure IV.4.
GROWTH AND THE EVOLUTION OF NATIONALLY DEFINED POVERTY DURING THE 1980s AND 1990s[a]

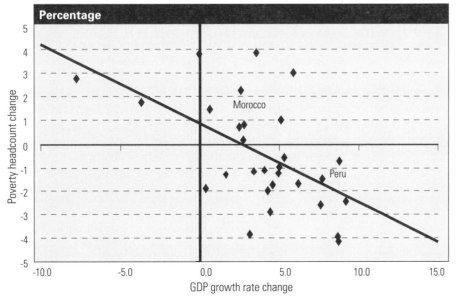

Source: UN/DESA, based on World Bank, *2002 World Development Indicators, CD-ROM* (Washington, D.C., World Bank, 2002).

[a] Nationally defined poverty is different from extreme poverty. The index is the percentage of the population living below the poverty line deemed appropriate for the country by its authorities.

in reducing nationally defined poverty headcounts with economic growth (indicated by the data points in lower right quadrant); but in eight countries, poverty, as measured by their poverty lines, did not fall even though their economies had grown (upper right quadrant), in some cases considerably. Three countries experienced negative growth with increased poverty (upper left quadrant).

At the country level, the evolution of poverty is further influenced by the situation where poverty incidence is being measured for the first time and by the policies that a Government adopts or abandons after that first measurement. This is particularly the case when the Government initiates a major economic reform, such as structural adjustment, liberalization or deregulation. For example, in cases where a country kept poverty (and income inequality) low in a pre-reform period by guaranteeing jobs for everyone, the introduction of market liberalization and greater openness to external trade would eliminate some jobs, at least temporarily, thus increasing poverty if no safety nets were in place. Countries with economies in transition fall into this category (see chap. VIII). On the other hand, in cases where a Government favoured the interests of the rich, where poverty was widespread and where inequality was high in a pre-reform era, market and trade reforms might have income-equalizing effects, benefiting the poor. For example, Peru cut its poverty rate and reduced income inequality during the mid-1990s while implementing reform policies that had been initiated in the mid-1980s.[24] Regional averages may cancel out such differing experiences, hiding the interactions between the initial conditions and the policies undertaken subsequently. While the reform policies helped alleviate poverty in Peru during the mid-1990s, some countries in Latin America and the Caribbean, which were slow to adopt such policies, experienced a rising incidence of poverty, even with positive growth.

The extent of differentials between urban and rural development, or economic dualism (which is often approximated by the relative productivity of the non-agricultural sector as compared with the agricultural sector), also influences the growth-poverty relationship at the country level.[25] Growth of the rural sector—farm yields plus non-farm incomes—matters for poverty reduction:[26] macroeconomic growth without development of the rural sector does not necessarily translate into poverty reduction as effectively as otherwise. Morocco, for example, experienced positive growth with rising poverty during the 1990s, mainly because of the deterioration in rural areas. Droughts in the second half of the decade were a major contributor, but widespread planting of crops that commanded higher prices in markets but were less resistant to drought aggravated the situation.[27] On the other hand, growth in many Asian countries, such as Japan, the Republic of Korea and Taiwan Province of China in the past and China and India at present, has led to significant poverty reduction. Strong productivity increases in agriculture and the transformation of the rural non-farm sector have come about as a result of reforms in land ownership or usage, the introduction of highly productive seeds combined with new technologies, and improvements in physical infrastructure.[28]

Mobility in and out of poverty

At a more fundamental level, averages hide not only countries' different initial conditions and sectoral characteristics, but also the movement of individual

[24] For the income distributions of Peru and other countries in Latin American and the Caribbean, see Barbara Stallings and Wilson Peres, *Growth, Employment, and Equity: The Impact of the Economic Reforms in Latin America and the Caribbean* (Washington, D.C., Brookings Institution/ECLAC, 2000), chap. 5.

[25] François Bourguignon and Christian Morrisson, "Inequality and development: the role of dualism", *Journal of Development Economics*, vol. 57, No. 2 (December 1998), pp. 233-257.

[26] Ibid. and Martin Ravallion and Gaurav Datt, "Why has economic growth been more pro-poor in some states of India than others?", *Journal of Development Economics*, vol. 68, No. 2 (August 2002), pp. 381– 400.

[27] IMF, "Morocco; 2001 Article IV consultation: staff report; public information notice; and statement by the Executive Director for Morocco", Country Report, No. 01/205, 13 November 2001.

[28] *World Economic and Social Survey, 2000 ...*, chap. V.

people or families in and out of poverty over time. Aggregate data collected at the national or regional level are useful for examining macroeconomic growth and poverty incidence and identifying a stylized, or general, relationship between the number and the average income of the poor. Among the poor covered by aggregate time-series data, however, there are some people who escape from poverty, while others become impoverished. This transient (or transitory) poverty has important implications for designing poverty reduction strategies. Even when an economy grows as a result of successful macroeconomic policies, not everyone benefits in the same manner; thus, complementary policies targeted at subnational regions or socio-economic groups are required to help the impoverished (see chap. VIII). Aggregate data are not informative when addressing the issues of transient poverty and relevant coping mechanisms at the household or individual level.

Such movements are illustrated by the experience of a region of Pakistan (not included in figure IV.4). Household surveys were conducted in 1996 and 1999 in rural areas of the North-West Frontier Province (Peshawar district)—a region with limited scope for agriculture-led growth, a low education level and a high infant mortality rate. Despite an average annual growth of 3.6 per cent for GDP and of 1.2 per cent for per capita GDP during the period 1996–1999, the region showed an increased incidence of poverty and the churning of people in and out of poverty.[29] During the period, the average income of the 299 households surveyed had declined by 23 per cent. The poor/non-poor status of three-quarters of the sample had remained unchanged,[30] but 33 households had escaped from poverty, while 46 non-poor families in 1996 had fallen into poverty by 1999. Income reductions were largely caused by job losses or significant drops in farm and non-farm wages (but not in crops harvested) which affected all the households. However, those who were severely constrained in respect of credit access had no means to smooth out consumption, making them impoverished in consumption.[31]

In general, transient poverty is as widespread a phenomenon as chronic poverty[32] and, in several cases, transient poverty is more prevalent than chronic poverty (see table IV.2).[33] An individual's or a household's income at any particular moment of time depends on its human and non-human capital endowments, its past perception of the returns to capital, idiosyncratic shocks (such as death, ill health and accidents) and common shocks (such as economic decline and natural disasters). Seasonal factors—more jobs at harvest time, for example—greatly contribute to income fluctuations within a year as well. The poor and people slightly above the poverty line, who typically have low human and non-human capital endowments, are always exposed to greater risks, not only of substantial income loss but also of hunger and even death, when adverse events affect them. Vulnerability—the risk of being negatively affected by shocks—is an important determinant of movements in and out of poverty.

Income fluctuation does not directly translate into consumption variability, because households or individuals can, to some extent, use coping mechanisms to smooth consumption. In many low-income developing countries that lack publicly managed programmes or market-based insurance schemes, the coping mechanisms are informal. They consist of reciprocal "gift" exchanges within local communities and extended families, self-insurance activities such as saving, asset accumulation and borrowing, and remittances from migrants living

[29] Takashi Kurosaki, "Consumption vulnerability and dynamic poverty in the North-West Frontier Province, Pakistan", mimeo., Hitotsubashi University, Tokyo (July 2002).

[30] Thirty-one households stayed above the poverty line (set at $189 per person per year in 1996) and 189 remained below the line, constituting cases of chronic poverty.

[31] Those impoverished households also stopped sending their girls (but not their boys) to school. Parents thought that girls' education would be expensive relative to the expected private returns from it. See Kurosaki, loc. cit.

[32] Some researchers define chronic poverty as a situation where average consumption over time is below the poverty line. This definition is less stringent than that in which the chronic poor are taken to be those whose consumption level is always below the poverty line. See Lawrence Haddad and Akhter Ahmed, "Chronic and transitory poverty: evidence from Egypt, 1997-1999", *World Development*, vol. 31, No. 1 (January 2003), pp. 71-85.

[33] Bob Baulch and John Hoddinott, "Economic mobility and poverty dynamics in developing countries", *Journal of Development Studies*, vol. 30, No. 6 (August 2000), pp. 1–24.

Table IV.2.
PROPORTION OF HOUSEHOLDS IN CHRONIC AND TRANSITORY POVERTY, VARIOUS COUNTRIES

Country	Study period	Welfare measure	Percentage of households		
			Always poor	Sometimes poor	Never poor
South Africa	1993-1998	Expenditures per capita	22.7	31.5	45.8
Ethiopia	1994-1995	Expenditures per capita	24.8	30.1	45.1
India	1968/1969-1970/1971	Income per capita	33.3	36.7	30.0
India	1975/1976-1983/1984	Income per capita	21.8	65.8	12.4
Côte d'Ivoire	1985-1986	Expenditures per capita	14.5	20.2	65.3
Côte d'Ivoire	1986-1987	Expenditures per capita	13.0	22.9	64.1
Côte d'Ivoire	1987-1988	Expenditures per capita	25.0	22.0	53.0
Zimbabwe	1992/1993-1995/1996	Income per capita	10.6	59.6	29.8
China	1985-1990	Expenditures per capita	6.2	47.8	46.0
Pakistan	1986-1991	Income per adult equivalent	3.0	55.3	41.7
Russian Federation	1992-1993	Income per capita	12.6	30.2	57.2
Chile	1967/1968-1985/1986	Income per capita	54.1	31.5	14.4
Indonesia	1997-1998	Expenditures per capita	8.6	19.8	71.6

Source: Bob Baulch and John Hoddinott, "Economic mobility and poverty dynamics in developing countries", *Journal of Development Studies,* vol. 30, No. 6 (August 2000), table 1.

[34] See chapter VIII of the present *Survey;* and Jonathan Morduch, "Between the state and the market: can informal insurance patch the safety net?", *World Bank Research Observer,* vol. 14, No. 2 (August 1999), pp. 187–207. According to the latter, these mechanisms are more prevalent in rural than in urban areas.

abroad or in another part of the country.[34] Such private mechanisms can help to buffer both common shocks to incomes and shocks that are specific to an individual. These mechanisms do not, however, completely protect people from falling into poverty. If a whole community was hit by a natural disaster, there would be no one who could provide an immediate "gift" exchange, as most assets in the community, such as land, crops, livestock and houses, would have been destroyed. In cases of long illness or the death of a main income-earner within the family, support from the community is lost eventually. Households or individuals who are detached from these mechanisms, and thus constrained in their access to credit, are at higher risk of becoming consumption-poor.

Evolution of poverty in the short run

Movements of people into and out of poverty cause short-run fluctuations in the incidence of poverty at the national or subnational level. Such short-run movements, however, are not captured by macroeconomic variables and household surveys in many developing countries because the former are estimated only once a year and the latter are conducted only once every few years. The lack of data for tracking poverty over short periods makes it difficult to analyse separately the shorter- and longer-run impacts on poverty of economy-wide policies, such as trade liberalization and macroeconomic adjustment.

Yet differences between the short-run and long-run effects of a particular policy are often at the core of controversies about the impact on poverty of macroeconomic policies, for example, between economists and policy makers in international financial institutions on the one hand and local authorities and fieldworkers in developing countries on the other.[35] Analyses by the former group are largely based on macroeconomic indicators and survey data and, because of the frequency of data collection, their time-horizon is usually a year or longer. They assert that growth and the policies that support it are beneficial for the poor in the longer term. The latter group of local authorities and field-workers (including non-governmental organizations) have day-to-day, hands-on experiences with poverty, and their time-horizon can be as short as a day.[36]

The impact of growth or policy changes on the poor within the short time-frame may not be captured by long-term macroeconomic and survey data. For example, consider a monetary contraction that aims at restraining high infla-tion, but also slows economic activity. Stable and low inflation is key for growth and thus for poverty reduction in the long run (see chap. V).[37] However, economic slowdowns may adversely affect the poor disproportionally through a rise in unemployment in the short run. Those who focus on a short time-hori-zon are concerned that the poor are on the edge of survival; to them, the possi-bility that the welfare of the poor will improve in a year or more is of little importance or relevance.

As discussed previously, there is strong evidence that growth is beneficial for the poor on average in the long run, but there is little systematic evidence regarding changes in the welfare status of the poor during short-run fluctua-tions, especially in developing countries. Most of the available evidence is con-fined to anecdotes. To make short-run analyses of poverty evolution that are comparable with longer-run analyses requires quarterly or semi-annual data on macroeconomic variables and poverty surveys conducted at least twice a year. Such data are generally unavailable in many developing countries because of the scarce human and fiscal resources of Governments.

One exception is Indonesia where the Asian financial crisis that erupted in August 1997 and affected the lives of many people in the country invited inten-sified research on economic crises, policy changes and poverty. The country, with the collaboration of the World Bank, tracked short-run changes in pover-ty over the course of the crisis (see figure IV.5). Its Government conducted a number of large-scale (but not necessarily nationally representative) household surveys covering between 10,000 and 65,000 households, starting in 1996.[38] While these different surveys used different sampling methods and poverty lines, researchers estimated a fairly consistent series of poverty rates for the period before and throughout the crisis.

Four findings emerge from a consideration of figure IV.5. First, changes in the level of economic activities have significant impacts on the evolution of poverty even in the short run: the poverty rate had declined steadily while the economy was growing, but the rate almost doubled in the six months after the third quar-ter in 1997, when the crisis hit the country.[39] Second, the response of the pover-ty rate to growth was asymmetric with respect to the boom and recession peri-ods; during 1996 and the first three quarters of 1997, the economy is estimated to have grown by 6 per cent and the poverty rate to have declined from 9.8 to a low of 6.6 per cent, implying that each percentage point of growth had led to a 0.5 percentage point reduction in the poverty rate. After the crisis, however, the economy shrank by 13 per cent in 1998 and the poverty rate increased from a low of 6.6 per cent in the third quarter of 1997 to 17.4 per cent in the fourth quarter of 1998, implying that 1 percentage point of output decline had led to an almost

[35] Such a sharp division oversimplifies a complex and wide spectrum of analytical and policy posi-tions held by those who are concerned with poverty issues. The purpose of such a simple clas-sification is to highlight disagreements in regard to the status of poor people and policy prescrip-tions. See Kanbur, loc. cit., sect. 2.

[36] Ibid., sect. 5.

[37] See, for example, William Easterly and Stanley Fischer, "Inflation and the poor", *Journal of Money, Credit and Banking*, vol. 33, No. 2 (May 2001, part 1), pp. 160-178.

[38] For details, see Asep Suryahadi and others, "The evolution of poverty during the crisis in Indonesia, 1996 to 1999", Social Monitoring and Early Response Unit, Jakarta (September 2000). See also Menno Pradhan and others, "Measurements of poverty in Indonesia: 1996, 1999 and beyond", Social Monitoring and Early Response Unit, Jakarta (n.d.).

[39] A survey conducted during August-October in 1997 suggests that the impacts of the crisis were not yet felt at that time.

Figure IV.5.
SHORT-TERM EVOLUTION OF POVERTY, FIRST QUARTER
1996-THIRD QUARTER 1999, INDONESIA (Percentage)

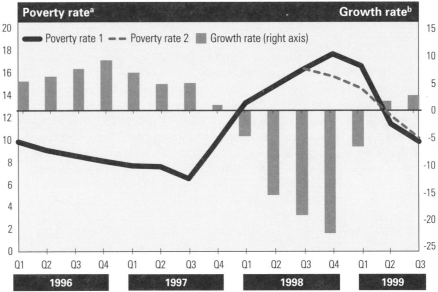

Source: UN/DESA, based on Asep Suryahadi and others, "The evolution of poverty during the crisis in Indonesia, 1996 to 1999", Social Monitoring and Early Response Unit, Jakarta (September 2000); and Statistics Indonesia, "Country paper: Indonesia: quarterly national accounts in Indonesia", paper presented at the OECD/Asian Development Bank/ESCAP Workshop on Quarterly National Accounts, 17-21 June 2002, Bangkok.

[a] Starting from the fourth quarter of 1998, there are two series. Series 1 is based on the surveys conducted by the Social Monitoring and Early Response Unit, Jakarta, and series 2 is based on the surveys conducted by the Central Bureau of Statistics of Indonesia.

[b] Based on changes in seasonally unadjusted quarterly GDP of the same quarter of two consecutive years.

0.8 percentage point increase in poverty, which was 1.6 times larger in absolute terms than the decrease in poverty when the economy had been growing. Thus, the downside risks to the poor were larger than the upside benefits: the poor were exposed to malnutrition and hunger during the downswing.

The third point is that the two different types of surveys show that the poverty rate had begun to decline in the first quarter of 1999, even before macroeconomic conditions improved in the second quarter. One explanation for this decline may be that the poor were not passive, but managed to find ways to secure a minimal consumption level by using some of the coping mechanisms discussed previously. Another explanation may lie in the underestimation of GDP: some economic activities might have become "informal",—possibly, in part, to avoid taxes—with the result that the statistical agencies, which also faced fiscal retrenchment, did not capture these activities in the national accounts after the crisis. The fourth point is that while the poverty rate declined as economic growth resumed in 1999, the rate was still about 1.5 times higher in the third quarter of 1999 than just before the crisis.

The experience of Indonesia highlights some developments that may be applicable to other crisis situations. A negative shock seems to have a larger impact on poverty than a positive one, in absolute terms. The benefits of sustained growth appear to trickle down to the poor slowly, but negative shocks affect them almost instantly. However, the adverse effects of the crisis may not fall disproportionately on the poor. Between 1996 and 1999, the Gini coefficient in Indonesia decreased—from 0.36 to 0.33 (or 0.32 depending on the price deflator used)—indicating that the non-poor had been affected more adversely than the poor, in relative terms. Finally, it seems that the poor have "private mechanisms", including self-help, to cope with negative shocks, at least in the short run. No evidence is available about the extent to which such coping mechanisms protect the poor, but the faster turnaround of the poverty rate than of GDP growth in Indonesia hints at the effectiveness of such mechanisms.

Although there exists a large volume of empirical studies on growth and the evolution of poverty in the long run, short-run analyses of how economic fluctuations affect poverty and to what extent coping mechanisms—public and private—influence the welfare of the poor are still scarce. More such analyses could help fill the void in respect of knowledge about the connections between short-run movements into and out of poverty and the long-run evolution of poverty. They also could help in assessing the immediate versus the long-lasting effects of policies on poverty.

CONCLUDING REMARKS

This chapter has argued that assessing the extent to which growth—which is generally desirable for poverty reduction—affects the incidence of poverty is influenced by the definition of poverty, the social and geographical level of aggregation of poverty, and the time-horizon employed for the assessment. As argued above, improvements in the material dimensions of poverty do not necessarily go hand in hand with improvements in the non-material dimensions of poverty. Even when poverty is defined solely in terms of its material dimensions, economic growth has been found not to affect all social or geographical groups uniformly and, in some cases, the same growth has affected two groups of people contrarily. Unsustainably high growth tends to reduce poverty incidence in the short run, but it eventually ignites high inflation, eroding the welfare of the population, particularly the poor with little stock of wealth. Furthermore, as noted in box IV.3, the choice of poverty line influences the general characterization of growth-poverty linkages: if the poor are defined as the people in the lowest bracket of a country's income distribution, then they benefit from growth as much as the average income-earner does but if, instead, the poor are defined in absolute terms (as in the Millennium Development Goals), such distributional neutrality disappears. In short, a simple statement such as "growth is beneficial for the poor" conveys a powerful message, but it can be misleading if not understood in the specific context of an assessment framework.

The extent to which growth affects the incidence of absolute poverty critically depends on various socio-economic conditions, such as initial distributions of income and physical and human capital, and the economic and political regimes that prevailed at the time of economic growth. In contrast with growth in East Asia, which led to a large decline in the poverty rate, economic growth in Latin America and the Caribbean during the 1990s did not reduce the poverty rate at all. While it is not easy to single out the most important determinants, an income distribution highly skewed against the poor and the large pool of chronic poverty, both rooted in the economic, social, political and cultural history of Latin America and the Caribbean, are factors that explain the weak linkages between growth and poverty reduction. In sub-Saharan Africa, income inequality aside, the presence of a large number of extremely poor people, who do not possess human and non-human capital, and the isolation of the subsistence sector from the formal sector of the economy, make it difficult for the benefits of growth to trickle down to the extreme poor, even when the economy grows.

The following chapters of the Survey examine the effects of policies on the incidence of poverty via their effects on the growth of a particular sector or the growth of an economy as a whole. They will argue that the complexity of the linkage between growth and poverty carries over to the relationship between policies and poverty. The policies to be examined are fiscal and monetary policies, trade policy and two key agricultural reforms, all conducted within the framework of a market-based economy. These policies are not necessarily designed to combat poverty directly, but they can have significant impacts on the incidence of poverty. The complexity of the linkage between policies and poverty stems from the complex reactions of the market to the policies implemented and from the economic, social, political and cultural conditions that underlie the state of poverty and income inequalities. Like the assessment of the relationship between growth and poverty, the determination by policy makers and researchers of the extent to which a policy is good for the poor needs to be undertaken in terms of three dimensions: the definition of poverty, the level of aggregation and the time-horizon employed.

V MACROECONOMIC POLICY AND POVERTY

Links between macroeconomic policies and poverty are complex. In theory, "good" macroeconomic policies are growth-enhancing,[1] and sustained growth reduces poverty in the long run; in practice, however, the extent to which growth affects poverty varies considerably among countries and over time, as was seen in chapter IV. In addition to the effects of growth, macroeconomic policies have their own direct effects on poverty. For this reason, it becomes a challenge to evaluate the overall effects of a particular macroeconomic policy on poverty.

Macroeconomic policy is used to manage aggregate demand in the short run and to bring the economy to a higher-growth trajectory in the long run. By these means, policy makers attempt to enhance the well-being of society as a whole, including the poor. In the short run, fiscal and monetary policies are used to balance aggregate demand and supply (see part one of the present *Survey* for a discussion of current practice). In the long run, structural changes are implemented to influence one or more of the three sources of growth:[2] growth in the factors of production, increased efficiency in the allocation of these factors across economic activities, and innovation that increases efficiency in the use of these factors or leads to new products or new uses for existing products. Trade liberalization, for example, can increase efficiency in the use of a country's resources, by exploiting comparative advantage, and introduces new products and technologies from abroad.[3] Deregulation of the economy and privatization of State-owned enterprises aim at improving allocation and production efficiency based on market mechanisms. However, the effects of macroeconomic policies, especially in the short run, do not always favour the condition of the poor. Therefore, other measures are necessary to protect the poor until favourable macroeconomic conditions are restored.

The present chapter will first analyse the theoretical relationships between macroeconomic policy and poverty in the short and long run. It will then focus on these relationships when changes in macroeconomic policy occur, especially during times of economic crises, when the poor are most vulnerable. The experiences of East Asia and Latin America during the past 10 years will help illustrate some of the possible effects on poverty of sudden changes in macroeconomic policies and conditions. The importance of maintaining stability during times of growth in order to have greater freedom to manoeuvre during times of crises and to be able to protect the socially and economically vulnerable will be examined. The focus will then be placed on the urban poor, since they have been identified as more vulnerable in times of economic crises (especially financial) than the rural poor. It will then be argued that, since macroeconomic policies

1 Stanley Fischer, "The role of macroeconomic factors in growth", *Journal of Monetary Economics*, vol. 32, No. 3 (December 1993), pp. 485-512.

2 T. N. Srinivasan, "Growth and poverty alleviation: lessons from development experience", mimeo, February 2001.

3 Trade and poverty are examined in chap. VI.

**alone are not sufficient to address the problems of the poor, direct comple-
mentary measures are necessary. Examples from the two regions will be
studied. Finally, based on the observations made, policy recommendations
at different levels of actions will be presented.**

MONETARY POLICY AND POVERTY

Monetary policy is utilized to affect aggregate demand, and price and employment levels, through a management of the monetary system that uses any or
all of its main tools, namely, open-market operations, the setting of an official
discount (or other) rate, and transactions in the foreign exchange market. The
degree to which the monetary authorities depend on individual tools and the
combination chosen will vary depending on the economic situation, the set of
objectives and the exchange-rate regime. Each tool and combination of tools
has an effect on prices (including interest rates and exchange rates), wages
and employment. Each of these variables, in turn, has a different effect on
poverty. Therefore, one cannot define one general relationship between monetary policy and poverty. However, one could simplify the analysis by examining the effects of monetary policy on poverty through observing two basic
macroeconomic variables, namely, output and inflation.

Expansionary monetary policy tends to raise both output and inflation in the
short run. This affects the poor in two main ways. First, high and unanticipat-
ed inflation induces an unintended redistribution of income. It can harm the
poor by reducing the real value of wages and transfers (such as pension
incomes and other government-sponsored schemes), but it can benefit the nominal debtor—a typical role assumed by the poor—at the expense of creditors.
Second, and most importantly, the rise in total output can reduce poverty
directly, as the experience of East Asian countries prior to the 1997 crisis
shows (see below). A cyclical expansion creates jobs, the majority of which are
likely to be low-skilled or to have low education requirements.

However, an expansionary monetary policy cannot continue indefinitely. It
decreases unemployment and increases output above the trend capacity in the
short run. On the other hand, low unemployment and high output, relative to
the trend capacity, cause inflation to rise, in response to which the monetary
authorities eventually have to contain inflation by shifting to a contractionary
policy, which will harm the poor, along with other groups, in the short run. If
not contained, inflation would accelerate further, leading to hyperinflation and,
eventually, economic decline. Therefore, although expansionary policies, in
general, may seem more beneficial towards the poor, restraining inflation and
preventing abrupt output fluctuations would be of greater benefit to them in the
long run.[4]

Prolonged high inflation has several effects on poverty. First, as in the short
run, it causes a redistribution of income, whose net effects can be either positive or negative for the poor, depending on the combined effect on their wages,
transfer payments and debt. Second, uncertainty associated with high inflation
discourages physical investment in general, thus raising the marginal and average returns on capital and consequently lowering market-based wages; however, if the average return on capital rises and if the tax authorities capture this,
the tax burden may shift away from labour and towards capital, partially off-

[4]   Christina D. Romer and David H. Romer, *Monetary
policy and the well-being of the poor*, National
Bureau of Economic Research Working Paper
Series, No. 6793 (Cambridge, Massachusetts,
November 1998).

setting the loss in wages. Third, economic uncertainty also discourages the poor from investing in their own human capital (for example, health and education), which is an important means for them to escape from poverty. Finally, high inflation may harm some industrial sectors more than others. For example, it is likely that inflation has adverse impacts on export-oriented sectors in many developing countries, such as agriculture and light manufacturing which are labour-intensive and employ the labour-abundant poor. On the other hand, these export sectors may become more competitive depending on the degree of depreciation of the currency.

Because these factors affect the poor in different directions and with different intensities, the net impact of prolonged high inflation on the poor cannot be determined a priori. To observe the actual effects, researchers have often used the so-called cross-country regression analysis, in which the statistical relationship between prolonged inflation and the incidence of poverty is estimated based on many countries' experiences. In those studies, higher inflation rates have been associated with lower average incomes of the poor.[5] While average inflation and the variability of nominal growth of gross domestic product (GDP) are highly correlated, making it difficult to isolate the effects of inflation on the income of the poor from those exerted by GDP growth, it is apparent that monetary policy—through lower inflation, less volatile growth or both—has contributed to the well-being of the poor. [6]

The strong inflation-aversion of the poor that has been revealed in international polling data substantiates this macrolevel observation:[7] the likelihood of mentioning inflation as a top concern increases as level of income and level of education decrease. Thus, while the rich or highly educated are more informed about the damage that inflation can cause, their physical, financial and human capital work as a hedge against inflation, making it less of a concern for them than for the poor or less well educated. With the least amount of human capital (education) and/or a negligible supply of non-human assets, the poor clearly do not have the means to buffer the shocks associated with inflation, and consequently make it a top concern.

The dilemma of policy makers, who are prone to choose expansionary policies to favour the poor, cannot be resolved within the framework of monetary policy alone. The poor prefer low inflation in the long run, but may accept high inflation in the short run if it is associated with expansionary policy and greater employment opportunities, provided that they have some source of income and have expectations of taking advantage of these new opportunities. However, expansionary policy must be abandoned sooner or later, to prevent inflation from accelerating.

FISCAL POLICY AND POVERTY

The macroeconomic policy that is most closely related to more direct poverty reduction strategies is fiscal policy, since it affects the amount to be spent on social needs. Social expenditures usually comprise expenditures for education, health and nutrition, housing, social security and welfare. Social security has relatively less relevance to poverty reduction since a larger percentage of the beneficiaries are typically at income levels above the poverty line.

[5] Ibid.

[6] William Easterly and Stanley Fischer, "Inflation and the poor", *Journal of Money, Credit and Banking*, vol. 33, No. 2 (May 2001, part 1), pp. 160-178.

[7] Ibid.

The pursuit of the main objectives of fiscal policy, namely, allocation of resources, general stabilization and distribution, has an effect on poverty levels. Two types of analysis can be performed: at the aggregate level and by composition. The impact of changes in fiscal policy could be assessed by examining the impact on economic growth of changes in total expenditure or in the deficit, if these were the only variables that mattered in poverty reduction.[8] An increase of fiscal expenditure or reductions of taxes will tend to increase national income in the short run, when the supply constraint is slack. Such a rise in national income tends to reduce poverty, as discussed above. In the long run, however, continuing fiscal expansion without accompanying increases in tax revenue will lead to structural fiscal deficits—crowding out private investment, accelerating inflation and slowing growth—particularly if the deficits are financed by the monetary authorities. Furthermore, when domestic savings are not large enough to cover domestic investment plus the fiscal deficit (as is often the case in many developing countries), the current-account balance deteriorates, creating the so-called twin deficits—fiscal and external. Tax reductions, without reductions in fiscal expenditure, will lead to the same situation. Thus, persistent fiscal imbalances over the long run may have adverse impacts on the economy as a whole and on poverty, if these deficits accumulate and reach unsustainable debt levels. It should also be noted that, even if the balances are maintained, unproductive fiscal expenditures that do not facilitate the accumulation of capital and consequent productivity growth could lower potential economic growth over the long run.

However, the total impact of fiscal policy on poverty cannot be predicted accurately solely on the basis of total expenditure and revenue or the size of the fiscal deficit. The composition of the entire fiscal package—current and capital spending, the functional distribution of expenditure (for example, on education, health and nutrition, social security and welfare, defence, interest payments etc.) and the types and distribution of financing (taxes, fees and external assistance)—greatly influences the nature and outcome of the policy. When interest payments take a large share of total expenditure, the Government has less money to channel towards other objectives, including poverty reduction. On the revenue side, fees of health or educational services limit the opportunities of the poor to receive these services.[9] The burden of value-added (or consumption) taxes can be disproportionately high for poorer people. On the other hand, social expenditures may have a positive impact on the poor, if they are effectively targeted. In order for there to be funds available for the expansion of social programmes when required, the fiscal situation must be stable during times of growth. In the following sections, issues concerning social expenditures in different countries will be analysed.

In sum, because of the sensitivity of poverty outcomes to the composition of fiscal expenditure and taxes, it is not possible to establish a single general linkage between fiscal policy and poverty. In recognition of the complex relationship between policy and poverty reduction, Governments are agreeing to approach the challenge by means of the greater participation of civil society, partially basing their decision on positive experiences with the participation of, for example, non-governmental organizations during the process of decision-making on fiscal budgets in developing countries. This is reflected in the formulation and adoption of Poverty Reduction Strategy Papers (PRSPs) (See box V.1).

[8] For relationships between economic growth and the size of fiscal expenditures or the size of fiscal deficits, see Fischer, loc. cit.; and Robert J. Barro, *Determinants of Economic Growth: A Cross-Country Empirical Study* (Cambridge, Massachusetts, MIT Press, 1997), chap. 1.

[9] See *World Economic and Social Survey, 2002* (United Nations publication, Sales No. E.02.II.C.1), chaps. VII and VIII.

The international community's increasing awareness that the linkage between economic growth and poverty incidence is not clear-cut, together with the current domestic and international recognition of the need for national ownership of development programmes, has led to efforts to revise the roles of the State and civil society in formulating poverty reduction policies. In respect of the Poverty Reduction Strategy Papers (PRSPs)—the statements of recipient-government objectives, whose preparation is required for all International Monetary Fund (IMF) and World Bank lending to low-income countries—the new consensus is to invite wide, active participation by civil society and the private sector in formulating national public policy—including both macroeconomic and sectoral policies—for the reduction of poverty. The international financial institutions, in turn, have introduced new lending instruments designed to support the implementation of poverty reduction strategies.[a] Bilateral donors have increasingly reorganized their own aid programmes with reference to the national policies and goals set out in the PRSPs.[b] This signifies a fundamental shift, at the domestic and international levels, in the way in which Governments and international organizations formulate international development strategies.

In the PRSPs, it is recognized that macroeconomic stability could help the poor benefit from growth, if accompanied by structural adjustment, adequate social policies (on health, education, employment and social inclusion) and effective governance (including budgetary processes and monitoring systems). The PRSPs have strengthened the reform efforts of developing countries. The use of PRSPs has also expanded reform efforts beyond the social sector, which was the main area targeted by previous adjustment programmes. Ministries of finance are now central figures in coordinating countries' principal policy instruments, linking poverty reduction strategies to medium-term national budget processes for domestic and external resources. In these processes, poverty reduction is considered a goal of all sectors, cutting across most if not all macroeconomic and other policy areas.

The participation of civil society in the formulation of all policies that affect the incidence of poverty, including macroeconomic policy, is an underlying principle of the PRSPs, drawing on previous positive experiences at the national and local levels in some developing countries.

For example, Uganda's effort to devise a participatory national strategy for poverty reduction was a model both for the use of PRSPs by the World Bank and IMF, and for the enhanced Heavily Indebted Poor Countries (HIPC) Initiative. In formulating its Poverty Eradication Action Plan in 1996-1997, the Government sought participation from "central and local governments, the donor community, non-governmental organizations and civil society, and academia", and quickly used the results to reallocate public expenditure towards basic services in 1997.[c] Opportunities for local citizens and non-governmental organizations to participate in policy-making have increased since 1998, when responsibility for providing many services was devolved to local authorities and relevant budget data were presented to the public through the press.[d] Along these lines, when consulted by the Government in 1998, poor urban and rural communities pleaded for greater access to clean water, leading to greater priority for this in Uganda's central budget.[e]

If the PRSP initiative is not to be "ephemeral, a passing fashion in the ever-changing world of international development",[f] Governments, the international community and civil society have to strengthen their capabilities in various areas. These include gathering more accurate information on the poor, examining the conditions and causes of poverty, understanding better the links between poverty incidence and the policies considered in the PRSPs (including fiscal policy in general and allocation of budget funds) and establishing systems for tracking poverty-reducing public spending.[g] Such actions could greatly strengthen the participation of the civil society groups that represent the poor, and thus the ability of the entire development community to reduce poverty.

[a] Notably, the Poverty Reduction and Growth Facility of IMF and the Poverty Reduction Support Credit of the World Bank/International Development Association (IDA).

[b] David Booth, "Introduction and overview", *Development Policy Review*, vol. 21, No. 2 (Special issue on "Are PRSPs making a difference? The African experience") (March 2003), pp. 131-159.

[c] John Mackinnon and Ritva Reinikka, *Lessons from Uganda on Strategies to Fight Poverty*, Policy Research Working Paper, WPS 2440 (Washington, D.C., World Bank, 30 September 2000).

[d] Derick W. Brinkerhoff and Arthur A. Goldsmith, "How citizens participate in macroeconomic policy: international experience and implications for poverty reduction", *World Development*, vol. 31, No. 4 (April 2003), p. 696.

[e] Ibid., p. 690.

[f] David Booth, loc. cit., p. 135.

[g] IMF and International Development Association (IDA), "Tracking of poverty-reducing public spending in heavily indebted poor countries", 27 March 2001 (http://www.imf.org/External/np/hipc/2001/track/track.pdf); and IMF and IDA, "Actions to strengthen the tracking of poverty-reducing public spending in heavily indebted poor countries", 22 March 2002 (http://www.imf.org/External/np/hipc/2002/track/032202.htm).

MACROECONOMIC POLICY IN TIMES OF CRISIS

Shocks to the domestic economy can come in different shapes and sizes. They can be caused either by non-economic factors such as natural disasters, internal political turmoil and wars, or by economic factors like sudden changes in the prices of commodities, domestic banking crises or fiscal crises, which could create an outflow of capital leading to balance-of-payments crises. Additionally, a crisis in one country may be triggered by events in another: a flight of capital may assume regional dimensions, affecting other neighbouring countries and their currencies. Although both non-economic and economic shocks can have important effects on the economy and poverty, focus will be directed towards shocks caused by economic factors, since they are more closely related to economic policy.

Such economic shocks have become more commonplace as economies have become more open and thus more sensitive to changes in the international economy. On the one hand, without liberalization, capital flows would have been smaller and would have provided less support to the development process; on the other hand, liberalization also meant an increase in vulnerability, demanding greater care in both the macroeconomic and sectoral management of the economy in order for it to be able to reap the benefits of liberalization.[10]

Economic crises, which are often associated with sharp increases in poverty, induce Governments and international financial institutions to introduce various measures to reduce economic volatility. Given the importance and severity of the crises in the 1990s, more analysis is required on the extent to which increases in poverty have differed among crisis-affected countries and on why there have been such differences. An important policy question concerns the priority attached to reducing poverty, since measures to protect the poor (increasing social expenditure, for example) may worsen the fiscal balance in the short run. Policy makers have to consider the trade-offs between different policies and measures, for example, social and macroeconomic policies, when prioritizing objectives. Another important issue is whether any increase in poverty during a crisis will turn out to be just transitory or (in part or in its entirety) chronic.

While a review of recent country experiences can give policy makers some hints on the relationship between policy and poverty, more systematic and more comprehensive understanding is required to make the tolls of macroeconomic policy a more effective part of poverty reduction strategies.

Economic crises magnify the effects of changes in growth and short-term macroeconomic policy on poverty. The crises during the 1990s serve as recent case studies of this relationship and confirm the limitations of macroeconomic policy in reducing poverty in times of crises. Experiences on two continents, Asia and Latin America, in countries with different economic structures show both similarities and differences, but at the same time provide some insight into the prevention of future crises and their consequences. The following sections will briefly describe the macroeconomic responses to these crises, analyse the possible effects on poverty, and discuss the supplementary measures that had to be taken in light of the limitations of macroeconomic policies in times of shock.

[10] For a further discussion on vulnerability, refer to the *World Economic and Social Survey, 2001* (United Nations publication, Sales No. E.01.II.C.1), part two.

Macroeconomic policy responses to crises in East Asia and Latin America

Several East Asian countries were directly affected by the financial crisis of 1997-1998. In five of those countries, Indonesia, the Republic of Korea, Malaysia, the Philippines and Thailand, an increase in poverty followed the crisis. All of these economies enjoyed high-sustained growth for most of the 1990s. In 1998, GDP fell 0.5 to 13 per cent. Inflation in these economies rose in 1998, but still within the single-digit range, except for Indonesia where it rose to 58 per cent.[11]

In response to the crisis, macroeconomic policy in these East Asian countries was initially restrictive in order to restore domestic stability; but as it became apparent that the magnitude of the crisis was greater than initially expected, macroeconomic policies became expansionary from the latter half of 1998.[12] In most countries, a general decline in revenues acted as an automatic stabilizer, while social expenditures increased along with the rise in total expenditures during the crisis as the need for emergency programmes grew.[13] As a result, fiscal balances deteriorated by between 2 and 4 per cent of GDP between 1997 and 1998 (see table V.1).

Monetary policy was geared to stabilize the exchange rates of the respective currencies, which quickly lost value as capital fled from the region. Interest rates, especially in the money market, had jumped, particularly during the latter half of 1997 and the first half of 1998, after which rates began to decrease in an attempt to prevent a further decline in economic activity and to support fiscal efforts.

Although the macroeconomic trends of the major economies of Latin America did not tend to converge as neatly as those of the East Asian countries, three shocks during the 1990s shaped to some degree the economic conditions of the region. The Mexican devaluation at the end of 1994 dragged down the

[11] For a more detailed analysis of the macroeconomic effects of the crisis, see, for example, *World Economic and Social Survey, 1998* and *1999* (United Nations publications, Sales Nos. E.98.II.C.1 and E.99.II.C.1, respectively).

[12] There has been much debate on the appropriateness of the policy responses after the East Asian crisis and the role of the international financial institutions. The present section will limit itself to referring to the results of these policies relevant to poverty.

[13] *World Economic and Social Survey, 1999 ...,* box III.2.

Table V.1.
MACROECONOMIC POLICY RESPONSES TO CRISES IN SELECTED COUNTRIES IN ASIA AND LATIN AMERICA

Country and year of reference	Fiscal balance (percentage of GDP)		Interest rate (lending)	
	Previous year	Reference year	Annual rate in the reference year (percentage)	Percentage change from previous year
Indonesia (1998)	-0.7	-2.9	32.1	47
Republic of Korea (1998)	-1.5	-4.2	15.3	29
Malaysia (1998)	2.4	-1.8	10.6	12
Philippines (1998)	0.1	-1.9	16.8	3
Thailand (1998)	-0.3	-2.8	14.4	6
Argentina (1995)	-0.7	-0.6	14.0	146
Brazil (1999)	-10.0	-4.6	49.1	-3
Mexico (1995)	0.0	-0.5	19.3	54

Sources: UN/DESA based on data from IMF, *International Financial Statistics;* and ECLAC, *Economic Survey of Latin America and the Caribbean* (various issues).

Argentine economy in 1995. Brazil had not been directly affected at that time, but the East Asian crisis followed by the Russian crisis of August 1998 put pressure on the Brazilian real, which had remained within a band since the beginning of the Real Plan in 1994 but had to be devalued in 1999. At the turn of the century, Argentina underwent its own crisis, while economic activity in Mexico and Brazil remained anaemic owing to the general global slowdown.

Inflation was rampant in the region during the first part of the 1990s; it surged in 1995 in Mexico, while Argentina managed to control its hyperinflation with the introduction of the Convertibility Plan, pegging the peso to the dollar one to one. The inflation situations in the three economies in the beginning of the new century had seemed to converge, although Brazil's inflation was slowly rising again in 2002. The Mexican peso had fallen in 1995, while the Argentine peso remained pegged until Argentina's abandonment of its Convertibility Plan in 2002, after which it plummeted. The real experienced more fluctuations during this period. Despite different exchange-rate paths, the current-account balances of the three largest economies in the region converged into deficits ranging between 1 and 5 per cent of GDP during the latter half of the 1990s. This meant a reduction in the current-account deficits of Argentina and Mexico compared with those of their pre-crisis period that was brought about by an increase in exports. Brazil's current-account deficit expanded between 1994 and 1999 and stabilized at about 4 per cent of GDP during the post-crisis years.

In general, macroeconomic policy in Latin America during the 1990s was largely conditioned by the swings in the economy. For example, on the fiscal side, since government revenues closely followed the trends in growth, and expenditures tended to follow revenues, Governments tended to spend more in times of growth and to cut down in times of trouble. Given the potential of fiscal policy to positively affect growth, this pro-cyclical tendency became counterproductive.[14]

Similarly, monetary policy in Latin America in general has not been able to smooth the volatile tendencies of the economies of the region. Usually, after a sharp fall in GDP accompanied by a significant outflow of capital, domestic currencies quickly began to lose their value. In an attempt to adjust and to prevent the inflationary effects of the depreciation, monetary authorities were forced to raise interest rates. This, in turn, dampened investment and made indebtedness more expensive in the medium term, with particularly adverse effects on domestic financing. In consequence, this type of monetary policy could only exacerbate the contractionary effect of fiscal policy, at a time when the entire economy was shrinking from the effect of the shock.

In the absence of domestic and external finance, this policy combination may be the only means to return to price stability and eventually regain the path of growth. However, the impact on the economy and society may have long-lasting repercussions.

Of the three Latin American countries discussed here, Mexico had a relatively stable fiscal situation throughout the decade of the 1990s, even during the crisis of 1994-1995. In general, primary expenditures remained fairly stable and fiscal deficits did not experience visible increases during the crisis. At the beginning of the 1990s, Argentina's fiscal situation had been stable but, afflicted by problems in the real domestic economy, the external sector and

[14] Ricardo Martner, "Los estabilizadores fiscales automáticos", *Revista de la CEPAL* (Santiago), No. 70 (April 2000).

provincial finances, it deteriorated during the latter part of the decade until 2002. This accumulation of problems ended up with the abandonment of the Convertibility Plan, and the cutting of expenditures during declines in economic activity. Brazil's public sector had suffered a large fiscal deficit fuelled by the increasing costs of servicing its debt in 1998. This was followed by a quick contraction in 1999, following recommendations of the international financial community to put limits on primary expenditures.[15]

Monetary policy in these three countries was attempting to ease the fall of the value of their currencies, to attract short-term capital and/or to attenuate the imminent sharp rise in prices. Interest rates had been raised to a much higher level in Argentina and Mexico during the crisis of 1995 and in Brazil in 1998 and 1999. The first two lowered their rates the following year, while Brazil was more hesitant in easing its monetary policy, given that the real value of its currency had dropped 36 per cent in 1999.

Comparing policy responses

While only one major economic shock, that of 1997-1998,[16] affected the East Asian region, Latin America and the Caribbean experienced the Tequila crisis at the end of 1994, the repercussions of the Asian and Russian crises in the 1990s, the devaluation of the Brazilian real in 1999 and the series of Argentine crises. This greater vulnerability of Latin America and the Caribbean also translated into the greater volatility of its economies during this period, not allowing much time or space for recovery. In addition to this constant short-term volatility, domestic savings in Latin America during the 1990s remained practically stagnant, partly owing to the lower savings of the public sector.[17] Furthermore, all five East Asian countries discussed here ended up with current-account surpluses, while each of the major Latin American countries still had to finance a deficit in its current account after the crises.[18]

Given these differences in the need for capital flows and degree of volatility, the macroeconomic policy responses varied among regions. As seen above, the Asian countries were able to pursue a fiscal policy that would help prevent a further fall in growth. Similarly, on the monetary side, interest rates were lowered to help reactivate the economy, except in Indonesia where inflationary pressure was much greater. In the case of Latin America, lack of financing obliged Governments to tighten their belts, putting off reactivation policies. Monetary authorities in Latin America were required to adopt contractionary policies and fiscal expansion was limited (see table V.1).

This delay in regaining the growth path had repercussions on poverty. Moreover, since the specific crises mentioned affected primarily urban activities, the urban poor were the most afflicted.

The channels of transmission to the poor will vary, depending on the policy responses taken and the effects on the economic sectors. Two of the most relevant variables for the poor are changes in wages and unemployment. The relative degree of adjustment of these variables will depend on inflation, which in turn is affected by the macroeconomic policies. For example, in Argentina, while the Convertibility Plan was still in effect, fiscal deficits had been kept under 2 per cent of GDP while interest rates were higher than in pre-crisis years. Thus, inflation was under control and real average wages (although fluc-

[15] Total expenditures without including debt-servicing.

[16] All five East Asian countries were growing at high sustained rates before the crisis. The Philippines was growing at a lower rate, but also experienced the smallest fall in growth. Although the shock in terms of the magnitude of the fall in growth in East Asia was larger than in the major Latin America countries, recovery came relatively quickly to the region.

[17] Economic Commission for Latin America and the Caribbean (ECLAC), *Una Década de Luces y Sombras: América Latina y el Caribe en los Años Noventa*, Alfaomega and ECLAC (Bogotá and Santiago, 2001), p. 89.

[18] Except for the 2002 Argentine crisis, which ended up with a current-account surplus owing to a contraction of its imports.

tuating) were maintained, but they plunged when Argentina abandoned the Plan and let the peso float freely (in January 2002). Hence, during the period of the Convertibility Plan, the adjustment was made mostly via unemployment, which remained consistently high after the initial shock in 1995. In 2002, unemployment also increased greatly but at a slower rate than after the crisis of the mid-1990s. During the Tequila crisis and at the end of the Brazilian Real Plan, the devaluation and consequent inflation also saw wages in Mexico and Brazil fall behind the rapid growth of prices. However, wages in Mexico recovered and unemployment was decreased under an expansionary macroeconomic policy, whereas wages in Brazil kept falling and unemployment remained high under strict contractionary measures.

In the aftermath of the Asian crisis, all five countries had experienced higher unemployment for a few years before it returned to pre-crisis levels, except for Indonesia and the Philippines where unemployment continued to rise. In these two countries, monetary policy during the post-crisis years was more restrictive than in the other countries (that is to say, official and lending interest rates remained at higher levels). However, all five countries pursued expansionary fiscal policies during the years immediately after the crisis. Of the main sectors with employment data, manufacturing had the biggest fall in employment in absolute terms in these countries during the crisis years. In contrast, employment in agriculture rose, despite the fall in output in the sector in 1998, except in Thailand where employment in all sectors fell.[19] Real average wages took a dive especially in Indonesia and the Republic of Korea, which also experienced large depreciation of their currencies and inflation.

POVERTY AFTER THE CRISES

It has been argued that the single most important cause of short-term increases in urban poverty (with possible medium- and long-term repercussions) is economic shocks that are typically produced by external or domestic imbalances and the policy responses to those imbalances.[20] Cities, given the nature of the activities, investments and industries that are usually concentrated in them are consequently more susceptible to certain types of shocks than other areas. Falls in investments are a first reaction to crises and as a result, unemployment, especially in the construction and manufacturing sectors, rises. Terms-of-trade shocks could affect rural or urban areas, depending on the location of the good's production. Whatever the shock, the first victims are usually low-skilled workers, who are also at the bottom of the income ladder and the most needy.

Although evidence is neither complete nor conclusive, in general, the rural sectors in East Asia seem to have been more resistant to the effects of the crisis in 1997 owing to their reliance on the agricultural sector which was largely unaffected by the crisis. In Latin America (see below), the majority of the population and the poor are concentrated in the urban areas. In addition, the agricultural sector in Latin America, similar to that of most of the East Asian countries, was much more resistant to the shocks than the urban-based sectors, and continued to grow throughout the crisis periods.[21] Therefore, the scope of the present discussion is limited to the effect of changes in the macroeconomic environment on the urban areas.[22]

[19] Since mining does not employ large amounts of labour, its decrease was not significant in terms of the economically active population or the increase of poverty. See Asian Development Bank, "Key indicators of developing Asian and Pacific countries" (http://www.adb.org).

[20] For further discussion of this argument, see, for example, Camilo Arriagada, *Pobreza en América Latina: Nuevos Escenarios y Desafíos de Políticas Para El Hábitat Urbano*, Serie Medio Ambiente y Desarrollo, No. 27 (Santiago, ECLAC, October 2000); and Nora Lustig, "Crises and the poor: socially responsible macroeconomics", presidential address given at the Fourth Annual Meeting of the Latin American and Caribbean Economic Association, Santiago, 22 October 1999.

[21] Based on data from ECLAC, *Estudio Económico de América Latina y el Caribe* (Santiago, various issues).

[22] Another factor, rapid demographic growth, affects the situation of urban poverty in the medium and long term in an important way. At the present growth rate, the urban population will soon surpass the rural population (*World Urbanization Prospects: The 2001 Revision* (United Nations publication, Sales No. E.02.XIII.16). Studies have also shown that if urban poverty continues its present rate of growth, it will surpass its rural counterpart. (Martin Ravallion, "On the urbanization of poverty," *Journal of Development Economics*, vol. 68 (2002), pp. 435-442; see also chap. VII of the present *Survey* for a discussion on rural poverty). Thus, urban poverty may become a problem if the appropriate policies are not implemented.

Disaggregated data on urban poverty are scarce, as they are not collected with much frequency, and pose problems of coverage and measurement. However, at least a partial description of urban poverty after the crises can be made. The highest proportions of urban population among the five East Asian countries discussed in this chapter are found in Malaysia, the Philippines and the Republic of Korea, where they are equivalent to between 57 and 82 per cent of the population.[23] In Indonesia, 42 per cent of the population live in urban areas, while in Thailand only one fifth do. As table V.2 shows, it was in Indonesia and the Republic of Korea that urban-dwellers were hardest hit by the crisis, with urban poverty rates doubling and almost tripling, respectively, during the crisis. About one fifth of all Indonesians were living in poverty, out of which one third lived in the urban areas. Urban poverty in the Philippines increased after the crisis to 25 per cent in 2000, eroding the progress made during the pre-crisis years (when poverty had been reduced from 28 to 21.5 per cent of the urban population between 1994 and 1997). Figures for Thailand before the crisis show that only about 10 per cent of urban-dwellers had lived under the poverty line. Although poverty in Thailand did increase during the crisis, most of this increase was concentrated in the rural areas, especially the north-eastern region.[24]

All three selected countries from Latin America suffered increases in urban poverty immediately after the economic shocks, reversing the progress made in

[23] Data from World Bank, *World Development Indicators* (Washington, D.C., various issues).

[24] For more details on the social impacts of the crisis, see for example, Michelle Gragnolati, "The social impact of financial crisis in East Asia: evidence from Philippines, Indonesia and Thailand", World Bank, East Asia Environment and Social Development Unit, EASES Discussion Paper Series, June 2001.

Table V.2.
EFFECTS OF ECONOMIC CRISES IN SELECTED COUNTRIES IN ASIA AND LATIN AMERICA

Country and year of reference	Macroeconomic indicators annual rate (percentage)				Other indicators					
	GDP per capita	Inflation	Exchange rate[a]	Current-account balance change[b]	Unemployment		Real Wages[c]	Urban poverty[d]		Most affected sectors[e]
					Rate	Percentage change	Percentage change	Rate	Percentage change	
Indonesia (1998)	-14.4	57.6	-70.9	6.0	5.5	36.2	-41.0	19.5	101.0	C, F
Republic of Korea (1998)	-7.4	7.5	-32.1	14.4	6.8	161.5	-9.3	19.2	180.0	C, T
Malaysia (1998)	-9.5	5.3	-28.3	19.1	3.2	41.7	-1.1	..	..	C, M
Philippines (1998)	-2.7	9.7	-27.9	7.7	9.6	21.5	-2.0	25.0	16.3	C, F
Thailand (1998)	-11.4	8.1	-24.2	14.7	3.4	277.8	-7.4	..	small increase	C, M
Argentina (1995)	-4.1	3.4	-0.1	2.3	17.5	52.2	-1.1	17.8	34.8	C, M
Brazil (1999)	-0.3	8.9	-33.6	-0.5	7.6	0.0	-4.4	26.4	7.5	M, S
Mexico (1995)	-7.8	35.0	-47.4	6.5	6.2	67.6	-13.0	37.5	29.3	C, S

Source: UN/DESA, based on data from Asian Development Bank, World Bank, ECLAC and other official sources.

[a] Percentage change in value of domestic currency per United States dollar. Negative sign denotes depreciation of the currency; positive numbers, appreciation of the currency.

[b] Change in percentage points of GDP.

[c] Data for Asian countries from Gordon Betcherman and Rizwanul Islam, eds, *East Asian Labor Markets and the Economic Crisis: Impacts, Responses and Lessons*, (Washington, D.C., and Geneva, World Bank and International Labour Office, 2001), p. 14.

[d] Percentage of urban population living under the national poverty line, pre- and post-crisis years of reference varying depending on availability of data.

[e] Sectors that had experienced the greatest fall in growth: C: construction; F: finance; M: manufacturing; S: services; T: trade.

terms of poverty reduction before the crises occurred, as was the case in East Asia. The majority of the population in these countries (75-88 per cent), as in most Latin American countries, live in urban areas, as do about 60-75 per cent of the total poor population.[25] Argentina and Mexico had managed to reduce urban poverty before 1994, especially the former, from almost 19 per cent of the total population in 1990 to a little over 11 per cent by 1994. After a sharp increase in urban poverty in Mexico in 1996, the level fell close to the pre-crisis level. However, the urban poverty level (29 per cent of the total population) remains high in Mexico. Argentina's urban poverty problem continued to worsen during the second half of the 1990s and into the new decade, along with the macroeconomic downturn. In the Greater Buenos Aires area alone, the population below the nationally established poverty line increased from about 30 to 50 per cent between October 2000 and May 2002.[26] The rate of poverty in urban areas of Brazil decreased from 36 to 24 per cent between 1990 and 1996[27], but this reduction was reversed during the crisis of 1999 when the poverty rate rose to over 26 per cent.

DIRECT MEASURES TO ADDRESS URBAN POVERTY

The degrees of freedom in the macroeconomic policy arena that authorities may earn during times of growth affect the availability of resources when they are most required to attend to social needs during times of crisis. The pre-crisis accumulation of surpluses in the East Asian countries allowed them to undertake fiscal expansion in times of crisis and create measures to protect the needy, since such measures had not existed before the crisis.[28] The Latin American examples illustrate how greater fiscal constraints even before the crisis and the unmet needs of the large number of the chronic poor limited the extension of existing social protection programmes when the crisis occurred.

In general, Governments in Latin America increase the amount directed towards social expenditures in times of growth. During the times of contraction and slower growth during the 1990s, many countries in the region found it difficult to protect the budgeted social expenditures. The degree of the adjustment differed among countries but, in general, its pro-cyclical pattern corresponded to the pattern of the Governments' total expenditures. Although attempts were made to protect funds budgeted towards social objectives, this could not always be achieved in the presence of financial constraints. Total expenditures are sensitive to the changes in revenues which, at the same time, are conditioned by the growth of the economy. As markets have become more open to foreign capital, fluctuations in the economy occur more often and more abruptly, making fiscal expenditures also volatile and thus hard to manage.[29]

Thus, the fiscal situation may affect the number and size of social protection schemes. There are two broad types of schemes which can be categorized by their objectives: those focused on assisting the affected people in generating income or compensating for its loss and those aimed at preserving human or physical capital and/or recuperating any such capital that was lost. The former include programmes such as workfare, unemployment insurance systems, severance payments and microcredit assistance. The latter includes programmes in education, health, nutrition and housing, sometimes referred to as livelihood protection.[30] Although the social service in the areas in the latter category could

[25] World Bank, *World Development Indicators*, …

[26] *World Economic Situation and Prospects 2003* (United Nations publication, Sales No. E.03.II.C.2), box III.1, entitled "Poverty in Argentina today".

[27] ECLAC, *Social Panorama of Latin America, 2000-2001* (United Nations publication, Sales No. E.01.II.G.141).

[28] Economic and Social Commission for Asia and the Pacific (ESCAP), *Protecting Marginalized Groups during Economic Downturns: Lessons from the Asian Experience* (United Nations publication, Sales No. E.03.II.F.2).

[29] For a more detailed elaboration of this argument, refer to ECLAC, *Social Panorama of Latin America, 2000-2001* …; and ECLAC, *The Fiscal Covenant: Strengths, Weaknesses, Challenges* (United Nations publication, Sales No. E.98.II.G.5), pp.125-129

[30] In public financing terms, both types of programmes are budgeted under social expenditures of the government. The income-related programmes are usually part of the social security expenditures, while livelihood protection pertains to the rest of the budget.

also be regarded as constituting monetary assistance, similar to that in the first group of programmes, the focus is nevertheless on investing in human capital and preventing permanent damage to it. Housing is physical capital, but at the same time it helps preserve the quality of human capital and the livelihood of people. Governments now see housing not merely as a spatial or physical issue, but as an integral part of efforts to reduce poverty and social isolation, as will be explained below. Since urban poverty presents multidimensional (income and non-income) challenges and each country faces specific problems and constraints, Governments have applied different measures according to their circumstances. These two types of programmes should complement each other, especially when the income generated by the poor alone is not sufficient to compensate for the human capital lost during a crisis or to provide access to services (see table V.3, which categories policies applied after crises).

Indonesia and the Republic of Korea experienced a much higher increase in the incidence of urban poverty than the Latin America countries (see table V.2). However, on average, poverty rates in Latin America have been higher than in East Asia. Much progress has been made in poverty reduction in East Asia during the sustained high-growth period before the crisis. This means that there was a greater surge in the number of people who became poor after the East Asian crisis. In addition, most of these "new poor" had been employed in the formal sector before they lost their jobs. Therefore, income-generating programmes were executed in the region to help these new poor return to their previous situations. In contrast, the proportion of the poor had been higher in Latin America before the crisis years, although progress was also made in poverty reduction in those years.[31] However, much of the poverty in Latin America is structural or chronic in nature, and existed even in times of growth. Hence, a variety of programmes have been in place in the region to attend to both income and non-income types of needs.

Several "income-type" programmes were implemented in South-East Asia to assist the population affected by the crisis of 1997.[32] The programmes included proactive measures, that is to say, measures aimed at generating

[31] ECLAC, *Social Panorama of Latin America, 2000-2001 ...*

[32] ESCAP, *Protecting Marginalized Groups during Economic Downturns ...*

Table V.3.
SOCIAL POLICY RESPONSES TO ECONOMIC CRISES

Types of policies	
Income generation/compensation	Livelihood protection
Active	Human capital
Workfare programmes Training programmes Micro credit programmes	Health provision Nutrition programmes Educational programmes
Passive	Physical capital
Unemployment insurance Severance payment Subsidies	Housing programmes

Source: UN/DESA.

income and creating employment, such as public works programmes, micro-credit and small and medium-sized enterprise (SME) credit, and "passive" programmes such as unemployment insurance schemes. In general, these measures partially achieved their goal of alleviating the loss of income of the needy directly affected by the regional financial crisis. However, they all encountered problems of coverage and efficiency. Many of these programmes had to be created and implemented after the crisis began, since many of them had not existed or had been discontinued while the region was growing rapidly and did not have an urgent need for them. In addition, reliance on existing close-knit and strong family relations and support, that is to say, "social capital", often took the place of government protection, especially during good times, in the five East Asian countries discussed in this chapter. Thus, many of these programmes were ad hoc in nature and lacked the institutionalization and planning necessary to confront this sudden surge in poverty.

Public works programmes implemented in Indonesia and Thailand generated jobs and expanded necessary infrastructure at the same time. However, given the nature of the jobs offered, namely, heavy construction work, women and the elderly were not always able to participate in such activities. In addition, most of these programmes were located in the rural areas, and did not attract those who had lost their jobs in the formal sector in the urban areas. Indonesians found that the duration of such programmes was too short and left many people still jobless and in need. The arguments in favour of these programmes emphasized their easy execution, the good response from workers with low levels of education and the rise in income while the work lasted. In the Republic of Korea, the Government combined public works and job training with cash and in-kind transfers of food, clothing, housing, education and health care, for those eligible for its Livelihood Protection Programme.[33] In this way, the Programme served the dual purpose of providing income-generating capacity, and offering assistance in protecting human capital as needed.

Microcredit programmes executed in Indonesia and Thailand benefited, in particular, women with low education levels.[34] Through this credit, beneficiaries were able to finance income-generating activities with short gestation periods. However, like the public works programme, the microcredit failed to reach those most directly affected by the financial crisis—the unemployed in the formal urban sector. One of the reasons for this was the requirement of creating groups in order to receive credit. The urban unemployed were not able to form these groups in a short period of time. Another shortcoming of the programme was that credit was used by the recipients to finance consumption rather than productive investment, reflecting their difficulties in meeting basic requirements.

The unemployment insurance schemes in the Republic of Korea managed to give just enough relief to the beneficiaries in the formal sector to cover their basic needs[35] but, as with most insurance schemes, they failed to cover the informal sector. In the other countries, unemployment insurance was not developed at the time of the crisis.

An important problem with the SME credit programme applied in the Republic of Korea was that the SMEs most afflicted by the crisis received the least amount of assistance, while those in better financial standing were approved for larger loans. Because standard credit criteria were used to select the beneficiaries,[36] the most vulnerable had the least access.

[33] World Bank, International Monetary Fund (IMF), Asian Development Bank and Inter-American Development Bank (IDB), "Social safety nets in response to crisis: lessons and guidelines from Asia and Latin America," submitted to the Asia-Pacific Economic Cooperation (APEC) Finance Ministers, February 2001, pp. 13-14.

[34] ESCAP, Protecting Marginalized Groups during Economic Downturns ..., pp. 44-45.

[35] Ibid., p. 52.

[36] Ibid., p. 59.

Social protection schemes of the income-generating type have also been executed in Latin America. As in East Asia, targeting is a major challenge in the region, but for a different reason. Unlike the South-East Asian new poor, many of the poor in Latin America were not part of the formal sector even before the crises. Therefore, these programmes, which are closely related to the formal sector, often failed to reach them. Indonesia and the Philippines have relatively small informal sectors, accounting for about a fifth of total employment.[37] Data for Thailand vary but indicate that the informal sector in the cities is small, accounting for less than one tenth of total employment. In contrast, the informal sector in cities of Argentina, Brazil and Mexico accounts for from 45 per cent to over half of total urban employment.

Some Governments in Latin America and the Caribbean have thus undertaken various programmes that target workers in the informal sector and address long-term structural problems.[38] Examples of long-term solutions for unskilled poor workers are training programmes such as the Retraining Programme on Employment and Wages (Programa de Becas de Capacitación para los Desempleados (Probecat)) in Mexico, which has trained nearly half a million urban workers per year since the late 1980s. However, each training programme, owing to its brevity, does not seem to have provided the required long-term skills. In Brazil, the Government is implementing an innovative professional training programme called the National Worker Qualification Plan (Programa Nacional de Qualificação do Trabalhador (PLANFOR), which is not linked to the formal sector. With the participation of local government and nongovernmental organizations, the programme aims to target the poor who are mostly engaged in the informal sector.[39]

Unemployment insurance programmes are rarer in Latin America, although severance payments are implemented. However, the high level of informality of the labour market limits the coverage of such programmes, especially among the poor. A case in point is Brazil's unemployment insurance programme, funded by earmarked contributions from the employers, which benefits mostly the unemployed at higher-income levels.[40]

The credit programmes in Brazil try to combine two objectives: to support small enterprises, and also to generate employment for the poor through these enterprises, which are administered and staffed by the poor. The same fund that has been reserved for the unemployment insurance schemes, the Workers' Assistance Fund (Fundo de Amparo ao Trabalhador (FAT)), established in 1990, supports these employment-generation programmes.[41]

Standards of living are also affected during times of crisis, and their decline may have long-term effects. A decrease in funding for livelihood protection can make access to basic services more difficult. Livelihood protection programmes in education, health, nutrition and housing, like income-related social protection schemes, have experienced coverage problems. Many of these are targeted at the entire population and miss the really needy. Thus, often the better-off benefit more from these programmes since they have more direct access to them. This can be a problem in times of crisis, when deterioration in human capital may cause permanent damage to the livelihood of the poor. For example, a decision to drop out of school in order to start working early because of loss of income in the household may have lasting repercussions in the future for the individual and his/her future household. Newly poor tenants may be

[37] International Labour Organization (ILO), *Key Indicators of the Labour Market, 2001-2002* (Geneva, 2002).

[38] There are also work programmes that target workers in the formal sector. For example, "workfare" programmes, such as Trabajar in Argentina, offered construction jobs for public infrastructure at wages set not higher than 90 per cent of the market rate in order to attract only the needy and to encourage a return to the market when the demand recovered. The advantage of this type of programme is the ability to expand quickly in times of crisis, target poor areas and attract the poor. However, the cost assumed by the Government could be high. See Norman Hicks and Quentin Wodon, "Social protection for the poor in Latin America", *Revista de la CEPAL*, No. 73 (April 2001); and Jyotsna Jalan and Martin Ravallion, *Income Gains to the Poor from Workfare: Estimates for Argentina's Trabajar program*, World Bank Policy Research Working Paper, No. 2149 (Washington, D.C., July 1999).

[39] For a review of poverty reduction policies in Brazil, see World Bank, *Attacking Brazil's Poverty: A Poverty Report with a Focus on Urban Poverty Reduction Policies*, vols. 1 and 2, Report No. 20475-BR (Washington, D.C., World Bank, 31 March 2001).

[40] Ibid., pp. 78-79.

[41] Ibid., p. 39.

forced to leave their dwellings and live in more precarious conditions. In the medium to long term, social expenditures can create positive externalities that may permeate other sectors of society. However, a regressive or poorly targeted programme would not be able to address the post-crisis needs of the lower deciles of the population.

The recent experience of Mexico in education and health programmes is illustrative of some of these problems of appropriately reaching the poor. Studies have shown that public education expenditures in Mexico have favoured the better-off and are highly concentrated in the urban areas, although this distribution became less skewed during the period 1994-2000. Expenditures per student at higher levels of education were disproportionately higher than expenditures at the primary level. In addition, the higher the levels of education, the more regressive the expenditures. Only at the primary level was it found that the poorest 40 per cent of the households were receiving more than 40 per cent of total public expenditures. Similarly, lower-income deciles have little access to health services, since they do not have medical insurance. Under reform programmes, the Government is attempting to increase access by offering medical insurance to workers outside the formal sector.[42]

Strategies with multiple objectives, that is to say, incentives to encourage the poor to try to protect or build various aspects of their "human capital" simultaneously, have also faced targeting problems. For example, food subsidies have been implemented to encourage school attendance and health treatment. However, lack of access to education and health facilities still impedes the poor's participation despite the incentives. Conditional cash transfers are instruments with similar problems in respect of targeting and reaching the appropriate groups.

Housing problems are probably the most visible result of urban poverty. Insufficient income and lack of access to credit force the poor to illegally claim land and build their living quarters with whatever means they have available. These large slums, well known in cities of Brazil (favelas) and Mexico (colonias populares), not only pose urban policy problems to the authorities, but can also perpetuate the precarious conditions of the poor living in them. Since land is claimed haphazardly, appropriate infrastructure is not in place, creating unhealthy, unsanitary, crowded and even dangerous conditions (such as steep hillsides vulnerable to landslides) for the inhabitants. In addition, such living quarters create physical and social isolation from the rest of the urban area and community. The mere provision of housing does not reduce urban poverty although it does improve living conditions.

In Brazil, several different approaches have been taken to address the housing problem of the urban poor.[43] One approach is offering credit to either households or communities. The credit programmmes for households target groups with different income levels under different conditions. Programmes covering communities include many non-poor households, but some municipalities are not eligible for credit at all owing to their low creditworthiness. Thus, the truly needy communities still remain without access to credit, while some non-poor households in eligible communities receive benefits.

A second type of programme is geared to the general improvement of the conditions of slums. These programmes provide the infrastructure necessary for basic services to be received and also provide support and advice in order

42   Ana Corbacho and Gerd Schwartz, *Mexico: Experiences with Pro-Poor Expenditure Policies,* IMF Working Paper WP/02/12 (Washington, D.C., January 2002).

43   Further analysis of these programmes can be found in World Bank, *Attacking Brazil's Poverty* ..., vol. 2.

to enhance the livelihoods of the dwellers in the favelas. One multisector favela improvement project in Rio de Janeiro has the objective of enabling the dwellers to integrate socially and physically with the rest of the neighbourhoods of the city covering all medium-sized settlements. The Favela Bairro is an ambitious project, which includes the construction of infrastructure, schools, training centres, commercial establishments, sports facilities, provision of basic services etc. Although this project reflects a new type of approach to the housing problem of the poor by attempting to improve not only their living conditions but also their social integration, the complexity in respect of achieving these objectives has caused the project to fall short of its objectives.[44]

A third means of addressing the housing problem of the poor in Brazilian cities is to reform land regulations by either legalizing illegally claimed land or easing up on land-use regulation.[45] According to the World Bank, strict land-use regulations in Brazil's urban areas promote the growth of informal neighbourhoods, since the poor cannot meet the requirements and conditions for using legal land.[46]

In sum, programmes for both income-generation and the protection of poor people's livelihoods have encountered problems in reaching their target population, particularly in cases where the informal section is large. Many of the problems arise from the lack of access to formal institutions. While many of the newly poor can be aided through programmes related to the formal sector, the chronic poor remain neglected and are more difficult to mobilize. Programmes that target workers in the informal sector or long-term structural problems are required to address chronic poverty. Such programmes provide a "safety net" for the poor in times of crisis.

POLICY IMPLICATIONS AND RECOMMENDATIONS

As can be seen, economic shocks can be very detrimental to the urban poor and recovery can be slow and costly. Therefore, the best macroeconomic policy is one that can soften or prevent these shocks. In times of crisis, the immediate and primary goal of economic policy is macroeconomic stabilization, and the direct results may or may not coincide with a reduction in poverty. Furthermore, financial constraints can also limit the space for manoeuvre for fiscal policy and determine the course of the subset of policies at the social level. Hence, measures to prevent crises at the macrolevel can and should be taken during times of growth, when constraints are fewer and space for manoeuvre is more ample.

The principle motivation behind taking preventive measures is to avoid excesses during both good and bad times by "saving for a rainy day". There has been greater consensus in this respect, especially after the experiences during the crises of the 1990s. However, it is also recognized that one set of measures is not sufficient to prevent crises and that policies must adjust to the specific economic situation. Applying sound macroeconomic policies is a necessary but not a sufficient condition for preventing crises. For example, regulation and supervision of the domestic banking system and appropriate capital controls can complement the macroeconomic policies in their efforts directed towards, crisis prevention.[47]

[44] Elizabeth Riley and others, "Favela Bairro and a new generation of housing programmes for the urban poor", *Geoforum*, No. 32 (2001), pp. 521-531.

[45] Hernando de Soto would also argue, as he has in *The Mystery of Capital: Why Capitalism Triumphs in the West and Fails Everywhere Else* (New York, Basic Books, 2000), that the poor not only need property rights but also the access to the market mechanisms that would allow them to increase the value of their acquired assets.

[46] World Bank, *Attacking Brazil's Poverty ...*

[47] For a discussion on financial vulnerability in a globalizing world, see chap. IV, entitled *"Financial vulnerability in a globalizing world"*, *World Economic and Social Survey, 2001* (United Nations publication, Sales No. E.01.II.C.I).

48 For a discussion on such policies, see J. A. Ocampo, *Developing Countries' Anti-cyclical Policies in a Globalized World*, Serie Informes y Estudios Especiales, No. 4 (United Nations publication, Sales No. E.00.II.G.115).

49 Some studies have calculated the cost of crises in terms of an increase in urban poverty. For some recent examples and further discussion on the social impact of economic crises, see Nora Lustig, loc. cit.

50 World Bank, IMF, Asian Development Bank and IDB, "Social safety nets in response to crisis ...

Ideally, such preventive measures would allow Governments to continuously pursue policies that resulted in relatively smooth and uninterrupted growth. In other words, counter-cyclical policies in periods of growth should allow for expansionary policies when they are required unexpectedly.[48] This is essential for an effective process of poverty reduction, since this process requires long-term stability and an interruption would mean losing ground in respect of the progress already made. [49]

Such policies would help attenuate the volatility of the economy, which makes policy response more difficult in times of crisis. Fiscal constraints during recessions usually directly reduce the budget assigned for social purposes, thereby impeding assistance to the needy. Hence macroeconomic policy can also directly affect the efficacy of social protection schemes, and the social impact of changes in macroeconomic policy in times of crisis should also be an important consideration for policy makers.

Social protection schemes are necessary to assist the vulnerable sectors of the population in case preventive measures, that is to say, macroeconomic policies, fail to protect the overall economy from either an internal or an external shock, and to help the chronically poor eventually escape their situation. Ideally, curative measures should not be necessary. Moreover, if structural problems (such as the pro-cyclical tendencies of fiscal policies) were reduced, especially during periods of growth, there would be more resources available during times of slow or negative growth for social protection schemes. Although such schemes do not guarantee complete shelter from economic fallout, they may help soften the shock.

Governments have faced many challenges in their pursuit of the reduction of urban poverty. The gap between the efforts made through policies and the results demonstrate the complexity of the problem. Problems exist at all stages of the process: from the design, planning, funding and targeting to the execution and monitoring.

One general difference between the Asian and Latin American economies concerns those who became poor as a result of the crises. In Asia, the newly poor were predominantly those in the formal sector who suddenly faced poverty as a result of losing their employment, but who could expect to escape poverty as a result of re-employment when the crisis subsided. In Latin America, the newly poor were often in the informal sector and joined the ranks of the chronically poor. This structural difference can determine the effectiveness of policies. For example, some policies directed at the poor who are or who were working in the formal sector may not reach the rest of the urban poor, who may not have access to formal sector institutions. To reach the chronically poor, other types of programmes may be needed.

East Asian countries had to resort to new ad hoc measures, since many social protection programmes were either discontinued or non-existent in the region. These were deemed unnecessary since the region had enjoyed more than a decade of high growth and relied more on family relationships in times of trouble—so-called social capital. In contrast, Latin American countries relied on extending existing programmes, since the countries had always had poverty problems, even during periods of high growth.[50]

Social expenditures in Latin American countries have followed the cycles of economic activity, which have been very volatile in nature, causing social expenditures to decrease in times of recession.[51] Hence, as is the case for preventive measures at the macrolevel, social protection programmes should be set up during times of growth when resources are available.

Besides all of the above-mentioned problems of implementation, the major challenge is to reach the most needy through programmes funded by social expenditures. Even though access to health, education and nutrition facilities is usually greater in urban areas than in rural areas owing to the population dispersion and the difficulties of reaching distant locations in rural areas, these urban-based programmes often reach only the middle—and higher-income individuals in the cities. Most programmes can reach only those who are already in the formal sector, while the extreme poor are often in the informal sector with little access to educational and health facilities.[52] In addition, the social structure of many cities in developing countries, especially those with a more uneven distribution of income, creates segregation of different types. Large slums are an example of spatial or residential segregation (or concentration, depending on the viewpoint). The schools near these areas tend to be of a lower standard than the average. The informal sector creates its own dynamic away from the formal labour market, perpetuating a system of isolation.[53] Thus, conventional programmes are not sufficient for reaching the entire targeted population.

Grass-roots activities have been organized to try to fill this gap and bring needed services to the urban poor. Given the isolation of the urban poor from the formal sector, including institutions and local government, non-governmental organizations serve as a natural bridge. Non-governmental organizations have shown that they can build social capital among low-income neighbourhoods and obtain financial capital to invest locally.[54]

The reduction of urban poverty requires the participation of many actors at all levels of society and is as complex a process as economic development itself, as well as an essential part of that process. At the highest macrolevel, prevention of shocks is essential, but macroeconomic responses to crises do not always favour the protection of the poor, particularly since financial constraints can limit the degrees of freedom of macroeconomic policy. Therefore, at a second level, preventive and curative measures within a social protection scheme should be in place at all times with varying degrees of intensity depending on the need. In theory, social programmes would be able to cover the needs of the poor if they were integrated in the formal sector. However, since the informal sector is very large in most developing countries, grass-roots-level involvement is also necessary to facilitate the access to services of the whole community.

[51] ECLAC, *Social Panorama of Latin America, 2000-2001* ...

[52] For a study on the case of Mexico, see for example, Ana Corbacho, and Gerd Schwartz, op. cit.

[53] For a sociological discussion of this phenomenon of isolation of the poor in Latin America, see for example, Rubén Kaztman, "Seducidos y abandonados: el aislamiento social de los pobres urbanos", *Revista de la CEPAL* (Santiago), No. 75 (December 2001).

[54] For a review of grass-roots activities for the urban poor, see for example, Diana Mitlin, "Addressing urban poverty through strengthening assets", *Habitat International* (forthcoming).

VI TRADE POLICIES, GROWTH AND POVERTY

John Stuart Mill, writing in the middle of the nineteenth century, noted the crucial role that trade can play in the process of development, maintaining that "the opening of foreign trade ... sometimes works as a sort of industrial revolution in a country whose resources were previously underdeveloped".[1] At the beginning of the twenty-first century, this link has taken on a slightly different emphasis. The current focus is heavily on the impact of trade policy on an economy and, specifically, on the potential role of trade policy in poverty reduction. A variety of factors have conspired to bring this connection to the forefront in recent decades. First, there has been the strong export performance of a number of East Asian economies, commencing in the 1970s, and the vigorous economic growth that came in the wake of their export drives.[2] Moreover, beginning in the 1990s, concern with the process of globalization began to capture the attention of policy makers and the public. In particular, a great deal of attention has been directed at the question whether income gaps are widening between those countries that are successfully integrating themselves into the world economy via their trading patterns and those that are falling by the wayside. Increasing concern is being expressed at the lack of progress of these poorest economies and their possible marginalization. The need to include the poorest has been articulated in the United Nations Millennium Declaration.[3] The Millennium Declaration emphasizes the need for poverty eradication and underscores the need for an open trading system that is "rule-based, predictable and non-discriminatory" (para. 13) as one means to this end. Finally, the Monterrey Consensus of the International Conference on Financing for Development,[4] noting that international trade is "an engine of growth", stated that a "universal, rule-based, open, non-discriminatory and equitable multilateral trading system, as well as meaningful trade liberalization, can substantially stimulate development worldwide, benefiting countries at all stages of development"(para. 26).

The present chapter will examine the role of trade and trade policies in stimulating growth and thereby contributing to poverty reduction. Trade policies are government policies that directly influence the quantity of goods and services that a country imports or exports. Such policies can take various forms. For example, liberal trade policies are geared towards allowing a nation's residents to trade internationally with a minimum of government interference, whereas strategic trade policy is intended to

[1]   John Stuart Mill, *Principles of Political Economy* (London, Taylor and Francis Books, Ltd., 1996), book III, chap. VII. Originally published in 1848.

[2]   For example, between 1969 and 1999, the share of world exports of goods and services of Hong Kong SAR of China, China, Malaysia, the Republic of Korea and Thailand increased from under 2 to over 8 per cent.

[3]   See General Assembly resolution 55/2 of 8 September 2000.

[4]   *Report of the International Conference on Financing for Development, Monterrey, Mexico, 18-22 March 2002* (United Nations publication, Sales No. E. 02.II.A.7), chap. I, resolution 1, annex.

influence the trade policies of partner countries. Such policies are beneficial only if other countries respond by changing their trade policies, as anticipated. Trade policy liberalization entails such measures as tariff reductions, relaxing or removing import quotas (quantitative restrictions), reducing import taxes and dropping export subsidies. All such policies can be carried out to a greater or lesser degree so that trade liberalization does not imply a shift to complete laissez-faire.

The basic contention of this chapter is that trade liberalization is a necessary, but not sufficient, condition for economic growth and that it is via such growth that poverty can be reduced. The chapter will argue that trade effects—and the policies that instigate them—operate in the short, medium and long run. Moreover, trade can impact on poverty via a variety of channels—for example, changing the prices and availability of goods and services or influencing the distribution of income within a country. Many of the changes brought about by trade and trade policies incur adjustment costs. In the longer run, however, the benefits of expanded trade tend to outweigh the costs. Moreover, avoiding trade expansion because of a concern with potential adjustment costs would be a recipe for stagnation. Yet, trade policies have to be thought out, since trade is but one—sometimes a small—variable in the growth equation, and policies suited to one country cannot be easily translated for use by other countries because conditions are as individualistic as are individual economies. Thus, the trade policy experiences of one country cannot be used to produce a generally valid "policy prescription".

TRADE AND THE ECONOMY

The potential of trade to serve as a catalyst for development can be put into sharp relief by looking at the ratio of trade to gross domestic product (GDP) in a variety of country groups (see table VI.1). Exports—which are conventionally viewed as contributing to, rather than subtracting from, GDP—had grown over the course of the 1990s by 29 per cent. By 2000, the ratio of exports to world GDP was almost 26 per cent. The importance of exports is further documented by noting that the ratio of exports to GDP was almost 30 per cent in both low-income and low- and middle-income countries, and over 20 per cent in least developed countries. Moreover, in each case, exports had risen substantially during the decade, at least at double the rate for the developed countries. With figures such as these, the focus has to be not on whether trade can serve the interests of growth and poverty reduction, but rather on putting the policies in place to ensure that it does so.

There are a variety of difficulties inherent in trying to pinpoint the economic consequences of specific trade policies, as well as in ascertaining the effects of changes in such policies. The greatest problem lies in the fact that trade policies are variable, shifting as circumstances demand. In part, this is because such policies are a useful tool and often easier to implement than changes in either monetary or fiscal policies. For example, raising government revenue by levying an import duty may be politically more palatable than raising revenue by increasing taxes, since the former may hurt a much smaller subset of the population. Similarly, non-tariff barriers to trade, while economically ineffi-

Table VI.1.
RATIO OF TRADE TO GROSS DOMESTIC PRODUCT
IN DIFFERENT COUNTRY GROUPS, 1990 AND 2000

Percentage		
	1990	2000
Least developed countries		
Exports of goods and services	13.6	21.6
Imports of goods and services	22.7	29.6
Total trade	36.3	51.3
Low-income countries		
Exports of goods and services	17.8	28.7
Imports of goods and services	20.7	28.1
Total trade	38.5	56.8
Low- and middle-income countries		
Exports of goods and services	20.1	29.9
Imports of goods and services	19.6	27.8
Total trade	39.7	57.8
High-income countries (OECD)		
Exports of goods and services	18.0	22.6
Imports of goods and services	18.0	22.9
Total trade	36.0	45.5
World		
Exports of goods and services	19.9	25.6
Imports of goods and services	19.8	25.3
Total trade	39.7	50.8

Source: World Bank, *World Development Indicators* web site, Washington, D.C.

cient inasmuch as they incur a variety of costs especially for consumers, might be politically desirable since they protect domestic producers. Or, confronted by a balance-of-trade deficit, policy makers may see export subsidies and import tariffs as the easiest way to rectify the problem, especially if monetary policy is not an option. The latter may be the case for economies whose exchange rates are tied to another country's currency, rendering monetary policy or devaluation an impotent policy device. In all such instances, falling back on trade policies to steer economic changes, while not a first-best solution, may be the most practical—and most practised—option.[5]

A second major complication in trying to identify the results of specific trade policies on the economy arises from the fact that it is difficult—if not impossible—to pin down causality (as opposed to correlation). This is because trade policies are never implemented in a vacuum. There are always a large number of macroeconomic policies being pursued in addition to the trade policy stance. Consequently, it is extremely difficult to disentangle the effects of trade policies from other economic policies and events. For instance, a partner country's tariff reductions may spur exports. However, increased exports may also be due to a better product or to increased income, and hence greater demand, in the partner country.

[5] For example, the drive to expand exports may be driven by export subsidies and may result in subsequent charges of dumping by virtue of the importer's being brought before the World Trade Organization.

6 Rui Albuquerque and Sergio Rebelo, "On the dynamics of trade reform", *Journal of International Economics*, vol. 51 (2000), pp. 21-47.

7 Thomas F. Rutherford and David G. Tarr, *Trade Liberalization and Endogenous Growth in a Small Open Economy: A Quantitative Assessment*, World Bank Policy Research Working Paper, No. 1970 (Washington, D.C., World Bank, 1998).

8 See, for example, L. Alan Winters, "Trade and poverty: is there a connection?" in *Special Studies, No. 5: Trade, Income Disparity and Poverty* (Geneva, World Trade Organization, 2000).

9 Douglas A. Irwin and Marko Terviö, "Does trade raise income? evidence from the twentieth century", *Journal of International Economics*, vol. 58 (2002), pp. 1-18.

Attributing results to trade policies is also problematic because trade policy shifts are usually gradual (except in dire situations), hence their impact is correspondingly minor. For example, countries often switch between various forms of protection, instead of eliminating or raising the level of protection in one fell swoop. It is often feared that trade reforms, such as removing import quotas or reducing import tariffs, will have devastating effects on import-competing industries, while causing a boom in other sectors of the economy. Although experience indicates that the benefits of the expansion will outweigh the costs associated with the demise of any protected sectors, those who are more cautious voice the concern that the contraction of the import-competing sector will lead to a deep and prolonged recession. In practice, however, once trade reforms are implemented, the overall impact is often surprisingly small.[6] For example, several estimates of the impact of trade liberalization have found welfare increases of only ½ to 1 per cent of GDP, or relatively small gains compared with expectations.[7] However, incorporating dynamic impacts yields far larger welfare gains. Thus, going beyond the immediate, or static, situation, the potential gains from trade and trade reform, together with the growth-inducing impact of liberalization, can be quite significant for a country in the medium or longer run. Trade and trade policies can thus be a powerful tool in the poverty alleviation arsenal.

Openness and trade liberalization (which is synonymous with increasing openness) have increasingly become customary tenets of economic policy advice over the past two decades. While there is broad acceptance that openness is ultimately beneficial, examining and dissecting the effects of such policies can be complex. With the caveats noted above, trade impacts—to the extent that they can indeed be tracked—manifest themselves on three time-horizons. First, trade will have a bearing on overall growth in the long run. In addition, trade can impinge on the distribution of income and the welfare of the poor. Both of these are medium-run effects. However, trade policies can also have a variety of shorter-run consequences, producing adjustment problems and costs, and perhaps even economy-wide shocks.

Since neither trade liberalization nor poverty is easily measured and since there is only a limited number of historical instances in which liberalization could be singled out as the dominant economic shock, it is difficult to derive empirical relationships between the two.[8] Nonetheless, countries that trade more—as a proportion of their GDP—tend to have higher incomes, other things being equal. A perennial concern in interpreting this assertion is that countries may trade more because they are wealthier; that is to say, the trade share may be endogenous. However, countries that have traded more have had higher incomes over the course of the twentieth century.[9]

There are two aspects to the question of "openness". There is the issue of the extent to which a country's own economy is unfettered by protection, such as export subsidies or import tariffs or quotas. Countries have control over the policy choices they make in this regard, though such choices may sometimes be difficult to make. Increased openness—via its effects on imports and welfare—has consequences for poverty. These work through a variety of routes, such as changing the prices and availability of goods and services and the demand for labour, altering the incentives for investment and innovation, influencing government revenue, and affecting income distribution. Additionally, there is the issue of access to markets and the degree to which potential partner economies resort to protectionist measures of various sorts, such as quotas, tariffs and non-tariff barriers to trade. Here the role of exports in generating GDP growth becomes relevant. To recoup gains from trade, foreign markets have to be open. Nevertheless, this is something concerning which individual countries have very little leverage. It falls, rather, upon the partners themselves, the World Trade Organization and the international community to ensure that the multilateral trading system is open and equitable.

TRADE AND GROWTH

Economic growth is acknowledged as a key to permanent poverty alleviation. The first fundamental question, therefore, is whether opening an economy to trade is an important determinant of growth.[10] This trade opening-growth relationship must be examined before exploring whether the growth that is associated with trade liberalization is particularly pro- or anti-poor.

Liberalization and growth in theory and practice

The theoretical links between liberalization and growth are ambiguous. Robert Solow's 1956 neoclassical growth model is the standard-bearer in this regard. The implication of this model is that openness, by allowing for a more efficient allocation of resources, can—under specified conditions—raise the steady-state level of income and the growth rate. Over the past two decades, endogenous growth theory has built on this foundation, suggesting that openness may promote long-run growth in a variety of ways, such as through the diffusion of technology or learning-by-doing.

To assess the empirical evidence of the liberalization-growth link, it is first of all necessary to recognize the difference between the active opening up—or liberalization—of an economy and the existing state of openness. It is logical to seek a relationship between two dynamic variables, such as liberalization and growth. It is equally logical to look for a relationship between two static variables, namely, the degree of openness and the level of incomes. However, it would generally be a mistake to seek an association between the level of trade openness and growth.[11] The benefit of free trade—or openness—is a static efficiency benefit. Dynamic benefits, which emanate from liberalization, impact on growth.[12]

Casual empiricism attests to an association between export growth and GDP growth (see figure VI.1). Nevertheless, there are at least two problems that arise when examining the relationship from a policy perspective. It can be difficult to assess accurately the trade stance of a country, particularly when it is relatively closed. This is a definitional issue. In addition, the difficulty of establishing an empirical link is complicated by the fact that trade policies are usually part of a policy package.[13]

While the domestic impacts of liberalization or, conversely, the costs of protection, can be difficult to gauge, there is a great deal of cross-country and sometimes controversial evidence that documents a positive relationship between a liberal trade regime and GDP growth. This finding has been con-

[10] For a cogent exposition of these relationships, see Jagdish Bhagwati and T.N. Srinivasan, "Trade and poverty in the poor countries", *American Economic Review: Papers and Proceedings*, vol. 92 (2002), pp. 180-183.

[11] Andrew Berg and Anne Krueger, "Lifting all boats: why openness helps curb poverty", *Finance and Development*, vol. 39, No. 3 (September 2002).

[12] T. N. Srinivasan and Jagdish Bhagwati, "Outward-orientation and development: are revisions right?", Economic Growth Center, Yale University, New Haven, Connecticut, 1999.

[13] Neil McCulloch, L. Alan Winters and Xavier Ciera, *Trade Liberalization and Poverty: A Handbook* (London, United Kingdom Department for International Development and Centre for Economic Policy Research, 2001).

Figure VI.1.
RELATIONSHIP BETWEEN THE AVERAGE ANNUAL
RATES OF GROWTH OF GDP AND TRADE, 1990-2000

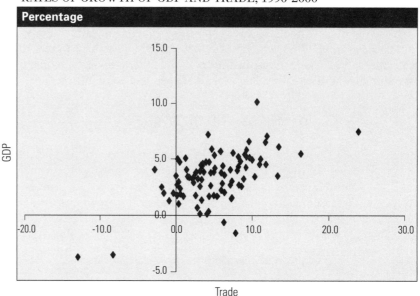

Source: World Bank, *World Development Indicators, 2002* (Washington, D.C., World Bank, 2002).

14   Kazi Matin, *Openness and Economic Performance in Sub-Saharan Africa: Evidence from Time-Series Cross-Country Analysis*, World Bank Working Paper, No. 1025; and Ann Harrison, *Openness and Growth: A Time Series, Cross-Country Analysis for Developing Countries*, NBER Working Paper No. 5221 (Cambridge, Massachusetts, National Bureau of Economic Research, 1995).

15   Gary Clyde Hufbauer, "Surveying the costs of protection: a partial equilibrium approach" in *The World Trading System: Challenges Ahead*, Jeffrey J. Schott, ed. (Washington, D.C., Institute for International Economics, 1996).

16   See, for example, Michael Michaely, "Exports and growth: an empirical investigation", *Journal of Development Economics*, vol. 4, No. 1, 1977, pp. 49-53.

17   Romain Wacziarg, "Measuring the dynamic gains from trade", Graduate School of Business, Stanford University, Palo Alto, California, 1998; and *The World Bank Economic Review*, vol. 15, No. 3 (2001), pp. 393-429.

18   Jeffrey D. Sachs and Andrew Warner, "Economic reform and the process of global integration", *Brookings Papers on Economic Activity*, No. 1 (Washington, D.C., Brookings Institution, 1995). The authors classify the developing economies into one of three sets: those that have always been open; those that had opened by 1994 after initial closure; and those that were closed as of the end of 1994.

firmed for a diverse set of countries, including a number of sub-Saharan African economies.[14] Looked at from the reverse perspective, findings suggest that trade barriers for agricultural and industrial goods impose major costs, both in developed and in developing economies.[15] High protection and large consumer costs are usually concentrated in a handful of industries in each country. Some sectors appear with regularity on inventories of highly protected activities. Agriculture, apparel and textiles are on practically every developed country's list, while automobiles and parts feature prominently on the protection schedules of developing countries. Transport, communications and finance are severely protected by many developed and developing countries.

A positive empirical association between openness and economic growth has been established, with evidence accumulating that outward-oriented countries grow faster. Some of these investigations have focused exclusively on developing countries.[16] Others have cast their net wider. A survey of 57 developed and developing countries over the period 1970-1989 concluded that openness supports growth.[17] Some analyses take the next logical step, looking at openness in more dynamic terms—that is to say, as synonymous with opening up or liberalization. One examination of the effects of liberalization focused on over 100 developed and developing economies from the post-Second World War period to the mid-1990s.[18] A strong relationship between liberalization and growth was evident. Within the group of developing countries, the more open economies grew at a rate of 4.5 per cent per year, whereas the relatively closed economies grew at a rate of 0.7 per cent per year. Within the group of developed countries, the results were a growth rate of 2.3 per cent per year for the "open" economies and a rate of 0.7 per cent per year for the "closed" ones. These findings also extend to the economies of Central and Eastern Europe that have been undertaking market reforms, including trade liberalization, since 1990: the strong trade reformers achieved positive economic growth by 1994.

These studies rarely differentiate between degrees of openness. Further results for a cross section of over 100 developed and developing countries over the last three decades, using two groups of trade openness measures, demonstrated that "trade liberalization does not have a simple and straightforward relationship with growth…".[19] Nevertheless, trade volume measures are found to be significantly and positively correlated with growth, while a second set of proxies for openness support the view that trade promotes growth through a variety of channels, such as technology transfers, scale economies and comparative advantage. An analysis of 93 developed and developing countries during 1980-1990, using nine different estimates of "openness", yielded similar results. Regardless of how openness is defined, "more open countries have indeed experienced faster … growth".[20] Moreover, while openness alone seems to be no guarantee of faster growth, the conclusions of most researchers involved in these studies is that lower trade barriers, in combination with a stable and non-discriminatory exchange-rate system, and prudent monetary and fiscal policies, as well as other elements of good governance, promote economic growth.[21]

Caveats concerning the trade-poverty link

A link exists between trade reform and the efficiency gains necessary for growth. Reduced average tariff levels, as well as lower quantitative restrictions on imports, are associated with increased output growth—even for given levels of investment and capacity use. However, the extent to which trade reform benefits a country reflects the initial conditions prevailing in that country. Countries with well-functioning markets and a better human capital base benefit more from trade reforms. For example, Ghana, Indonesia and Turkey had begun their respective trade reform programmes in the 1980s under different conditions. While all three carried out extensive reforms, Indonesia and Turkey benefited more because, at that time, they had more diversified production structures and better-functioning markets than had Ghana.[22] Initial conditions are thus extremely important.

Moreover, a concomitant of "initial conditions" is the considerable variation that can exist between countries depending on what is and can be exported. The impact of manufacturing exports on economic growth is likely to be greater than the impact of primary commodity exports because the former typically generate greater externalities and learning effects. Such external effects in commodity-exporting economies tend to be small. Furthermore, the export growth-economic growth relationship has often been fragile for mineral-exporting economies. Several explanations have been proffered for this, including the "Dutch disease" phenomenon, where surges in mineral export revenues lead to an appreciation of the real exchange rate and consequently to reduced competitiveness in other tradables.[23]

Another qualification is that the correlations between trade openness and a variety of other variables are frequently high. For example, the quality of a country's institutions, sustained long-run growth and high levels of trade often go together. There are findings that suggest "an important joint role for both trade and institutions in the very long run…".[24] Thus, liberalization is but one element in an array of variables important for growth, and its relative importance may vary depending on the time-horizon.

[19] Halit Yanikkaya, "Trade openness and economic growth: a cross-country empirical investigation", *Journal of Development Economics*, vol. X (2003).

[20] Sebastian Edwards, *Openness, Productivity and Growth: What Do We Really Know?*, National Bureau of Economic Research Working Paper, No. 5978 (Cambridge, Massachusetts, NBER, 1997); and *The Economist*, 21 March 1998.

[21] Robert E. Baldwin, *Openness and Growth: What's the Empirical Relationship?*, National Bureau of Economic Research Working Paper, No. 9578, (Cambridge, Massachusetts, NBER, 2003).

[22] Ejaz Ghani and Carl Jayarajah, *Trade Reform, Efficiency and Growth*, World Bank Policy Working Paper, No. 1438 (Washington, D.C., World Bank, 1995).

[23] United Nations Conference on Trade and Development, *The Least Developed Countries Report, 2002: Escaping the Poverty Trap* (United Nations publication, Sales No. E.02.II.D.13), box 11.

[24] David Dollar and Aart Kray, "Institutions, trade and growth", *Journal of Monetary Economics*, vol. 50X, No. 1 (2003), pp. 133-162.

25 Sarath Rajapatirana, *Trade Policies, Macroeconomic Adjustment, and Manufactured Exports: The Latin American Experience*, World Bank Policy Research Working Paper, No. 1492 (Washington, D.C., World Bank, 1995).

26 Methods in current use fall into four broad categories, namely, cross-country regression analysis, partial equilibrium/cost-of-living analysis, general equilibrium simulation, and micro-macro synthesis. These four groups encompass both the "bottom-up" and the "top-down" approaches that are employed by poverty and trade specialists, respectively. The first approach is based on detailed survey information and emphasizes the heterogeneity of individual households and commodity market links between trade and poverty. The second methodology begins with microeconomic theory's "representative household" assumption and usually incorporates additional links between trade and poverty, such as factor earnings and terms-of-trade effects. One general conclusion of those working in this field is that any thorough analysis needs to incorporate both approaches. See Jeffrey J. Reimer, "Estimating poverty impacts of trade liberalization", Center for Global Trade Analysis and Department of Agricultural Economics, Purdue University, West Lafayette, Indiana, 2002.

27 L. Alan Winters, "Trade and poverty: is there a connection?", background paper (2000) for World Bank, *World Development Report 2000/2001: Attacking Poverty* (New York, Oxford University Press, 2001).

28 With 95 per cent confidence, a 1 per cent rate of growth of consumption per person can yield anywhere from a 0.5 to a 3.5 per cent decline in the share of population living on less than one dollar per day. See Martin Ravillion, "Have we already met the millennium development goal for poverty?", *Economic and Political Weekly*, 16 November 2002.

29 David Dollar and Aart Kraay, "Trade, growth and poverty", Development Research Group, World Bank, 2001. See also Dani Rodrik, "Comments on trade, growth and poverty" (2000) for a critique of this paper.

30 Paul A. Dorosh and David E. Sahn, "A general equilibrium analysis of the effect of macroeconomic adjustment on poverty in Africa", *Journal of Policy Modelling*, vol. 22, No. 6 (2000), pp. 753-776.

31 Gaurav Datt and Martin Ravallion, "Is India's economic growth leaving the poor behind?", *Journal of Economic Perspectives*, Vol. 16, No. 3 (2002), pp. 89-108.

32 L. Allan Winters, "Trade liberalisation and poverty: what are the links?", *The World Economy*, vol. 25, No. 9 (2002), pp. 1339-1367.

Finally, trade policies are but a single element in the policy makers' arsenal of macroeconomic policy tools. More significantly, there are objectives that trade policy cannot—and should not be expected—to achieve. For example, an examination of the relationship between trade policies and macroeconomic adjustment in Argentina, Brazil, Chile, Colombia, Costa Rica and Mexico over the period 1965-95 confirmed the inability of trade policies to solve those countries' current-account difficulties. Other means had to be found to deal with this problem.[25]

ASSESSING THE EVIDENCE

One of the major problems in determining the trade growth-poverty reduction relationship is the fragility of the various statistical techniques that can be applied to an examination of this issue.[26] Although trade liberalization is generally viewed as a positive contributor to poverty alleviation, the evidence as regards the trade-poverty linkage is usually both fragmentary and often incomplete. Liberalization allows productive potential to be exploited, assists with economic growth and curtails arbitrary policy interventions. However, most reforms will create some losers—even in the longer run—and some reforms may temporarily exacerbate poverty.[27]

Moreover, while poverty reduction typically comes hand in hand with economic growth (see chap. IV), there is considerable variation in the impact of a given rate of growth on poverty.[28] One explanation is that differences in the impact of growth on poverty are a function of the initial level of inequality. Higher inequality results in the poor's receiving a lower share of the gains from growth.

Numerous investigations have found that the poor gain as trade expands. For a set of "post-1980 globalizers", which includes China and India, no systematic relationship was found between large increases in trade volumes and small changes in household income inequality. The conclusion was that the increase in growth rates that had accompanied expanded trade on average translated into more or less proportionate increases in the incomes of the poor.[29]

Comparable results have also been established for individual countries. For example, simulations for Cameroon, the Gambia, Madagascar and the Niger suggested that trade (and exchange-rate) liberalization tended to benefit poor households in both rural and urban areas, as rents on foreign exchange were eliminated, demand for labour increased and returns to the production of agricultural tradables rose.[30]

A further example is provided by a study of India in the 1990s. This suggested that economic growth in India had typically reduced poverty prior to the 1990s and that the 1980s rate of poverty reduction was most likely maintained through the last decade. At the same time, however, achieving higher aggregate economic growth was only one element of an effective poverty reduction strategy for India. Had the sectoral and geographical composition of growth been more balanced, and had existing inequalities in human resource development and between urban and rural areas been better redressed, the rate of poverty reduction would have been considerably higher.[31]

Overall, therefore, while trade liberalization alone cannot be linked incontrovertibly to poverty reduction, the general tendency of the evidence, comprising both cross-sectional and case studies, is strongly in the direction of such a linkage.[32]

ADJUSTMENT

Trade liberalization may involve adjustment problems and costs. Examples include the loss of jobs that existed only by virtue of a subsidy or distortion, lower wages in contracting activities or higher prices for certain imports when their importation is no longer subsidized. For example, estimates of the effects of the Uruguay Round of multilateral trade negotiations found large potential gains in East Asian World Trade Organization members—such as Indonesia, Malaysia, the Republic of Korea and Thailand—as well as in the South Asia region. However, the Middle East and North Africa had relatively small gains, while a loss was projected for sub-Saharan Africa, reflecting the lack of liberalization in the area, and likely increases in prices for some foodstuffs, as well as higher prices of imported textile and apparel products.[33] Similarly, all the evidence shows that abolishing the Multifibre Arrangement would generate enormous benefits for importers, but that two groups of exporters would suffer, namely, those whose quotas are large relative to their comparative advantage and those that may have been induced by the Arrangement to enter the production of textiles and clothing without possessing a true comparative advantage in those goods.[34]

In each liberalizing country, there are always winners and losers if trade policy shifts to a significant extent, because of the need for the changes to work themselves through. Two problems can emerge during the adjustment process. The first occurs when adjustment is constrained and prolongs the dependence on products with poor export prospects for them.[35] Similarly, trade adjustment assistance—designed to overcome political opposition to trade liberalization— reduces policy makers' incentives to press for such liberalization and may thus slow down the pace of needed reform.[36] This problem arises when there is a lack of social safety nets to ease and mitigate the adjustment process. This is especially critical because those who are harmed the most in the short term typically lack political power.[37]

It has been suggested that international trade policies have a "gender-differentiated" impact: strong export performance in manufactures in developing countries is secured via reliance on female labour in such areas as textiles, apparel, electronics, leather products and food processing. By contrast, in most industrialized economies, increased trade with developing countries has led to a loss of employment in such industries as textiles, apparel and leather goods, in which women are heavily represented.[38]

Adjustment costs in a diversified economy are small relative to the benefits for several reasons. Adjustment costs related to unemployment are typically short-term and terminate when workers find new employment. The benefits of trade reform, meanwhile, grow with the economy. Second, in most industries, estimates indicate that the duration of unemployment of their workers is not long, especially, in cases where workers were not earning substantial wages in their original jobs. Third, in many industries, normal labour turnover exceeds the dislocation from trade liberalization, so that downsizing—where necessary—is accomplished without much forced unemployment. Moreover, in many instances in which a dynamic role is played by micro- and small-scale enterprises, which are quick to respond to new opportunities, a significant portion of the resource reallocation after trade liberalization has been observed to occur through inter-industry shifts, thereby minimizing the dislocation of labour.

[33] G.W. Harrison, T.F. Rutherford and D.G. Tarr, "Quantifying the Uruguay Round", *Economic Journal*, vol. 107, No. 444 (1997), pp. 1405-1430.

[34] Will Martin and L. Alan Winters, *The Uruguay Round: Widening and Deepening the World Trading System* (Washington, D.C., World Bank, 1995).

[35] Mark S. Leclair, "Fighting the tide: alternative trade organizations in the era of global free trade", *World Development*, vol. 30, No. 6 (2002), pp. 949-958.

[36] Christopher Magee, "Endogenous tariffs and trade adjustment assistance", *Journal of International Economics*, vol. 60 (2003), pp. 203-222.

[37] Bernard Hoekman and others, "Trade policy reform and poverty alleviation", Development Research Group, International Trade Team, World Bank, Washington, D.C., 2002.

[38] Nilüfer Cagatay, "Gender, poverty and trade", background paper (2001) for the UNDP Report on Trade and Sustainable Human Development, 2001, UNDP, New York.

[39] Steven J. Matusz and David Tarr, "Adjusting to trade policy reform", Trade, Development Research Group, World Bank, Washington, D.C., 1999.

[40] Constantine Michalopoulos, "Trade and development in the GATT and WTO: the role of special and differential treatment for developing countries", paper presented to the World Trade Organization Seminar on Special and Differential Treatment for Developing Countries, Geneva, March 2000.

[41] Raymond Robertson and Donald Dutkowsky, "Labor adjustment costs in a destination country: the case of Mexico", Journal of Development Economics, vol. 67 (2002), pp. 29-54. See also Dani Rodrik, Has Globalization Gone Too Far? (Washington, D.C., Institute for International Economics, 1997).

[42] For more on this point, see Geoffrey J. Bannister and Kamau Thugge, International Trade and Poverty Alleviation, IMF Working Paper WP/01/54 (Washington, D.C., 2001).

[43] World Trade Organization, "Market access: post-Uruguay Round inventory and issues", Special Studies, No. 6 (Geneva, 2001), p. 48 and table III.3.

Finally, developing countries typically have a comparative advantage in labour-intensive industries, hence trade liberalization, resulting in greater trade, tends to favour labour. This may partially explain why manufacturing employment has typically increased in developing countries after trade liberalization.[39]

Because the adjustment process may entail difficulties, which can be relatively more pronounced at lower income levels, many developing countries, including (but not only) the least developed countries, have been provided with longer transition periods in which to implement a variety of World Trade Organization liberalization agreements. These fall into such categories as safeguards, subsidies and countervailing measures, anti-dumping, sanitary and phytosanitary measures and trade related intellectual property rights (TRIPs). However, developing countries, especially those confronted by fiscal constraints, often have limited resources to direct towards the areas of public administration responsible for overseeing the implementation of these agreements, which can be both time-consuming and costly. A number of these transition periods expired before the developing countries in question could overcome their difficulties in establishing the institutions necessary for the implementation of the agreements.[40] Institutional weaknesses of this sort thus add greatly to the costs of adjustment, despite the fact that longer transition periods are set up precisely to reduce such adjustment costs. Therefore, special and differential treatment for developing countries should encompass more than just longer periods of implementation.

Finally, adjustment costs depend on individual circumstances and the external environment. The estimated adjustment costs in Mexico for the period 1987-1995 were found to be small—a result consistent with an earlier finding.[41] That adjustment costs vary between countries has been documented in analyses of developed economies, though few studies exist for developing countries.

THE CHANNELS FOR ASSURING THE WELFARE OF THE POOR

Prices and availability of goods and services

David Ricardo, in the early 1800s, demonstrated several important "gains from trade". Foremost among these was the ability of consumers to buy goods and services at prices lower than original home prices. However, a secondary advantage of a country's being open to trade is consumer access to goods and services that would otherwise not even be available for purchase and certainly not at prices that would prevail were these products to be produced domestically.

The removal of import tariffs, as well as any non-tariff barriers to trade, affects the prices and availability of goods and services. The prices of imports are thereby lowered. Additionally, the prices of substitutes for such imports are also kept down, effectively increasing the real incomes of the poor. Imported goods that might be of particular importance to the poor include basic foods, pharmaceuticals and other basic health products.[42] However, high import tariffs on agricultural products are a continuing reality in both developed and developing economies.[43] To counter the problem of high import tariffs on pharmaceuticals and other basic health products, at the African Summit on Roll Back Malaria held in Abuja in April 2000, Governments pledged to reduce or waive taxes and tariffs for the mosquito nets, insecticides and anti-malarial drugs necessary for malaria control.

Another strategy that results in changed prices and availability of goods and services—and one that has burgeoned in recent years—consists in joining a regional trading arrangement. Such schemes are frequently trade-creating and can therefore be favourable from a welfare-enhancing perspective. In addition, there may be dynamic gains to be realized. For example, production will be possible on a larger scale and greater exposure to other markets may mean greater efficiency, which in turn, may lead to greater output at lower prices.

Joining a trading arrangement is a policy choice and, from that perspective, it is important to gauge whether it is the best choice that could be made. There are indications that the new wave of regionalism that had occurred during the 1990s—during which decade a number of preferential trading arrangements were either created (the Southern Common Market (MERCOSUR) and the North American Free Trade Agreement (NAFTA)) or revamped (the Association of the Southeast Asian Nations (ASEAN), the Central American Common Market (CACM) and the Andean Community (ANDEAN))—did little to boost intra-bloc trade significantly, above and beyond what historical trade trends would have predicted.[44] Moreover, evidence for a data set for about 40 developed and developing economies for the period 1950-1992 compares the growth performance of countries that liberalized broadly with those that joined a regional trading arrangement. Economies grew faster when they undertook broad-based liberalization than when they limited their liberalization efforts to participation in a regional trading arrangement.[45] Nevertheless, numerous countries have joined, or have expressed an interest in joining, a variety of regional trading arrangements. In Eastern Europe, a number of countries are waiting to join an enlarged European Union (EU).

Regional arrangements may have negative welfare implications for nearby countries that are excluded. For example, Argentina's beef and cattle exports to Peru fell when Peru established a pact whose members included Colombia, an exporter of the same products.[46] Another example was the reduction of prices on exports from Brazil—a non-member State of MERCOSUR—to member States of MERCOSUR, following the formation of this regional trading bloc. Because of high tariffs levied on exports from outside the trading bloc, Brazil's exporters had to reduce the prices of their products significantly, compared with prices of exports to countries outside the trading bloc, in order to maintain price competitiveness in markets of the member States.[47]

Sub-Saharan African countries have pursued regional integration schemes for over three decades in order to accelerate industrialization and growth. However, the problems associated with African regional trade arrangements as a means to this end are daunting, since Africa's exports are highly concentrated in a few products, so that the economies in question appear to have very little to trade with one another.[48]

Several Asian economies have used accession to a regional arrangement as part of their respective reform strategies in pursuit of the export and income growth necessary for poverty reduction. For Cambodia, the Lao People's Democratic Republic, Myanmar and Viet Nam, forging regional linkages has been an important part of their export growth dynamic. Meeting the requirements of accession to the ASEAN Free Trade Area[49] has helped these countries to modernize their trade regulations and, at the same time, has required wide-ranging preferential trade liberalization.[50]

[44] Isidro Soloaga and L. Alan Winters, *Regionalism in the Nineties: What Effect on Trade?*, World Bank Working Paper, No. 2156 (Washington, D.C., 1999).

[45] Athanasios Vamvakidis, *Regional Trade Agreements Versus Broad Liberalization: Which Path Leads to Faster Growth? Time Series Evidence*, International Monetary Fund Working Paper, No. WP/98/40 (Washington, D.C., IMF, 1998).

[46] The Andean Pact was created in 1969 between Bolivia, Chile, Colombia, Ecuador and Peru. Venezuela joined in 1973 and Chile withdrew in 1976. See Ana Gupta and Maurice Schiff, *Outsiders and Regional Trade Agreements among Small Countries*, World Bank Policy Research Working Paper, No. 1847 (Washington, D.C., World Bank, 1997).

[47] Won Chang and L. Alan Winters, "Preferential trading arrangements and excluded countries: ex-post estimates of the effects on prices", *The World Economy*, vol. 24, No. 6 (2001), pp. 797-807.

[48] Alexander Yeats, *What Can Be Expected From African Regional Trade Arrangements?: Some Empirical Evidence*, World Bank Policy Research Working Paper, No. 2004 (Washington, D.C., World Bank, 1998).

[49] ASEAN members are Indonesia, Malaysia, the Philippines, Singapore, Thailand and Viet Nam.

[50] *The Least Developed Countries Report, 2002...*, box 11; and Will Martin , *Trade Policy Reform in the East Asian Transition Economies*, World Bank Policy Research Working Paper, No. 2535 (Washington, D.C., World Bank, 2001).

[51] Trade creation results when domestic production is replaced by imports from a lower-cost and more efficient producer within the trading arrangement. Trade diversion results when higher-cost suppliers from within replace imports from lower-cost, more efficient producers outside a trading arrangement.

[52] Emiko Fukase and Will Martin "Economic effects of joining ASEAN Free Trade Area (AFTA): the case of the Lao People's Democratic Republic", World Bank, Development Research Group (Washington, D.C., 1999); and Emiko Fukase and Will Martin, *Free Trade Membership as a Stepping Stone to Development: The Case of ASEAN* (Washington, D.C., World Bank, 2001).

[53] Helena Johansson and Lars Nilsson, "Export processing zones as catalysts", *World Development*, vol. 25, No. 12 (1997), pp. 2115-2128. The 10 economies in the study were: the Dominican Republic, Egypt, Hong Kong SAR of China, Malaysia, Mauritius, the Philippines, the Republic of Korea, Singapore, Sri Lanka and Tunisia.

[54] Kankesu Jayanthakumaran, "Benefit-cost appraisals of export processing zones: a survey of the literature", *Development Policy Review* (Overseas Development Institute, London), vol. 21, No. 1 (2003), pp. 51-65.

[55] See Demetrios Papageorgiou, Armeane Choksi and Michael Michaely, *Liberalizing Foreign Trade in Developing Countries: The Lessons of Experience* (Washington, D.C., World Bank, 1990). The period examined was from the Second World War to 1984.

[56] See Ronald Parker, Randall Riopelle, and Wiliam Steel, "Small enterprises adjusting to liberalization in five African countries", World Bank Discussion Paper, No. 271, Washington, D.C., 1995.

[57] Sanjukta Mukherjee and Todd Benson, "The determinants of poverty in Malawi, 1998", *World Development*, vol. 31, No. 2 (2003), pp. 339-358.

[58] The Stolper-Samuelson Theorem, so named after the two economists who proved it algebraically.

There is a dilemma that arises, however, centering around the fact that costly trade diversion has been introduced alongside healthy trade creation.[51] Such a problem is particularly serious if the external trade barriers in the bloc are high. However, even in ASEAN—where external trade barriers are relatively low—welfare gains from trade creation have been substantially undermined for the new members of the group by their losses from trade diversion.[52]

While regional trade agreements (RTAs) have garnered a great deal of attention in recent years, there are other stratagems that affect liberalization and the level of trade and hence can affect growth and reduce poverty. One such stratagem entails the creation of an export processing zone (EPZ). Malaysia, the Republic of Korea and Thailand initiated their EPZs as part of a shift in policy from an inward to an outward orientation. China initiated its open-door policy and economic reforms by introducing special economic zones. In addition to fostering job creation, such zones have an indirect impact on poverty by promoting linkages with the domestic economy and encouraging technology transfers. The spillovers can affect the entire economy. The export-generating effect of the Malaysian EPZs has been significant, and foreign affiliates attracted to these EPZs stimulated local firms to begin to export by assisting them in producing, marketing and distributing manufactures internationally.[53] Zones in China, Indonesia, Malaysia, the Philippines, the Republic of Korea and Sri Lanka have been an important source of employment and have encouraged local entrepreneurship in some cases.[54]

Labour markets

Trade liberalization impinges on the labour market in a variety of ways. First and foremost, such reforms can lead to changes in the demand for labour, that is to say, to employment creation or contraction. Reforms may also have an effect on wages, including changing the relative wages of skilled versus unskilled labour. Trade liberalization can change conditions of work in the labour market. For example, when transnational corporations are allowed into a country, they may have more or less stringent health and safety standards than do local companies.

Trade liberalization is consistent with continued growth of employment. Following such liberalization in a sample of 19 countries, 12 of them developing, all but 1 experienced higher manufacturing employment during, as well as a year after, the liberalization. Moreover, the strongest liberalizers—Brazil and Chile—experienced the strongest employment gain.[55] Similar results have been observed in five African economies—Ghana, Malawi, Mali, Senegal and the United Republic of Tanzania,[56], as well as in Costa Rica, Peru and Uruguay. In Malawi, the welfare advantages were due to the increase in the number of traders and vendors throughout the country.[57]

Trade liberalization also exerts an influence on employment via wages. Under certain restrictive conditions, the opening of trade can be expected to increase the relative price of labour in the labour-abundant country as it decreases the relative price of labour in the capital-abundant country.[58] Empirical evidence from East Asia—especially from Hong Kong Special Administrative Region (SAR) of China, the Republic of Korea, Singapore and Taiwan Province of China—has lent credence to the view that greater openness in countries with large reserves of unskilled labour has benefited this type of labour. However, in a number of Latin American economies—including Argentina, Chile, Colombia, Costa Rica, Mexico and Uruguay—increased openness has done little to elevate the wages of unskilled labour. Mexico actually experienced a substantial rise in the premium paid to skilled labour—and therefore an increase in overall wage inequality—following the trade reform of the mid-1980s. This reflected improved productivity in reformed industries and a shift towards the use of more skilled labour.[59] The consequence of trade liberalization of Mexico in the mid-1980s, prior to its joining the General Agreement on Tariffs and Trade (GATT), differed from the consequences of Mexico's entry into NAFTA in 1994. In the former episode, the wages of skilled Mexican workers had risen, while in the latter case, the wages of unskilled labour increased. This was because Mexico is a skill-abundant country vis-à-vis the rest of the world (comprising the relevant partner countries when Mexico joined GATT), but a labour-abundant country vis-à-vis its NAFTA partners.[60]

Brazil's trade liberalization between 1988 and 1994 contributed to the growing skill premium through technological change, instigated by increased foreign competition. Moreover, industry-specific returns to skill increased by a larger amount in industries that had undergone larger tariff reductions. Overall, however, the effects of trade liberalization on wage inequality were relatively modest.[61]

Wages in the Chilean cosmetics industry since it began to be liberalized in 1974 have also shown higher returns to skilled labour. One explanation hinges on the fact that the region as a whole had reduced trade barriers in the 1990s, leading to far greater competition and a surge in imports. Seeking to be more competitive, multinationals often closed local factories, forcing the dismissal of the mostly low-skill workforce, employed in simple, labour-intensive tasks. Many multinationals also outsourced non-core personnel, such as maintenance staff, who were then rehired through subcontractors at a lower salary. Meanwhile, the workers that had kept their jobs in multinational firms were employed in management, marketing and sales—all well-paid positions for educated workers. The net result was a large upward shift in the relative demand for skilled compared with unskilled workers in multinationals. Domestic firms, meanwhile, made every effort to keep costs down, resulting in employment gains for low-skill workers in these companies which were not, however, matched by wage gains, in large part because of union weakness.[62]

Increased openness also impacts on labour conditions. Among the outcomes ascribed to trade openness is the expansion of the categories of part-time, temporary and subcontracted labour, whose members do not receive the benefits enjoyed by those employed full-time and regularly. Also observed is an increase in the female labour force and an expansion of middle-salaried workers, especially in the service sectors. Several of these trends were observed in Brazil in the late 1990s. One startling statistic derived from data published in 2000 indicates that the economically active population in Brazil totalled 71 million workers, only one third of whom were found in the formal job market. The remaining two thirds worked in the informal sector, with few of the benefits that formal employment confers.[63] In Indonesia, wages are low by world standards and a sizeable portion of the workforce consists of young females,

[59] Ana Revenga, *Employment and Wage Effects of Trade Liberalization: The Case of Mexican Manufacturing*, World Bank Policy Research Working Paper, No. 1524 (Washington, D.C., World Bank, 1995).

[60] Raymond Robertson, "Relative prices and wage inequality: evidence from Mexico", Macalester College, Department of Economics, St. Paul, Minnesota.

[61] Nina Pavcnik and others, *Trade Liberalization and Labor Market Adjustment in Brazil*, World Bank Working Paper, No. 2982 (Washington, D.C., World Bank, 2003).

[62] Janine Berg, "Technology versus trade versus social institutions: rising wage inequality in the Chilean cosmetics industry", Center for Economic Policy Analysis, The New School (2002), New York.

[63] Ricardo Antunes,"Global economic restructuring and the world of labor in Brazil: the challenges to trade unions and social movements", *Geoforum*, vol. 32 (2001), pp. 449-458.

who are frequently less activist than their male counterparts. However, while there may be a correlation between openness and sub-standard working conditions in Indonesia, this does not imply causality. In fact, working conditions in foreign-owned plants are frequently considerably better than in locally owned enterprises. Standard procedures in the former—for shift times, and medical leave, as well as health and safety precautions—often conform to global rather than local standards.[64]

While increased openness is conducive to increasing employment (both male and female), it is not clear how it benefits women differently from men. In some cases, for example, greater female secondary schooling has been found to have had a negative impact on levels of female employment. This may be because enterprises introduce technologies that require a small number of highly specialized employees and a large workforce with little training.[65]

Empirical estimates for the Philippines using data for the period from 1980 to 2000 indicate that, at both the aggregate and manufacturing sub-industry levels, increases in the propensity to export shift the demand for labour upward. In terms of the employment structure, the impact of openness on women workers, in particular, was not significant in the aggregate. However, at the manufacturing industry sub-level, the increase in the propensity to export has been a boom, especially for women workers. Finally, increases in export propensity increased the proportion of low-skilled production workers, at both the aggregate and manufacturing sub-industries levels.[66]

The effects of trade on women vary by socio-economic characteristics, sector and country. In Bangladesh, for instance, women's participation in market activities had traditionally been low and confined to a narrow range of casual jobs on the margins of the labour market.[67] With the establishment of a large number of garment factories in the 1980s (ready-made garments provide some 60 per cent of total foreign earnings), there were significant increases in female labour-force participation rates.

Investment and innovation: capital inflows and direct foreign investment

Increased openness might impact positively on growth through its effect on the rate of investment.[68] An increase in foreign investment impacts on growth and poverty reduction via improved efficiency and the adoption of new technologies. For example, in India, where liberalization began in July 1991, following a long-standing policy of fostering self-reliance, "liberalization has driven competition and competition has driven technical change".[69] Firms have therefore responded to post-1991 liberalization by improving their efficiency, by importing technology and by increasing in-house research and development. An analysis using data from Hong Kong SAR of China-based garment manufacturers, which had invested in mainland China in the 1990s, showed that such firms were endowed with valuable managerial technology and had acted as effective channels for the transfer of such technology to mainland China.[70]

After the Second World War, Mexico, like India, pursued an import substitution policy in order to reduce its dependence on both exports of raw material and imports of manufactured goods. The nascent manufacturing sector was protected from competition by heavy tariffs and quantitative restrictions on

[64] Debora Spar, "Trade, investment and labor: the case of Indonesia", *The Columbia Journal of World Business* (Winter 1996)

[65] Karin A. Siegmann, "Effects of foreign direct investment in manufacturing: gender-specific employment in Indonesia", Centre for Development Research (ZEF), University of Bonn, Germany, 2002.

[66] Aniceto C. Orbeta, "Globalization and employment: the impact of trade on employment level and structure in the Philippines", Philippine Institute for Development Studies, Discussion Paper Series, No. 2002-04, Manila.

[67] Marzia Fontana, " Modelling the effects of trade on women, at work and at home: a comparative perspective", International Food Policy Research Institute, Washington, D.C., 2002.

[68] Romain Wacziarg, "Measuring the dynamic gains from trade", background paper for World Bank, *Global Economic Prospects and the Developing Countries, 1997* (Washington, D.C., 1997).

[69] Naushad Forbes, "Technology and Indian industry: what is liberalization changing?", *Technovation*, vol. 19 (1999), pp. 403-412. See also: T.N. Srinivasan, "Economic liberalization and economic development: India", *Journal of Asian Economies*, vol. 7, No. 2 (1996), pp. 203-216.

[70] Edmund R. Thompson, "Technology transfer to China by Hong Kong's cross-border garment firms", *The Developing Economies*, vol. 41, No. 1 (2003), pp. 88-111.

imports. Managers viewed this environment as "a means of avoiding technological change and pressures for greater competitiveness".[71] Much of this has changed since 1985, when reforms were initiated in anticipation of Mexico's 1986 admission to GATT. Most firms polled have reported significant revisions in their competitive strategies. Moreover, in addition to focusing on competitiveness, many firms saw the need to retool technologically—for example, by modernizing plant and equipment.[72] An examination of the development of technological capabilities by Vitro, a Mexican firm in the glass industry, confirms this finding. Under an import substitution regime, innovation efforts had been slow. As the Mexican market opened up, however, major innovative efforts were instigated. Not only were these efforts more specialized, but there was also an attempt to master production engineering faster and to adapt when this was required to increase Vitro's exports.[73]

Trade liberalization also has a role to play in increasing productivity. Studies on manufacturing productivity and costs in Japan found that the rapid increases in volume, due to freer trade, led to dramatic improvements in output per hour, especially in large plants, as well as reductions in average cost per unit.[74] Evidence from India, based on the sizeable 1991 trade liberalization, supports this link. Firm-level data from a variety of industries over the period 1986-1993 show large increases in the growth rate of productivity in three of the four industries investigated: electronics, non-electrical machinery and electrical machinery (transport equipment was the fourth). One explanation for these increases invokes a traditional efficiency argument.[75] Additional substantiation comes from an investigation of 30 Indian industries over the period 1973-1988 which found that trade liberalization had raised total factor productivity growth.[76]

The potential for greater openness to increase investment flows to a country is of particular importance because of the likelihood that foreign investment will bring with it new technologies and greater innovation. The causality runs both ways. Increased investment can bring in new technology, enhance productivity and increase innovation, as in the case of the Mexican firm Vitro. At the same time, these domestic developments can induce greater foreign investment. Hence, the process becomes a "virtuous circle", spurring poverty reduction via growth. However, for investment to be encouraged, the trade liberalization and reforms being undertaken have to be credible. Investor confidence in the viability of liberalization and reform is thus decisive for the success of these measures.[77]

Government revenue

Although trade liberalization generates greater efficiency and potentially higher levels of output and welfare, some real trade-offs, involving, for example, the impact on government revenues, have to be considered.[78] For countries with fiscal imbalances, any loss of revenue is an important consideration, especially since this may translate into reduced spending on the poor.

Frequently, a first step in trade liberalization is to replace quantitative restrictions with tariffs. The process then continues with the gradual reduction of tariffs. However, such tariff reductions can lower government revenue. The impact can be considerable. In 1997, trade taxes accounted for 24 per cent of central government revenue in developing countries overall and for 33 per cent

[71] Len J. Trevino, "Strategic responses of Mexican managers to economic reform", *Business Horizons*, May-June 1998.

[72] Ibid.

[73] Cristina Casanueva, "The acquisition of firm technological capabilities in Mexico's open economy: the case of Vitro", *Technological Forecasting and Social Change*, vol. 66 (2001), pp. 75-85.

[74] Donald J. Daly, "Canadian research on the production effects of free trade: a summary and implications for Mexico", *North American Journal of Economics and Finance*, vol. 9 (1998), pp. 147-167.

[75] Pravin Krishna and Devashish Mitra, "Trade liberalization, market discipline and productivity growth: new evidence from India", *Journal of Development Economics*, vol. 56 (1998), pp. 447-462. The contention of X-efficiency is that firms seek to produce the maximum output technically possible from any given inputs.

[76] Satish Chand and Kunal Sen, "Trade liberalization and productivity growth: evidence from Indian manufacturing", *Review of Development Economics*, vol. 6, No. 1 (2002), pp. 120-132.

[77] Halvor Mehlum, "Zimbabwe: investments, credibility, and the dynamics following trade liberalization", *Economic Modelling*, vol. 19 (2002), pp. 565-584.

[78] Andrea Cattaneo and others, "Costa Rica trade liberalization, fiscal imbalances and macroeconomic policy: a computable general equilibrium model", *North American Journal of Economics and Finance*, vol. 10 (1999), pp. 39-67.

79 *World Public Sector Report: Globalization and the State 2001* (United Nations publication, Sales No. E.01.II.H.2). See also Liam Ebrill, Janet Stotshy and Reint Gropp, *Revenue Implications of Trade Liberalization*, IMF Occasional Paper, No. 180 (Washington, D.C., IMF, 1999).

80 David Bevan, *Fiscal Implications of Trade Liberalization*, IMF Working Paper No. 95/50 (Washington, D.C., IMF, 1995).

81 Zhi Wang and Fan Zhai, "Tariff reductions, tax replacement, and implications for income distribution in China", *Journal of Comparative Economics*, vol. 26, issue 2 (1998), pp. 358-387.

82 Andrew Feldenstein, *Tax Policy and Trade Liberalization: An Application*, IMF Working Paper, No. 92/108 (Washington, D.C., IMF, 1992).

83 See Hubert Escaith and Keiji Inoue, "Small economies' tariff and subsidy policies in the face of trade liberalization in the Americas", *Integration & Trade* (Inter-American Development Bank, Buenos Aires), vol. 5. No. 14 (2001).

84 See Jagdish Bhagwati and T.N. Srinivasan, *Lectures in International Trade* (Cambridge, Massachusetts, The MIT Press, 1983).

85 See, for example, Ebrill, Stotshy and Gropp, op. cit.; and George T. Abed, *Trade Liberalization and Tax Reform in the Southern Mediterranean Region*, IMF Working Paper, No. 98/49 (Washington, D.C., IMF, 1998).

in Africa.[79] The problem can be great in those economies for which tariff revenue makes the largest contribution to government revenue: in 1997, tariff revenues amounted to over 12 per cent of GDP in the Gambia and over 26 per cent of GDP in Lesotho. The specific impact of a tariff reduction varies by country, depending on a country's initial conditions and its reform strategy. An examination of the relationship between trade liberalization and the budget position in Kenya concluded that liberalization may be strongly budget-enhancing because of increased trade flows.[80] An analysis of the case of China suggests the use of various tax instruments to compensate budget losses arising from trade liberalization.[81]

If import values are unchanged, the short-term effect of tariff reductions is to lower government revenue. However, increased demand for now-cheaper products could compensate for this loss—eventually even outweighing it, depending on the elasticity of demand for the goods in question. In the case of differentiated tariffs, by reducing higher tariffs and increasing lower ones to create a more uniform average rate, Governments may increase revenues (depending upon which goods are affected). In addition, such a uniform tariff rate alleviates administrative difficulties and discourages tariff evasion, thus allowing for increased—rather than decreased—revenue, since the lower the tariff rate, the smaller the motivation to seek exemptions. Mexico's 1985 liberalization plan serves as one example. Tariffs gradually replaced quantity restrictions. Tariff rates were, in turn, reduced and their range and coverage were made more uniform, with positive results in terms of the productivity of the export sector. Moreover, total revenues from import duties remained approximately constant in real terms, while overall budgetary revenues rose.[82]

Reducing tariffs has important implications for the fiscal position of many countries, especially smaller economies, which are traditionally more dependent on this type of revenue. For this reason, a reduction in tariffs should be a part of the package through which the overall tax structure is changed.[83] Since domestic taxes and the expanded tax base provided by economic growth eventually compensate for the role of tariff revenues in GDP, strengthening domestic taxes is very important, especially during the initial stages of liberalization. In this regard, taxes on international trade should play a minimal role since using trade taxes/subsidies to raise government revenue is not a first-best policy from a welfare perspective.[84] From a welfare standpoint, trade tariffs and/or subsidies should be levied only to affect trade-related variables. To raise government revenue, personal and corporate and excise taxes are the more appropriate tools. However, personal and corporate income taxes need to be simplified, modernized and reformed. Finally, a simplified and streamlined tax process is often a necessity.[85]

Several case studies highlight specific examples of the impact of tariff reduction on government revenue. In Malawi, the initial focus on reducing quantitative restrictions and tariff dispersion, together with the favourable impact of foreign exchange market liberalization and enhanced tax administration, resulted in both strengthened revenue mobilization and a more liberal trade regime. Following reform in the Philippines, imports increased significantly as a percentage of GDP. The increase in imports, coupled with a reform strategy, resulted in an increase in trade taxes as a percentage of GDP and of total tax revenue, even as the tax rate declined. Argentina and Morocco, like the Philippines and

Malawi, consolidated tariffs and reduced the range that they covered.[86] In Argentina, following post-1991 reforms, overall revenue rose. Morocco, commencing with its initial reforms in the 1980s, coupled an overhaul of the domestic tax system with trade liberalization. It had reduced its maximum tariff rate from 400 to 35 per cent between 1982 and 1993 and the number of tariff bands was reduced from 47 to 6 in 1996. The combination of tax charges and tariff reductions resulted in relatively stable government revenues.[87] Numerous examples suggest that it is possible to undertake domestic fiscal reform so as, over time, to offset any revenue losses from reductions in trade taxes.

The distribution of income

There is a debate on whether trade liberalization is associated with a narrowing or widening of the intra-country distribution of income. Evidence garnered from over 40 developed and developing economies between 1978 and 1994 suggests that reduced protection worsened the distribution of income in the developing countries examined, but did not contribute significantly to increased income inequality in the developed economies.[88] On the other hand, observations covering 137 countries over the past four decades led to the conclusion that several determinants of growth, including openness to international trade, had had little systematic effect on the share of income accruing to the bottom quintile.

A focus on individual countries indicates that China, for example, dramatically increased its openness over the 1980s and 1990s. Income inequality rose as well. According to one estimate, China's Gini coefficient rose from 28.8 in 1981 to 38.8 in 1995.[89] However, disaggregating the data further shows that regions that had experienced an increase in openness between 1988 and 1993 also experienced a faster decrease in inequality. Embracing trade openness created opportunities for rural areas not only to grow, but to grow faster, than their urban neighbours. However, evidence for the Republic of Korea, using annual data for the period 1975-1995, showed that changes in the openness ratio had not been significant in influencing the distribution of income.[90] Meanwhile, there is evidence, using the 1996 Mexican National Household Income and Expenditure Survey, that, in Mexico, the impact of tariff reform on welfare was positive in general for all income deciles, with poor individuals having benefited relatively more than rich ones.[91]

Cross-country evidence suggests that, on balance, trade liberalization benefits the poor via its beneficial impact on economic growth, particularly when accompanied by other policies that are generally considered to foster growth;[92] but trade openness may not have systematic effects on the poor beyond its effect on overall growth and thus on overall poverty reduction. Micro-evidence from a large number of individual liberalization episodes shows that there is no clear-cut relationship between trade liberalization and income distribution. Even if trade liberalization results in aggregate welfare gains over all households, it is possible that the poorest households might not benefit as much in relative terms. Such a scenario has been of concern in Turkey as it deepens its relationship with EU.[93]

The policy implication—and the explanation for the diverse findings—lie in the distinction between "necessary" and "sufficient" conditions. Thus, trade

[86] This is referred to as reduced "dispersion" and is typically consistent with a reduction in average effective protection.

[87] Ebrill, Stotshy and Gropp, op. cit.

[88] Andras Savvides, "Trade policy and income inequality: new evidence", *Economics Letters*, vol. 61 (1998), pp. 365-372.

[89] Shang-Jin Wei, "Is Globalization good for the poor in China?", *Finance and Development*, vol. 39, No. 3 (September 2002).

[90] Jai S. Mah, "A note on globalization and income distribution: the case of Korea, 1975-1995", *Journal of Asian Economics*, vol. 14 (2003), pp. 157-164.

[91] Elena Ianchovichina, Alessandro Nicita and Isidro Soloaga, "Trade reform and poverty: the case of Mexico", *World Economy*, vol. 25, No. 8 (2002), pp. 945-972.

[92] Andrew MaKay, L. Alan Winters and Abbi Mamo Kedir, "A review of empirical evidence on trade, trade policy and poverty", report to the Department for International Development (DFID), prepared as a background document for the Second Development White Paper, London, 2000.

[93] Glenn W. Harrison, Thomas F. Rutherford and David G. Tarr, "Trade liberalization, poverty and efficient equity", *Journal of Development Economics*, vol. 71 (2003), pp. 97-128.

94   Ramkishen S. Rajan and Graham Bird, "Trade liberalization and poverty: where do we stand?",
University of Adelaide, Australia, 2002.

95   Lance Taylor, "External liberalization, economic
performance, and distribution in Latin America
and elsewhere", United Nations University, World
Institute for Development Economics Research,
Helsinki, 2000.

96   Zhi Wang and Fan Zhai, "Tariff reduction, tax
replacement, and implications for income distribution in China", *Journal of Comparative Economics*,
vol. 26 (1998), issue 2, pp. 358-387.

97   Dani Rodrik, "The global governance of trade: as if
development really mattered", background paper
for the Project on Trade and Sustainable Human
Development, UNDP, New York, 2001.

liberalization can be expected to help the poor overall. However, trade liberalization, while necessary, may not by itself be sufficient to achieve this end.[94]
The outcome may differ depending on the route that is taken. For example,
prior to 1990, the distributional impacts of the liberalization measures undertaken by Chile had been relatively unfavourable for the poor. However, post-
1990, Chile managed to combine high growth with decreasing inequality.[95]
Similarly, it has been suggested that trade liberalization enhanced both economic efficiency and income equality in China: the extent of the efficiency
gains appear to have depended on which instrument the Government chose to
balance its budget. Imposing a progressive household income tax reduced the
Gini coefficient while retaining most of the efficiency gains.[96]

Concomitant policies are then critical to whether liberalization will actually
result in poverty reduction. It is especially the case that these policies need to
be appropriate and balanced. In particular, the success of trade liberalization
and its impact on the poor depend critically on the extent to which product and
labour-market reforms are synchronized.

The focus on domestic reforms and policies in areas other than trade raises
another issue. Increasingly, the two goals of promoting development and max-
imizing trade are viewed as identical by policy makers. However, an alternative account of economic development questions the centrality of trade and
trade policy and emphasizes instead the critical role of domestic institutional
innovations. This train of thought argues that imported blueprints rarely spark
economic growth and that opening up the economy is hardly ever critical at the
outset. Rather, policy reforms must be "targeted to domestic investors and tai-
lored to domestic institutional realities".[97] However, liberalization and institutional reform do not constitute the terms of an either-or proposition. Both are
necessary for a successful development strategy.

THE ROLE OF THE INTERNATIONAL COMMUNITY

Thus far, the discussion has reviewed the various internal mechanisms whereby
trade expansion and trade liberalization can have an impact on poverty in a
developing country. However, intrinsic to this process is the ability of the economy in question to integrate with the global economy. This, in turn, raises the
question of the role of developed countries—to which 55 per cent of developing
economies' exports were directed in 2001—in facilitating such integration.

Trade policy of developed countries is key, since shutting out the exports of
developing countries condemns the poor to remaining poor. It has been estimated that developed countries' trade barriers cost developing countries more
than 100 billion dollars per year, roughly twice what is provided in aid. Among
the most protected sectors in industrialized countries are agriculture, textiles
and apparel—exactly those where developing economies are most competitive
and where they could create the most jobs, including jobs for low-skilled and
poor people, were such protection absent. Producers in industrialized countries
often benefit from a combination of government subsidies and import tariffs
and quotas.

The issue of the need for specific market access advantages for developing
countries was first raised at the Second Session of the United Nations
Conference on Trade and Development (UNCTAD) in 1968. Special treatment

specifically geared to the least developed countries has been provided by developed countries through the Generalized System of Preferences (GSP) schemes, and by developing countries through the Global System of Trade Preferences among Developing Countries (GSTP).[98] While these schemes are designed to assist developing countries in promoting faster export growth, the fact that preferences are granted does not guarantee that they will be effectively utilized.

Nevertheless, various attempts to ascertain levels of market access have been made, most recently in mid-2003. A Commitment to Development Index (CDI) has been compiled whose trade component measures developed countries' barriers to developing country exports, as well as the income that poor countries forgo owing to internal production subsidies in richer economies. Protection against developing countries is lowest in Australia, New Zealand and the United States, intermediate in EU and highest in Japan and Norway.[99]

A number of developing countries have successfully seized the export opportunities presented to them as a consequence of trade preferences from developed countries. Two prominent measures in this regard are the United States African Growth and Opportunity Act (AGOA) and the EU's Everything But Arms Initiative. The former had been signed into law in May 2000 and as of January 2003, 38 sub-Saharan African countries were eligible for tariff preferences.[100] The Everything But Arms Initiative was approved in February 2001 and will eventually eliminate quotas and duties on all products, except arms, from the world's poorest countries. In September 2000, the Canadian Government enlarged the product coverage of its GSP scheme to allow 570 products originating in the least developed countries to enter its market duty-free. Some countries are already benefiting from these measures. For example, Ghana, whose main trading partner is EU, has been developing a furniture-manufacturing export sector (see box VI.1). Lesotho benefits from at least two agreements—the Southern African Development Community Protocol and AGOA (see box VI. 2). These agreements have enabled Lesotho to expand clothing and textile exports to its two main export markets, South Africa and the United States.

A wider window of opportunity currently exists to assist all developing economies in the trade arena in the wake of the Fourth Ministerial Conference of the World Trade Organization which took place in Doha in November 2001. The outcome of the Conference was a Ministerial Declaration (see document A/C.2/56/7, annex) and ministerial decisions which set out the elements of a work programme with important development components, referred to as the Doha Development Agenda—The low-income countries, in particular, have much to gain from these negotiations, especially in the areas of agriculture and textiles. One of the more important deadlines in the Doha trade round slipped by, however, on 31 March 2003 when the 145 members of the World Trade Organization were unable to agree on a framework for cuts to farm subsidies and import duties on agricultural goods.[101] It has been estimated that abolishing Organisation for Economic Cooperation and Development (OECD) agricultural subsidies would provide developing countries with three times their current official development assistance (ODA) receipts. The elimination of all tariff and non-tariff barriers could result in static gains for developing countries of about $182 billion in the area of services, $162 billion in manufactures and $32 billion in agriculture.[102]

[98] *The Least Developed Countries Report, 2002 ...*, pp. 223-228.

[99] For most countries, the results are driven by estimates of agricultural protection, which is so high that it dominates the results despite the fact that the share of agriculture in total developed country imports is modest. See William R. Cline, "An index of industrial country trade policy toward developing countries", Working Paper, No. 14 (Washington, D.C., Center for Global Development, 2002).

[100] Paul Brenton, "Integrating the least developed countries into the world trading system: the current impact of EU preferences under everything but arms", World Bank, International Trade Department, Washington, D.C., 2003; and www.whitehouse.gov/news/releases/2003. See also, *World Economic and Social Survey, 2001* (United Nations publication, Sales No. E.01.II.C.1), chap. V.

[101] See IMF, "Developments in the Doha round and selected activities of interest to the Fund", 8 April 2003 (available at http://www.imf.org/external/np/pdr/doha/2003/040803.htm).

[102] Economic Commission for Africa, *Economic Report on Africa, 2003: Accelerating the Pace of Development* (United Nations publication, Sales No. E.03.II.K.1).

Box VI.1

BEYOND AGRICULTURE: FURNITURE MANUFACTURING IN GHANA

[a] N. Rankin, M. Söderbom and F. Teal, "The Ghanaian Manufacturing Enterprise Survey 2000", Centre for the Study of African Economies (CSAE), University of Oxford, Oxford, November 2002, p. 31.

[b] World Trade Organization secretariat, "Trade Policy: Ghana", Trade Policy Review Body (WT/TPR/S/81), p. 1.

[c] Ibid., p. 8

[d] N. Rankin, M. Söderbom and F. Teal, loc. cit., p. vi.

[e] United Nations Statistical aggregated country data, 1991-2001.

[f] R. Kaplinsky, M. Morris and J. Readman, "The globalization of product markets and immiserizing growth: lessons from the South African furniture industry", *World Development*, vol. 30, 7: 1159–1177, p. 1173.

[g] M. Söderbom and F. Teal, "Can African manufacturing firms become successful exporters?", Centre for the Study of African Economies (CSAE) in cooperation with United Nations Industrial Development Organization, CSAE-Unido Working Paper No. 4, Vienna and Oxford, United Kingdom, 2001.

[h] N. Rankin, M. Söderbom and F. Teal, loc. cit., p. 9.

For much of the world's population, the growing integration of the global economy has provided an opportunity for substantial income growth. Manufactured exports are seen as a key factor in a small number of African economic "lions" that have pursued sound macroeconomic policies—Ethiopia, Ghana, Mozambique, Uganda and the United Republic of Tanzania—enabling them to achieve higher and sustainable levels of economic growth.[a]

Like many African countries, Ghana is still predominantly an agrarian economy heavily dependent upon primary production, especially if subsistence agriculture is taken into account. Trade is relatively concentrated, both in commodities and in markets. Primary production (especially agriculture), and services each account for over 40 per cent of gross domestic product (GDP), while manufacturing represents about 10 per cent. Government policy has been aimed at diversifying the economy's export base away from the traditional commodities of cocoa, logs, gold and electricity.[b] To this end, the focus has shifted from the production of mainly agricultural products to manufactured products with a higher value added.

Ghana's main trading partner is the European Union (EU), accounting for almost half of total exports—partly owing to trade preferences—and imports. Within EU, Italy, the United Kingdom of Great Britain and Northern Ireland and France are the main European sources of imports.[c]

Firms in the wood and furniture sector have a higher export intensity than those in other sectors.[d] The high probability of exporting in the wood sector was due to comparative advantage. Ghana has a relative abundance of natural resources, including wood, and labour. Ghana's furniture exports increased almost 250 per cent over the last decade.[e] This was despite the global furniture industry's being characterized by increased competition, with unit prices converging across countries and falling overall.[f]

Some of the characteristics to which this export success can be attributed are: size of firms, their age and their technical efficiency. For example, there is a strong positive relationship between size and export success, as firms face large fixed costs in entering the export market.[g] Such costs include establishing an overseas supply network, market research in foreign markets, and specific product design for overseas markets.

Larger firms tend to be older and are more likely to invest and export. However, in the case of Ghana, firm age has been found to have a significant—but negative—impact on the probability of exporting. This may be attributed to the fact that recently established firms are more outward-oriented than are older firms. Alternatively, it may be because the newer firms have more advanced capital equipment and are thus better able to produce goods for export. This suggests that these factors may overshadow the benefits of "learning-through-exporting", if there are any.

The lesson to be learned from Ghana's furniture industry is that both macroeconomic policy and firm-level efficiency are key ingredients in enabling firms to enter the export market. Policies that improve the performance of firms can greatly enhance the growth prospects of developing economies, including those facing problems in respect of taking the first step into the export market in labour-intensive sectors, such as furniture manufacturing[h].

Box VI.2

BEYOND AGRICULTURE:
CLOTHING AND TEXTILE
MANUFACTURING IN
LESOTHO

Landlocked and completely surrounded by South Africa, Lesotho's main economic activity has been subsistence farming. However, the manufacturing industry in Lesotho constituted 44 per cent of gross domestic product (GDP) in 2000, compared with just over 25 per cent in 1985 and 33 per cent in 1990. It now employs a quarter of the workforce. Future development of the manufacturing sector is therefore seen as vital for improving the living standards of the population of 2.2 million. Clothing and textile companies have led the way in growth terms. In 1999, the sector employed about 18,000 people and contributed 30 per cent of total value added in manufacturing. Companies export to the United States of America, the European Union (EU) and South Africa.[a] With the nationwide unemployment rate estimated at 45 per cent, job creation is central to government policy, which places the future expansion of the clothing and textile sector—with its high labour-intensiveness—in sharp focus.

[a] South African Ministry of Finance, "Lesotho", 1999, p. 3.

The growth of Lesotho's textile sector can be attributed mainly to external factors: Lesotho is too small to sustain a manufacturing sector on its own. Gaining a foothold in the overseas market is therefore all-important for boosting the economy. Although trade linkages exist among the members of the States of the Southern African Development Community (SADC), most are more integrated with EU and the United States than they are within SADC, though Lesotho is an exception in this respect owing to its strong reliance on South Africa.

The textiles and clothing industry is mainly influenced, or regulated, by a plethora of different bilateral and multilateral trade arrangements that have been largely geared towards greater market access and an expansion of market boundaries. The sector mainly benefits from two agreements—the Southern African Development Community Trade Protocol and the African Growth and Opportunity Act (AGOA) of the United States. It further continues to benefit from preferential access to markets in EU under the Lomé Convention, though quotas limit access to this market.

Promotion of a SADC free trade area will yield benefits to all participants, but the small size of SADC relative to the global economy and trade imbalances among its members are likely to limit the medium-term scope for trade expansion.[b] However, AGOA offers sub-Saharan African countries duty-free and quota-free status into the United States for those products meeting the eligibility requirements. Since April 2001, Lesotho has been eligible for duty-free access to United States markets for textiles and apparel under AGOA.

[b] Samson Muradzikwa, "Textiles and clothing in SADC: key issues and policy perspectives", Policy Brief, No. 01/P20, Development Policy Research Unit (DPRU), University of Cape Town, Cape Town, 2001, p.10.

For the firms in this sector, the benefits have been significant and have provided a huge boost. Lesotho has established a growing presence in the United States clothing and textile market. About one third of Lesotho's exports are sold there, and 90 per cent of those sales are of jeans and T-shirts. Since April 2001, apparel and textile exports to the United States from Lesotho have risen by nearly 40 per cent.[c] The jump in Lesotho's exports of apparel to the United States from $140.3 million in 2000 to $215.3 million in 2001, has led to the soaring of investment to $122 million. For example, the Taiwan Province of China textile firm Nien Hsign is building a clothing factory outside Maseru, scheduled for completion in 2004. Some 20,000 extra jobs in the textile industry have been created as a result of AGOA—jobs that pay 5 to 10 times the average wage.[d]

[c] http://www.finance.gov.za/documents/fiscu/summits/1999/lesotho.pdf.

Although the clothing and textile industry in Southern Africa is large, directly employing up to 260,000 workers and contributing 6 per cent towards the region's

[d] Samson Muradzikwa, "The Southern African regional clothing and textile industry: case studies of Malawi, Mauritius and Zimbabwe", Working Paper, No. 01/58, Development Policy Research Unit (DPRU), University of Cape Town, Cape Town, 2001, p.9.

Box VI.2 (continued)

national output, in a global context the industry is still very small; and even though the benefits of bilateral trade agreements like AGOA have started to materialize, African clothing manufacturers exported only 3 per cent of the apparel they had been entitled to ship into the United States tariff-free—suggesting that there is still a huge potential for SADC producers to seize the opportunities presented by this market. At present, the United States imports 85 per cent of its clothing. Of the total clothing imports amounting to $60 billion, approximately $600 million are from Africa.[e]

The presence of spinners and weavers, garment manufacturers, and cross-border formal and informal trade means that this sector has both vertical and horizontal growth possibilities. By creating an attractive investment climate, Lesotho continues to encourage foreign investors with the financial, managerial and technical skills to expand the country's industry.

There are, however, concerns related to the success of the sector. Weak tax administration continues to give scope to smuggling and undervaluation of imports, thereby causing market instability within Lesotho. Customs authorities and border/port controls need to be strengthened so as to combat smuggling, especially of illegal second-hand clothing.[f] Although legal and illegal imports of second-hand clothing imports provide cheap clothing for scores of relatively poor people in Southern Africa, these imports have devastating effects on clothing and textile producers in the region.[g] Finally, there is growing unease regarding the chemical effluent from textiles production, which is fed virtually untreated into the Caledon River, an important source of drinking water, downstream, for both Lesotho and South Africa[h].

[e] *Business Day*, 16 February 2001.

[f] Muradzikwa, "The Southern African regional clothing and textile industry" ..., p. 23.

[g] Muradzikwa, "Textiles and Clothing in SADC" ..., p. 13. Used clothing accounted for 51 per cent of total United States exports of textiles and apparel to sub-Saharan Africa (United States, Department of Trade, "US trade and investment with sub-Saharan Africa", 2002, p. xv.

[h] *EU Courier*, Country report 194 (2002), p. 91.

In Doha, ministers had also agreed to negotiate on improved market access for non-agricultural goods. The aim was to reduce or eliminate tariff peaks and tariff escalation (said to exist when tariff rates rise as the level of the processing of a product increases) as well as to abolish non-tariff measures. These measures would be particularly important to poor African countries because the region as a whole is highly dependent on external trade. Tariff escalation makes it difficult for African countries to diversify their economies towards high-value-added processed goods. Tariff peaks are often concentrated in products of export interest to developing countries. In respect of the two sectors of particular importance to these exporters, textiles and agriculture, tariff barriers in textiles remain high, while high tariffs for agricultural commodities and the continued subsidization of agriculture repel agricultural exports.

For many developing countries, a successful outcome to the Doha round will necessitate obtaining significant concessions on special and differential treatment (SDT). While there are a wide assortment of SDT and implementation proposals, most seek either to exempt eligible countries from World Trade Organization disciplines (or soften them) or to deal with capacity shortfalls in meeting such regulations. One key concern is the criteria for eligibility—at present, developing-country status in the World Trade Organization is conferred through self-declaration. The group of least developed countries, however, is an exception, their identification being carried out by the United Nations.

Since almost 40 per cent of developing-country exports in 2001 were directed to other developing countries, a discussion of the role of the international community in assisting developing countries on the trade front no longer can—nor should—focus exclusively on the developed economies. The average unweighted tariff rates in developing economies in Africa, East Asia, Latin America, the Middle East and North Africa, and South Asia were 17.8, 10.4, 11.1, 19.3 and 30.7 per cent, respectively, in 1996-1999 (in contrast with a rate of 6.1 per cent in the developed countries). While these tariff rates came down in the 1990s, non-tariff barriers persist. For example, not only have developing countries become frequent users of anti-dumping measures, a predominant non-tariff barrier to trade, but on a per-dollar-of-import basis, they are the most intensive users.[103]

CONCLUSIONS

While increased openness is conducive to economic growth, and growth, in turn, is conducive to poverty reduction, openness and liberalization are not a panacea for poverty reduction. The prime explanation for this lies in the fact that the impact of trade on an economy is generally rather small, particularly in the short run. Trade policy is but one element in the relationship between growth and poverty reduction.

The effects of liberalization can manifest themselves in the short, medium and long run. In the short-to-medium term, adjustment costs are of major concern to policy makers. Stabilization schemes and other safety nets capable of being quickly implemented—such as temporary income support, and relocation assistance—are called for. All reforms—and there is no reason that trade liberalization should be an exception—create winners and losers. Indeed, this notion is built into conventional trade theory, the argument being that the "gains from trade" will be so great that the winners will be able to compensate the losers so that the welfare of both groups will rise. Reality is, unfortunately, not so neat, and appropriate policy responses are therefore required to mitigate hardships and facilitate adjustment. Potential safety net measures include targeted subsidies, cash transfers (such as fee waivers for basic services or child allowances), retraining for workers laid off from non-competitive firms, and public works employment.

In the longer run, however, due to their dynamics, trade liberalization and increased trade contribute to growth, which is necessary for poverty reduction. One lesson, therefore, is that the appropriate reaction to any of the short- and medium-run problems engendered by trade liberalization is to devise suitable policy responses, such as the introduction of retraining programmes for displaced workers, rather than to abort the trade reform process. Identification of hardships arising from generally desirable policy reforms should spur the search for complementary policies to minimize adverse consequences, such as providing training and disseminating best business practices so that new market opportunities can be exploited, and gradually phasing in trade reforms in sectors that are likely to have a particularly large impact on the poor. Rejecting all reforms that could adversely affect any poor person would be a recipe for long-run stagnation, which would ultimately increase—rather than reduce—poverty. Such a policy is not only undesirable but unnecessary, since it is possible to design approaches to trade liberalization that preclude losses by the

[103] J. Michael Finger, Francis Ng and Sonam Wangchuk, *Antidumping as safeguard policy*, World Bank Policy Research Working Paper, No. 2730 (Washington, D.C., World Bank, 2001).

poorest households. One such method is selective, rather than across-the-board, tariff reform; but while tariff exemptions can redress the adverse distributional impacts of tariff reform, they incur the danger of inducing rent-seeking practices.

Finally, the results of trade policies tend to be country-specific because effects are contingent on individual conditions. This makes it extremely difficult to gauge and predict the outcome of trade liberalization on poverty by applying the results derived from a given country at a given time to other countries and periods. Nevertheless, there are two compelling arguments for trade liberalization and the importance of trade to economic growth and, via growth, to poverty reduction. The first is that trade liberalization is generally not undertaken in isolation; rather, it is part of a "package" of complementary reforms—all of which may be necessary for, and conducive to, growth. The second argument attesting to the importance of trade reform is based on the fact that there are virtually no "counter-examples"—that is to say, cases of *closed* economies that have thrived in the long term. Countries that have performed well as regards economic growth over the past 20 years or so have made opening up part of the reform process. Given today's ever more globalized world economy, it is difficult to imagine that any country hoping to prosper and reduce poverty in the future could do otherwise.

VII MARKET-BASED APPROACHES TO RURAL DEVELOPMENT IN SUB-SAHARAN AFRICA

Policies to improve the economic efficiency of agriculture can play a critical role in the implementation of rural development strategies, including efforts to combat rural poverty. The present chapter focuses on selected market-based policies, namely food marketing reform and land redistribution, intended to increase agricultural efficiency and identifies the indirect impacts of such policies on the achievement of more equitable patterns of rural development, particularly in sub-Saharan Africa, a region in which the total number of people living in extreme poverty is expected to rise between 1990 and 2015. Although market-based policies are not usually adopted primarily to reduce rural poverty, they can have overall positive impacts on poverty alleviation.

Better access to staple food markets is especially important for the rural poor, who often generate the bulk of their income from producing staple foods. Particular attention should thus be paid to the role of food marketing in rural economic growth. Until the mid-1980s, the marketing of major food crops in many African countries was carried out by ad hoc State agencies, notably marketing boards. State intervention in food marketing, however, created economic inefficiencies and unsustainable fiscal costs, besides proving generally ineffective in ensuring sustained rural economic growth. This led to greater emphasis on market-based approaches aimed at improving the efficiency and cost-effectiveness of agricultural marketing. The case studies of marketing reform presented in this chapter suggest that providing the enabling environment for improved marketing efficiency—through a better transport network, food storage capacity and credit provision for poor farmers—can be a more effective form of government involvement in food marketing than direct intervention through marketing boards.

The chapter also argues that market-based land redistribution policies can promote greater economic efficiency and more equitable rural growth. When small-scale farmers have secure access to arable land—in the form of land titles or long-term rental—they are likely to increase investment in their land, produce more food and raise their incomes. Expanded land-use or ownership rights also increase their chances of securing cheaper and more extensive credit by using land as collateral. At the same time, success with redistributive land reform depends, to a large extent, on the implementation of complementary measures to foster rural development.

Market-based schemes can be considered one of the most innovative approaches to land reform that have emerged over the last decade, and provide a useful alternative to more conventional, State-controlled land redistribution programmes. The chapter concludes, however, that when countries opt for market-based approaches to land redistribution, the State still has an important role to play, without necessarily deciding which land parcels change hands.

RURAL DEVELOPMENT AND POVERTY REDUCTION IN SUB-SAHARAN AFRICA

The need for greater emphasis on rural poverty reduction

Approximately 75 per cent of the world's extreme poor live and work in rural areas and two thirds of them depend for their livelihoods mainly on farming or farm labour.[1] Although rural poverty rates fell sharply in many developing countries during the 1970s and 1980s, the decline has slowed down around the world since then. It is estimated that 60 per cent of the world's poor will still live in rural areas by 2020, even though the world urban population is likely to have overtaken the rural share.[2] Substantial progress on rural poverty reduction in developing countries will thus be crucial for the attainment of the Millennium Development Goal for poverty.

Rural poverty is a multidimensional phenomenon that is reflected by low income, inequality in access to resources, low education standards, poor nutrition, inadequate health services and vulnerability to shocks, among other factors. Sustainable development strategies to combat rural poverty must reflect its multidimensional nature and thus be targeted at different economic, social and environmental objectives. This implies that social policies to improve poor people's access to health, nutrition, education and training should become an integral part of rural development strategies, even though a discussion of these issues lies beyond the scope of this chapter.[3] The chapter examines selected market-based policies to improve the economic efficiency of agriculture—and looks at their indirect impact on the promotion of more equitable patterns of rural development—as opposed to broad socio-economic policies to combat rural (and urban) poverty.

The relationship between rural and urban poverty is a critical underlying factor in the analysis of poverty issues, given that persistently high levels of rural poverty in developing countries have stimulated migration of the rural poor to urban areas. A significant share of urban poverty can be seen as a result of the personal poverty alleviation strategies of poor rural people who have few options other than migrating to urban areas.[4] In many developing countries, economic policies primarily based on urban development seem unlikely to alleviate poverty as effectively as policies that also incorporate rural development strategies. Furthermore, government policies that penalize the agricultural sector and neglect the social and physical infrastructure in rural areas have been major contributors to both rural and, through migration, urban poverty.[5] Examples of policies that negatively affect the rural poor include urban bias in the public provision of social services and infrastructure; and bias in favour of large landowners and agribusinesses with respect to land ownership rights, publicly provided extension services and subsidized access to credit and irrigation water. Unequal land distribution is one of the greatest obstacles to rural poverty reduction in developing countries.

[1] International Fund for Agricultural Development (IFAD), *Rural Poverty Report 2001: The Challenge of Ending Rural Poverty* (New York, Oxford University Press, 2001). The United Nations Millennium Declaration (See General Assembly resolution 55/2 of 8 September 2000) defines people in extreme poverty as those whose income is less than one dollar a day.

[2] M. Ravallion, "On the urbanization of poverty", *Journal of Development Economics*, vol. 68 (2002), pp. 435-442.

[3] See, for example, *Report of the World Summit for Social Development, Copenhagen, 6-12 March 1995* (United Nations publication, Sales No. E.96.IV.8); and *Report on the World Social Situation, 2001* (United Nations publication, Sales No. E.01.IV.5).

[4] M.H. Khan, *Rural Poverty in Developing Countries: Issues and Policies*, IMF Working Paper, No. WP/00/78 (Washington, D.C., International Monetary Fund, April 2000).

[5] See R. Sobhan, "Eradicating rural poverty: moving from a micro to a macro agenda", mimeo, Centre for Policy Dialogue, Dhaka, June 2001.

It can be argued that the success of efforts to combat rural poverty depends on at least two economic factors: granting the rural poor legally secure entitlement to assets—notably land—and improving their access to agricultural markets.[6] Inadequate access to arable land is probably the most important cause of rural poverty, and redistributive land reform is increasingly seen as crucial in many developing countries. There is an urgent need, therefore, to focus attention on the implementation of land redistribution policies as a means to promote more equitable rural growth patterns. Similarly, better access to staple food markets is especially important because staples farming often accounts for a large proportion of the income of the rural poor. Particular attention should thus also be paid to the role of food marketing reform in rural economic growth, even if this type of policy reform is not designed to reduce poverty directly.

Focusing on sub-Saharan Africa

The latest poverty projections suggest that the Millennium Development Goal of halving extreme poverty between 1990 and 2015 (see document A/56/326, annex, goal 1, target 1) is likely to be achieved on a global level, although there will be considerable regional disparities. While the largest share of the world's extremely poor people live in South Asia (41.7 per cent in 1999), the highest proportion of poor people within a region is found in sub-Saharan Africa, where over 315 million people (approximately 40 per cent of the population) lived on less than one dollar a day in 1999. Moreover, sub-Saharan Africa is the only developing-country region in which the total number of people living in extreme poverty is expected to *rise* considerably between 1990 and 2015.[7] With more than 400 million people projected to be in extreme poverty in Africa in 2015, this region will have a total number of extremely poor people equal to that of all other developing-country regions put together (see figure VII.1).

Non-income poverty indicators have also deteriorated in sub-Saharan Africa. For example, while East Asia has made significant progress in reducing the proportion of people who suffer from hunger, the estimated number of undernourished Africans rose by 27 million during the 1990s.[8] Similarly, sub-Saharan Africa has the highest share of its population below the minimum level of dietary energy consumption; the lowest net enrolment ratio in primary education; the highest under-five mortality rate; the highest prevalence and death rates associated with human immunodeficiency virus/acquired immunodeficiency syndrome (HIV/AIDS), malaria and other diseases; and the highest proportion of its population without access to safe drinking water.

This significant deterioration of poverty indicators calls for systematic action to deal with the dire situation in sub-Saharan Africa. The international community and sub-Saharan African Governments must pull together to promote sustained economic growth and combat poverty. In other words, just as there is an urgent need to give greater emphasis to rural poverty reduction around the world, international efforts to achieve the Millennium Development Goal for poverty reduction should also give greater priority to sub-Saharan Africa.

A greater international focus on rural poverty alleviation would strengthen poverty reduction efforts in sub-Saharan Africa, where the vast majority of the

[6] In addition to social factors based on improved access to human assets, such as health, nutrition, education and skills. See *Rural Poverty Report, 2001 ... .*

[7] See World Bank, *Global Economic Prospects and the Developing Countries, 2003* (Washington, D.C., World Bank, 2002), p. 30.

[8] Report of the Secretary-General entitled "Implementation of the United Nations Millennium Declaration" (document A/57/270 and Corr.1).

Figure VII.1.

SHARE OF DEVELOPING-COUNTRY REGIONS IN WORLD EXTREME POVERTY,[a] 1999 AND 2015

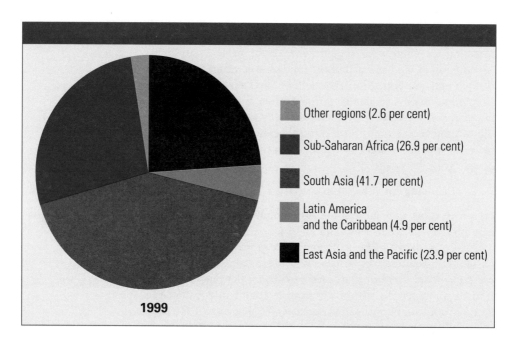

Other regions (2.6 per cent)

Sub-Saharan Africa (26.9 per cent)

South Asia (41.7 per cent)

Latin America
and the Caribbean (4.9 per cent)

East Asia and the Pacific (23.9 per cent)

1999

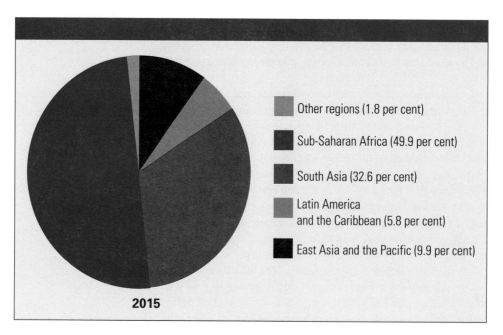

Other regions (1.8 per cent)

Sub-Saharan Africa (49.9 per cent)

South Asia (32.6 per cent)

Latin America
and the Caribbean (5.8 per cent)

East Asia and the Pacific (9.9 per cent)

2015

Source: UN/DESA, based on *Global Economic Prospects and the Developing Countries, 2003* (Washington, D.C., World Bank, 2002), p. 30.

a Regions are defined by the World Bank. The country data necessary to compute these aggregates according to the country grouping used elsewhere in the *Survey* are not available.

poor live and work in rural areas. In Eastern and Southern Africa, at least four fifths of the extreme poor live in rural areas and 85 per cent of the poor depend on agriculture for their livelihood.[9] In the United Republic of Tanzania, for example, income from agriculture—including crops, livestock and wage labour—is the main income source for 96 per cent of the households in the bottom income quintile.[10] Even in Central and Western Africa—where urban poverty has been rising rapidly—the incidence of poverty is still much higher in rural (as opposed to urban) areas in most countries.[11] In Ghana, for instance, 83 per cent of the poor lived in rural areas in 1998-1999 and most of them were food crop farmers.[12] The most recent projections indicate that in only two African countries—Ghana and Madagascar—are rural poverty rates likely to decline at a pace adequate to achieve the Millennium Development Goal for poverty.[13]

Sustained growth of the farm sector could offer an opportunity for many Africans to escape from poverty. One of the most important means for reducing rural poverty in Africa would be to raise the incomes of poor farmers by increasing their agricultural productivity and output. For example, the significant reduction of rural poverty in the developing countries between 1970 and 1990 was closely associated with increased agricultural productivity, arising primarily from the expansion of irrigated croplands and the introduction of other forms of enhanced agricultural technology during the so-called green revolution, between the mid-1960s and the mid-1980s.

At the regional level, however, the implementation and success of both these policies were highly unbalanced. For example, East Asia's and South Asia's considerable agricultural growth and poverty reduction during that period are partly explained by their expansion of irrigation agriculture. Conversely, the persistence of rural poverty and agricultural stagnation in most of sub-Saharan Africa has been partly caused by its meagre 5 per cent of irrigated cropland area.[14] Similarly, although the green revolution did reach sub-Saharan Africa, the region failed to benefit from it as much as Asia, which experienced a significant agricultural "technology shift" that increased the productivity of staple foods, notably rice, wheat and maize.[15] Higher crop yields arising from technological progress achieved during the green revolution contributed to the rapid decline of rural poverty in many Asian developing countries.

For the rural economy to be Africa's growth engine, appropriate economic policies to promote agricultural growth are thus crucial. Over the past two decades, many sub-Saharan African Governments have introduced significant macro- and microeconomic policy changes that have had a direct impact on agricultural productivity and rural development. While agricultural policy reform throughout the continent has been closely associated with aid conditionality in general, and structural adjustment programmes in particular, there are also key endogenous dimensions of economic policy change. The heavy fiscal burden of State intervention and the need to improve efficiency were particularly instrumental in encouraging African Governments to introduce different approaches to agricultural development in their countries.

Among the economic policies that can promote agricultural development in Africa are agricultural market reform; policies to provide better access to physical assets (mainly land) and financial assets, and to improve extension services, transport and irrigation infrastructure; pricing, tax and exchange-rate policies

[9] IFAD, *Assessment of Rural Poverty: Eastern and Southern Africa* (Rome, IFAD, 2002).

[10] Ibid.

[11] IFAD, *Assessment of Rural Poverty: Western and Central Africa* (Rome, IFAD, December 2001), p. 24. One country (Cameroon) currently has a higher poverty incidence rate in urban than in rural areas.

[12] C.K. Dordunoo and G.Y. Dogbey, "Globalization and economic reforms in Ghana", in *Globalization and the Developing Countries: Emerging Strategies for Rural Development and Poverty Alleviation*, D. Bigman, ed. (Wallingford, United Kingdom, Centre for Agriculture and Biosciences International/ International Service for National Agricultural Research (CABI/ISNAR) 2002), chap. 4.

[13] D.E. Sahn and D. C. Stifel, "Progress toward the Millennium Development Goals in Africa", *World Development*, vol. 31, No. 1 (2003), pp. 23-52.

[14] *Rural Poverty Report, 2001...* .

[15] See *World Economic and Social Survey, 2002* (United Nations publication, Sales No. E.02.II.C.1), chap. V.

that do not penalize agriculture; agricultural trade liberalization; and the expansion and dissemination of agricultural technology research. This chapter argues that innovative market-based approaches aimed at increasing agricultural efficiency in Africa have emerged under the first two of these sets of policies, namely, marketing reform and a market-based approach to land reform.

FOOD MARKETING REFORM IN SUB-SAHARAN AFRICA

The role of food markets in rural poverty alleviation

Agriculture is vital to most of Africa's rural population as their major source of both food and income. Furthermore, while the urban poor derive their main source of income from the urban informal sector, smallholder agriculture is by far the main source of income of the rural poor in sub-Saharan Africa.[16] Farming of basic food crops (staples), in particular, account for a considerable share of the income of Africa's rural poor, although an increasing proportion of them also generate income from other sources, notably cash crops, livestock and some non-farm activity. In addition, the rural poor usually obtain 70 to 80 per cent of their calorie intake from staple foods.[17]

Domestic production of basic food crops also has considerable impacts on domestic inflation in poor African countries in view of their significant effect on (national) retail price index baskets of goods and the well-being of the poor. In sum, properly functioning food markets are crucial for poverty alleviation in Africa, for three major reasons: food purchases tend to dominate the expenditure of the poor; the sale of staples is one of the major sources of income of the rural poor; and poorly organized food markets and food distribution systems often result in heavy socio-economic costs, including famine, in both rural and urban areas.

There is plenty of evidence to show that food marketing uncertainty in sub-Saharan Africa contributes to stagnation in agricultural output and productivity.[18] Grain markets in the region are prone to instability owing to a series of unique physical and economic characteristics that set them apart from other agricultural markets. First, staple grains are subject to large differences between import and export prices because their value tends to be low relative to transportation costs, notably in areas with poor transport infrastructure. Second, since grains can be stored at relatively low cost, price expectations have considerable influence on current price movements in grain markets. Third, low short-run price elasticity of aggregate demand and supply of grains means that even moderate changes in output are likely to lead to large price fluctuations.

In addition, international grain markets tend to be dominated by the activities of a relatively small number of countries whose surplus disposal policies are a further source of price instability.[19] International price fluctuations for some staple food commodities, such as rice, for example, tend to be much greater than domestic fluctuations. Greater alignment between domestic and international grain prices arising from agricultural trade liberalization can thus increase domestic price volatility. Nonetheless, as chapter VI illustrates, there have been several "success stories" that can be at least partly associated with agricultural trade liberalization in Africa.[20] The present section, however, will

[16] The term "smallholder" is often used to refer to poor small farmers without formal land titles, sometimes tilling poor-quality soils—inter alia, on plots owned by large landlords—and who depend directly on this activity for their subsistence. This broad definition thus includes tenants and share-croppers but not landless farm labourers, many of whom subsist on very low wages and the pay derived from insecure jobs, and are thus also part of the rural poor. See, for example, E. R. Wolf, *Peasant Wars of the Twentieth Century* (New York, Harper and Row, 1969).

[17] *Rural Poverty Report, 2001... .*

[18] J. Coulter and G. Onumah, "The role of warehouse receipt systems in enhanced commodity marketing and rural livelihoods in Africa", *Food Policy*, vol. 27 (2002), pp. 319-337.

[19] There has been, however, a long-term downward trend in international grain prices in general, sometimes interrupted by sharp price rises, as in 1995. See also S. Jones, *Liberalized Food Marketing in Developing Countries: Key Policy Problems* (Oxford, United Kingdom, Oxford Policy Management (OPM), May 1998), p. 2.

[20] For a criticism of the assumed connection between agricultural trade liberalization and poverty reduction, see the Special Contribution by J. Stiglitz in United Nations Development Programme, *Human Development Report, 2003* (New York, Oxford University Press, 2003), p. 80.

focus on food production for domestic markets, in view of its close links to rural poverty through smallholder production and the dominant share of food staples in the consumption of the rural poor.

Although State intervention in food markets is generally aimed at stabilizing domestic prices, it is often justified on three main grounds: (a) to avoid interruption of food supply and to ensure food access for the poor; (b) to protect consumers (both urban and rural) from sharp price rises; and (c) to protect producers from sharp price falls associated with imbalances in demand and supply. State intervention has thus often involved granting price-reducing subsidies to consumers and price-raising subsidies to producers. However, restraining retail food prices has not always been compatible with guaranteeing minimum producer prices, especially in poor countries with limited budgets. Despite the fiscal costs arising from State intervention in food markets, marketing and storage of major food crops in most African (and many other developing) countries tended to be in the hands of State agencies until the 1980s. Furthermore, State institutions in many countries also controlled both international purchases and domestic distribution of critical inputs, such as fertilizers and pesticides.

This intervention in food production and marketing was often carried out through State marketing boards that had a statutory monopoly over key domestic marketing functions, as well as (external) agricultural trade. Marketing boards in Africa have usually been associated with export cash crops—such as cocoa, coffee, cotton, groundnuts and tea—and with their price stabilization functions. However, at least one of these (cash crop) marketing boards—as well as several ad hoc food marketing boards—also intervened in the purchasing, processing and distribution of staple food crops, such as maize, millet, rice, sorghum and yam. Regardless of their intervention in food staple or cash crop markets, most marketing boards in sub-Saharan Africa either have failed to achieve their price stabilization objectives—mainly because of financial or managerial constraints—or have achieved them only temporarily, at the cost of fiscal destabilization.[21] As a result of these domestic constraints, the 1980s and 1990s witnessed a redefinition of the State's role in food marketing and a marked trend towards food (and agricultural) marketing reform throughout Africa. There were therefore critical endogenous reasons for this reform, notably the unsustainable fiscal cost of pricing intervention by State agencies.

At the same time, policy reform has been closely associated with the implementation of the structural adjustment programmes promoted by the Bretton Woods institutions and bilateral aid programmes from the early 1980s onward. For example, a World Bank report published in 1981 advocated a series of actions for African economies caught in a downward spiral, including a recommendation that African Governments reduce control over food markets and increase the role of market forces.[22] Aid conditionality thus also contributed to shaping policies on food (and agricultural) marketing reform in Africa over the past two decades.[23] The main features of this reform have been (a) the partial or complete withdrawal of State agencies from staple food marketing; (b) the reduction or removal of consumer and producer pricing subsidies, including input subsidies; (c) a gradual movement away from State-controlled prices towards market-determined pricing; and (d) relaxation of regulatory controls over private marketing activities.

[21] See S. Jones and S. Wickrema, "Price stabilization policies in the context of market liberalization", *OPM Policy Briefing Note 2* (Oxford, United Kingdom, OPM, n.d.).

[22] World Bank, *Accelerated Development in Sub-Saharan Africa: An Agenda for Action* (Washington, D.C., World Bank, 1981). This document is widely referred to as "The Berg report" after its senior author, E. Berg.

[23] Many African countries have also liberalized markets of non-staple commodities, such as cotton and coffee, but their analysis lies outside the scope of this chapter. See, for example, T. Akiyama and others, "Commodity market reform in Africa: some recent experience", *Economic Systems* (forthcoming, 2003); and A. W. Shepherd and S. Farolfi, "Export crop liberalization in Africa: a review", *FAO Agricultural Services Bulletin 135* (Rome, FAO, 1999).

Food marketing reform in selected African countries

The implementation of food marketing reform in sub-Saharan Africa has varied considerably across countries and the achievement of reform objectives has often been closely associated with the degree of political commitment. Reform measures have focused mainly on reducing State involvement in marketing and price-fixing, or on increasing the efficiency of the remaining marketing boards. By the end of the 1990s, these boards were either "generally losing out in competition with the private sector" throughout sub-Saharan Africa or had "been converted into non-trading industry boards for the purpose of promotion and regulation".[24]

Some countries, such as Ghana and Mali, had already had significant private sector involvement in food marketing (often in contravention of marketing boards' monopoly status) before reforms were introduced. In many Western African countries, State marketing boards nominally had statutory monopsonies and monopolies over food marketing but rarely handled more than a fifth of total marketed staples output. Well-established private grain trading networks operated extensive parallel markets, both within countries and across borders. In these cases, reform eventually focused on providing the enabling environment for the expansion of private trading, inter alia, by improving physical infrastructure, extension services and access to credit.

Countries that had more effective State intervention in food marketing before reform, notably in Eastern and Southern Africa, embarked on market liberalization as a result of fiscal constraints and aid conditionality, but several of them did so without full political commitment to reform. Frequent policy reversals in some of these countries have undermined the attainment of major reform objectives and also have created a good deal of uncertainty for the emerging private sector. For example, a comprehensive review of marketing reform in Kenya, Malawi and the United Republic of Tanzania found out that private agricultural traders repeatedly complained about the unpredictability of Government policies.[25] However, South Africa—and, to a lesser extent, the United Republic of Tanzania—have succeeded in making a transition from a State-controlled food marketing system to an increasingly market-based one. In addition, as will be shown below, the transition in South Africa has led to greater reliance on existing private commodity markets to correct price fluctuations arising from the withdrawal of marketing boards from price stabilization.

The following seven case studies illustrate the varied extent of marketing reform in sub-Saharan Africa, and their different degrees of success in improving food marketing efficiency and reducing the real prices of staple foods, as well as the indirect impacts of the reforms on household food security and poverty alleviation.

Ghana

Even prior to reform, small private traders were already responsible for the bulk of food marketing in Ghana, including staple foods such as maize. Partly in response to the food shortages associated with the drought of 1982-1983, the Government sought to expand the role of the Ghana Food Distribution Corporation (GFDC) in maize marketing activities, notably through pricing stabilization;[26] but the inability of GFDC to maintain this pricing policy—

[24] Food and Agriculture Organization of the United Nations, "A guide to maize marketing for extension officers", *Marketing Extension Guide 2* (Rome, FAO, 1999).

[25] P. Seppälä, ed., *Liberalized and Neglected? Food Marketing Policies in Eastern Africa*, World Development Studies, No. 12 (Helsinki, United Nations University (UNU) World Institute for Development Economics Research (WIDER), March 1998).

[26] See M. Kherallah and others, *Agricultural Market Reforms in Sub-Saharan Africa: A Synthesis of Research Findings* (Washington, D.C., International Food Policy Research Institute (IFPRI), August 2000), chap. 4.

mainly because of its deteriorating finances—contributed to a rapid reversal of State intervention and greater marketing liberalization.

The Economic Recovery Programme (ERP), initiated in 1983 with the support of the Bretton Woods institutions, introduced several market-based macro- and microeconomic reforms. These included the elimination of guaranteed minimum maize prices and the creation of an enabling environment for the expansion of private sector grain trading, including small-scale traders. In the early 1990s, the Government introduced a medium-term agricultural development programme (MTP), covering the period 1991-2000, whose aim was "to establish and support market-led growth in agriculture".[27] MTP reforms included the Government's withdrawal from price fixing and price support operations in the agricultural sector—with the notable exception of cocoa—and a significant reduction in Government subsidies for State agencies, such as GFDC.

Marketing reform has changed the Government's role from that of intervening in food pricing and marketing to one of implementing measures in support of private sector expansion, such as the provision of better storage services to both maize farmers and traders and the construction of rural feeder roads and other infrastructure essential for agricultural and marketing expansion. Improvements in local storage capacity and transport systems have helped to reduce both long-term food prices and their variability.[28] GFDC is now focused on the provision of marketing support services—notably grain drying, cleaning and storage—to private sector clients. Support for small-scale marketing has also had positive gender effects, given that women traders are particularly active in small-scale food marketing in Ghana.[29]

Marketing reform, however, has had mixed results for agricultural development. For example, real grain prices have fallen since 1984 and agricultural output per capita also declined between the mid-1980s and mid-1990s.[30] In addition, the expansion of small-scale agricultural marketing activities has often been hampered by the inability of commercial financial institutions to serve rural areas and the rural poor adequately. In order to deal with this problem, the Government, in cooperation with bilateral donors and multilateral agencies, is currently implementing a programme aimed at strengthening microfinance institutions and improving rural access to financial services, particularly for the poorest segments of the rural population.[31]

Political resistance to further restructuring of GFDC has limited the potential benefits of food marketing reform in the country. Particular problems have arisen from the Government's unwillingness to deal with overstaffing in GFDC and the latter's resistance to making its warehouses fully available to the private sector.[32] It has been recommended that "serious consideration should be given to ... selling off or leasing (GFDC) stores and grain handling equipment to the private sector".[33] However, the privatization of grain storage facilities may raise problems of monopoly power in cases where other storage opportunities are limited. As a result, efforts to increase the efficiency of food distribution should address such problems by leasing storage facilities to the private sector and by obliging private operators to facilitate competition by making grain storage services available to third parties on commercial and non-discriminatory terms.[34]

[27] See Dordunoo and Dogbey, loc. cit.

[28] O. Badiane and G. E. Shively, "Spatial integration, transport costs and the response of local prices to policy changes in Ghana", *Journal of Development Economics*, vol. 56 (1998), pp. 411-431.

[29] F. Lyon, "Trust, networks and norms: the creation of social capital in agricultural economies in Ghana", *World Development*, vol. 28, No. 4 (2000), pp. 663-681.

[30] T.S. Jayne and others, *Trends in real food prices in six Sub-Saharan African countries*, MSU International Development Working Paper, No. 55 (East Lansing, Michigan, Michigan State University, n.d.).

[31] See *Assessment of Rural Poverty: Western and Central Africa...*, p. 61.

[32] See J. Coulter and A. W. Shepherd, "Inventory credit: An approach to developing agricultural markets", *FAO Agricultural Services Bulletin 120* (Rome, FAO, 1995), case study 4.

[33] Ibid., sect. 7.

[34] See, for example, S. Jones and S. Wickrema, "Defining the role of the State in staple food markets", OPM *Policy Briefing Note 3* (Oxford, United Kingdom, OPM, n.d.).

Kenya

Kenya has had a slow and uneven process of marketing reform, for several economic, social and political reasons. Until the 1980s, State intervention in food marketing was exercised through a monopoly, granted to the National Cereals and Produce Board (NCPB), over grain movements between different districts of the country, sales to large grain mills and international agricultural trade. The Government also set a fixed national price for producers. Despite the monopoly status of NCPB, private sector trading (both legal and illegal) accounted for a significant share of marketed maize output. Because of this private involvement in food marketing, as well as restrictions on internal grain movements, NCPB was unable to eliminate disparities between official and parallel market prices, and there were large price differentials among different areas of the country.

In 1980, the country's first structural adjustment programme included limited reform of producer prices, but pressure to reform NCPB met with stiff political resistance. Increased producer prices and a threefold increase in NCPB personnel associated with the establishment of local buying centres in the mid-1980s made that marketing board a considerable fiscal burden to the country. By 1987, NCPB accumulated debt was equivalent to 5 per cent of Kenya's gross domestic product (GDP).[35] Radical reform of NCPB was repeatedly emphasized in structural adjustment and bilateral aid programmes throughout the 1980s and early 1990s, but never fully implemented owing to a lack of political commitment.

Grain marketing reform has, however, made significant progress in other areas. The partial implementation between 1986 and 1991 of a Cereal Sector Reform Programme (CSRP)—with the financial support of the European Union (EU)—allowed grain millers to purchase an increasing proportion of their supplies from the private sector. By 1992, about 50 per cent of (national) millers' requirements were purchased from non-NCPB sources. In addition, small-scale (hammer) mills gained a significant market share from large-scale (subsidized) millers. By the mid-1990s, urban hammer meal consumption had increased to as much as 40 per cent of total maize meal consumption. Given that a large proportion of low-income families own or work in those small urban mills, this is likely to have had a positive impact on poverty alleviation.

Another important outcome of reform has been the partial lifting of controls on grain movements within the country. As a result, consumer prices have fallen in most parts of Kenya as trade flows between surplus and deficit areas rose, and increased private sector efficiency has been encouraged by a "spatial configuration of agricultural production more in line with regional comparative advantage".[36] In addition, the parallel liberalization of the country's fertilizer market has produced broad efficiency gains in the farming sector. There is also evidence that the liberalized maize milling has improved the sector's competitiveness—notably through the expansion of small-scale hammer mills—and contributed to lower maize flour (real) prices.[37]

Nonetheless, in key reform areas, such as NCPB restructuring, price liberalization and allowing licensed buying agents to operate legally in the food market, Kenya's marketing reform programme has suffered from erratic implementation. Opposition to reform by past Kenyan Governments meant that private marketing was liberalized only during the 1990s and only after concerted donor

35   S. Jones and S. Wickrema, "The use of conditionality in reform: food markets in Africa", OPM Policy Briefing Note 1 (Oxford, United Kingdom, OPM, n.d.).

36   S. Were Omamo and L. O. Mose, "Fertilizer trade under market liberalization: preliminary evidence from Kenya", Food Policy, vol. 26 (2001), pp. 1-10. See also J. K. Nyoro and others, "Evolution of Kenya's marketing system in the post-liberalization era", paper presented at the Workshop on Agricultural Transformation in Africa, Nairobi, 27-30 June 1999.

37   Seppälä, op. cit.

pressure. Lack of political commitment, and major weaknesses in the formulation and implementation of the reform programme, have been the two main reasons for the relatively slow pace of reform so far. Although real grain prices gradually fell during the 1990s, further success in marketing reform will require policies to intensify marketing liberalization, including the creation of favourable economic conditions for private sector expansion in food marketing.

Malawi

Malawi's agricultural sector includes a smallholder subsector—which accounts for 70 per cent of agricultural output, including the bulk of food staples—and the private commercial subsector, which mainly produces cash crops.[38] In 1971, the Government set up the State-owned Agricultural Development and Marketing Corporation (ADMARC) to intervene in the purchasing and marketing of agricultural produce. ADMARC had monopsonist powers only in the purchase of non-food crops, such as cotton and tobacco. However, it became increasingly involved in the purchasing and marketing of food products that were supposed to be freely traded, which led to some crowding-out of private traders.[39]

The marketing activities of ADMARC aimed at providing a reliable market for smallholder output; setting uniform national prices that cross-subsidized less competitive farmers living in areas lacking adequate transport networks; and providing subsidized agricultural inputs. It also provided large subsidies for the consumption of maize and rice.[40] The activities of ADMARC during its first decade played an important role in sustaining the smallholder sector and contributing to household food security. However, from the early 1980s onward, ADMARC had increasing difficulty in sustaining its pricing policy, with increasing losses in its food marketing activities, owing to several micro- and macroeconomic problems, including exogenous shocks. These problems included the escalating fiscal cost of producer and consumer subsidies; the inflated number of ADMARC employees and their decreasing productivity; Malawi's falling or negative economic growth rates and deteriorating terms of trade; increasing transport costs arising from the civil war in Mozambique; and falling world prices for tobacco, whose export tax revenues were used to subsidize the marketing board's maize support operations.

As a result of these economic difficulties, as well as aid conditionality, Malawi launched a series of structural adjustment programmes during the 1980s and 1990s, which led to the gradual liberalization of grain pricing and marketing. In fiscal year 1981/82, the producer price of maize was increased by two thirds and the ADMARC statutory monopsony in smallholder agriculture purchases was officially eliminated in 1987, although the State marketing board still remained active in food markets. Despite the considerable pressure exerted by international financial institutions to promote extensive price and marketing liberalization, Malawi has been one of the African countries that most resisted the dismantling of a State marketing agency.

Although price and marketing liberalization led to a considerable increase in maize production, it did not guarantee household food security. While smallholders who are net food sellers have gained from liberalization, small farmers who are net food buyers or who live in remote areas appear to have become worse off.[41] Small-scale traders as a whole—a significant proportion of whom

[38] See W. Chilowa, "The impact of agricultural liberalization on food security in Malawi", *Food Policy*, vol. 23, No. 6 (1998), pp. 553-569.

[39] The increasing involvement of ADMARC in food marketing was facilitated by its establishment of 1,400 marketing points by the early 1980s. See T. S. Jayne and S. Jones, "Food marketing and pricing policy in Eastern and Southern Africa: a survey", *World Development*, vol. 25, No. 9 (1997), pp. 1505-1527.

[40] Chilowa, loc. cit., p. 557.

[41] Chilowa, loc. cit.

have relatively low incomes—have benefited from marketing reform, even though they have also faced serious constraints that have hindered their ability to improve marketing efficiency. These constraints include poor and costly transport infrastructure, inadequate storage facilities and lack of credit, training and extension services, including insufficient technical advice. Greater Government (and donor) efforts are thus needed in order to accelerate food marketing reform and ensure that the benefits of improved private marketing efficiency are passed on to consumers, especially the poor.

Mali

The establishment of Mali's agricultural marketing board—*L'Office malien des produits agricoles* (OMPA)—dates back to the mid-1960s. Before marketing reforms, it had a statutory monopoly over grain trade and the authority to set uniform prices for both producers and consumers throughout the country. Food pricing policy was primarily aimed at providing "cheap food to the army, State employees, and the urban population".[42] During the 1960s and 1970s, OMPA was also the main State agency responsible for the distribution of food aid.

Partly as a result of its ineffective monopoly status, questionable food pricing policy and inefficient marketing operations, private traders developed an extensive parallel grain market. By the early 1980s, the OMPA "monopoly" accounted for as little as 15 per cent of total marketed production, although its operational deficit had increased significantly, mainly as a result of its food import operations and (consumer) price subsidies. The increasing fiscal drain of OMPA on the Malian Government's financial resources drove the Government to adopt marketing reforms—with the support of donors—in 1981.[43] Reform has taken place over the past two decades through the gradual implementation of different phases of the Cereal Market Restructuring Programme (*Programme de restructuration du marché céréalier*), known by its French acronym, PRMC.

Phase I of PRMC (1981-1986) aimed at increasing the role of the private sector in official grain trading and reducing subsidies to both producers and consumers. During this phase, physical grain losses were sharply reduced and the operational deficit of OMPA was cut by two thirds. However, the marketing board was unable to maintain the official price at the end of this phase, eventually leading to its withdrawal from price stabilization in order to comply with the fiscal terms of an International Monetary Fund (IMF) structural adjustment programme. The major objectives of OMPA for phase II (1988-1990) included managing a national food security buffer stock and food aid distribution. In addition, donor aid support was channelled into a credit programme for private grain traders. Phase III (1991-1994) focused on extending credit to farmers associations (administered by a State-owned development bank) and promoting the expansion of private sector storage, including the privatization of State-owned storage facilities.

PRMC succeeded in removing OMPA from price stabilization activities and reducing its role in (non-aid) food distribution, together with ensuring greater competition and private sector involvement in food marketing. The increasing fiscal costs of the State marketing system were reversed and average grain output over the period 1985-1991 was 40 per cent larger than the averages for the

[42]   Jones and Wickrema, "The use of conditionality in reform".... .

[43]   See, in particular, N.N. Dembele and J.M. Staatz, "The impact of market reform on agricultural transformation in Mali", paper presented at the Workshop on Agricultural Transformation, Egerton University, Nairobi, 27-30 June 1999.

periods 1975-1979 and 1980-1984.[44] There is also evidence that marketing reform contributed to an increase in competition, lower grain distribution costs and improved physical access to grains by consumers.[45] In addition, reduced marketing costs and improved market integration associated with the reform have benefited both urban and rural consumers by improving food access for the poor and by ensuring lower grain prices.

Nonetheless, the continuing responsibility of OMPA for food aid distribution and the national food security stock has continued to be a fiscal burden and has contributed to a distorting of prices. For example, the national food security stock has suffered from "political pressure to provide price support (subsidies) to some producers and to favour certain suppliers in the awards of contracts".[46] In addition, there are still substantial problems in ensuring reliable access to cereals by low-income consumers owing to structural problems that marketing reform alone is unlikely to resolve, including, in particular, poor transport infrastructure in many parts of the country.[47] While some progress has been achieved to date, the future success of the marketing reforms is likely to be compromised unless those problems are dealt with by the Government, with the cooperation of its international partners.

South Africa

South Africa's food marketing system has undergone a decisive transition from being State-controlled to being predominantly market-based, notably in maize marketing. For over five decades up to the mid-1990s, the South African Maize Board (SAMB) operated a price stabilization scheme that provided significant subsidies to maize farmers.[48] The Government began to curtail the activities of this maize marketing board in 1995, although it continued to collect a stabilization levy and to support maize exports. In 1996, new legislation still allowed certain types of market intervention, including the collection of stabilization levies and export controls, although there are important checks and balances. In particular, the Minister of Agriculture must be satisfied that any proposed intervention advances the improvement of market access and the optimization of export earnings, without being significantly detrimental to specific socio-economic objectives, including household food security.

Statutory intervention in the South African maize market ceased in 1997, when SAMB was closed down. Controls over who buys or sells maize, or on the prices at which maize is traded, were abolished, together with all restrictions on maize exports. In addition, the South African Futures Exchange (SAFEX) has been trading future maize contracts on a regular basis for several years. One of the reasons for the growth of SAFEX is that maize market liberalization created a great deal of spot market price volatility and this caused "farmers, traders, and millers to use forward contracts and futures contracts to manage their price risk".[49] However, small-scale, black farmers still contribute a very small part of the marketed grain production of South Africa which, in this respect, is unlike most other countries in Southern Africa.

The effectiveness of SAFEX as a food commodity market was first tested during the 1997 El Niño/Southern Oscillation (ENSO) event.[50] The expected drought in the region caused a sharp rise in futures prices of white maize as millers tried to secure supplies for the following season. The price of yellow maize (not used for human consumption)—which had always been pegged to

[44] Jones and Wickrema, "The use of conditionality in reform"... .

[45] Coulter and Shepherd, loc. cit., case study 3.

[46] Jones and Wickrema, "The use of conditionality in reform"... .

[47] See Dembele and Staatz, loc. cit.

[48] See, in particular, B. Bayley, *A Revolution in the Market: The Deregulation of South African Agriculture* (Oxford, United Kingdom, OPM, January 2000).

[49] S. Jones, op. cit., p. 33.

[50] See Jones and Wickrema, "Price stabilization policies in the context of market liberalization"... .

white maize prices under the State marketing regime—increased very little by comparison. This led to a considerable shift to white maize planting by many farmers. As fears of drought receded, futures contract prices fell, showing that markets are often better prepared than State-controlled systems to respond to shocks. The range of risk-hedging opportunities allowed by SAFEX futures contracts thus provides a solution to increased price instability arising from food market liberalization. Other countries in the region—including those with a significant proportion of smallholders—are also considering the use of similar futures markets.

United Republic of Tanzania

Despite initial resistance to marketing reform, the United Republic of Tanzania eventually liberalized maize trading decisively, particularly during the 1990s. Marketing reform in the country can be traced to the "collapse after 1981 of the official marketing system as a result of the unsustainable pricing policies implemented by the National Milling Corporation (NMC)".[51] Even prior to liberalization, parallel markets were handling a significant share of grain trading owing to the inability of NMC to enforce its statutory monopoly status. Illegal trade among different regions was also encouraged owing to differences among local prices arising from Government restrictions on interregional trade.

Although the Tanzanian Government had tried to suppress illegal private trading until 1983, restriction of private marketing was afterwards gradually reduced, as it had become clear that the inefficient and costly State marketing system could neither compete with the (legal or illegal) private sector nor maintain official prices. Marketing liberalization thus merely legalized rapidly expanding parallel grain markets. In 1984, liberalization policies were launched and, as part of structural adjustment programmes, the Government eliminated subsidies for maize. Between 1987 and 1990, restrictions on interregional trade were also removed. Private trading was fully liberalized in 1990, and NMC activities were basically limited to milling maize.

The private marketing system has expanded throughout the country but, partly because of a lack of investment in both greater storage capacity and better transport infrastructure, price fluctuations are still large. The private marketing system has faced other obstacles to its further expansion, notably the lack of credit for purchases and investment. Most of the operators are small traders with a limited amount of capital. The lack of both capital and transport facilities means that many small farmers also have difficulties selling their crops at reasonable prices. Nonetheless, it can be argued that the liberalization of the maize market "has been one of the success stories of agricultural liberalization in Tanzania".[52] Furthermore, while the withdrawal of subsidies has sometimes caused urban riots in other African countries, the availability of maize generally kept pace with demand during and after marketing reform.[53]

Zambia

The main priority of State intervention in food marketing in Zambia has been to benefit urban consumers. The Government established the National Agricultural Marketing Board (Namboard) shortly after independence in the mid-1960s. Namboard monopolized maize marketing and fixed producer and consumer prices until the late 1970s.

[51] Jones and Wickrema, "The use of conditionality in reform".... .

[52] B. Cooksey, "Marketing reform? the rise and fall of agricultural liberalization in Tanzania", Development Policy Review, vol. 21, No. 1 (2003), pp. 67-91.

[53] Ibid.

Marketing reform was initiated in 1981, when the Government partially transferred maize marketing to cooperatives and allowed maize meal and fertilizer prices to rise in order to comply with an IMF structural adjustment programme. The Government attempted to reduce maize subsidies in the mid-1980s but the design and implementation of the subsidy reduction programme were badly mishandled and resulted in a reduced supply of maize meal products and sharp consumer price increases.[54] Serious food riots at the end of 1986 prompted the Government to increase subsidies and nationalize large-scale private maize mills. Further attempts to reduce subsidies were made through the introduction of food coupons in the late 1980s but another policy U-turn eliminated the food coupon system in the early 1990s. In addition, Namboard was abolished, the national milling industry was privatized and many production and consumption subsidies were eliminated at around the same time.

Although the State's involvement in marketing was significantly reduced during the first half of the 1990s—following the abolition of Namboard—the State-owned Food Reserve Agency, established in 1995, has continued to use public funds to sell maize to industrial millers below market prices. While this agency's grain sales have been relatively small—given the lack of funding to support its expanded operation—they have contributed to the disruption of private marketing and trading in some local markets. At the same time, the expansion of smallholder production and private marketing has been hindered by poor road infrastructure, and lack of credit and adequate provision of inputs and extension services. This has been particularly detrimental to the rural poor, as it has contributed to a rise in grain (consumer) prices in rural areas. Furthermore, the party winning the 2001 election had run on the premise of reintroducing a food marketing board to provide subsidized maize prices to farmers and consumers and the legislation for the new Crop Marketing Authority was set for parliamentary consideration in 2002.[55]

The rural poor in Zambia will be able to derive significant benefits from liberalized maize marketing only if such policy reversals are avoided, the Government's pro-urban bias is reduced and further reform measures are implemented decisively, including policies to increase agricultural output and productivity, and the provision of the necessary infrastructure and extension services for efficient marketing, as well as adequate technical and financial support by donors. However, the implementation of these policies is likely to fail unless there is full political commitment to reform.

An assessment of food marketing reform in Africa

An examination of reform experiences in selected African countries shows that food marketing liberalization has produced several positive (as well as negative) socio-economic results. One general point is that in most, if not all, cases, there was private sector food marketing, whether legal or not. This itself suggests that food marketing boards were not performing their statutory functions effectively.

The withdrawal of marketing boards from food pricing and trading activities has generally contributed to increasing the efficiency and thus reducing the cost of grain distribution. It has also reduced the fiscal burden of State-controlled food marketing systems, which is a particularly important issue in poor countries

[54] S. Jones, op. cit., p. 8.

[55] T.S. Jayne and others, "False promise or false premise? the experience of food and input market reform in Eastern and Southern Africa", *World Development*, vol. 30, No. 11 (2002), pp. 1967-1985.

with scarce financial resources. Greater spatial market integration arising from the removal of State restrictions on private grain trading between contiguous regions (both subnationally and internationally) has also contributed to lower prices and an increase in the range of food products available. Both rural and (especially) urban consumers in many African countries now have a greater availability of food products as a result of the increased entry of private traders into the food and agricultural marketing sector. While consumer vulnerability to price fluctuations arising from marketing liberalization has sometimes increased in the short run, this negative impact has often been eventually mitigated by greater private investments in grain processing and distribution, as well as inter-regional or cross-border trade, which contributed to the expansion of consumer choice and the ability to stabilize expenditures on maize meal.[56]

Consumers in many countries have generally benefited from efficiency gains of private marketing through lower prices, notably by small-scale hammer mills.[57] A survey of grain and grain meal prices in six African countries that have liberalized food marketing (to different degrees) shows that real prices declined in five of them during the 1980s and 1990s: Mali, since 1982; Ghana, since 1984; Zambia, since 1987; Kenya, since 1988; and Ethiopia, since 1990.[58] There were, however, different reasons for the decline in real consumer food prices in these countries, including increased competition and lower costs in food marketing and processing in Kenya, Mali and Zambia; and better transmission of falling real world prices into the domestic economies by removal of trade barriers in Ghana and Mali. Nonetheless, in all five countries, increased efficiency arising from greater private sector involvement in grain distribution contributed to lower real prices.

At the same time, food market liberalization has given rise to some critical problems that require corrective policy action. First of all, withdrawal of the State marketing boards from food marketing has sometimes made net purchasers of food more vulnerable to short-run price fluctuations, given that State intervention had some success in ensuring price stabilization, even if the benefits of such policies had often been limited by fiscal constraints on marketing boards' ability to defend official prices. Since price fluctuations sometimes have a negative impact on rural (and urban) poverty, corrective measures are required to maintain household food security, including the distribution of (means-tested) food coupons.

Second, some small farmers have been negatively affected by the withdrawal of guaranteed official purchasing at fixed prices, particularly when marketing boards are abolished before an adequate private food marketing system is in place. In addition, the abolition or streamlining of State marketing boards has sometimes disrupted the provision of essential support services to smallholders. The above-mentioned case studies underline that the adequate provision of both credit[59] and extension services is vital for agricultural development in Africa. Similarly, improving infrastructure—notably roads and storage facilities—is critical for raising the efficiency of food marketing activities (carried out by either the public or private sectors). There is particular evidence that lack of rural feeder roads is a major cause of high transportation costs and poor market integration in most African countries.[60]

Third, it is also argued that the removal of fertilizer subsidies arising from food marketing reform has reduced their use by smallholders. This, in turn, has

---

[56] See T.S. Jayne and others, *Successes and Challenges of Food Market Reform: Experiences from Kenya, Mozambique, Zambia and Zimbabwe* (East Lansing, Michigan, Michigan State University, 1999). Those negative short-term impacts, however, suggests a need for targeted action, such as the provision of food stamps for the poor.

[57] Ibid.

[58] T.S. Jayne and others, *Trends in real food prices*... .

[59] It is worth noting, however, that credit provision by marketing boards (and agricultural banks) in the past was not only officially subsidized but sometimes constituted unofficial subsidies through the failure of farmers, many of them politically well connected, to repay loans.

[60] See S. Jones (op. cit., pp. 21-22), who also proposes a "road funds" tax earmarked to finance road improvements and maintenance in poor countries.

often had negative effects on agricultural output and productivity, and thus on rural income and poverty. However, evidence from both Kenya and the United Republic of Tanzania indicates that subsidized fertilizer supply benefited primarily commercial farms, as opposed to smallholders.[61] As often happens with general price subsidies granted by public water agencies for both irrigation and household consumption, larger farmers (and higher-income urban-dwellers) tend to benefit disproportionately from such subsidies.[62] Nonetheless, since marketing boards often played a significant role in the supply of (subsidized) inputs to farmers as a whole, their reduced role has sometimes created obstacles for the expansion of agricultural output.

Last, but by no means least, a drop in per capita food production in many African countries in the post-reform period could imply that marketing reform has been generally detrimental to agriculture. As figure VII.2 shows, grain production per capita fell in all five Eastern and Southern African countries covered in this section, although the drop in the first half of the 1990s is partly attributed to the drought that hit Southern Africa in 1991-1992. In addition, this drop in per capita food production is partially associated with some diversification beyond food crops into cash crops, which is generally considered a risk-minimization strategy. In any case, a drop in per capita output does not necessarily entail a welfare loss, given that in most of these countries output levels before market liberalization had been propped up by State subsidies. The operation of marketing boards basically shifts the costs of maintaining economically inefficient State-controlled food systems from one social group to others and, in many cases, large-scale (and wealthier) farmers have benefited disproportionately from such subsidies, including input subsidies.[63]

61   Cooksey, loc. cit., p. 71. See also Omamo and Mose, loc. cit.

62   See *World Economic and Social Survey, 1996* (United Nations publication, Sales No. E.96.II.C.1 and Corr.1), chap. XI.

63   See, in particular, T.S. Jayne and others, *Trends in Real Food Prices...* .

Figure VII.2.
COARSE GRAIN OUTPUT PER CAPITA IN
SELECTED AFRICAN COUNTRIES, 1980-1994

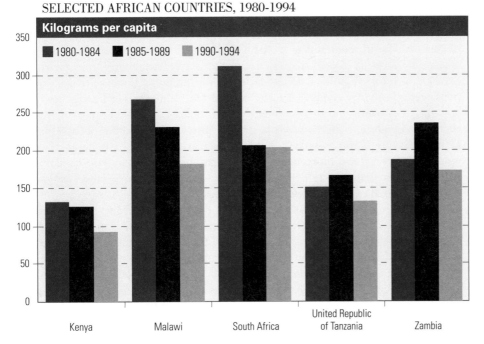

Source: UN/DESA, based on T.S. Jayne and S. Jones, "Food marketing and pricing policy in Eastern and Southern Africa: a survey", *World Development*, vol. 25, No. 9 (1997), p. 1518.

Similarly, negative impacts of reforms on smallholders in isolated areas raise the question whether cross-subsidies are preferable to providing an enabling environment for increasing their economic efficiency vis-à-vis more competitive farmers, inter alia, through the State provision of better transport and grain storage infrastructure. Following marketing reform and the withdrawal or reduction of producer subsidies, the production of staple crops in excess of subsistence requirements is not economically viable to many smallholders in remote areas, given that transport costs may exceed the value of the crops themselves. While improved road networks can help to reduce costs, marketing liberalization also has encouraged remote farmers "to change their cropping patterns and identify new crops which have higher value-for-weight ratios and can thus absorb higher transport costs".[64] Marketing boards' withdrawal from—or reduced involvement in—food pricing, purchasing, transport and distribution has thus encouraged food production to be more responsive to demand and consumer preferences.

While food marketing liberalization may have adverse impacts on less efficient farmers, the reversion to State marketing systems with their associated operational inefficiencies, pricing distortions and heavy fiscal cost would be a worse alternative. The move towards greater liberalization in Africa was a result of not only aid conditionality, but also the unsustainable fiscal burden and inefficient operation of State marketing boards. There is, however, concern that, since many sub-Saharan African countries had little experience with market-oriented food systems before the 1980s or 1990s, pricing and marketing liberalization should be implemented gradually.

The case studies show that corrective Government policies to reduce market instability and increase efficiency in both food production and marketing include: (a) improving the transport infrastructure and food storage capacity in rural areas; (b) adequate provision of extension services and credit to both small farmers and private traders; (c) dissemination of reliable market information to smallholders;[65] (d) market-based measures to reduce the effects of price fluctuations, as reflected, for example, in South Africa's innovative experience with future commodity exchanges; and (e) regional trade integration measures, such as those supported by the New Partnership for Africa's Development (NEPAD) (see document A/57/304, annex).[66] Some of these functions were, in theory, supposed to be carried out by marketing boards but, in practice, they were poorly provided by such boards, partly because of their central focus on (and problems with) pricing intervention and direct food marketing. It is now also recognized that food security objectives can be achieved more effectively (and more economically) through targeted socio-economic policies rather than through State marketing boards that have other primary objectives and are often inefficiently operated.

Finally, the development of a competitive (and more efficient) private food marketing calls for effective regulation to deal with potential market failures, detrimental activities by powerful traders and food quality control. Since these functions—notably quality control for food and non-food export crops—were partly carried out by marketing boards, it is critical that other Government agencies enforce food quality regulation after the abolition or streamlining of marketing boards. Effective regulation is important not only to secure export markets but also to ensure adequate standards of human health for domestic

64 Food and Agriculture Organization of the United Nations, "Understanding and using marketing information", *Marketing Extension Guide 2* (Rome, FAO, 2000), p. 3.

65 FAO has produced several useful guides to assist extension workers in sub-Saharan Africa in advising small farmers and traders how best to use market information for marketing maize and other food crops. See, for example, "Understanding and using marketing"…; and "A guide to maize marketing"….

66 See Declaration on Democracy, Political, Economic and Corporate Governance of 18 June 2002 (NEPAD, n.p.), paras. 3 and 24. See also *World Economic and Social Survey, 2002*, pp. 111-112.

food consumers. The development of a legal framework should also include the clear definition of property rights and a legitimate authority to enforce these rights.[67] In this context, as will be argued in the next section, there is a particularly strong case to be made for strengthening the land-use and ownership rights of small farmers as a means of increasing agricultural productivity and promoting more equitable rural growth patterns.

A MARKET-BASED APPROACH TO LAND REFORM

The central role of land reform in rural poverty alleviation

In most developing countries, agriculture makes a significant contribution to employment, income and economic growth. Policies to promote more efficient and equitable agricultural growth should thus play a central role in rural poverty reduction strategies. Increasing agricultural productivity and output is particularly critical for improving living standards and reducing rural poverty in sub-Saharan Africa, where most of the poor depend on farming for their livelihood.

While much economic research on agricultural productivity focuses on increased mechanization, revolutionary technology shifts and increased soil fertility, higher yields can also be derived from redistributive land reform. Small farms in developing countries tend to be more productive than larger farms per unit of land, notably because hired labour on large farms is usually less productive than family labour, unless there is effective supervision or appropriate incentives—both of which can be very costly.[68] In north-east Brazil, for example, farm yields rose by between 10 and 40 per cent on non-irrigated land and between 30 and 70 per cent on irrigated land that was redistributed to small farmers.[69]

In the 1960s, some economists argued that redistributing land to small farmers would lead to lower crop yields, but subsequent empirical research showed that land redistribution to the poor increased agricultural output per hectare in many developing countries, at least in the medium to long run, for three main reasons.[70] First, small farms often use more labour per hectare—extra labour that might not have otherwise been used—and thus tend to be more productive. Second, as noted above, the costs of supervising farm labour increase with the size of the farm. Third, when small farmers have secure land titles, they are more likely to obtain cheaper and more extensive credit—by using land as collateral—and undertake farm improvements and increase output. More equal patterns of land ownership thus often contribute to faster, as well as more equitable, aggregate economic growth.[71]

Redistributive land reform has traditionally been carried out by (a) distributing unused State lands to the rural poor; (b) expropriating large private landholdings—with or without compensation—for division and distribution to landless peasants and small farmers without land titles; and (c) strengthening the land rights of smallholders. Strengthening the land-use or property rights of small farmers, in particular, has made a significant contribution to the production of greater food output per hectare and thus to poverty alleviation in several Asian developing countries, including the world's two most populous ones.

In India, greater increases in food output and faster poverty reduction were achieved in States that had implemented redistributive land reform.[72] While

[67] Jones and Wickrema, "Defining the role of the State".... .

[68] See R. A. Berry and W. R. Cline, *Agrarian Structure and Productivity in Developing Countries* (Baltimore, Maryland, Johns Hopkins University Press, 1979); and A. V. Banerjee, "Land reforms: prospects and strategies", mimeo (Cambridge, Massachusetts, Massachusetts Institute of Technology, n.d.).

[69] UNDP, *Human Development Report, 2003*..., p. 89.

[70] For a detailed discussion of these factors, see *World Economic and Social Survey, 2000* (United Nations publication, Sales No. E.00.II.C.1), chap. V; and E. Wayne Nafziger, *The Economics of Developing Countries* (Upper Saddle River, New Jersey, Prentice Hall, 1997), chap. 7.

[71] A recent analysis of incentives conducive to economic growth across countries stresses that more unequal land distribution patterns are often associated with lower growth. See W. Easterly, *The Elusive Quest for Growth: Economists' Adventures and Misadventures in the Tropics* (Cambridge, Massachusetts, MIT Press, 2001), chap. 13.

[72] *Rural Poverty Report, 2001*... .

increased agricultural productivity in the country is often associated with the green revolution in the late 1960s and 1970s, empirical research covering the period between 1955 and 1988 also shows a clear link between poverty reduction and land reform, notably tenancy reform.[73] The Indian experience indicates, in particular, that a more adequate legal title to ownership or tenancy of land provides an incentive for small farmers to invest in the land and enables them to use land as collateral in accessing the credit market.

China provides one of the most remarkable examples of the positive impacts of land reform on agricultural growth and rural poverty reduction. The household responsibility system (HRS), introduced during the 1978-1984 land reform, was based upon the distribution of collectively owned land to households, mainly according to family size.[74] While collective land ownership was officially maintained, the granting of land-use rights to peasant households linked their remuneration to output. This contributed to reducing costs and boosting agricultural production and rural incomes. Between 1978 and 1984, output of the three main types of crops—grain, cotton and oil-bearing seeds—increased at annual rates of 4.8 per cent, 7.7 per cent and 13.8 per cent, respectively, compared with the average annual growth rates of 2.4 per cent, 1.0 per cent and 0.8 per cent between 1952 and 1978.[75] Similarly, while the per capita income of farmers had risen at an average annual rate of 3.9 per cent between 1949 and 1978, the rate increased to 13.1 per cent between 1978 and 1986.[76] Although there were other reasons for this significant rise of productivity and incomes during the 1980s, such as the expansion of irrigated croplands, land reform played a crucial role in agricultural expansion and socio-economic development. The resulting fall in rural poverty is ultimately attributed to the "combined impact of egalitarian distribution of communal lands, better seeds, more irrigation and less repression of farm prices".[77]

In Viet Nam, rapid growth of agricultural output, achieved through land redistribution and market liberalization, is considered the main reason for the country's success in reducing poverty during the 1990s.[78] The liberalization of the agricultural sector began in the late 1980s with the granting of long-term land leases, the lifting of price controls and the gradual removal of restrictions on agricultural trade. A 1993 law allowed landholders to sell, lease and inherit land, and use it as collateral. Private ownership of agricultural machinery and farm animals, as well as the right to buy and sell them, was also permitted. These reforms allowed the development of a private land market and the eventual privatization of agriculture. Greater security of tenure, particularly from the distribution of collective farmlands to small-scale farmers, has been responsible for increased productivity and agricultural diversification, notably into cash crops with large export potential, such as rice and coffee. Recent research also indicates that land reform led to a considerable increase in the total area devoted to (more productive) multi-year crops between 1993 and 1998.[79]

The strengthening of land property rights achieved under Viet Nam's decollectivization programme can be considered a type of *market-oriented* land reform in that it has led to the development of private land markets. Tenure reform is based on the recognition that rural economic development requires a secure system of property rights for small farmers that encourages investment and facilitates access to credit. In cases where land markets do not function satisfactorily, and where it is impossible to enforce land repossession, formal land

[73] See *Human Development in South Asia 2002: Agriculture and Rural Development* (Karachi, Oxford University Press, 2003).

[74] See *World Economic and Social Survey, 2000...*, p. 144.

[75] Fu Chen, L. Wang and J. Davis, "Land reform in rural China since the mid-1980s", *Land Reform*, No. 2 (1998), pp. 122-137. While HRS has succeeded in raising agricultural productivity and output, the authors identify several institutional weaknesses and propose measures to strengthen land use or property rights. See also J. M. Zhou, "Principal forms of land consolidation and expansion in China", *Land Reform*, No. 1 (2000), pp. 89-107.

[76] See United Nations University (UNU), *The Impact of Economic Development on Rural Women in China* (United Nations publication, Sales No. E.92.III.A.2).

[77] *Rural Poverty Report, 2001...*, chap. II, p. 28, see also chap. III. According to this report, the rural Poverty Head Count Index in China fell from 33.0 in 1978 to 11.5 in 1990 and to 4.6 in 1998 (see table 2.1).

[78] See, for example, *World Economic and Social Survey, 2000...*, box VIII.3; and World Bank, "Viet Nam: Delivering on Its Promise", Development Report 2003, No. 25050-VN (Washington, D.C., World Bank, November 2002), pp. 45-50.

[79] See Q.T. Do and L. Iyer, "Land rights and economic development: evidence from Viet Nam, mimeo (Cambridge, Massachusetts, MIT, July 2002).

titles tend to be useless as collateral.[80] Secure access to land—in the form of ownership or long-term rental—also tends to reduce landless peasants' dependence on poorly paid and volatile rural labour markets.

Land tenure reform is particularly suitable to countries with large numbers of labourers working on State farms or small farmers working on State-owned lands. Market-oriented land reform can also be used to settle landless peasants and smallholders without land titles in countries with large tracts of unused State land that are suitable for agriculture. By contrast, countries with large numbers of landless peasants—or small farmers without land titles—and whose most arable land is formally owned by private landlords, have often redistributed such land through coercive measures. While coercive land reform is normally associated with expropriation without compensation, land redistribution can also be based on compulsory purchase below market prices.

Japan, for example, was one of the first countries to successfully implement this type of land redistribution in the modern world, during the late 1940s and early 1950s. The State played a central role in that programme by redistributing land owned by large landholders in equal lots to landless peasants and smallholders for individual ownership. The Government also implemented a range of complementary policies, including the adequate provision of credit and extension services for small farmers. More controversial measures—such as Government subsidies, tax preferences and import barriers—also contributed to the success of land reform in the country. Since many of the new (small-scale) landowners had been tenants working the land prior to reform, the implementation of the programme was further facilitated by the fact that the beneficiaries had a proved capacity to work (and even manage) the farms they received.

Japan's pioneering programme was different from other coercive types of land reform—notably those associated with widespread political upheaval[81]— in that former landowners were at least partially compensated for the expropriated land by the Government, "which reconveyed the fields at nominal prices to the small sharecroppers already working on them".[82] Japan's land redistribution programme contributed to increasing productivity and raising the small farmer's income substantially.[83] Successful land reform programmes—sometimes even State-controlled programmes, as in Japan—can thus lead to both greater aggregate economic growth and a more equitable income distribution among farmers as well as between farmers and non-farmers.[84]

Although land reform programmes similar to the one implemented by Japan were subsequently introduced successfully in the Republic of Korea and Taiwan Province of China, other forms of land reform have been used more extensively in developing countries, ranging from more radical coercive approaches to market-based land reform. The rest of this section focuses on the latter approach.

The case for market-based land reform

Interest in market-based land reform has increased because of the problems with coercive forms of land reform—notably land expropriation without compensation—in many developing countries. First of all, because land expropriation is fundamentally inconsistent with the protection of private property rights, it tends to undermine private investment and even "international confi-

80 See H. de Soto, *The Mystery of Capital: Why Capitalism Triumphs in the West and Fails Everywhere Else* (New York, Basic Books, 2000), who argues that the formal recognition of property rights would enable property currently held informally to be used as collateral and thus unlock the "hidden" capital assets of the poor.

81 In the past, most (coercive) large-scale land redistribution was associated with socio-political revolts or the demise of colonial rule. See H. Binswanger, K. Deininger and G. Feder, "Power, distortions, revolt and reform in agricultural land relations", in *Handbook of Development Economics*, vol. III, J. Behrman and T. Srinivasan, eds. (New York, Elsevier, 1995), pp. 2659-2772.

82 M.G. McDonald, "Agricultural landholding in Japan: fifty years after land reform", *Geoforum*, vol. 28, No. 1 (1997), p. 58.

83 *World Economic and Social Survey, 2000...*, p. 139.

84 Recent research, however, point to long-term problems with Japan's pioneering land reform programme, including lower efficiency arising from land fragmentation and political obstacles to the expansion of the non-farm economy. See, for example, M. G. McDonald, loc. cit. and J. M. Zhou, loc. cit.

85   K. Deininger and J. May, "Is there scope for growth with equity: the case of land reform in South Africa", mimeo (Washington, D.C., World Bank, 2000).

86   See, for example, A. de Janvry and E. Sadoulet, "A study in resistance to institutional change: the lost game of Latin American land reform", *World Development*, vol. 17, No. 9 (1989), pp. 1397-1407.

87   K. Deininger, "Making negotiated land reform work: initiatives from Colombia, Brazil and South Africa", *World Development*, vol. 27, No. 4 (1999), pp. 651-672.

88   See United Kingdom Department for International Development (DFID), "Better livelihoods for poor people: the role of land policy", consultation document (London, DFID, November 2002).

89   E. Wayne Nafziger, op. cit., p. 194.

90   See S. M. Borras, "Towards a better understanding of market-led agrarian reform in theory and practice: focusing on the Brazilian case", *Land Reform*, vol. 33, No. 1 (2002), pp. 32-50.

91   Deininger and May, loc. cit., p. 20.

92   See A. de Janvry and others, "Access to land and land policy reforms", in *Access to Land, Rural Poverty and Public Action*, A. de Janvry and others, eds. (Oxford, United Kingdom, Oxford University Press, 2001), pp. 1-26; and K. Deininger and H. P. Binswanger, "The evolution of the World Bank's land policy: principles, experiences and future challenges", *World Bank Research Observer*, vol. 14, No. 2 (1999), pp. 247-276.

dence in the economy".[85] In addition, landowners and other local elites often use political power to weaken the implementation of coercive land redistribution programmes. Reaction to the confiscatory nature of these programmes has led powerful landowners to slow down their implementation through various legal or other means, including subdividing their land to evade expropriation or submitting the plots unsuitable for agriculture for compulsory purchase.[86] Resistance to expropriation, in turn, has often led to political instability and more radical, undemocratic responses by Governments.

Second, Governments sometimes attempt to introduce coercive land reform as a response to immediate socio-political pressure rather than as part of a long-term rural development strategy. For example, Government efforts to redistribute land are often made in regions where well-organized and politically active land reform movements exist.[87] As a result, such efforts tend to ignore the needs of the poorest peasants, who are often disorganized. In addition, efforts to placate the most vigorous peasant organizations may open the way for political manipulation, the inappropriate selection of both the beneficiaries and the tracts of land expropriated, and even the exacerbation of social conflict.[88]

A third problem is that many land reform programmes became inefficient because they were often accompanied by a considerable expansion of agrarian reform bureaucracies at the central Government level. Political interference can also contribute to the undermining of land redistribution and lower land-use efficiency when land is allocated for speculative rather than productive purposes. It is argued, for example, that this was a major problem in Kenya's attempt to replace the colonial land tenure system with a new system in which Africans purchased land from Europeans between 1954 and 1974. Although huge tracts of land were transferred to Africans in the central and western highlands, "the political leadership redistributed most of the land to itself, allies, and clients, many of whom had no experience in farming".[89]

Similarly, it can be argued that coercive land reform tends to be supply-driven and thus to lead to greater economic inefficiency.[90] This aspect is significant because coercive forms of land reform usually begin by identifying farmland for expropriation and then looking for potential landless beneficiaries to receive and settle on this land. Lower land-use efficiency results when productive farms (as opposed to underutilized land) are expropriated and given to settlers who lack the knowledge and means to become efficient producers or when environmentally fragile land is distributed by the State. Even in countries with a long history of smallholder agriculture, State institutions have been ineffective at targeting underutilized land and in achieving the intended gains in economic efficiency.[91]

The final—and arguably most significant—problem is that coercive forms of land reform often distort the operation of land markets. Two of the most useful functions of (arable) land markets are to allow more efficient producers to purchase or increase their landholdings and, conversely, to allow inefficient farmers to exit from agriculture. While there are structural obstacles that hinder the rural poor from obtaining land through the market, evidence also shows that State institutions in many developing countries use regulatory tools to restrict (rather than facilitate) land use, sales and rental, as part of coercive land reform programmes.[92] In the absence of these restrictions, "land rental markets tend to be friendlier to the rural poor ... in allowing them access to land", owing to lower transaction costs and greater opportunities for mitigating the market failures to which the rural poor are exposed.[93]

[93] A. de Janvry and others, op. cit., p. 15.

When coercive land reform programmes create or exacerbate socio-economic tensions among central or local Governments, large landowners and small-holders or landless peasants, they tend to escalate social conflict and undermine agricultural development, as was the case in parts of Brazil, the Philippines and Zimbabwe. There are, however, several non-coercive alternatives for improving land distribution—without resorting to expropriation of private landholdings—that may also increase agricultural productivity and reduce rural poverty. These include (a) the distribution of unused State lands that are neither environmentally fragile nor unsuitable for agriculture, (b) the introduction of progressive land taxes to discourage ownership of large tracts of land for non-productive purposes over the long run and (c) market-based land reform.

Market-based land reform could be particularly suitable for countries with little unused State lands and with large numbers of landless peasants and small farmers without satisfactory claims to (arable) land rights. Its main innovation is to enable beneficiary farmers to receive grants from State institutions in order to purchase land from voluntary sellers at market prices. This "willing seller-willing buyer" approach differs markedly from land expropriation, as it can encourage landowners to sell idle land, and provide an alternative to illegal occupation by landless peasants.

A market-based approach to land redistribution is thus, to a large extent, *demand-driven* in that it involves voluntary exchanges between willing buyers—initially assisted by a Government grant—and land sellers in the market. Rather than depend on Governments' deciding who will benefit from expropriated land—sometimes on political grounds—the potential beneficiaries themselves "compete" for available land in the market. The potential beneficiaries who want land the most, and who are best prepared to farm it, are likely to navigate the screening process for obtaining the Government grants better than other segments of the peasantry. This would lead not only to more effective targeting but also to higher productivity, given that the most skilled potential farmers are likely to be more successful in obtaining land than those with little interest in or knowledge of farming.

This approach is intended to stimulate the operation of rural land markets from both the supply and the demand sides. On the supply side, it encourages landowners to undertake the reduction of their holdings of (underutilized) farmland, which could be reinforced by the introduction of progressive land taxes and other fiscal mechanisms. On the demand side, it provides Government grants to poor small farmers or rural labourers with farming experience to purchase land through the market. In order to strengthen the bargaining position of potential beneficiaries and to reduce transaction costs, beneficiaries are encouraged to join community organizations designed for those purposes. These organizations, sometimes in cooperation with local Governments or rural financial institutions willing to provide loans to beneficiaries, can help to screen applicants, negotiate purchases on their behalf and provide follow-up technical assistance.

Several developing countries, such as Brazil, Colombia, Ecuador and South Africa, have experimented with market-based land reform. Since implementation is most advanced in South Africa, the following section will examine its experience with this innovative approach to land reform and assess its effectiveness as an alternative to coercive forms of land reform.

Market-based land reform in South Africa

As in most sub-Saharan African countries, there is a much higher incidence of poverty in rural (as opposed to urban) areas in South Africa. As shown in table VII.1 in 1995, 71 per cent of all rural-dwellers were classified as poor, compared with 29 per cent of urban-dwellers. Furthermore, rural households headed by women are likely to suffer from poverty more than male-headed households: estimates show that female-headed households accounted for 77 per cent of all poor households living in rural areas in 2000.[94] This is partly explained by the existence of a relatively developed non-agricultural sector—notably mines and manufacturing—which has encouraged migration of rural adult males to urban and mining areas, leaving many women, children and elderly persons in rural areas.[95]

Poverty in South Africa is not only associated with gender but also very much race-related: over 60 per cent of black South Africans were poor in the mid-1990s, compared with only 1 per cent of whites (see also table VII.1). Many of the reasons for this race-related, as well as rural, characteristic of poverty in South Africa can be traced to past apartheid policies. One of the most important causes was the exclusion of black South Africans from owning or renting land outside so-called homelands covering less than 15 per cent of the country's area. In 1997, there were at least 900,000 black households living in former homelands without access to arable land and it is estimated that more than 80 per cent of arable land was still owned by white farmers in the late 1990s.[96]

In order to deal with this highly unequal pattern of land ownership, the South African Government began to implement an extensive programme of land reform in the mid-1990s. This programme consisted of three main components: (a) the restitution of or compensation for land lost by black citizens due to colonial or apartheid policies; (b) the redistribution of white-owned farmland to black farmers; and (c) land tenure reform to provide more secure access to land in the former homelands.[97] Given the large number of black households that wanted to gain access to land, but lacked the required documentation or were otherwise ineligible to participate in either the restitution or the tenure compo-

[94] M. Aliber, "Chronic poverty in South Africa: incidence, causes and policies", *World Development*, vol. 31, No. 3 (2003) pp. 473-490.

[95] In many African countries, there are also institutional obstacles to women's access to land ownership titles. See, for example, African Development Bank, "Achieving the Millennium Development Goals in Africa: Progress, Prospects and Policy Implications" (n.p., June 2002).

[96] See M. Aliber, loc. cit., p. 480; and J. Kirsten, S. Perret and J. van Zyl, "Land reform and the new water management context in South Africa: principles, progress and issues", paper prepared for a seminar of the Natural Resources Management and Land Policy Thematic Group (Washington, D.C., World Bank, September 2000).

[97] For details of this comprehensive land reform programme, see L. Cliffe, "Land reform in South Africa", *Review of African Political Economy*, No. 84 (2000), pp. 273-286; and M. Aliber, loc. cit.

Table VII.1.
POVERTY IN SOUTH AFRICA, 1995

Indicator	Number of people (thousands)	Proportion of population (percentage)
National poverty	19 700	49.9
Poverty in rural areas	13 700	70.9
Poverty in urban areas	6 000	28.5
Poverty among black population	18 300	60.7
Poverty among white population	44	1.0

Source: K. Deininger and J. May, "Is there scope for growth with equity: the case of land reform in South Africa", mimeo (Washington, D.C., World Bank, 2000). table 1a.

nents, redistribution became the major pillar of land reform in the country. The Government set ambitious targets for land redistribution: the (voluntary) transfer of almost 30 million hectares of farmland—that is to say, 30 per cent of the country's total arable land area—between 1995 and 1999.

Particular efforts were made to formulate a land redistribution programme that avoided the above-mentioned problems connected with coercive forms of land reform—notably expropriation, compulsory acquisition below market prices and the expansion of agrarian reform bureaucracies. Greater emphasis was thus placed on assisting potential beneficiaries, including landless peasants who had been dispossessed during apartheid, to purchase land through the development of land markets. This innovative approach to land redistribution was based upon the provision of a Government grant—known as the Settlement and Land Acquisition Grant (SLAG)—to enable rural households to purchase arable land in the market. The SLAG was originally equal to the maximum subsidy under the national housing programme, that is to say, 16,000 rand (R) (equivalent to approximately US$ 2,000 at present). The grant was available only to potential beneficiaries with a monthly income below R 1,500.

Potential beneficiaries could use the grant to purchase land on offer from private owners so long as the purchased land was intended for an agricultural use, such as cultivation of cash crops, grazing or even subsistence farming intended to improve household food consumption. Large landowners could initiate transactions, for example, by dividing a portion of a commercial farm into small parcels for sale under the programme. In addition, property developers could purchase arable land (with private funds, rather than Government grants), build basic infrastructure, divide it into parcels and then sell it to beneficiaries under the programme. Potential beneficiaries were otherwise responsible for designing their own projects, although they could use grant money to hire consultants for that purpose.

In practice, beneficiaries have often grouped together in order to obtain the grant, design projects and acquire land collectively. This type of collective action was particularly encouraged after the Government enacted the Communal Property Associations Act in 1996. This Act established mechanisms to finance and facilitate community initiatives to purchase land on behalf of groups of landless citizens. However, an unexpected degree of State interference in providing assistance to these community initiatives had an adverse impact on the implementation of the market-based land redistribution programme. The Department of Land Affairs (DLA), established by the Government to implement the land reform programme, played a central role in mobilizing community associations, on behalf of potential beneficiaries, to access different types of grants available for land purchases. The paternalistic way in which proposed projects were dealt with by DLA slowed down the programme's implementation: it is estimated that it took an average of two years to approve a project.[98]

As a result, the land redistribution programme failed to avoid one of the major problems faced by coercive programmes as "it has become an over-centralized and bureaucratic process where the public sector tries to do everything".[99] Bureaucratic delay in the implementation of the programme was partly responsible for its failure to meet the land redistribution targets. Between 1995 and 2000, less than 1 per cent of the country's commercial farmland was

[98] Deininger and May, loc. cit., p. 24.

[99] See Kirsten, Perret and van Zyl, loc. cit.

100 See M. Aliber, loc. cit. Since under municipal com-monage schemes, landownership is vested in the municipality and is made available to low-income households, mainly for the grazing of their live-stock, it is particularly difficult to quantify the exact number of beneficiaries.

101 See F. J. Zimmerman, "Barriers to participation by the poor in South Africa's land redistribution", *World Development*, vol. 28, No. 8 (2000), pp. 1439-1460.

102 Although this is usually a requirement of land redistribution programmes—both market-based and State-controlled ones—in practice, large plots of redistributed land often end up in the hands of speculators without farming experience.

103 Deininger and May, loc. cit., p. 14.

willingly sold by private landowners under the programme: 0.6 per cent to less than 60,000 beneficiaries and another 0.3 per cent in the form of municipal commonages.[100] This disappointing rate of land transfer was also associated with other obstacles to participation by the poor in market-based land reform. These obstacles included (a) upfront costs not covered by the Government grant, (b) human capital constraints associated with modern farming, (c) low geographical mobility of certain groups of landless peasants and small farmers without land titles and (d) inadequate provision of rural and extension services required for the success of small-scale farming.[101]

The poor rate of delivery during the second half of the 1990s was mitigated, however, by the fact that most of the transferred land was used for cultivation and other agricultural purposes,[102] with less than 5 per cent being left idle in 1999 (see figure VII.3). This supports the argument that market-based land reform reduces the incentive for maintaining farmland for speculative purposes, and successfully targets smallholders and landless peasants who are better pre-pared to use redistributed land productively. In addition, a considerable propor-tion of successful beneficiary farmers were also able to (collectively) obtain complementary private loans. This is significant for two reasons: (a) it proves that beneficiaries with land titles can gain access to sources of credit other than the Government grant and (b) it encourages private lenders to help to strength-en the screening process so as to ensure that the most suitable applicants pur-chase redistributed land. There is also evidence that the programme succeeded in reaching the rural poor: a survey conducted in 1999 shows that three quarters of land reform beneficiaries were below the national poverty line.[103]

In addition, significant progress has been made in improving access to irri-gation water for small farmers, a particularly important prerequisite for the

Figure VII.3.
DISTRIBUTION OF LAND TRANSFERRED UNDER THE SOUTH
AFRICAN REDISTRIBUTION PROGRAMME, BY TYPE OF USE

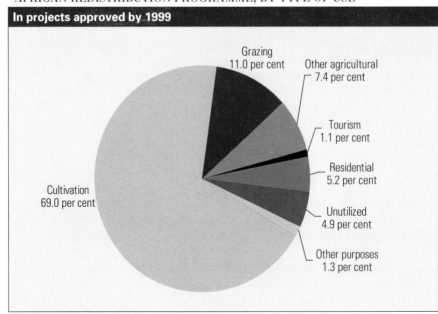

In projects approved by 1999

Grazing 11.0 per cent

Other agricultural 7.4 per cent

Tourism 1.1 per cent

Residential 5.2 per cent

Unutilized 4.9 per cent

Other purposes 1.3 per cent

Cultivation 69.0 per cent

Source: UN/DESA, based on data supplied by the South African Department of Land Affairs (as men-tioned in Cliffe, "Land reform in South Africa", *Review of African Political Economy*, No. 84 (2000), p. 281).

success of land reform. The South African National Water Act of 1998 recognized that water must be used to promote socio-economic development and introduced a series of innovative measures to tackle the highly unequal patterns of access to water resources in the country, including the strengthening of water user associations and smallholding irrigation schemes.[104] Although there are difficult transition issues arising from past apartheid water resource policies, the new water policy formulated in the Act can be "a powerful tool to achieve equity, poverty alleviation and development in rural areas".[105]

Furthermore, market-based land reform took place in the context of broader economic liberalization in the country. Relevant liberalization policies included the withdrawal of State agencies from agricultural marketing activities and a movement from State-controlled prices towards market-determined pricing, as the experience of the above-mentioned SAFEX market illustrates. It also included the reduction or removal of input subsidies to commercial (white-owned) farms that created distortions in the agricultural sector. These subsidies contributed to South Africa's focus on the production of low-value crops (such as wheat), rather than "specialization in labour-intensive production of high value crops and agro-exportables that one would expect given the country's natural endowment".[106] In addition, there was a major restructuring of financial institutions, including rural financial agencies, and greater public investment in physical and social infrastructure, notably rural roads, schools and hospitals. These complementary economic policies to promote macroeconomic and sectoral liberalization were essential for the introduction of market-based land reform in the country. This broad process of economic liberalization was closely associated with an increase in the number of land transactions: while an annual average of 4.5 per cent of arable land had changed hands during apartheid, this figure increased to more than 6 per cent in both 1997 and 1998.[107]

Nonetheless, by the late 1990s, it became clear that the major challenges were how to accelerate the redistribution of land and to provide more effective extension services to farmers already resettled under the programme. It became increasingly recognized that the long-term economic viability of the land reform programme required new measures to create greater opportunities in small-scale commercial agriculture and to streamline programme implementation. The revised market-based programme, entitled "Land Reform for Agricultural Development", was launched in 2001 with a number of key adjustments, summarized below.[108]

In order to increase the pace of land redistribution and reduce bureaucratic delay, implementation has been decentralized. While district-level officials now provide assistance to applicants in the preparation of project proposals, a committee at the provincial (as opposed to national) level has become responsible for approval of those project proposals. As a result, beneficiaries can now join the programme, purchase land from willing sellers and obtain land titles more swiftly than in the original programme. By speeding up the effective transfer of underutilized land to small farmers, the revised programme is expected to accelerate the growth of agricultural output and income, and thus contribute to alleviating rural poverty.

The most significant adjustment is that all beneficiaries must now make a contribution—in cash, labour and/or kind—in order to obtain the grant. The minimum grant amount requires a minimum personal contribution of R 5,000

[104] See S. R. Perret, "Water policies and smallholding irrigation schemes in South Africa: a history and new institutional challenges", *Water Policy*, No. 4 (2002), pp. 283-300; and Kirsten, Perret and van Zyl, loc. cit.

[105] See, in particular, Perret, loc. cit., p. 298.

[106] Deininger and May, loc. cit., p. 6.

[107] Ibid., p. 7.

[108] See Kirsten, Perret and van Zyl (loc. cit.) for details of the revised programme.

(approximately US$ 650 at 2003 exchange rates). Greater grant amounts are available to beneficiaries on a sliding scale, according to the size of their contribution (see table VII.2). As the amount of the grant and the amount of the contribution increase, there is a decline in the size of the grant as a proportion of total project cost. Both the grant and the contribution are calculated on a household basis. If beneficiaries decide to apply collectively, the personal contribution and the total grant are both scaled by the number of households represented in the group.

While the programme continues to focus on achieving a more equal distribution of land ownership (between black and white landholders), the introduction of personal contributions is intended not only to strengthen the commitment of beneficiaries in their projects, but also to increase the average grant amount (and thus the personal contribution) per beneficiary. This may make it harder for some potential (very poor) applicants to access the Government grant. The personal contribution mechanism thus implies that the revised programme is aimed more towards farmers intending to undertake the establishment or expansion of small and medium-sized commercial farms than towards poor landless peasants without any assets. As a result, there has been some concern that the poorest segments of the peasantry will be priced out of the revised land redistribution programme. One preliminary analysis of the revised programme, for example, concludes that a "clear danger under the demand-led rationing scheme is that the wealthier segments of the rural population will prove more apt to participate, and will therefore be the major beneficiaries, while the poorer segments will be left largely without programme benefits".[109]

To assess whether the revised programme will have a significant positive impact on rural poverty alleviation in South Africa would be premature. It is evident, however, that by increasing access options to (different amounts of) grants, the revised programme should facilitate structural change in the long run with the establishment of greater numbers of competitive small and medium-sized farms producing food and cash crops. It is also expected that the best-prepared beneficiary farmers will use the distributed land more productively.

That a cash contribution is provided by beneficiaries means that the new landowners now have a greater incentive to use the land for the most productive uses so as to maximize returns on personal investment. The minimum contribution to the total costs of projects will also help to screen out applicants who are

[109] F.J. Zimmerman, loc. cit., p. 1441.

Table VII.2.
LAND REDISTRIBUTION IN SOUTH AFRICA: SLIDING SCALE OF GRANTS AND PERSONAL CONTRIBUTIONS

Government grant (rand)	Own contribution (rand)	Total project cost per household (rand)	Share of grant (percentage)	Share of own contribution (percentage)
20 000	5 000	25 000	80	20
40 871	35 000	75 871	54	46
68 888	145 000	213 888	32	68
100 000	400 000	500 000	20	80

Source: J. Kirsten, S. Perret and J. van Zyl, "Land reform and the new water management context in South Africa: principles, progress and issues", paper prepared for a seminar of the Natural Resources Management and Land Policy Thematic Group (Washington, D.C., World Bank, September 2000), p. 10.

interested in an easy transfer of wealth but do not have the intention of farming the redistributed land. As a result, the share of unutilized land in approved projects is likely to drop even below the 5 per cent figure recorded in the original land redistribution programme. In addition, by promoting the growth of small and medium-sized commercial farms, the programme is also expected to encourage increased involvement of private financial institutions in project implementation through the provision of complementary (private) loans. This will not only reinforce beneficiaries' commitment to the success of their farms, but also encourage private lenders to strengthen the screening process and to provide independent monitoring of projects after they come on-stream.

The revised programme is intended to increase agricultural output, stimulate rural income growth—notably the income of beneficiaries—and improve land-use efficiency, given that small-scale beneficiaries often convert underutilized farmland to productive purposes. By ensuring greater agricultural output and productivity by small farmers, market-based land reform can indirectly contribute to growth in rural areas and more equitable rural development patterns (notably with respect to white and black farmers). It cannot, however, eradicate rural poverty on its own. In order to maximize its effectiveness, the revised programme, like all forms of land reform, also needs to be complemented by better infrastructure, such as rural roads, the provision of agricultural support services and adequate financial resources for its implementation.

While it has sometimes been argued that the implementation of market-based land reform would be hindered by its cost, the annual capital expenditure on the original South African land redistribution programme at the peak fiscal year (1998/99) was equivalent to only 0.2 per cent of the total annual government budget.[110] Although this relatively insignificant share of Government expenditure can also be associated with the poor rate of delivery of the original land redistribution programme, the annual expenditure on the provision of the physical and social infrastructure required to support, for example, 40,000 small-scale beneficiaries under the revised programme would be less than 1 per cent of general Government expenditure in 2001.[111] The provision of infrastructure and agricultural support services—in addition to the provision of Government grants—is thus within the budget of many developing countries. What is required is the political will to give greater priority to redistributive land reform within broader rural development strategies and to invest in the infrastructure and services required to support the activities of land redistribution beneficiaries, with the aim of turning many rural people into landowners.

An assessment of market-based land reform

It is increasingly recognized that market-based land redistribution programmes can be a useful alternative to coercive forms of land reform in many developing countries. While the implementation of market-based land programmes can be slowed down by teething problems, the South African experience shows that this type of land reform can be adjusted to respond to such problems without compromising the shift towards greater economic efficiency in the operation of land and agricultural markets. Market-based schemes also tend to be far less politicized than coercive approaches.[112]

[110] See A.V. Banerjee, loc. cit., p. 31; and M. Aliber, loc. cit., p. 486.

[111] See Kirsten, Perret and van Zyl, loc. cit. This estimate includes water supply and sanitation, electricity, and rural roads, as well as health and education. At this rate, it would take 11 years to successfully settle as many as half of the 900,000 landless households living in the former homelands in 1997. The term "general government expenditure" is used as defined in *World Development Report, 2003* (Washington, D.C., World Bank, Oxford University Press, 2003).

[112] It is worth noting, however, that similar initiatives have been fiercely opposed by landless or revolutionary movements in other developing countries, such as Brazil, Colombia and the Philippines.

At the same time, market-based approaches to land redistribution are likely to be implemented more effectively when targeted towards beneficiaries with agricultural skills and at least a little financial capital reserve. By encouraging the most dynamic segments of the peasantry to obtain arable land, market-based programmes can thus increase agricultural efficiency (a particularly important objective in countries with relative scarcity of arable land), output and rural incomes. In addition, market-based schemes often contribute to the development of land markets and make them more accessible to peasants with lower incomes, even when the poorest landless peasants experience difficulty in participating in those schemes.

As a result of this focus on increased productivity, the poorest (and least competitive) segments of the peasantry may have difficulty participating in schemes such as the South African one. Market-based programmes, on their own, are thus unlikely to transfer enough land to meet the needs of all poor rural people with the desire and the ability to farm it. When countries opt for market-based approaches to land redistribution, the State still has an important role to play, without necessarily deciding which land parcels change hands. In this regard, Governments need: (a) to draw up the criteria for selecting beneficiaries; (b) to reserve areas that are environmentally inappropriate for farming; (c) to provide grants and loans for land purchases; (d) to provide extension services and better transport infrastructure; and (e) to consider complementary policies to reach landless peasants unable to benefit from existing programmes. Market-based land reform can be a more effective policy tool when it becomes an integral part of a larger rural development and poverty alleviation strategy.

Market-based reform could be particularly useful in countries such as South Africa with little unused arable land and many landless peasants and smallholders without clear-cut claims to land rights. South Africa's experience with land reform could thus be relevant to other developing countries—not only in sub-Saharan Africa, but also in Latin America and parts of Asia—with highly unequal patterns of land distribution. In Southern Africa, for example, market-based land schemes could be implemented, at least to a limited extent, in countries such as Malawi and Namibia—where land reform is urgently needed—and could have offered a less conflictual option for land reform in Zimbabwe.[113] In other countries—such as Angola, Mozambique and the United Republic of Tanzania—where there are large tracts of unused State-owned land suitable for agriculture—smallholder expansion does not require land reform measures, as much as credit, extension services and improved rural infrastructure.

CONCLUDING REMARKS

Over the past two decades, the Governments of many poor countries have realized that certain types of State intervention in the agricultural sector have created economic inefficiencies and unsustainable fiscal cost, besides proving generally ineffective in ensuring sustained rural economic growth. In addition, bilateral and international donor or lender institutions have become increasingly unwilling or unable to fund the rising cost of direct State intervention in agricultural production and marketing, as well as the maintenance of inefficient land-use policies. This has led to greater emphasis on market-based approaches aimed at improving both the efficiency and the cost recovery of

[113] There are, in fact, proposals for a market-based scheme intended to benefit 15,000-20,000 rural households in Malawi.

agricultural production and marketing. These approaches, however, have produced mixed results in respect of rural poverty alleviation. The major challenge for the future is therefore to implement corrective measures to deal with reform problems while maintaining the efficiency improvements, marketing cost reductions and fiscal savings that have resulted from market-based approaches to reform.

Future efforts to consolidate or intensify food marketing reform in African (and other developing) countries must thus be better integrated into broader rural development strategies focusing on household food security and poverty alleviation. It is crucial, however, to design and use alternative instruments to achieve the food security objectives that many developing countries have long pursued through food marketing boards. Reform should have increasing the efficiency of food marketing systems as its primary objective, as opposed to questionable objectives, such as propping up inefficient farmers, which have contributed to the disappointing performance (and eventual demise) of food marketing boards over the long run.

At the same time, the case studies show that poor transport infrastructure and high transport costs of marketing agricultural produce pose serious obstacles to the successful implementation of both marketing and land reform. It can be concluded, therefore, that Government intervention in food marketing should move away from monopsonistic approaches and price-fixing, towards efforts to provide the enabling environment conducive to improved marketing efficiency, which would include better transport infrastructure, improved food storage capacity and the development of rural markets. Improved access to rural markets can make a significant contribution to raising the incomes of the rural poor and thus combating rural poverty.

The rural poor will be able to increase their income significantly only if their access to available productive resources—the most important of which, in poor countries, remains land—is substantially expanded. Although land redistribution is only one of several options for raising agricultural productivity, it is increasingly seen as crucial in many developing countries with highly unequal patterns of land ownership, particularly in Southern Africa, Latin America and parts of Asia. While it is now broadly recognized that land redistribution can play a critical role in efforts to reduce poverty in rural areas and to promote more equitable growth patterns, there has been an increasing interest in market-based approaches to land reform, as a result of the problems associated with coercive forms of land reform in many developing countries. The path-breaking South African experience with market-based land reform shows that this approach is flexible enough to respond to country-specific problems without compromising efforts towards the development of land markets, greater economic efficiency in agriculture, improved rural incomes and rural poverty alleviation.

Inasmuch as land redistribution can make a significant contribution to poverty alleviation, market-based land reform cannot be considered the single solution to rural poverty, in isolation from other policies designed to increase agricultural productivity, and to promote integrated rural development. Success with market-based land reform depends, in particular, on the implementation of complementary measures to foster rural development and smallholder agriculture. Such measures must address the availability of credit, the provision of extension services, the dissemination of appropriate agricultural technology, the access to irrigation water and better transport infrastructure, among other factors. Governments therefore still have an important role to play in promoting more equitable patterns of rural development, not only in terms of ensuring effective regulation but also with respect to the creation of a favourable environment for increased private investment, in the context of a broader economic liberalization strategy.

As in other sectors, the move towards greater overall economic efficiency may produce adverse socio-economic impacts and may even mean the contraction of some economic sectors. The fundamental goal, however, must be to raise employment and production in the economy as a whole and thereby raise overall living standards and reduce poverty. How to reduce rural poverty is a complex issue, which requires a comprehensive set of economic (and social) policies; the promotion of market-based approaches to food marketing and land redistribution are two such policies that could be potentially helpful.

VIII TRANSITION ECONOMIES AND POVERTY

After more than a decade of reforms, most of the former centrally planned countries of Eastern Europe and the former Soviet Union have largely completed their transition from central planning to a market economy. [1] **However, only a few of these countries were able to restore and surpass the pre-reform level of output and employment. The transition was achieved at a very high human cost, leading to unprecedented increases in poverty and inequality. In the course of the 1990s, the region of the transition economies was the only region in the world that experienced an overall decline in living standards. The present chapter focuses on some of the key policy-related problems of poverty in the transition economies. The main questions the chapter tries to answer are: What caused the dramatic increase in poverty in the transition economies? What is the nature of poverty in the transition economies? What explains the major differences in poverty levels in different transition economies? How do Governments and individuals in transition economies cope with poverty? In what ways can these coping strategies be made more successful?**

The transition to a market economy that started in the Eastern European countries in 1989 and in countries of the former Soviet Union in 1992 led to a dramatic increase in poverty. Prior to the start of reforms, in 1989, the number of the poor in the region, as measured by those living on less than $4 a day at international prices, had been 13.6 million, about 4 per cent of the population, with 6.5 million in the Central Asian republics of the then Soviet Union, 3.6 million in Belarus, the Russian Federation and Ukraine, 3.6 million in the Balkans, and 0.1 million each in the Central European centrally planned economies and the Baltic States. By 1993-1994, the total number of poor in the region was 119.2 million, of whom 83.2 million were in Belarus, the Russian Federation and Ukraine, 19.9 million in the Central Asian Republics, 12.9 million in the Balkan countries, 3.0 million in the Baltic States and 0.4 million in Central Europe. [2]

These figures show that the countries and areas that were under central planning the longest, namely, the Russian Federation and the other parts of tsarist Russia, had a much higher rate of poverty both before and after the transition than the countries of Central Europe, namely, the Czech Republic, Hungary, Poland and Slovakia. The Central European countries had been forced to adopt

[1] In the present chapter, the region of the transition economies is understood to comprise 30 countries, including 15 Eastern European countries (Albania, Bosnia and Herzegovina, Bulgaria, Croatia, the Czech Republic, Estonia, Hungary, Latvia, Lithuania, Poland, Romania, Slovakia, Slovenia, the former Yugoslav Republic of Macedonia and the Federal Republic of Yugoslavia), the three Baltic States (Estonia, Latvia and Lithuania) and 12 countries members of the Commonwealth of Independent States (CIS) (Armenia, Azerbaijan, Belarus, Georgia, Kazakhstan, Kyrgyzstan, the Republic of Moldova, the Russian Federation, Tajikistan, Turkmenistan, Ukraine, and Uzbekistan). As of 4 February 2003, the official name of "Federal Republic of Yugoslavia" was changed to "Serbia and Montenegro". It will be noted that "Eastern Europe" refers to all the transition economies except the CIS member States and thus includes the Baltic States.

[2] United Nations Development Programme, Regional Bureau for Europe and CIS, *Poverty in Transition* (United Nations publication, Sales No. E.98.III.B.27), p. 15, figure 1.8. These figures were based upon a $4 purchasing power parity (PPP) per day poverty line.

the centrally planned system only after the Second World War. They were wealthier than the republics of the Soviet Union and still retained some of the institutions that were to make it easier to operate a market economy. If it had not been for the imposition of central planning, they would have been developed economies like their neighbours to the West and would almost certainly have become members of the European Union (EU) many years earlier. The Balkan countries were less advanced economically than the Central European countries and the Baltic States were among the wealthiest republics of the former Soviet Union. Thus, the relative states of impoverishment of the different transition economies could not be considered altogether surprising. However, what was unexpected to some observers—and to many of the inhabitants of the region—was that the transition, instead of lasting for a few years and resulting in faster growth and rising living standards once the inefficiencies of central planning had been removed and a futile and costly arms race with the developed countries abandoned, had actually led to mass pauperization in many countries. This was especially the case in those parts of the Soviet Union that, unlike the Baltic States, had no experience of independence in the modern era and had not been prepared for the shock that would be caused by attaining independence and being set free to operate in a world economy that was increasingly subject to market forces.

Table VIII.1 shows how, in the late 1990s, absolute poverty, defined as those living on less than $1 a day at international prices, was still less than 2 per cent in the countries of Eastern Europe, with the exception of Romania, which, apart from Albania, had the lowest gross domestic product (GDP) per capita in the region in 2001. Measured at $2 per day, the poverty rates in Bulgaria and Romania stand out as much higher than those of the other Eastern European countries. Not only were these countries poorer, in terms of average income per capita, than those set to enter EU in 2004, but they had still not recovered fully from the transition recession. Thus, while Poland's GDP per capita in 2002 was nearly 30 per cent above its level of 1989, Bulgaria's and Romania's was over 10 per cent lower.

None of the members of the Commonwealth of Independent States (CIS), with the exception of Uzbekistan, had surpassed its 1989 level of GDP per capita by 2002. Poverty rates, when measured by the percentage of the population living on less than $2 per day, were considerably higher in CIS countries than in Eastern Europe. The problems confronting the CIS countries in tackling poverty are of a different order of magnitude from those confronting the Eastern European countries: they must recover their output levels of before the transition and ensure that the fruits of economic growth are enjoyed by the poorer members of society. Much of the analysis in this chapter, then, will be concerned with the CIS countries rather than with the Eastern European countries.

The shock that was followed by a rise in poverty in the transition economies was primarily a result of political factors—the breakdown of Soviet control first over the nominally independent countries of Central and Southern Europe and then, later, over the individual republics within the Soviet Union. These political factors had economic roots—the poor performance of the centrally planned system as compared with the market economy system in terms of delivering the goods and services that the citizens of these countries actually

Table VIII.1.
ABSOLUTE POVERTY RATES IN TRANSITION ECONOMIES, 1992-1999

Country	Survey year	Population below $1 a day (percentage)	Population below $2 a day (percentage)	Real GDP, 2002 (1989=100)
Eastern Europe				103.4
Albania		..	..	113.9
Bulgaria	1997	<2	21.9	82.9
Croatia	1998	<2	<2	86.4
Czech Republic	1996	<2	<2	105.8
Estonia	1998	<2	5.2	93.6
Hungary	1998	<2	7.3	111.7
Latvia	1998	<2	8.3	80.6
Lithuania	1996	<2	7.8	74.1
Poland	1998	<2	<2	129.6
Romania	1994	2.8	27.5	87.4
Slovakia	1992	<2	<2	108.7
Slovenia	1998	<2	<2	117.3
The former Yugoslav Republic of Macedonia		…	…	78.5
Commonwealth of Independent States				68.0
Armenia	1996	7.8	34.0	79.3
Azerbaijan	1995	<2	9.6	63.1
Belarus	1998	<2	<2	95.2
Georgia	1996	<2	<2	35.1
Kazakhstan	1996	<2	15.3	85.4
Kyrgyzstan		..	..	73.2
Republic of Moldova	1997	11.3	38.4	38.6
Russian Federation	1994	7.1	25.1	70.2
Tajikistan		..	..	43.1
Turkmenistan	1998	12.1	44.0	98.4
Ukraine	1999	2.9	31.0	47.3
Uzbekistan	1993	3.3	26.5	106.3

Sources: Economic Commission for Europe, *Economic Survey of Europe, 2003, No 1.* (United Nations publication, Sales No. E.03.11.E.26); and World Bank, *World Development Indicators* (Washington, D.C., World Bank, various issues).

wanted. Dismantling the centrally planned system and erecting a market system was bound to result in shocks, and historians will continue to discuss whether the steps that individual countries took minimized the disruption and maximized the possibilities for future growth. While there were great differences in the path to the market that the various countries followed, in the early days of transition this path had several common elements, which are analysed below. Those elements were: (a) a transformational recession, which could have been foreseen as overmanned and inefficient State enterprises reduced employment and which led to a sharp reduction of GDP; (b) hyperinflation which destroyed the savings of the population and helped to depress real wages in many transition economies; (c) an increase in income inequality across social groups, regions and sectors of the economy; and (d) the disintegration of the Soviet-era social protection system. In addition, in almost half of the countries in the region, people suffered severe losses of income from civil and ethnic conflicts. Given that, before the transition, incomes of a large part of the population in transition economies had been relatively low, any one of the above factors could have pushed them under the poverty line. This was even more likely when these factors worked in concert.

The negative factors were particularly evident in the poorest countries of CIS, which suffered greatly from the loss of federal subsidies that had been terminated with the dissolution of the Soviet Union.[3] In addition, during the 1990s, five of these countries were affected by wars and civil conflicts and had to accommodate sometimes hundreds of thousands of refugees and internally displaced persons (IDPs). Moreover, some countries suffered from extensive natural disasters and from recurring political crises (see box VIII.1, for the example of Armenia).

[3] For example, for Kyrgyzstan in the last years of the Soviet Union, these subsidies were equivalent to 30 per cent of the government budget and 10-12 per cent of the GDP, while in Uzbekistan subsidies constituted 18.5 per cent of GDP. See *World Economic and Social Survey, 2001.*(United Nations publication, Sales No. E.01.11.C.1), chap. VI, subsect. entitled "Increased vulnerability: poverty and deteriorating social conditions"; and Martin C. Spechler, "Hunting for the Central Asian tiger", *Comparative Economic Studies*, vol. 42, issue 3 (fall 2002), p. 17.

Box VIII.1

POVERTY IN ARMENIA

The Republic of Armenia, with a population of 3.8 million, was one of the 15 constituent republics of the former Soviet Union and is a current member of the Commonwealth of Independent States (CIS). Relatively poor in natural resources and landlocked, it nevertheless was one of the more prosperous republics in the Soviet Union, where Armenians enjoyed the reputation of being a well educated, industrious and entrepreneurial people.

The break-up of the Soviet Union at the end of 1991 dealt a severe blow to the well-being of Armenia. The transfers from the federal Government, mostly in the form of low-priced energy, which in 1989-1991 had constituted 31 per cent of fiscal revenues and 12 per cent of the gross domestic product (GDP) of Armenia, were abruptly ended. The timing was most unfortunate, as at the time Armenia still had to deal with the consequences of the devastating earthquake of 1989. The simultaneous collapse of inter-republic trade virtually cut off Armenian exports to the rest of the Soviet Union. To aggravate the situation, hostilities with Azerbaijan over the disputed enclave of Nagorny Karabakh escalated into a full-scale war, further draining the budgetary resources, and causing refugees to flow in both directions. Close to 300,000 refugees entered Armenia.

In the first four years of transition, Armenia's GDP dropped by 63 per cent. During the worst years of the crisis, in the mid-1990s, with almost no electricity or heating, many Armenian cities looked like ghost towns. In the capital city of Yerevan, with a population of over 1 million, people cut down trees in city parks for use as fuel.

The shrinking economy and the war meant that government spending on social protection had to be drastically reduced. At the end of the 1990s, pension spending was just 3.1 per cent of GDP, with the average pension dropping to less than one fifth of the average per capita income. Public spending on education fell to 2 per cent of GDP, and that on health care to 3.5 per cent of GDP. Faced with the economic crisis and inability

THE MACROECONOMIC BACKGROUND

The transformational recession

During the 1990s, the main cause of mass poverty in transition economies was the deep recession that had followed the collapse of the centrally planned economies. The length of the transformational recession across the 27 countries of the region ranged between three years (Poland) and nine years (Ukraine). The fall in GDP ranged from 15 to 70 per cent, although the fall cannot be attributed entirely to the transformation. In the CIS countries, the recession led to a fall in incomes surpassing that of the Great Depression and comparable only with the situation during periods following the Russian (Bolshevik) Revolution of 1917 and the Second World War.

In view of the widespread suffering of the poor in the transition economies, in particular the successor States of the former Soviet Union, the following question is often asked: Was it possible to escape the massive increase in poverty in the course of market reforms?

Box VIII.1 (continued)

of the State to protect them from poverty, hundreds of thousands Armenians left the republic for the Russian Federation and countries further away. Many of those who stayed turned to the informal economy.

The recovery started in Armenia earlier than in most other members of CIS and in the last seven years GDP has been growing at 6 per cent annually, helped by foreign assistance and remittances from Armenians abroad which constitute an estimated one eighth of GDP. Still, the per capita GDP of Armenia is just over $2,000 at purchasing power parity (PPP) valuation. In 1999, the poverty headcount, measured at the international poverty line of $4.30, was 86.2 per cent of the population, while acute poverty, measured at half that line, was 43.5 per cent of the population. This high incidence of poverty was also to a large degree the result of an extremely sharp disparity of incomes. Between 1987-1990 and 1996-1998, the Gini coefficient of inequality in Armenia had gone up from 0.27 to 0.61, with 50.6 per cent of incomes going to the richest, and only 5.5 per cent to the poorest quintile of the population.

In the last several years, thanks to economic recovery, large remittances from migrants and substantial international assistance, massive transitory poverty in Armenia has diminished. Government efforts to rebuild the social protection system are also bringing results. Armenia has become one of the leaders in CIS in the volume and efficiency of the distribution of targeted subsidies to the poorest families. Targeted means-tested subsidies constitute 2 per cent of GDP, a figure much higher than that in other CIS countries, where such subsidies constitute between 0.1 and 1.5 per cent of GDP. The poor in Armenia should also benefit from the new international "CIS-7" Initiative, launched in 2002 by the World Bank, the International Monetary Fund (IMF), the European Bank for Reconstruction and Development (EBRD), the Asian Development Bank and the Governments of the Netherlands and Switzerland to provide assistance to the seven poorest countries of CIS (Armenia, Azerbaijan, Georgia, Kyrgyzstan, the Republic of Moldova, Tajikistan and Uzbekistan).

Sources: *World Economic and Social Survey, 2001* (United Nations publication, Sales No. E.01.II.C.1), chap. VI entitled "The challenge to small, landlocked transition economies"; *Transition: The First Ten Years. Analysis and Lessons for Eastern Europe and the Former Soviet Union* (Washington, D.C., World Bank, 2002); *Making Transition Work for Everyone: Poverty and Inequality in Europe and Central Asia* (Washington, D.C., World Bank, 2000); and Sam Vaknin, United Press International, 23 January 2003.

4 Janos Kornai, *Highways and Byways: Studies on Reform and Postcommunist Transition* (Cambridge, Massachusetts, and London, England, The MIT Press, 1995); World Bank, *Making Transition Work for Everyone: Poverty and Inequality in Europe and Central Asia* (Washington, D.C., World Bank, 2000); Vladimir Popov, "Shock therapy versus gradualism: the end of the debate", *Comparative Economic Studies*, vol. XLII, No. 1 (spring 2000), pp. 1-58; and Jan Svejnar, "Transition economies: performance and challenges", *Journal of Economic Perspectives*, vol. 16, No. 1 (winter 2002), pp. 3-28.

5 Joseph Stiglitz, *Globalization and Its Discontents* (New York, W.W. Norton, 2002); World Bank, *From Plan to Market* (Washington, D.C., World Bank, 1996); Marek Dabrowski, Stanislaw Gomulka and Jacek Rostowski, *Whence Reform? A Critique of the Stiglitz Perspective* (London, Centre for Economic Performance, London School of Economics and Political Science, 2000); and Stanley Fischer and Ratna Sahay, "Taking stock", *Finance and Development*, vol. 37, No. 3 (September 2000), pp. 2-6.

6 "Much of the reform policy has been driven by the weakness of the Government and by the desire to preserve freedom through preventing a return of the communists", admits one of the leading Western consultants on the market transition. See Richard Layard, "Why so much pain?", in *Emerging From Communism: Lessons from Russia, China and Eastern Europe*, Peter Boone, Stanislaw Gomulka, and Richard Layard, eds. (Cambridge, Massachusetts and London, The MIT Press, 1998), p. 5. See also: Joseph Stiglitz, *Whither Socialism* (Cambridge, Massachusetts, The MIT Press, 1994); Marek Dabrowski, Stanislaw Gomulka, and Jacek Rostowski, op. cit.; Stanley Fischer and Ratna Sahay, loc. cit.; Leszek Balcerowicz, "Poland's transformation", *Finance and Development*, vol. 37, No. 3 (September 2000), pp. 14-16; and Gerald Roland, "The political economy of transition", *Journal of Economic Perspectives*, vol. 16, No. 1 (winter 2002), pp. 29-50.

7 "Inflation is a regressive and arbitrary tax, the burden of which is typically borne disproportionately by those in lower income brackets", *A Sourcebook for Poverty Reduction Strategies*, Vol. 2, p.5. See also *Poverty in Transition ...*, p. 23.

8 Richard Layard, loc. cit., p. 8.

9 Simon Commander, Andrei Tolstopiatenko and Ruslan Yemtsov, "Channels of redistribution", *Economics of Transition*, vol. 7, issue 2 (July 1999), p. 24.

10 In the last several years, depositors in the Russian Federation, Ukraine and some other CIS countries have started to receive limited compensation on deposits for the losses in the hyperinflation of the early 1990s. However compensation is partial and is limited only to the oldest of surviving depositors.

Most specialists agree that the initial sharp drop in output in the transition economies was caused by the combination of the demand shock brought about by the change in relative prices, the reduction of Government orders and the disruption of foreign trade, and the supply shock resulting from the inability of producers to quickly reallocate resources to the new uses. The poor quality of market institutions and a high degree of corruption in many transition economies contributed to the depth of the recession.[4]

There is still disagreement about the speed and sequencing of reforms. Some argue that the more rapid reforms would have been more beneficial to growth, while others think that the more rapid reforms, while more painful in the short run, were more conducive to higher longer-term growth.[5] With the benefit of hindsight, it would appear that the course that the reforms took in a particular country was largely predetermined by the distribution of political power.[6] Thus, in the republics of the former Soviet Union, practically all power on the eve of reforms was concentrated in the hands of the former Communist Party bureaucracy and managers of large State-owned enterprises. The majority of the population had little role in determining the reform agenda. In many Eastern European countries, in contrast, civil society was quite vocal and grass-roots organizations, such as the "Solidarity" trade union in Poland, were important players in their own right. As a result, in Eastern Europe the working population could count on poverty alleviation measures, being incorporated in the reform programme from the very start.

Inflation

Political differences were significant in the case of inflation. The poor suffer from inflation more than the well-to-do, as they usually lack the information and skills to protect their incomes and assets from rapidly rising prices. As a result, hyperinflation generally leads to an increase in poverty and income inequality.[7] However, in the transition economies, the success of stabilization policies generally depended on political factors. Governments of the leading Eastern European countries, operating under national consensus, were able to contain inflation relatively quickly. In the CIS countries, the struggle with inflation was frequently complicated by the presence of powerful political interests. In the Russian Federation, in the first years of reform, the lobbying by enterprise directors secured a massive flow of Government credits to their firms which helped fuel the hyperinflation. By some estimates, in 1992-1993, these credits had resulted in a net transfer of wealth to enterprises of about 15 per cent of GDP.[8] The net losers from hyperinflation were private savers, mostly pensioners. Overall, the destruction of private savings in the Russian Federation eliminated up to one fourth of household wealth.[9]

Inflation damaged or destroyed private savings in many other transition economies, in most of which deposits were not indexed or otherwise compensated for inflation. However, in Eastern European countries such as in Hungary and the Czech Republic, where levels of inflation were lower, and in countries such as Poland where most savings were kept in foreign currencies, losses of depositors were relatively small.[10]

Private sector investment

With privatization and the sharp reduction of the role of the State in the economy, much of the responsibility for generating growth has naturally shifted to private, including foreign, investment. In this matter, however, the situation in the transition economies is far from satisfactory. The level of investment in most of these countries is less than 20 per cent of GDP. For the CIS countries, the problem is often not a lack of savings, but rather the relatively poor business climate and the low quality of institutional support. Thus, in 1999-2001, domestic savings in the Russian Federation surpassed 30 per cent, while domestic investments were less than 20 per cent, with a good part of the difference explained by capital flight. The business climate in CIS affects the inflow of foreign direct investment (FDI). During the period 1999-2001, in the EU accession countries of Eastern Europe, FDI constituted almost 5 per cent of GDP, or about $200 per capita, while in the CIS countries, the comparable figures were less than 1 per cent of GDP, or less than $40 per capita.[11]

In recent years, investment and the general business climate in many transition economies have improved. According to the extensive survey of enterprises conducted in the transition economies jointly by the World Bank and the European Bank for Reconstruction and Development (EBRD) since 1996, in almost all countries of the region, between 1999 and 2002, economic governance and the general business environment have improved. Progress was particularly significant in the countries of South-Eastern Europe and CIS, partly from the impact of the change in the Government of the former Federal Republic of Yugoslavia and the accession to power of the new leadership in the Russian Federation. However, the overall scores for the quality of the business environment in the countries of South-Eastern Europe and in CIS remain lower than those for the countries of Central and Eastern Europe. On average, the scores for the two former groups of countries in 2002 were equal to those of the latter group of countries for 1999.[12]

Income distribution

Over the course of transition, income inequality, measured at the household level, increased rapidly and significantly in almost all of the transition economies. In the Russian Federation and Ukraine, the Gini coefficient of inequality rose to over 45 per cent (see table VIII.2). The rise in income inequality, in its turn, was directly linked to a major increase in wealth inequality, resulting from the way in which the privatization of government assets had been carried out. This was particularly true in resource-rich countries such as Azerbaijan, Kazakhstan and the Russian Federation. Here a whole class of instant millionaires and even billionaires was created, as a result of the highly questionable method by which the privatization of oil and other natural resources had been achieved (see box VIII.2). Measured by the Gini inequality coefficients, the level of inequality in the Eastern European countries was much lower than in the CIS countries: in 1999-2000, the coefficients were in the range of 0.30-0.34, or close to that in the Organisation for Economic Cooperation and Development (OECD) member countries.

[11] European Bank for Reconstruction and Development (EBRD), *Transition Report, 2002: Agriculture and Rural Transition* (London, EBRD, 2002), pp. 54-55.

[12] Ibid., pp. 22-31.

Table VIII.2.
GINI COEFFICIENTS IN TRANSITION ECONOMIES, 1987-1998

Country	1987-1990	1993-1994	1996-1998
Eastern Europe	0.23	0.29	0.33
Bulgaria	0.23	0.38	0.41
Croatia	0.36	..	0.35
Czech Republic	0.19	0.23	0.25
Estonia	0.24	0.35	0.37
Hungary	0.21	0.23	0.25
Latvia	0.24	0.31	0.32
Lithuania	0.23	0.37	0.34
Poland	0.28	0.28	0.33
Romania	0.23	0.29	0.30
Slovenia	0.22	0.25	0.30
Commonwealth of Independent States	0.28	0.36	0.46
Armenia	0.27	..	0.61
Belarus	0.23	0.28	0.26
Georgia	0.29	..	0.43
Kazakhstan	0.30	0.33	0.35
Kyrgyzstan	0.31	0.55	0.47
Republic of Moldova	0.27	..	0.42
Russian Federation	0.26	0.48	0.47
Tajikistan	0.28	..	0.47
Turkmenistan	0.28	0.36	0.45
Ukraine	0.24	..	0.47

Source: EBRD, *Transition Report, 2002: Agriculture and Rural Transition* (London, EBRD, 2002), p. 9.

Fiscal policy

The transition to a market economy has led to the significant reduction of the government's role in many economic activities. Between 1989-1990 and 1999-2000, government revenues as a percentage of GDP declined on average from 50 to 40 per cent in Eastern Europe and from 40 to 25-30 per cent in the CIS countries.[13] In most of the transition economies, this decline was accounted for primarily by the reduction in centralized investments and military spending, while spending on social programmes, education and health care expressed as a percentage of GDP remained largely intact.[14] Owing to the transformational recession, however, the actual volume of spending on social protection went down, unless the share of this spending was increased to compensate for the fall of GDP. The reduction of actual spending was particularly deep in the CIS countries, where real GDP dropped in the 1990s by 40-70 per cent.

The difference between Eastern Europe and the CIS countries lay not only in the overall extent of fiscal retreat but also in how it was accomplished. In many Eastern European countries, the reduction of government spending was managed in a relatively orderly manner, while in many CIS countries, this was not the case.[15] In many CIS countries, the effectiveness of the State in coping with poverty was further undermined by the power of special interests, which

[13] Vladimir Popov, loc. cit., p. 54; *Transition report, 2002...*, p. 62; and *Transition: The First Ten Years. Analysis and Lessons for Eastern Europe and the Former Soviet Union* (Washington, D.C., World Bank, 2002), p. 47.

[14] However, in most Central Asian and Transcaucasian countries of CIS, spending on social protection, education and health care fell in proportion to GDP, often significantly (*Poverty in Transition ...*, pp. 94-95).

[15] "Instead of completely shutting down some Government programs and concentrating limited resources on the others with the aim of raising their efficiency, some Governments kept all programs half-alive, half-financed and barely working. The political pressures for maintaining services across the board outweighed the need for more selective streamlining of priorities" (*Poverty in Transition.*, p. 36).

Box VIII.2

THE RUSSIAN FEDERATION:
LAND OF BILLIONAIRES?

In the 2003 *Forbes*' list of the world's richest individuals, the Russian Federation boasted 17 billionaires, a figure lower than those of only three countries—the United States of America, Germany and Japan. By the number of its super-rich, the Russian Federation has surpassed such countries as Canada (15 billionaires), the United Kingdom of Great Britain and Northern Ireland (14) and France (13)—countries with a 2002 gross domestic product (GDP) per capita of $25,000-27,000, compared with the Russian Federation's GDP per capita of $4,000 (at the market exchange rate). It has also left China (no billionaires) far behind and, even more tellingly, Brazil. With a population and per capita income very similar to those of the Russian Federation, Brazil has a much longer history of market capitalism, but accounted for only four billionaires.

Almost all the super-rich in the Russian Federation derive their wealth from the control of oil and other natural resources. Unlike the fortunes of billionaires in the mature market economies, which were based on unique entrepreneurial talents such as those of Bill Gates of Microsoft, or on wealth accumulated over several generations, the fortunes of Russian billionaires have been created essentially by government decrees. The largest Russian private companies were not built from scratch; rather, they came into existence as a result of insider-controlled privatizations and rigged auctions of already existing government companies. In effect, all Russian billionaires (and many, if not most of the "ordinary" millionaires) were "nominated" as such by the political decisions of government bureaucrats.

The jury is still out on the longer-term outcome of Russian privatization. Pointing to other countries of CIS, some Russian economists argue that keeping the prize government assets in the hands of the State would have brought about even worse results. However, it is clear that some controversial privatizations contributed to the growth of income inequality in Russia.

Sources: *Forbes*, 17 March 2003; Francisco H. G. Ferreira, "Economic transition and the distributions of income and wealth", *Economics of Transition*, vol. 7 (World Bank), No. 2 (July 1999), pp. 377-410; and Michael Alexeev, "The effect of privatization on the wealth distribution in Russia", *Economics of Transition*, vol. 7 (World Bank), No. 2 (July 1999).

prevented the redistribution of income towards the more vulnerable members of society. For example, while in Eastern Europe spending on pensions and unemployment benefits averaged 10 per cent of GDP, in CIS such spending was only 5 per cent. Continuation of selected price subsidies and the old enterprise-based system of provision of social services helped the poor survive the worst periods of the transition, but, overall, the fiscal policies in the CIS countries failed to perform their social protection function.

Between 2001 and 2003, several CIS countries, in particular the Russian Federation, embarked on the path of fiscal reform, aimed at increasing government revenues and stopping the disorganized fiscal retreat of the Government. In the Russian Federation, the simplification of the tax structure and the introduction of a flat 13 per cent income tax have reportedly brought positive results in terms of increased tax compliance and revenue collection. It remains to be seen, however, if an improvement of the fiscal situation will translate into better-funded and more efficient poverty alleviation programmes.

Trade and foreign exchange policy

Trade liberalization and the removal of currency controls that accompanied market reforms in transition economies were pursued in order to stimulate long-term economic growth. In this way, trade policy would contribute to combating poverty. However in the short-run perspective, an open-trade regime creates not only winners but also losers. The poor depend upon foreign trade as consumers and their welfare increases when the opening up of trade gives them access to foreign goods, services and food supplies that were previously unavailable or too expensive. As producers, the poor who are employed in export or export-related industries also gain from freer trade. At the same time, the poor may lose as producers when the industries in which they have been employed are affected by competition from foreign imports.[16]

In the first years of market reforms, the opening of domestic markets in transition economies to foreign competition inflicted serious damage on domestic industries. Unable to compete with foreign producers, they had to reduce output, employment and/or wages. At the same time, exporters from some transition economies were making hefty profits by taking advantage of sharp differences between the domestic and world prices of raw materials, such as oil, timber and metals. Very soon, protectionist pressures in the transition economies forced the Governments to retreat from the path of full liberalization and to start increasing tariffs and imposing quotas and other forms of import containment and export control. To protect their domestic markets, some countries, such as Uzbekistan, also preserved multiple exchange rates.

The benefits of trade liberalization depend on many factors in the country itself (whether it has a diversified economy, its geographic position and the state of its institutions) and in its trading partners. Costs might also be incurred when liberalizing trade; jobs could be lost in industries competing with imports before new jobs are created.[17]. However, the introduction of low uniform tariffs has proved to be quite effective for some countries. The leader here is probably Estonia, with its uniform zero-level tariffs, similar to those in Hong Kong Special Administrative Region (SAR) of China and Singapore. Kyrgyzstan has also introduced a progressive tariff system with a small dispersion of rates, comparable with those in Chile.[18]

In the field of exchange-rate regulation, a pro-growth, and therefore pro-poor, policy calls for maintaining an undervalued rather than an overvalued real exchange rate vis-à-vis a country's main trade partners. An undervalued exchange rate helps promote exports. Historically, the policy of having an undervalued national currency had helped to spur export growth in South-East Asia and Japan, China and other countries that were successful in overcoming or reducing poverty. At the same time, however, the benefits of an overvalued exchange rate in terms of cheaper imports are enjoyed less by the poor than by the rich, since imported goods constitute a smaller share of the consumption of the poor.[19]

The situation in resource-based economies, such as the Russian Federation, is more complex. Here, the massive inflow of foreign currency from the export of raw materials creates a constant risk of the overvaluation of the national currency—the so-called Dutch disease. In the Russian Federation, the large appreciation of the ruble prior to the 1998 crisis had served as a major drag on growth. As a result, the 1998 devaluation, while disrupting the country's financial system, was nevertheless quite beneficial for economic growth and, overall, was arguably a positive development for the poor. The fact that, in the last few years, the currency has appreciated again in real terms is becoming a major policy concern.

[16] "Trade liberalization can be expected to help the poor overall, given the positive association between openness and growth. However, in the short run, liberalization may have a negative impact on some of the poor, depending on their sources of income and the impact of liberalization on the prices of goods and services the poor consume." See Bernard Hoekman and others, "Trade policy". In *A Sourcebook for Poverty Reduction Strategies*, vol. 2…, p. 30.

[17] See Joseph E. Stiglitz, "Globalization and Growth in Emerging Markets and the New Economy", *Journal of Policy Modeling*, vol. 25 (2003), p. 513.

[18] See Bernard Hoekman and others, loc. cit., pp. 33-34.

[19] See Brian Ames and others, "Macroeconomic Issues", in *A Sourcebook for Poverty Reduction Strategies*, vol. 2, p. 9.

TRANSIENT VERSUS CHRONIC POVERTY

The emergence of chronic poverty

Government shortcomings in coping with poverty in the early days of the transition forced people in the poorer transition economies to resort heavily to self-help methods of economic survival. The private response to coping with poverty included increased employment in the informal economy, cultivation of family plots, and heavy reliance on intra-family transfers. Lack of opportunity at home led to massive labour migration to better-off economies of the region and to other countries. As a last resort, large numbers of people engaged in crime and prostitution.

Since the mid-1990s, the poverty situation in the transition economies region has improved, led by an economic recovery in Eastern Europe. Economies of CIS have been growing rather vigorously since the 1998 devaluation of the ruble. However, this general improvement has been accompanied by a concentration of poverty in particular regions and sectors of the economy, and among specific groups of the population. Thus, while the recession-induced "transient" poverty has subsided, the smaller-scale but entrenched pockets of chronic poverty have not disappeared. The emergence of concentrated and acute long-term poverty is a relatively new phenomenon.[20]

Owing to the various levels of poverty, the problems experienced by the leading reformers of Eastern Europe in coping with it are significantly different from those confronting the CIS countries. In the Eastern European countries, in particular the EU accession countries,[21] transient poverty is subsiding now that income levels are surpassing their pre-transition levels and market-based economic growth is being achieved. The goal of the Governments consists largely of improving the existing social protection mechanisms and rooting out the pockets of concentrated poverty. In the poorest CIS countries, the main challenge is to alleviate their acute poverty and to prevent the collapse of the existing health-care and education systems. For other CIS countries, the task consists of reducing the still massive transient poverty via stimulative economic policies while at the same time containing the dangerous increase in concentrated long-term poverty.

At the present time, poverty in transition economies has many unique features (see box VIII.3). Prior to the transition, poverty was largely prevented by Government-guaranteed employment, free health care and education, and heavily subsidized food, housing and utilities. In line with its collectivist ideology, the Government ensured a fairly egalitarian distribution of wages and severely restricted other sources of incomes. At the same time, Governments provided fairly generous social protection systems for children and families. Extensive health and education services were also provided to all households, ensuring a high level of human capital. In addition, most households in transition economies inherited from the centrally planned period valuable physical capital in the form of formerly State-owned apartments complete with a full set of amenities. This made them relatively assets-rich in contrast with comparable households in developing countries. Another feature of the centrally planned economies was the main provision of some of the key services and social protection, such as housing, childcare and social security, by enterprises rather than by the government.

[20] Attesting to the recent emergence of this phenomenon is the fact that it was not mentioned as a major problem neither in the comprehensive 1996 World Bank report on the transition economies nor in the 1998 UNDP report on poverty in transition, which stated that there was "little indication as yet" of the emergence of an underclass in the region (see *From Plan to Market...*; and *Poverty in Transition ...*, p. 18).

[21] The EU accession countries are: Bulgaria, the Czech Republic, Estonia, Hungary, Latvia, Lithuania, Poland, Romania, Slovakia and Slovenia. Eight of them are scheduled to join EU in May 2004. Bulgaria, and Romania are scheduled to be admitted in 2007.

Box VIII.3

MEASUREMENT OF POVERTY
IN TRANSITION ECONOMIES

Sources: Simon Johnson, Daniel Kaufman and Andrei Shleifer, "The unofficial economy in transition", *Brookings Papers on Economic Activity*, vol. 2 (1997), pp.159-221; J. Flemming, and J. Micklewright, "Income distribution, economic systems and transition", in *Handbook of Income Distribution*, Anthony Atkinson and François Bourguignon, eds. (Amsterdam, Elsevier, 2000), pp. 843-910; Carola Grun and Stephan Klasen, "Growth, income distribution and well-being in transition countries", *Economics of Transition*, vol. 9, No. 2 (2001), p. 378; Aline Coudouel, Jesko S. Hentschel and Quentin T. Wodon, "Poverty measurement and analysis", in *A Sourcebook for Poverty Reduction Strategies*, vol.1, Jeni Klugman, ed. (Washington, D.C., World Bank, 2002), pp. 27-74; *Bulgaria Poverty Assessment*, World Bank Report, No. 24516 (Washington, D.C., 29 October 2002), pp.3-7; and *Trud*, 11 January 2003.

While no one doubts the overall massive increase of levels of poverty in the transition economies, questions exist with regard to its measurement. Owing to such unique features of transition economies as socialized health care and education, subsidized utilities and large intra-family transfers, the measurement of poverty in those economies is more difficult than in developing economies at a comparable level of development. Measurement of poverty in transition economies is further complicated by major fluctuations in output and prices, the large size of the unofficial economy, massive migration of the population, and statistical systems that are still adjusting to the market environment. In the present chapter, the analysis of poverty in transition economies relies primarily on absolute indicators, based on "fixed" poverty lines, usually defined in international dollars. In addition, use has been made of relative poverty indicators, based on "moving" poverty lines, defined by individual countries in proportion to the average wage, or to the average per capita income.

A particularly difficult problem in poverty measurement in transition economies is how to account for the large unofficial sector, estimates of which range between 6 per cent in Slovakia to over 60 per cent in Georgia and Azerbaijan. Government statistical agencies are making increasing efforts to account for the size of the unofficial economy's contribution to GDP. For example, in the Russian Federation, the size of GDP is periodically adjusted upward to include output of the unofficial economy and small family plots. However, a significant part of the unofficial economy escapes government data-gatherers and can be estimated only approximately, based on indirect indicators, such as electricity consumption. Existence of a large unofficial sector is one of the reasons why poverty measurement using household expenditures is more reliable compared with measurement based on reported incomes.

Low income alone cannot convey the overall level of deprivation suffered by the poor. Broader measures of well-being can include degree of equality, access to health care and education, and political participation. The resulting indicators are generally well related, but can show somewhat different trends. For example, indicators combining poverty and inequality show much larger deterioration of well-being in transition economies compared with measures based on poverty alone. This, of course, is explained by the sharp increases in income inequality in transition economies in the 1990s.

For the formerly egalitarian communist societies, the sudden arrival of income disparity was quite painful psychologically. The survey-based "subjective poverty" in these countries increased in the 1990s to much higher levels than did "measured poverty". Thus in Bulgaria in 2001, 73 per cent of the population called themselves poor, compared with 12.8 per cent based on the national poverty line. In a 2002 survey in the Russian Federation, over 50 per cent called themselves poor, roughly twice the headcount based on the national poverty line.

A significant segment of poverty in transition economies appears to be transient in nature. With a fairly equal distribution of income before the transition and with many families clustered near the poverty line, a large number of people had been pushed below this line when incomes fell. When economies in the region started to recover, the incomes of many of these families recovered to levels above the poverty line, thus making poverty a transient experience for them.

However, along with the decline of transient massive poverty, the transition economies have witnessed the growth of chronic and concentrated poverty.

This came about as a result of several interrelated income differentiation processes linked to regional, sectoral, demographic and other characteristics of the population. As could be expected, different groups of people (urban/rural, educated/uneducated, employed/unemployed/self-employed) fared differently during the transformational recession. Some groups were able to climb out of poverty relatively quickly, while others have remained stuck in poverty since the start of the transition.

In all countries, transient poverty is brought about by unfavourable but temporary *macroeconomic* conditions, such as a decline in overall GDP, hyperinflation or a massive depreciation of the national currency. Wars and other non-economic factors, such as natural disasters, can also cause transient poverty. As opposed to this type of poverty, chronic poverty is primarily the result of microeconomic factors, such as the characteristics of a particular region or industry, or the characteristics of individual household members, such as level of education, professional occupation, age, gender and ethnicity.[22]

A recent study of chronic poverty in several transition economies based on longitudinal surveys of household expenditures concluded that chronic poverty accounts for about one half of the overall poverty headcount.[23] According to this study, in which the poor were defined as being in the bottom 20 per cent of the income or expenditure distribution, about 10 per cent of the population in Hungary, Poland and the Russian Federation can be considered to be chronically poor and thus candidates for the permanent underclass (see table VIII.3).

Sectoral and geographical differentiation of incomes

In the centrally planned era, in addition to making cross-country and inter-republic transfers, central Governments had actively engaged in cross-subsidization at the regional level. The collapse of central planning led to a significant weakening of regional cross-subsidization. Along with the opening of

[22] Michael Lokshin and Barry M. Popkin. "The emerging underclass in the Russian Federation: income dynamics, 1992-1996", *Economic Development and Cultural Change,* vol. 47, No. 4 (1999), pp. 822-823. Separating the transient from the chronic components of poverty is fraught with difficulty, as it calls for observation over a long period of time and panel data. Such data are available in comparable format for only just a few of the transition economies. Most measurements of poverty are thus effectively snapshots inasmuch as a poverty per capita count for a particular year does not reveal anything about the previous income status of those registered as poor or about their income situation the following year.

[23] This corresponds to a similar proportion found in the study of long-term poverty in China and India. See World Bank, *World Development Report, 2000/2001: Attaching Poverty* (New York, Oxford University Press, 2001), p. 140.

Table VIII.3.
TRANSIENT AND CHRONIC POVERTY: HUNGARY, POLAND AND THE RUSSIAN FEDERATION, 1994-1996[a]

Percentage			
Share of the population	Hungary (income)	Poland (expenditure)	Russian Federation (expenditure)
A. Share of the population based on measured poverty			
Always poor (4 out of 4 rounds)	8.8	5.9	3.4
Sometimes poor (1, 2 or 3 out of 4 rounds)	26.3	31.6	41.9
Never poor (0 out of 4 rounds)	65.0	61.5	54.7
B. Share of the population based on simulations using "underlying" poverty transition problems			
Always poor (4 out of 4 rounds)	9.7	10.7	10.0
Sometimes poor (1, 2 or 3 out of 4 rounds)	22.6	20.1	21.8
Never poor (0 out of 4 rounds)	67.8	69.2	68.2

Source: *Transition Report, 2000* (London: EBRD, 2000), p. 98.

[a] Based on data from four rounds of national longitudinal household surveys in Hungary, Poland and the Russian Federation conducted in 1994-1996. Panel A shows poverty headcounts directly observed by the surveys. In panel B, headcounts are adjusted to control for the impact of general transitory shocks and to reflect the "underlying" long-term poverty. In every round of the surveys, poverty was defined as being in the bottom 20 per cent of the income or expenditure distribution.

[24] See: V. Popov, " Reform strategies and economic performance of Russia's regions", *World Development*, vol. 29, No. 5 (2000), pp. 865-886; N. Mikheeva, "Differentiation of social-economic situation of Russian regions and problems of regional policy" (Moscow, Economics Education and Research Consortium (EERC), 1998); Irina Dolinskaya, *Transition and Regional Inequality in Russia: Reorganization or Procrastination?*, IMF Working Paper, No. 02/169, (Washington, D.C., October 2002, Leonid Fedorov, "Regional inequality and regional polarization in the Russian Federation, 1990-99", *World Development*, vol. 30, No.3 (2002), pp. 443-456; and Simon Commander, Andrei Tolstopiatenko and Ruslan Yemtsov, loc. cit.

national economies to the outside world, this produced major changes in the fortunes of individual regions, cities and districts. This was particularly true for the regions of the former Soviet Union, many of which lost valuable energy subsidies and other federal aid; but in the course of their transition to the market, even the wealthier transition economies witnessed the emergence of numerous depressed regions within their borders. These were regions that were hit particularly severely by market reforms, such as changes in relative prices, the elimination of subsidies, drops in State orders and increases in transportation costs. Examples include the northern territories and defence-producing regions in the Russian Federation (see box VIII. 4).

On the other hand, the transition to a market economy led to the relative increase in the well-being of most capital cities and the emergence of newly prosperous regions, such as oil-rich western Siberia. Generally, the winners are regions rich in natural resources, with a large population and close proximity to the main economic centres.[24]

The resulting differences in poverty levels can be substantial. For example, a resident of Warsaw is six times less likely to be poor than residents of the rest

Box VIII.4

THE RUSSIAN DEFENCE INDUSTRY: THE CASE OF A SHRINKING GIANT

In the course of the 1990s, the Russian defence industry was hit by the triple shock of severe budget cuts, radical market reforms and the breakdown of traditional economic ties with partners in the other former Soviet republics. Between the peak of the Soviet military build-up of the late 1980s and the lowest point reached in 1996, the share of defence spending in Russian GDP dropped from 15-17 to 3-4 per cent, the military industry's output fell by 80 per cent, and employment in the defence industry fell by two thirds.

Defence industry enterprises are found in the majority of the Russian provinces. However, most of them are concentrated in just a few regions, in particular in Moscow and Saint Petersburg, the Urals and western Siberia.

In the Soviet era, defence enterprises had many advantages in comparison with the rest of the economy: they possessed the highest-skilled personnel, both workers and engineers, and developed the best research and development (R&D) and innovations. Higher wages were the main factor in attracting and retaining better workers. In addition, defence enterprises owned extensive facilities that provided social services— retail outlets, hospitals, kindergartens and summer camps for children, sport stadiums, seaside resorts and libraries.

As a result of the severe reduction of military orders, defence enterprises found themselves in a more disadvantageous position than the rest of the economy. This was reflected in particularly deep cuts in wages, wage arrears, losses of personnel and tension in labour-management relations. During the transition period, some of the social service facilities were closed down or sold off as enterprises were no longer able to fund them.

Throughout the decade of reforms, average wages in the defence industry constituted only 40-60 per cent of average wages and 50-80 per cent of average wages in manufacturing. Among other branches of the economy, only education, agriculture and health care had lower average wages than the defence industry. In recent years, wages in the defence industry have started to catch up with those in other sectors of the economy. However, the gap remains. In 2002, based on a survey of defence enterprises, average wages therein amounted to 3,135 rubles (just over US$ 100 at the market exchange rate) per month, which was equivalent to 60 per cent of the level of average wages in

of Poland; the poverty level in Saint Petersburg in the Russian Federation is eight times lower than that in the Russian republic of Tuva.[25] As a result, per capita income disparities among the 89 administrative regions of the Russian Federation are much larger than, for example, disparities among the 50 States in the United States of America, with a coefficient of variation of 51.9 per cent as compared with one of 14.8 per cent for the United States.[26]

In transition economies, rural areas remain poorer compared with urban areas. However, the patterns are different in Eastern European and CIS countries. In most Eastern European countries, the levels of *rural poverty* are significantly (about 50 per cent) higher than the levels in the cities. In the CIS countries, the gap between urban and rural regions is not as pronounced. In some of these countries (for example, Georgia) poverty is actually lower in rural than in the urban areas. The reason for the relatively better situation of rural areas in the CIS countries is a much deeper fall in industrial production in these countries compared with that in the Eastern European countries. In some of the CIS regions, the dire economic crisis in manufacturing made even depressed farming areas appear attractive. In extreme cases, it led to de-urban-

[25] *Making Transition Work for Everyone...*, p. 74; and Simon Clarke, "Poverty in Russia", *Problems of Economic Transition*, vol. 42, No. 5 (September 1999), p. 21.

[26] Simon Commander, Andrei Tolstopiatenko and Ruslan Yemtsov, loc. cit., p. 34; and Jeni Klugman and Jenine Braithwaite, "Poverty in the Russian Federation during the transition: an overview", *The World Bank Research Observer*, vol. 13, No. 1 (February 1998), p. 39.

Box VIII.4 (continued)

industry, and 80 per cent of the level of average wages in manufacturing.

A low level of wages, however, is only one aspect of the wage problem in the Russian defence industry. Another aspect is persistent wage arrears. Even the most competitive enterprises suffer from this problem. For example, in 2002, wages on average in the Izhmash plant in the republic of Udmurtia producing the Kalashnikov guns were two months in arrears.

As a means of retaining workers while not paying them competitive wages, many defence enterprises continue to rely on enterprise-based social services. By presidential decree, control of all "social infrastructure objects" of defence enterprises was to have been transferred to the municipal authorities by 1997. In reality, the process of transfer has not been completed. By 2003, only part of the social infrastructure had been transferred to municipal budgets, sold or rented out.

Having begun the transformation of their social infrastructure, enterprises realized the importance of some of these properties for retaining personnel and decided to slow or halt the transition altogether. As of 2001, 60-70 per cent of the defence enterprises continued to own medical clinics, cafeterias and libraries; 35-55 per cent of enterprises owned stores, camps for children, recreation facilities, sports stadiums and housing; and about 20 per cent of the defence enterprises owned kindergartens.

Considerable differentiation exists among defence enterprises located in different regions of the Russian Federation. Enterprises located in, or in the vicinity of, the central cities generally enjoy better economic and social conditions than those located in the remote regions of the country, especially the far east, eastern Siberia and northern Caucasus. In the defence enterprises of Moscow and the Moscow region, average monthly wages in 2002 were more than 1.4 times higher than in other regions. This reflects the fact that, in central cities, the labour market is much more vibrant than in the provinces, hence defence industry workers unhappy with their pay or working conditions can simply leave for a better job. In provincial defence enterprises, in particular those based in the so-called closed cities, fewer workers have such an option. Yet, the fact that Moscow has a considerably higher cost of living largely offsets the differences in wage levels measured in real terms.

Sources: Clifford Gaddy, *The Price of the Past: Russia's Struggle with the Legacy of a Militarized Economy* (Washington, D.C., Brookings Institution Press, 1996); Ksenia Gonchar, "Russia's defence idustry at the turn of the century", Bonn International Centre for Conversion, Bonn, 2000; Alexei Izyumov and others, "Market reforms and regional differentiation of Russian defence enterprises", *Europe-Asia Studies*, vol. 54, No. 6 (2002), pp. 959-974; State Committee for Statistics of the Russian Federation, *Living Standards of Population* (available at: http://www.gks.ru/); and Udmurtia, "Weapons producers still suffer from wage arrears", 21 September 2002 (available at http://www.regions.ru/article/any/id/854061.html).

27 Kathryn H. Anderson and Richard Pomfret, "Relative living standards in new market economies: evidence from Central Asian household surveys", *Journal of Comparative Economics*, vol. 30 (2002), p.702.

28 Branko Milanovic, *Income, Inequality and Poverty during the Transition from Planned to Market Economy* (Washington, D.C., World Bank, 1998), pp. 4-5.

29 United Nations Development Programme, *Human Development Report, 2001: Making New Technologies Work for Human Development* and addendum, United Nations Development Programme and addendum (New York, Oxford University Press, 2001), pp. 205 and 207.

30 *Making Transition Work for Everyone...*,p. 52; and "Monitoring in Central and Eastern Europe, the Commonwealth of .Independent States and the Baltics", (MONEE Project), *Women in Transition*, Regional Monitoring Report, 6 (Florence, Italy, United Nations Children's Fund/International Child Development Centre, 1999), p.11.

31 Marcelo Bisogno and Alberto Chong, "On the determinants of inequality in Bosnia and Herzegovina", *Economics of Transition*, vol. 10, No. 2 (2002), p. 335.

ization, or a reverse flow of urban citizens back to rural areas, which occurred in the Central Asian countries of CIS.[27]

Conflicts and poverty

The breakdown of the centrally planned system had led to the creation of almost 20 newly independent States, but this was accompanied by numerous national and ethnic conflicts, several of which escalated to fully fledged military conflicts.

Wars and political crises resulted in major dislocations. In the course of the 1990s, close to 50 million people in transition economies were directly affected by wars and disturbances. Of these, 8 million had to flee their homes and became refugees or internally displaced persons (IDPs).[28] Half of these refugees came from within the former Yugoslavia because of the wars fought there, another 1.5 million from wars in Transcaucasus and the rest from conflicts in other CIS countries. Many of these countries have witnessed the formation of an urban underclass of beggars, including migrant children, and the creation of camps of refugees from ethnic conflicts, in, for example, the successor States of the former Soviet Union and the former Yugoslavia.

By the end of the 1990s, practically all the military conflicts in transition economies had ended or had entered a low-intensity stage. However, the number of IDPs and refugees remains very high. As late as 1999, based on the United Nations estimates, the population of IDPs was 570,000 in Azerbaijan, 279,000 in Georgia and 498,000 in the Russian Federation.[29] The consequences of wars and forced migration will be felt for many years to come. For example, in Azerbaijan in 1999, 75 per cent of IDPs lived in temporary accommodations. In Georgia, one third of displaced families had no regular income several years after resettlement.[30] In Bosnia, families of former soldiers and refugees were found to have a significantly higher risk of being poor.[31]

Ethnic-specific poverty

Not all ethnic-specific poverty in transition economies is related to civil conflicts. Groups experiencing peacetime poverty of this type include Roma and ethnic Turks in Eastern European countries and migrant workers from Central Asia in the Russian Federation and other successor countries of the former Soviet Union. Roma, numbering between 7 million and 9 million, are considered the largest ethnic minority in Europe.

In Bulgaria, ethnic minorities constitute less than 20 per cent of the population, but 60 per cent of the poor. The risk of poverty among ethnic Turks is 3.5 times greater, and among Roma more than 10 times greater, than among ethnic Bulgarians (see table VIII.4). Poverty among ethnic minorities is not only wider but also deeper. The poverty gap (the percentage increase in income necessary to bring income up to the poverty line) for the poor among the Roma is 25.9 per cent compared with just 1.1 per cent for the poor among ethnic Bulgarians. The high level of poverty among Roma in Bulgaria and other Eastern European countries has led to a recent initiative spear-headed by the European Commission, the George Soros Open Society Institute and the World Bank. A high-level conference on the subject was held in Budapest in June 2003.

In the Russian Federation, the poorest ethnic minorities are refugees from other CIS countries, IDPs created by ethnic conflicts, such as the Chechen con-

Table VIII.4.
POVERTY BY ETHNICITY IN BULGARIA

Percentage			
	Share in total population	Poverty rate of ethnic group[a]	Poverty gap of ethnic group[b]
Ethnic Bulgarians	82.3	5.6	1.1
Turks	7.1	20.9	5.3
Roma	8.8	61.8	25.9
Other	1.8	7.6	1.2
Total	100.0	11.7	3.6

Source: *Bulgaria Poverty Assessment*, World Bank Report, No. 24516, (Washington, D.C., 29 October 2002).

[a] Percentage of population below the poverty line.
[b] Difference between the poverty line and the average income of the poor, expressed as a percentage of the poverty line.

flict, and illegal immigrants. International relief groups reported that, as of 2002, there were 110,000 Chechen refugees in the territory of the Russian Federation, of whom up to 20,000 were living in tent cities in the bordering republic of Ingushetia.[32]

The majority of illegal immigrants to the Russian Federation are citizens of other CIS countries. A recent estimate for this category, given by the Ministry of Internal Affairs of the Russian Federation, is 10 million.[33] Of these, a significant part came from Central Asia, in particular from Uzbekistan and Tajikistan. Illegal immigrants are one of the most deprived segments of the population, earning low incomes, living in sub-standard housing and often subjected to persecution and extortion by local businessmen and police.

[32] *Moscow Times*, 19 December 2002.

[33] Newsru.com, 24 October 2001 (http://newsru.com/russia/24Oct2001/nelegaly.html).

Household characteristics and poverty

As in most other market economies, the risk of poverty in transition economies is sensitive to age, gender, education, number of children and other household characteristics. In the central planning period, Governments in the region of the transition economies prided themselves on caring for the young and the old alike. The system of old-age pensions and child support guaranteed a low but stable income, while free public education and health care provided for these basic needs. In the course of the transition, these benefits were reduced in absolute terms in some countries. In relative terms, however, the very young lost much more than the old.

The incidence of poverty increased with the number of children in the family. In the Russian Federation, for example, based on the 1997 national poverty line, the poverty headcount was 37 per cent for families with two children, 50 per cent for families with three children and 72 per cent for families with four or more children. In Armenia, based on a 1996 survey, families twice the size of the average registered twice the rate of extreme poverty.[34] Extreme poverty and an increase in the number of dysfunctional families have led to the emergence of a sizeable population of runaway street children. In the Russian Federation, homeless children are estimated to number 1 million, a figure attesting to a situation that can be compared only with the post-civil war period of the early 1920s.

[34] *Women in Transition...*, p. 10.

The risk of poverty for older citizens of transition economies is generally lower than for the average citizen. This is particularly true for Eastern European countries. In the course of transition, the share of pensions in GDP in these countries was preserved at the pre-market reform level and, in some countries, actually increased. In most CIS countries, spending on pensions in proportion to GDP was largely maintained. In view of the sharp drop of GDP, this meant a fall in real incomes. However, compared with other groups of the population, pensioners fared relatively well. A recent World Bank study found the poverty risk for pensioners lower than for the population at large in all of the Eastern European countries with the exception of Bulgaria and Croatia. In the CIS countries, the risk of poverty for the elderly was generally higher than the average, but not by a large amount, and in two countries, Turkmenistan and Tajikistan, the risk of poverty was lower.[35] Unlike young people, most retirees in transition economies could rely on accumulated assets, such as apartments and garden plots. In many of the poor families in CIS, pensioners actually share their monetary and in-kind resources with the younger members of their families.

Lack of education is a significant predictor of poverty risk. According to a recent study, people with only elementary education have a risk of being poor that is 20-60 per cent higher compared with the national averages. In contrast, people with a higher education have a lower-than-average probability of being drawn into poverty. This relationship is stronger in the more wealthy Eastern European economies, where returns to education are higher, but it also holds for the poorest economies such as those of Central Asia.

Overall, the links between individual and household characteristics and chronic poverty are stronger in Eastern European countries than in the CIS countries. This indicates the decline in indiscriminate mass transient poverty in the former and the dominance of such poverty in the latter.

EMPLOYMENT, UNEMPLOYMENT AND POVERTY

Because of their inefficiency and disregard for the true costs of production, the pre-transition economies operated under conditions of an apparent labour shortage and claimed an official unemployment rate of zero. In the early period of market reforms, the reduction of output in the transition countries that came about as much of the inefficient, wasteful and unwanted production was eliminated, was more pronounced than the increase in recorded unemployment. The reasons for this included the inertia of the full employment paradigm, the political fear of mass unemployment, the preservation of soft budget constraints in many of the State-owned and newly privatized enterprises, labour hoarding by firms accustomed to labour shortages, and the low geographical mobility of labour.[36]

By the mid-1990s, however, the legacy of the centrally planned economy had been largely destroyed, thereby weakening the strength of many of the above factors, especially in the countries most advanced in their transition. As a result, several years into market reforms, unemployment in the transition economies rose from less than 5 per cent to 10-15 per cent or more (for selected countries, see table VIII.5). The overall losses of employment were even larger than indicated by the unemployment figures alone, as millions of people withdrew from the labour force altogether. Between 1989 and 1998, an estimated 26 million jobs were lost in the transition economies—13 per cent of the pre-transition total. However, in contrast with the experience of the developed countries, where a drop in employment is generally not accompanied by a drop

[35] *Making Transition Work for Everyone...*, pp. 82-83.

[36] See *World Economic and Social Survey, 2002* (United Nations publication, Sales No. E.02.II.C.1), box IV.2, for the adverse effects of soft budget constraints. See also Janos Kornai, *Highways and Byways...*; Olivier Blanchard, *The Economics of Post-communist transition* (Oxford, United Kingdom, Clarendon Press (1998); Mark E. Shaffer, "Do firms in transition economies have soft budget constraints? a reconsideration of concepts and evidence", *Journal of Comparative Economics*, vol. 26, pp. 80-103; and Vahaly Izyumov, "The unemployment-output trade-off in transition economies: does Okun's law apply", *Economics of Planning* (forthcoming).

Table VIII.5.
OUTPUT, UNEMPLOYMENT, AND REAL WAGES IN SELECTED TRANSITION ECONOMIES, 1991-2001

Country	1991	1992	1993	1994	1995	1996	1997	1998	1999	2000	2001
Bulgaria											
Real GDP growth	-11.7	-7.3	-1.5	1.8	2.8	-10.2	-7.0	3.5	2.4	5.8	4.1
Unemployment rate (percentage)	11.1	15.3	16.4	12.8	11.1	12.5	13.7	12.2	16.0	17.9	17.7
Real wage (1989=100)	68.0	76.7	77.6	63.7	60.2	49.6	40.1	48.1	51.7	48.9	48.7
Czech Republic											
Real GDP growth	-11.6	-0.5	0.1	2.2	6.0	4.3	-0.8	-1.2	-0.4	2.9	3.1
Unemployment rate (percentage)	4.1	2.6	3.5	3.2	2.9	3.5	5.2	7.5	9.4	8.8	8.6
Real wage (1989=100)	68.9	76.0	78.8	84.9	92.2	100.4	102.3	101.0	107.4	108.1	117.0
Poland											
Real GDP growth	-7.0	2.6	3.8	5.1	7.1	6.0	6.9	4.8	4.1	4.0	1.0
Unemployment rate (percentage)	12.2	14.3	16.4	16.0	14.9	13.2	10.3	10.4	13.1	15.1	16.2
Real wage (1989=100)	75.4	73.3	71.2	71.6	73.3	77.9	82.4	85.2	90.1	97.4	102.1
Russian Federation											
Real GDP growth	-5.0	-14.5	-8.7	-12.7	-4.1	-3.6	1.4	-5.3	6.4	10.0	5.0
Unemployment rate (percentage)	..	5.2	6.1	7.8	9.0	10.0	11.2	13.3	12.2	9.8	8.7
Real wage (1990=100)	93.9	63.1	63.4	58.4	42.1	47.7	50.0	37.0	35.8	43.3	51.8

Sources: ECE, *Economic Survey of Europe: 2003, No.1* (United Nations publication, Sales No. E.03.11.E.26); European Bank for Reconstruction and Development (EBRD), *Transition Report, 2002:. Agriculture and Rural Transition* (London, EBRD, 2002), pp. 58, 65-66, 133, 141, 185 and 193; *EBRD Transition Report Update 2001* (London, EBRD, 2001), p. 15; *Making Transition Work for Everyone: Poverty and Inequality in Europe and Central Asia* (Washington, D.C., World Bank, 2000), p. 125; and Goskomstat of Russia (available at: http://www.gks.ru/).

in the real wages of those employed, in many transition economies, real wages also fell as nominal wage increases did not keep up with rapid inflation. This was particularly true for the countries of CIS, where they had declined by 40-50 per cent by the middle of the 1990s. Not only did real wages decline, but they were often paid in considerable arrears, sometimes up to one year.

Rampant inflation and a higher level of macroeconomic instability made workers in CIS countries less capable of defending their real wages than workers in Eastern Europe. Inflation, in particular, was much more severe in the CIS countries, than in Eastern Europe. In the first years of reforms, the largest CIS countries experienced inflation of above 2,000 per cent a year. In Eastern Europe, the worst inflation experience was of the order of 100-200 per cent. Relatively rapid macroeconomic stabilization helped workers in Eastern Europe to partially or fully restore their pre-transition wage levels. Having fallen by about 25 per cent in the period 1989-1991, real wages there have since increased and on average regained 15-20 per cent. In most of the CIS countries, where macroeconomic stabilization took several more years, real wages continued to decline until the mid-1990s.[37] Wages in CIS recovered somewhat in 1995-1997, but dropped dramatically in the wake of the 1998 ruble crisis. Since 1999 they have increased, but still remain much lower than in the pre-transition period, especially if frequent arrears and non-payments are taken into account.

[37] Tito Boeri and Katherine Terrell, "Institutional determinants of labour reallocation in transition", *Journal of Economic Perspectives*, vol. 16, No. 1 (winter 2002), p. 54; and Jan Sveinar, "Transition economies: performance and challenges", *Journal of Economic Perspectives*, vol. 16, No. 1 (winter 2002), p. 18.

Weaker trade unions, the inadequacy of unemployment protection and reliance on enterprise-specific non-wage benefits, such as subsidized housing, health care and childcare, force workers in CIS countries to hold on to low-paid jobs. Low geographical mobility of labour reinforces this tendency. Owing to such obstacles as undeveloped housing markets, high costs of transportation and legal restrictions, millions of workers cannot take advantage of job opportunities in other districts and are stuck with poorly paid jobs or no jobs at all.

CIS countries suffer from another major bottleneck in their labour markets—an inadequate number of small and medium-sized enterprises (SMEs), a situation rooted mainly in the poor legal and tax environments facing such enterprises and the preservation of soft budget constraints and other privileges for larger enterprises.[38] In contrast, in Eastern Europe, where SMEs are treated favourably, these enterprises serve as a major source of new jobs and thus as an important antidote to poverty. As a result, in Eastern Europe, employment and output in SMEs have grown quickly, making this sector the main engine of economic growth. By 1998, enterprises employing 50 workers or less produced 55-65 per cent of GDP in the Czech Republic, Hungary and Lithuania, in contrast with just 10-20 per cent of GDP in Belarus, Kazakhstan, the Russian Federation and Ukraine. The share of SMEs in CIS countries was still low despite the fact that their productivity had been higher than the average in the economy. This is significant as, according to a recent World Bank study, the positive impact of SMEs on overall employment and growth can be felt only after a threshold of 40 per cent in employment and value added is reached.[39]

Unemployment benefits and the minimum wage

The different ways in which the labour market adjusted to the transition—mostly through the reduction of employment in Eastern Europe and through reductions both in employment and in real wages in CIS—resulted from the different labour policies in these two groups of countries and had significantly different implications for poverty.

In Eastern Europe, in particular in those countries more advanced in their transition, from the start, Governments maintained relatively high unemployment benefits. In the CIS countries, on the contrary, unemployment benefits were meagre. For example, in Slovakia, in 2000, unemployment benefits generally ranged between 40 and 50 per cent of the average wage. The duration and coverage of unemployment benefits were also set longer and broader in Eastern Europe compared with CIS countries. For example, benefits had been limited to 24 months in the former Yugoslav Republic of Macedonia, as against a limit of 6 months in the Russian Federation. In Romania, even new entrants to the labour force are eligible for unemployment benefits if they cannot find work.

In the Russian Federation, the minimum wage is less than 10 per cent of the average wage, while unemployment compensation, instead of being based on the average wage before redundancy, is often paid at the minimum wage level.[40] With unemployment benefits being set so low, most unemployed do not even care to register. As a result, registered unemployment in the Russian Federation is about three or four times less than survey-based unemployment. The low level of benefits is only partially explained by limited funding: in the Russian Federation, the Federal Employment Service has recorded a budget surplus for a number of years.[41]

[38]   In the first three years of reforms (1992-1994), the number of small businesses increased in the Russian Federation from 268,000 to 897,000. Yet, macroeconomic instability, unfair competition from larger companies and highly unfavourable government policies stopped the growth of the small private businesses, effectively freezing them at the level of 1 million.

[39]   *Transition: The First Ten Years...*, pp. 39-42.

[40]   Poorly protected from inflation, the minimum wage in the Russian Federation and many other CIS countries had essentially lost its primary meaning and was turned by various Government agencies into a unique accounting unit.

[41]   *Making Transition Work for Everyone ...*, p. 345; and Tito Boeri and Katherine Terrell, loc. cit., p. 72.

Unemployment status is a fairly accurate predictor of poverty in the countries most advanced in their transition. In Poland and Hungary, households headed by an unemployed person are four times more likely to be poor than those headed by an employed person. In Hungary in the mid-1990s, 60 per cent of heads of poor households were unemployed; in Bulgaria, and Poland, 30 per cent; and in Estonia, 24 per cent. However, in CIS, the link between poverty and unemployment is weak. Only 11 per cent of the poor in the Russian Federation and only 5 per cent of the poor in Belarus came from the ranks of the unemployed.[42] The main reason for this seeming anomaly is the extremely low level of wages in CIS, making the difference between the employed and the unemployed less distinguishable there than in Eastern Europe.

Minimum wage legislation in Eastern Europe is different from that in CIS. In Eastern Europe, the minimum wage is set at between 30 and 40 per cent of the average wage, while in the CIS countries, it was allowed to shrink from close to 30 per cent of the average wage in 1990 to less than 10 per cent in 1996 and to less than 7 per cent in 2002.[43]

In principle, the minimum wage should be set at a level that provides the household with an income at least sufficient for its members to reach the national poverty line. For example, in the United States, the minimum wage is set at approximately four times the national poverty line. Thus, one working member in a family of four earning the minimum wage should generate just enough income to keep the family from falling below the poverty line. Even in the countries most advanced in their transition, this condition is met only by those earning the average, rather than the minimum, wage. Thus, in Poland in the mid-1990s, the ratio of the average wage to the official poverty line was almost 3:1. In the Russian Federation and Ukraine, this ratio was just 2:1.[44]

Higher minimum wage and unemployment benefits in Eastern Europe provided a wage floor, which allowed the working population to escape poverty. The costs of this policy were a reduction in the effective demand for labour, and higher taxation. In CIS, in contrast, the absence of the effective wage floor led to real wages dropping well below the poverty line and creating millions of "working poor".

In recent years, policy makers in CIS countries have increasingly recognized that low real wages are a major obstacle to both the struggle against poverty and the broader goal of economic restructuring: low minimum wages have discouraged the shedding of redundant labour and have thereby slowed down the badly needed restructuring of obsolete enterprises. In the Russian Federation, some of the participants in the "minimum wage debate" have called for a national tri-party agreement among labour unions, business and the Government, aiming at a substantial increase in the level of wages in the economy. In exchange for such a commitment, the Government would agree to an across-the-board reduction in taxes, while trade unions would guarantee higher productivity and labour discipline.[45] In 2000-2001, the Government of Slovenia, and employees and employers of both public and private sectors, entered into a "social partnership" agreement over wages. A similar partnership is being negotiated in Croatia.[46] In all such attempts to raise the minimum wage, the disincentive effects on investment and, particularly, FDI must be carefully assessed.

[42] Branko Milanovic, op. cit., pp. 98 and 117.

[43] Tito Boeri and Katherine Terrell, loc. cit., p. 65; and Russian State Statistical Agency (available at: http://www.gks.ru).

[44] Branko Milanovic, op. cit., pp. 97-99.

[45] Interview with Dr. Viktor Ivanter, Director of the Institute of Economic Forecasting of the Russian Academy of Sciences in Moscow (available at www.echo.msk.ru).

[46] EBRD, *Transition Report, 2001: Energy in Transition* (London, EBRD, 2001), p. 195; and *Transition Report 2002: Agriculture and Rural Transition...*, p. 135.

COPING WITH POVERTY: THE GOVERNMENT'S RESPONSE

The transition from a political, social and economic system based upon centrally planning to one based upon market forces necessitates changes in all aspects of the economy, including the provision of social services and social security. Under the previous system, poverty had been claimed to be largely a non-problem, as employment, basic housing, education and health care were guaranteed and provided by the State. Not only income but also a large proportion of social services were provided by the place of employment.[47]

The recession attending the transformation subjected the old social protection system to a test for which it was totally unprepared. In addition to the shrinking of GDP in all transition economies, there was also a shrinking of the share of the government in the economy. The dual shock of recession and fiscal retreat meant that Governments had to construct an alternative system for delivering social services and for reducing poverty—but with fewer resources. Between 1989 and 2000, in Eastern Europe, the share of aggregate Government expenditures in GDP fell on average from 53 to 42 per cent, while in the CIS countries, it fell from 50 to 26 per cent. In several of the poorest CIS countries, this share fell to a much lower level, for example, to 18 per cent in Georgia.[48] Much of this decline, however, was due to cuts in Government investment expenditures.

The response to the challenge of protecting the population during the transition differed markedly across the transition economies. In the countries most advanced in their transition, Governments played a proactive role in alleviating the shock of transition. In spite of recessionary pressures, the level of social protection was left largely intact, while the system itself was reoriented towards the needs of the market economy. The level of social protection was also largely maintained in some CIS countries, such as Belarus and Uzbekistan. Here, though, little restructuring of the system took place. In the rest of the transition economies, the social protection system was downsized while being reformed on an ad hoc basis. The situation is particularly difficult in several war-torn countries, such as Georgia, where social protection almost disintegrated.

The main components of the Government social protection system are: (a) social security (including pensions and unemployment benefits); (b) targeted welfare (family allowances); (c) untargeted subsidies; and (d) and the provision of health care and education. In addition to social protection, Government can undertake proactive measures to cope with poverty, such as job training and public works.

Pensions reform

Of all social protection programmes, pension programmes have probably survived the transition best. This is particularly true for Eastern Europe, where, in some countries, the share of GDP spent on pensions has surpassed its pre-transition level; but even in the poorest transition economies, pensions have played a very important income-stabilizing role for pensioners and their families. As previously discussed, the risk of poverty for pensioners is generally less than or close to that of the population at large and significantly less than for the unemployed or for residents of rural areas.[49]

[47] For a description of the pre-reform social protection systems, see, for example, Branko Milanovic, op. cit., pp. 12-19; and *Poverty in Transition...*, pp. 90-93.

[48] *Making Transition Work for Everyone...*, p. 132; *Transition: The First Ten Years...*, pp. 81-82.

[49] Branko Milanovic, op. cit.; and *Transition: The First Ten Years...*, pp. 39-42.

On average, during the 1990s, public spending on pensions constituted 10 per cent of GDP in Eastern Europe and 5 per cent of GDP in CIS. For individual countries, this proportion ranged from 15.5 per cent in Poland (in 1997) to just 2-3 per cent in Armenia and Azerbaijan (in 1996), Georgia (in 2000), and Tajikistan and Turkmenistan (in 1996) (see table VIII.6).[50] Cross-country comparisons of pension spending have to be treated with caution. While the average retirement age is similar in most countries with transition economies (55 years for women and 60 years for men), other eligibility requirements can be different. In some professional categories, workers in transition economies are eligible to retire at 45 years of age or even earlier. Moreover, the transition

[50] *Making Transition Work for Everyone...*, pp. 292-294.

Table VIII.6.
PUBLIC EXPENDITURES ON PENSIONS, 1994-2000

Percentage				
Country	Year	Share of GDP	Year	Average pension as proportion of per capita income
Eastern Europe				
Albania	1995	5.1	..	..
Bulgaria	1996	7.3	1995	39.3
Croatia	1997	11.6	..	..
Czech Republic	1999	9.8	1996	37.0
Estonia	1995	7.0	1995	56.7
Hungary	1996	9.7	1996	33.6
Latvia	1995	10.2	1994	47.6
Lithuania	1998	7.3	1995	21.3
Poland	1997	15.5	1995	61.2
Romania	1996	5.1	1994	34.1
Slovakia	1994	9.1	1994	44.5
Slovenia	1996	13.6	1996	49.3
The former Yugoslav Republic of Macedonia	1998	8.7	1996	91.6
Commonwealth of Independent States				
Armenia	1996	3.1	1996	18.7
Azerbaijan	1996	2.5	1996	51.4
Belarus	1997	7.7	1995	31.2
Georgia	2000	2.7	1996	12.6
Kazakhstan	1997	5.0	1996	18.8
Kyrgyzstan	1997	6.4	1994	35.0
Republic of Moldova	1996	7.5	..	..
Russian Federation	1996	5.7	1995	18.3
Tajikistan	1996	3.0	..	..
Turkmenistan	1996	2.3	..	..
Ukraine	1996	8.6	1995	30.9
Uzbekistan	1995	5.3	1995	45.8

Source: *World Development Indicators, 2002*, CD-ROM (Washington, D.C., World Bank, 2002).

economies were often generous in their requirements for disability pensions and so the number of disabled persons among pre-retirement-age pensioners increased. In Poland and Croatia, 60 per cent and 90 per cent, respectively, of those in their first year on a pension are under age 60.[51]

To complement their pension incomes, many retired people in transition economies continue to work. Of the total number of pensioners, between 10 and 12 per cent continue to work in the Czech Republic, Poland and the Russian Federation, but only between 4 and 6 per cent in Bulgaria, Hungary, Slovakia and Slovenia. The average rate of employment of pensioners for European OECD member countries is less than 4 per cent.[52]

While the level of pensions is inadequate in the poorest CIS countries, it is probably unsustainable over the longer run for the richest transition economies. This is all the more true given the demographics in most transition economies. The share of the elderly in the population is increasing more rapidly than that of the employed, making the dependency ratio grow quickly. In the late 1990s, in some Eastern European countries, the number of pensioners approached that of wage earners.

In recent years, most transition economies have started reforming their pension systems. The goal is to emulate the pension systems of some of the developed and developing countries, such as Chile, that have reformed the pension schemes by gradually reducing the pay-as-you-go component of pensions while adding to existing pensions employment-based defined contribution plans and individual private plans. In addition, most of these reforms propose the extension of the retirement age and stricter eligibility requirements. In 2001-2002, the retirement age was increased in Albania from 55 to 60 years for women and from 60 to 65 years for men. Estonia has started its move towards a universal retirement age of 63 years. Extension of the retirement age is a reasonable proposal for the richer Eastern European countries. However, in some CIS countries, such as the Russian Federation and Kazakhstan, by some estimates average life expectancy for men is already below the retirement age.[53] The problems caused by an ageing population are thus fading in significance when set against those caused by high morbidity among the working-age population.

Targeted social protection

Targeted welfare programmes (direct payment to poor families with children, individual housing, utilities and other subsidies) constitute a much smaller part of the social protection system than pensions. In Eastern Europe, spending on targeted assistance ranges between 0.5 and 2 per cent of GDP, while in the CIS countries, it is generally less than 0.5 per cent of GDP (with the exception of Armenia, where this spending is 2 per cent of GDP).[54]

Owing to the rapidly changing economic situation, the large size of the informal sector and little experience in means-testing, the effective administration of such programmes is difficult. As a result, a significant part of nominally targeted subsidies goes to well-to-do rather than poor households. The waste of resources is particularly large in countries where means-testing is not used at all.

There are, however, several successful examples of targeted welfare programmes in transition economies. One economy with such programmes is Romania, where targeted assistance to families with children is linked to

[51] *Poverty in Transition ...*, p. 98; and *Transition Report, 2002...*, p. 183.

[52] Alexandre Kolev and Anne Pascal, "What keeps pensioners at work in Russia?", *Economics of Transition*, vol. 10, No. 1 (2002), p.33

[53] Michael Ellman, "The social costs and consequences of the transformation process", in *Economic Survey of Europe, 2000*, No. 2/3 (United Nations publication, Sales No. E.00.II.E.28), p. 133.

[54] *World Development Report, 2000/2001...*, p. 293.

Table VIII.7.
TARGETING OF CASH BENEFITS IN TRANSITION ECONOMIES, 1996-1997

Percentage			
Country	Year	Social assistance	Child/family allowances
Albania	1996	47	..
Armenia	1996	..	25
Croatia	1998	25	28
Estonia	1995	44	40
Hungary	1997	46	20
Kazakhstan	1996	6	24
Latvia	1998	20	29
Romania	1997	79	51
The former Yugoslav Republic of Macedonia	1997	47	5
Uzbekistan	1999	23	..

Source: World Bank, *Making Transition Work for Everyone: Poverty and Inequality in Europe and Central Asia* (Washington, D.C., 2000), p. 298.

Note: The table shows what proportions of general cash benefits assistance and child/family allowances reach the poorest 20 per cent of the population in different countries. For example, in Latvia, Croatia and Uzbekistan, the poorest 20 per cent of households are receiving only between 20 and 25 per cent of total social assistance funds, which reflects poor targeting. In Romania, the poorest 20 per cent of the population receive 79 per cent of total social assistance, which indicates more accurate targeting.

school attendance. In Romania, almost 80 per cent of social assistance funds and over 50 per cent of family allowances reach the poorest quintile of the population, much higher proportions than in other countries (see table VIII.7).

Untargeted subsidies

In transition economies, untargeted subsidies come in the form of controlled prices on public utilities, including electricity, heating, telecommunications, water supply and some other services and goods, such as public transportation and basic food staples. The degree of subsidization varies greatly across different countries. Subsidies are minimal in the countries that are most advanced in their transition, but are very high in the CIS countries, especially in the resource-rich countries, such as Azerbaijan, the Russian Federation and Turkmenistan. In Azerbaijan, for example, electricity and gas subsidies amounted in 1999 to 6.2 per cent of GDP; in the Russian Federation, to 5 per cent of GDP.[55]

All transition economies inherited from the central planning period an extensive utilities infrastructure, providing practically all households with electricity and 50-90 per cent with running water, centralized gas, heating and sewerage systems. Prior to reforms, prices of energy in transition economies were held low, based on plentiful energy supplies from the former Soviet Union. With the break-up of the Council for Mutual Economic Assistance, subsidized energy flows to Eastern Europe ceased, thereby forcing these countries to pay prices at international market levels. At the same time, in most CIS countries, Governments tried to maintain low prices for utilities, claiming this policy to be a form of social protection. The subsidies are financed explicitly by government budget allocations or implicitly by the accumulation of arrears by energy suppliers, as a result of allowing non-payment by customers, and by forgiving the taxes due from energy-using enterprises. In the Russian Federation, subsidies from local governments to large energy using enterprises, ostensibly to maintain employment, amounted, in the mid-1990s, to 4 per

[55] Ibid., p. 135; and OECD, *Economic Survey: Russian Federation* (Paris, OECD, 2002), p. 20.

cent of GDP. Cross-subsidization is widespread. For example, in the Russian Federation, electricity tariffs for industrial users are approximately double those for households.[56]

Energy subsidies are extremely costly to the transition economies, in terms both of their fiscal impact and of the losses of macroeconomic efficiency. Moreover, the role of these subsidies in helping the poor is highly questionable. Even with prices based upon the true costs of production, expenditures on electricity and heat in most transition economies would constitute a fairly small proportion of the family budget—usually under 5 per cent.[57] In view of the fact that the poor are receiving only a fraction of the resources used to maintain energy subsidies, it can be seen that other, more selective programmes of social assistance are needed.

Among the alternative methods currently used in transition economies to help the poor pay for their utilities are: (a) lifeline tariffs, where an initial block of energy is supplied free or at a low price; (b) targeted energy subsidies; and (c) general income support. The efficiency of these programmes varies, as it depends upon accurate measurement of income and energy use; but in many transition economies, this measurement is highly imprecise. However, it is clear that the existing system of wasteful across-the-board subsidization prevalent in the CIS countries needs to be reformed.

Public spending on education and health

The role of good education and health in overcoming poverty is hard to overestimate. Universal education and health-care systems were the pride of the centrally planned countries. However, by the time that the centrally planned system had collapsed, the health and education systems were already failing, as shown by the lower life expectancy in those countries compared with the developed countries.

In the course of market reforms, even as GDP fell, most transition economies strove to maintain the level of public spending on education and health care measured as a proportion of their GDP. In some countries, such as Belarus, Latvia, Lithuania and the Republic of Moldova, the share even increased. However, in countries of Caucasus and Central Asia, the share fell (see table VIII.8). However, the transformational recession produced heavy declines in the amounts spent.[58]

In addition to lower spending on health and education, transition economies suffered from problems of low efficiency and a waste of resources. In education, those problems included overstaffing, low capacity utilization, a shift of resources in favour of tertiary education, falling quality of education and growing corruption.

The decline in spending and efficiency has already influenced the quality outcomes and disproportionately affected the poor. Enrolment rates in compulsory basic education and, in particular, in secondary education fell in the 1990s in many CIS countries. In Kazakhstan in 1998, 19 per cent of children aged 6-12 years were not attending school.[59] Between 1989 and 1997, enrolment in general secondary education fell by 15 per cent in Armenia, by 40 per cent in Georgia and by 45 per cent in Tajikistan.

Inequality in access to education has increased. In Armenia and Kazakhstan, the lowest income quintile of the population received less than 10 per cent of

[56] *Transition Report, 2001...*, p. 98.

[57] Ibid., p. 99.

[58] *Women in Transition...*, p. 16.

[59] *Poverty in Transition...*, p. 72; and *Making Transition Work for Everyone...*, p. 230.

Table VIII.8.

PUBLIC EXPENDITURES ON EDUCATION AND HEALTH AS A PROPORTION OF GDP, 1990, 1998 AND 2000

Percentage

Country	Share in GDP of public expenditure on education		Share in GDP of public expenditure on health	
	1990	1998	1990	2000
Eastern Europe				
Albania	5.9	..	3.4	2.1
Bulgaria	5.2	3.4	4.1	3.0
Croatia	7.2	4.2	9.5	8.0
Czech Republic	..	4.2	4.8	6.6
Estonia	..	6.8	1.9	4.7
Hungary	5.8	4.6	6.0	5.2
Latvia	3.8	6.8	2.7	3.5
Lithuania	4.6	6.4	3.0	4.3
Poland	4.6	5.4	4.8	4.2
Romania	2.8	3.5	2.8	1.9
Slovakia	5.1	..	5.0	5.3
Slovenia	4.8	..	..	6.8
The former Yugoslav Republic of Macedonia	..	4.1	9.2	5.1
Commonwealth of Independent States				
Armenia	7.0	..	..	3.2
Azerbaijan	..	3.4	2.7	0.7
Belarus	4.8	..	2.5	4.7
Georgia	..	5.2	3.0	0.8
Kazakhstan	3.2	4.4	3.2	2.7
Krygyzstan	8.4	5.4	4.7	2.2
Republic of Moldova	5.6	10.2	4.4	2.9
Russian Federation	3.0	3.5	2.5	3.8
Tajikistan	10.0	2.1	4.9	1.0
Turkmenistan	4.3	..	4.0	4.6
Ukraine	5.2	4.5	3.0	2.9
Uzbekistan	9.5	7.7	4.6	2.6

Sources: World Bank, *World Development Indicators*, CD-ROM (Washington, D.C., 2002); and United Nations Development Programme, *Human Development Report, 2001: Making New Technologies Work for Human Development* and addendum (Oxford University Press, New York, 2001), pp. 195-197.

public spending on education, while the top quintiles received 29 per cent and 26 per cent, respectively.[60] In Bulgaria, in 2001, the gap in the enrolment rates between children coming from the poorest and children coming from the richest quintiles of the population was 23 per cent for urban and 45 per cent for rural areas. In the Russian Federation, school enrolment of children aged 17-19 years from low-income families is one third below that of children from the high-income group, while university and college enrolment is one half. In the course of the 1990s, in Moscow State University, the largest university in the Russian Federation, the proportion of non-Moscow-based students dropped from 80 per cent of the total to 20 per cent.[61]

[60] *World Development Report, 2000/2001*, p. 80.

[61] *Bulgaria Poverty Assignment*, World Bank Report, No. 24516 (Washington, D.C., World Bank, 29 October 2002), p. 110; Milanovic, *Income, Inequality and Poverty during the Transition from Planned to Market Economy...*, pp. 12-19; *Poverty in Transition...*, p. 75; and *Making Transition Work for Everyone...*, p. 232.

62 For a fuller discussion of the poverty trap, see *World Economic and Social Survey, 2000* (United Nations publication, Sales No. E.00.II.C.1), chap. VI, entitled "Education as a prerequisite of sustained growth".

63 Peter S. Keller and Christian Heller, *Social Sector Reform in Transition Countries*, IMF Working Paper, No. 01/35 (Washington, D.C., IMF, 2001), pp. 21-22; *Poverty in Transition...*, pp. 86-87; and *Transition: The First Ten Years...*, p. 85.

64 For children of age group 6-7 to 14-15, based on UNICEF data and methodology. See: Michael Ellman, loc. cit., p. 130.

65 *World Development Report, 2000/2001...*, p. 80.

66 *Transition: The First Ten Years...*, p. 86; *World Development Report, 2000/2001...*, p. 81; and *Making Transition Work for Everyone...*, p. 259.

67 Peter Keller and Christian Heller, op. cit., pp. 21-23; *Poverty in Transition...*, pp. 57-63 and 87; and *Transition: The First Ten Years...*, p. 85.

Falling enrolments and rising inequality in access to education have long-term consequences: they undermine income-earning opportunities for children of poorer families and thus create a "poverty trap".[62] Proposals for the reforms of education call for increased emphasis on the provision of universal basic education (in particular in the poorer countries of CIS); the reallocation of public funding away from tertiary to primary and secondary education; the reduction of the personnel employed in the public education system; and the consolidation of school infrastructure.[63]

One of the few successful examples of a programme curbing the decline of human capital in the transition economies is the above-mentioned system of targeted family allowances for poor families in Romania which is tied to the school attendance of their children (similar to programmes used in the United States and some other countries). Introduced in 1993, this programme helped to increase school enrolment in Romania from 89.6 per cent in 1992 to 95 per cent in 1997.[64] Largely because of this programme, Romania also achieved the most equitable distribution of public spending on education: the lowest income quintile of the population received 24 per cent of public spending, while the top quintile received 15 per cent.[65]

The decline of the public health-care system also disproportionately affected the poorer transition economies and the poorer segments of the population within them. In Central Asia and Caucasus, health-care expenditures fell in both relative and absolute terms. In Georgia, the fall was from 3 per cent of GDP in 1990 to 0.8 per cent in 2000 (see table VIII.8). Moreover, a lack of structural reforms through which to adjust to the new market environment meant a loss of efficiency and accessibility to health care, in particular for the poor. The main problems of health care include overstaffing, an excess number of hospital beds, longer-than-necessary hospital stays and widespread informal payments from patients for medical services.

A growing problem is inequality in health-care access. In Bulgaria, the lowest income quintile of the population received 13 per cent of public spending on health care, while the top income quintile received 25 per cent. In the Russian Federation, in 1997, 11 per cent of patients could not afford medical treatment and 41 per cent of patients could not afford necessary drugs. In Kazakhstan, the coverage of immunization of children in the top income quintile is over 80 per cent, but for the bottom quintile just 40 per cent.[66]

The disarray in the health-care system contributed to the decline in health indicators. In the poorest regions of CIS countries and in the Balkans, malnutrition, anaemia and iodine deficiency are widespread among children and women. At the same time, tuberculosis, human immunodeficiency virus/acquired immunodeficiency syndrome (HIV/AIDS) and other infectious diseases are assuming epidemic proportions.

The health-care crisis is creating another dangerous poverty trap, as poor health is one of the main obstacles to productive economic activity. Measures proposed to overcome the crisis include: concentrating resources on preventive (rather than curative) primary care; putting the focus on children; consolidating facilities, thereby reducing the number of hospital beds; and rationalizing private payments.[67]

COPING WITH POVERTY: THE PRIVATE RESPONSE

As a result of the inadequacy of Government-provided poverty abatement pro-grammes in most of the transition economies, poor families and individuals have borne the brunt of the struggle with poverty. At the start of the transition, people in transition economies were not very well positioned to handle this task, as their knowledge of the rules of the market economy was minimal. Moreover, as mentioned previously, the savings of many people had been wiped out by the hyperinflation of the early 1990s.

Various coping strategies have come into play: the growth of self-employ-ment and of the informal economy; the cultivation of family plots to satisfy food needs; intra-family transfers; internal migration; and emigration to other countries. Each of these strategies has its benefits, and some proved to be more efficient than government transfers in alleviating poverty. For example, it is established that intra-family transfers to the poor are better targeted than simi-lar Government subsidies and thus, for a given transfer of resources, larger gains in welfare are generated.[68] At the same time, many of the private coping strategies lead to socially and economically questionable outcomes such as de-urbanization (migration of urban-dwellers back to farming areas), the growth of the informal economy and the spread of crime.

Self-employment and the growth of the informal economy

Faced with unemployment and/or falling wages, millions of people in the tran-sition economies turned to self-employment. Many of them formed unregis-tered one-person businesses in activities such as the resale of consumer goods, "shuttle trade" and in-home-based businesses, such as sewing, repairing, cleaning, providing day care and tutoring.[69]

Between 1990 and 1995, the share of GDP produced in the unofficial sector is estimated to have grown from 25 to 36 per cent in Bulgaria; from 12 to 35 per cent in Latvia; from 14 to 19 per cent in Romania; from 22 to 61 per cent in Azerbaijan; from 15 to 42 per cent in the Russian Federation; and from 16 to 49 per cent in Ukraine (see table VIII.9). However, the sector's growth was not universal. In the Czech Republic, Estonia, Hungary and Poland, as well as in the CIS countries of Belarus and Uzbekistan, the informal sector's share in the economy decreased or barely increased.[70]

The different growth patterns of the informal economy underscore differ-ences in the openness and dynamism of labour markets in transition economies. While in those countries that had been more advanced in their transition, the official economy provided increasing opportunities for employment and entre-preneurship, in other transition economies, the lack of these opportunities forced millions of people into the unofficial sector. For example, in the Russian Federation, over 12 million people are self-employed, most in one-person oper-ations. At the same time, the number of officially registered small businesses in the Russian Federation is less than 1 million, compared with 4 million in Poland and over 15 million in the United States. In fact, the total number of small private businesses in the Russian Federation is less than the number of new businesses opening up in the United States every year.

[68] *Bulgaria Poverty Assessment...*, p. 100; and Stanislav Kolesnikov and Ksenia Yudaeva, "Inequality and poverty in post-crisis Russia", *Economic Trends*, vol. 8, issue 3 (August 1999), p. 14.

[69] Shuttle trade is a term generally applied to describe the massive unregulated and unregis-tered commerce conducted by hundreds of thou-sands of individuals in transition economies. It involves buying goods abroad and selling them in the Russian Federation in street markets. In the Russian Federation in the mid-1990s, the turnover of the unregistered shuttle trade had reached an estimated $10 billion, comparable with the total annual revenue from Russian oil exports.

[70] Estimates of the size of the informal economy can, by definition, be only approximate. Every such estimate strongly depends upon the assumptions and methodology used. For a discussion see, for example: Simon Johnson, Daniel Kaufman and Andrei Shleifer, "The unofficial economy in transi-tion", *Brookings Papers on Economic Activity*, vol. 2 (1997), pp. 159-221; and Maria Lacko, "Hidden economy—an unknown quantity?", *Economics of Transition*, vol. 8, No. 1 (2000), pp. 117-149.

Table VIII.9.
ESTIMATES OF THE SHARE OF GDP PRODUCED IN THE UNOFFICIAL
ECONOMY IN SELECTED TRANSITION COUNTRIES, 1990 AND 1995

Percentage		
Country	1990	1995
Eastern Europe		
Bulgaria	25.1	36.2
Czech Republic	6.7	11.3
Estonia	19.9	11.8
Hungary	28.0	29.0
Latvia	12.8	35.3
Lithuania	11.3	21.6
Poland	19.6	12.6
Romania	13.7	19.1
Slovakia	7.7	5.8
Commonwealth of Independent States		
Azerbaijan	21.9	60.6
Belarus	15.4	19.3
Georgia	24.9	62.6
Kazakhstan	17.0	34.3
Republic of Moldova	18.1	35.7
Russian Federation	14.7	41.6
Ukraine	16.3	48.9
Uzbekistan	11.4	6.5

Source: Simon Johnson, Daniel Kaufman and Andrei Shleifer, "The unofficial economy in transition", *Brookings Papers on Economic Activity*, vol. 2 (1997), p. 183.

In addition to self-employment opportunities, the informal economy provides the bulk of second jobs for hire. For example, in the Russian Federation about 70 per cent of such jobs are estimated to be in the informal economy.[71]

[71] Byung-Yeon Kim, "The participation of Russian households in the informal economy", *Economics of Transition*, vol. 10, No. 3 (2002), p. 703.

Cultivation of family plots and de-urbanization

Widespread ownership of small family plots was one of the features of the centrally planned economies. Rooted in part in ideology (the Marxist dream of abolishing the distinction between the city and the village in the communist society of the future) and in part in practicality, this feature proved to be highly important in helping people to survive the transition back to capitalism. By some estimates, over two thirds of urban residents and practically all rural residents of the successor countries of the former Soviet Union own such family plots. The proportion is probably somewhat lower in Central and Eastern Europe but similar in the Balkans. In the Russian Federation, for a population of approximately 145 million people, the number of such plots in the mid-1990s was estimated at 55 million.[72] The role of family plots as poverty alleviation tools is hard to overestimate. Production from these plots generates 22 per cent of all food consumption in Bulgaria and 20-24 per cent in the Russian Federation.[73]

[72] Harm Tho Seeth and others, "Russian poverty: muddling through economic transition with garden plots", *World Development*, vol. 26, No. 9 (1998), p. 1612.

[73] *Bulgaria Poverty Assessment...*, p. 100; and Simon Clarke, loc. cit., p. 15.

In some countries, escape to rural labour became a longer-term solution to poverty, leading to resettlement of urban-dwellers in villages. This trend is most visible in the Central Asian republics of Uzbekistan and Tajikistan, in the

Russian Federation, in Ukraine and in the Balkans. In the first five years of reform, employment in agriculture actually increased in the Russian Federation and Ukraine, as well as in Romania and Bulgaria. Agriculture thus played a buffer role, softening the blow of the transformational recession for the poorest segment of the population.[74]

Migration and emigration

In spite of the relative immobility of labour markets, millions of people in transition economies tried to escape the threat of poverty by moving to other localities or other countries. Migration of people in response to economic and political disturbances was particularly heavy in CIS. During the 1990s, the Russian Federation alone admitted almost 11 million immigrants, almost all of them from CIS.[75] At the same time, in the period 1992-2002, close to 5.4 million Russian citizens emigrated to other countries. The actual number of emigrants and immigrants was probably much larger, as Government agencies have difficulty tracking illegal labour migration.

Illegal migration is widespread in other countries of CIS, as evidenced, for example, by the migration of Belarusians and Ukrainians seeking work in the Russian Federation and Poland, and the migration of Moldovans to Romania and countries of Western Europe as well as other countries. Migration from the countries of Eastern Europe has been less heavy, but still substantial. During the 1990s, between 50,000 and 90,000 people emigrated annually from Bulgaria, and between 10,000 and 20,000 from Poland (on a net migration basis). Characteristically, in this period, two of the richest transition countries, the Czech Republic and Hungary, registered positive net immigration.[76]

The role of intra-family transfers

Intra-family transfers, including remittances from emigrants, have been particularly important in the CIS countries, where government social protection systems proved to be especially weak. Thus in the Russian Federation, based on household surveys, intra-family transfers were received in 1997 by 25.2 per cent of all households and by 31.5 per cent of the poorest quintile of households; in Kazakhstan, similar ratios were 27.5 per cent and 33.8 per cent, respectively; and in Kyrgyzstan 35.5 per cent and 31.7 per cent.[77] In the Russian Federation, intra-family transfers constituted 4.7 per cent of overall household money income in 1993, 7.1 per cent in 1996 and 12 per cent in 1998. These transfers constituted 20 per cent of the income of net recipients of such transfers and from one third to one half of the income of the poorest quartile of all recipients.[78] Characteristically, while in the Russian Federation, in the course of the transition to the market, the role of intra-family transfers increased, in Poland, which had resumed economic growth much earlier, that role decreased.[79] In Bulgaria in 2001, 14 per cent of families received private transfers which amounted to 34 per cent of their average household consumption.

Intra-family transfers are generally better targeted than government assistance. A recent study found that in the Russian Federation, intra-family transfers reduced the overall poverty count per capita by 4 per cent compared with the 1.5 per cent reduction achieved by government transfers.[80] In Bulgaria,

[74] Liesbeth Dries and Johan F. M. Swinnen, "Institutional reform and labour reallocation during transition: theory evidence from Polish agriculture", *World Development*, vol. 30, No. 3 (2002), p. 458.

[75] *Russian Statistical Annual* (Moscow, Goskomstat, 1991), p. 128; and http://www.gks.ru.

[76] *Bulgaria Poverty Assessment...*, p. 102.

[77] *World Development Report, 2000/2001...*, p. 144

[78] Simon Clarke, loc. cit., p. 30.

[79] Jeni Klugman and Jenine Braithwaite, loc. cit., p. 54.

[80] Stanislav Kolesnikov and Ksenia Yudaeva, loc. cit., p. 14.

81 *Bulgaria Poverty Assessment...*, p. 100.

such transfers reduced the poverty rate among receiving households by 16 percentage points and the overall poverty rate in Bulgaria by 2 percentage points.[81]

CONCLUSIONS

Contrary to most expectations, the transition to the market proved to be longer and much more costly in social terms than had been envisaged in many countries at the outset. The transformational recession of the 1990s and a sharp decline in income for many households resulted in massive poverty and deprivation in the region. By the mid-1990s, almost 30 per cent of the 414 million people in the transition economies lived below the $4 a day poverty line in PPP terms.

The increase of poverty was contained in the Eastern European countries that moved most rapidly to a market economy. In these countries, the recession was shorter, income differentiation was not as drastic, and Governments made a concerted effort to provide social protection to the most vulnerable groups among the population, such as pensioners, the unemployed, single mothers and children. In most of the CIS countries, the situation was much more serious and in some countries, such as Armenia, Georgia, the Republic of Moldova and Tajikistan, the overwhelming majority of the population was poor.

While Governments of those Eastern European countries that were most advanced in their transition to a market economy generally achieved an adequate response to the challenge of mass poverty, the policy response of Governments of the CIS countries and other countries of Eastern Europe (such as those in the Balkans) was at best inadequate. To some degree, this government failure was predetermined by the lower level of development, the obsolete structure of the economy and other objective factors. However, policy choices also played an important role. In many of the CIS countries, particularly the resource-rich countries, special interests succeeded in channeling a large part of the already shrinking government funds away from social spending.

Faced with the inability of Governments to protect them from suffering, millions of people in transition economies resorted to private strategies of fighting off poverty. Those included unregistered employment and self-employment, migration to other countries and regions and, in extreme cases, engaging in crime. Thus, while in Eastern Europe, the struggle with poverty was dominated by government action, in CIS, it was dominated by the private response.

More than 10 years after the start of market reforms, all transition economies have returned to the path of economic growth, which has curbed further increases in poverty. However, many challenges remain.

One of these challenges is the emergence of chronic long-term poverty. This form of poverty exists in both the relatively well-to-do and the poorer transition countries and brings with it the risk of the development of a permanent new underclass. Chronic poverty is concentrated in depressed industries, and among specific regions and demographic and ethnic groups, as well as among rural families with many children. For the richer countries of Eastern Europe, the emergence of chronic poverty, some of it acute, is probably the single most important poverty challenge facing Governments and societies.

The use of targeted social protection, relying on successful experiences within developed countries and some early examples of such experiences in transition economies might prove to be beneficial to transition economies in their efforts to combat chronic poverty. Measures would include the development of regional poverty maps, investment in transportation facilities to help depressed regions access new markets and overcome labour-market restrictions and ethnic-specific social programmes. In some cases, more drastic actions may be in order, such as resettling the population of localities, like some of the northern territories and closed military cities in the Russian Federation, where no prospects of sustainable employment exist.

The broad challenge in the labour-market area is to provide people in transition economies with increasing opportunities for gainful and legitimate employment. Here, the policy tasks are different for Eastern Europe and CIS countries. In the former, where labour markets are relatively flexible, this task can be described as one of fine-tuning existing legislation, for example, through the introduction of stricter eligibility requirements for unemployment benefits. In CIS countries, on the contrary, the meagre unemployment benefits and minimum wages have to be increased and tied to a subsistence minimum. Labour markets in CIS would benefit from the removal of administrative and fiscal restrictions on SMEs and the curtailment of implicit subsidies to inefficient large enterprises. Government unemployment agencies might be encouraged to provide more proactive employment services such as job matching and job retraining.

The second generation of reforms in transition economies should include measures aimed at coordinating Government and private responses to poverty. These would include, for example, extending social security to the informal sector and the adoption of migration legislation that would deal with the problem of massive illegal migration.

In the area of social protection, the Governments in Eastern Europe face the task of adjusting existing levels of benefits, such as those of pensions, to the fiscal capacity of the State. This would mean, for example, a switch to multi-pillar pension systems and possible curtailment of unsustainable social security expenditures in countries like Poland and Slovenia, where they constitute a larger share of GDP than in the developed countries. In the CIS countries, the goal is to reduce or eliminate the wasteful across-the board energy subsidies, to lift the share of social security payments in GDP, and to bring the level of individual basic social protection closer to the subsistence minimum.

Some of the Governments of transition economies might find it beneficial to increase the share in GDP of public spending on education and health. A reasonable share is essential for the preservation of human capital, which is the key determinant of the income-generating prospects of the population.[82] The decline in the education and health levels of the population, which is particularly noticeable in the largest CIS countries (Kazakhstan, the Russian Federation and Ukraine,) should be arrested and reversed. Otherwise, poor health and low education will keep millions of young people in these countries in a vicious poverty trap.

The outlook for the eradication of mass poverty is quite encouraging for many of the Eastern European countries. Eight of these countries will join the EU in May 2004 and two others (Bulgaria and Romania) are scheduled to follow in 2007. By the end of the decade, the problem of poverty in these countries will be considerably reduced, with their own efforts being supported by EU.

82 *Poverty in Transition ...*, pp. 36-37.

The prospects for reducing poverty in CIS are much less clear. In the smaller and poorer countries of Central Asia and Caucasus, acute mass poverty will probably subside as their economies continue to recover. However, without the reversal of the extreme inequality of incomes and active policies of job creation, progress in poverty reduction will be slow. The role of international strategies, such as the multilateral "CIS-7" Initiative, can be very important in achieving poverty containment here.

In the largest of the CIS countries—the Russian Federation and Ukraine— much will depend upon the direction of the second stage of reform. To realize their growth potential, the Governments of these countries might consider liberalizing labour and capital markets, encouraging the growth of the SME sector, and eliminating wasteful subsidies to large enterprises. The achievement of these measures, in turn, will depend upon reducing the power of special interests and upon the maintenance of overall political stability.

The promise of a better life and the manifest failings of the centrally planned system led peoples of Eastern Europe and the Soviet Union away from that system, despite all of its security and social guarantees. Now, over 10 years into the transition to the market system, this promise is being fulfilled, but not for all. While some countries of the region are getting ready to join— or rejoin—the developed world, in others a third or more of the population live in poverty. At the present time, the worst is probably over but much remains to be done. Given the right tools and with appropriate government support and policies, millions of well-educated, hard-working people in the transition economies would be fully capable of pulling themselves out of their misery.

ANNEX STATISTICAL TABLES

ANNEX

STATISTICAL TABLES

The present annex contains the main sets of data on which the analysis provided in the *World Economic and Social Survey, 2003* is based. The data and the information are those available as of 15 May 2003.

The annex was prepared by the Economic Monitoring and Assessment Unit of the Department of Economic and Social Affairs of the United Nations Secretariat. It is based on information obtained from the United Nations Statistics Division and the Population Division of the Department of Economic and Social Affairs of the United Nations Secretariat, as well as from the United Nations regional commissions, the International Monetary Fund (IMF), the World Bank, the Organisation for Economic Cooperation and Development (OECD), the United Nations Conference on Trade and Development (UNCTAD) and national and private sources. Estimates for the most recent years were made by the Economic Monitoring and Assessment Unit in consultation with the regional commissions and participants in Project LINK (see directly below). Data presented in this *Survey* may differ, however, from those published by these other organizations and sources for a variety of reasons, including differences in timing, sample composition, and aggregation methods (see section on "Data quality" below for additional reason for data discrepancies). Historical data may differ from those in previous editions of the *Survey* because of updating and changes in the availability of data for individual countries.

Forecasts are based on the results of the April 2003 forecasting exercise of Project LINK, an international collaborative research group for econometric modelling, which is coordinated jointly by the Economic Monitoring and Assessment Unit and the University of Toronto. LINK itself is a global model that links the trade and financial variables of 79 country and regional economic models, which are managed by over 60 national institutions and by the Unit.[a] The primary linkages are merchandise trade and prices, as well as the interest and currency exchange rates of major countries. The LINK system uses an iterative process to generate a consistent forecast for the world economy in which international trade flows and prices, among other variables, are determined endogenously and simultaneously. The one exception is the international price of crude oil. The average price of the basket of seven crude oils of the Organization of the Petroleum Exporting Countries (OPEC) is estimated to increase by 12 per cent in 2003 and to decline by some 10 per cent in 2004.

[a] Additional information on Project LINK is available at: http://www.un.org/analysis/link/ index.htm.

COUNTRY CLASSIFICATION

For analytical purposes, the *World Economic and Social Survey* classifies countries into one of three categories: developed economies, economies in transition and developing countries. The composition of these groupings is specified in the tables presented below. The groupings are intended to reflect basic economic conditions in countries. Several countries (in particular the economies in transition) have characteristics that could place them in more than one category but, for the purposes of analysis, the groupings are mutually exclusive.

The **developed economies** (see table A) on average have the highest material standards of living. Their production is heavily and increasingly oriented towards the provision of a wide range of services; agriculture is typically a very small share of output and the share of manufacturing is generally declining. On average, workers in developed countries are the world's most productive, frequently using the most advanced production techniques and equipment. The developed economies are often centres for research in science and technology. Governments of developed countries are likely to offer development assistance to other countries and they themselves do not generally seek such assistance.

The **economies in transition** are characterized by the transformation that they began at the end of the 1980s, when they turned away from centralized resource allocation as the main organizing principle of their societies towards the establishment or re-establishment of market economies. Some of these

Table A.
DEVELOPED ECONOMIES[a]

Europe		Other countries	Major industrialized economies
European Union	Other Europe		
Euro zone			
Austria	Iceland	Australia	Canada
Belgium	Malta	Canada	France
Finland	Norway	Japan	Germany
France	Switzerland	New Zealand	Italy
Germany		United States of	Japan
Greece		America	United Kingdom of Great Britain
Ireland			and Northern Ireland
Italy			United States of America
Luxembourg			
Netherlands			
Portugal			
Spain			
Other EU			
Denmark			
Sweden			
United Kingdom of			
Great Britain and			
Northern Ireland			

[a] Countries systematically monitored by the Economic Monitoring and Assessment Unit of the United Nations Secretariat.

Table B.
ECONOMIES IN TRANSITION[a]

Baltic States	Central and Eastern Europe	Commonwealth of Independent States

Estonia
Latvia
Lithuania
	Central Europe
	Czech Republic
	Hungary
	Poland
	Slovakia
	Slovenia
	
	South-Eastern Europe
	Albania
	Bulgaria
	Croatia
	Romania
	Former Yugoslav Republic
	  of Macedonia
	Former Federal Republic
	  of Yugoslavia
		Armenia
		Azerbaijan
		Belarus
		Georgia
		Kazakhstan
		Kyrgyzstan
		Republic of Moldova
		Russian Federation
		Tajikistan
		Turkmenistan
		Ukraine
		Uzbekistan

[a] Economies systematically monitored by the Economic Monitoring and Assessment Unit of the United Nations Secretariat.

economies began this transformation with many of the characteristics of developed economies, while others had several characteristics of developing economies. However, for the purposes of the analysis in the *Survey,* their most distinguishing characteristic is the transition undergone by their economic structures.

The rest of the world is grouped together as the **developing economies**. This is a heterogeneous grouping, although one with certain common characteristics. Average material standards of living in developing countries are lower than in developed countries and many of these countries are characterized by deep and extensive poverty. Developing countries are usually importers rather than developers of innovations in science and technology and their application in new products and production processes. They also tend to be relatively more vulnerable to economic shocks.

Estimates of the growth of output in developing countries are based on the data of 95 economies, accounting for 97-98 per cent of the gross domestic product (GDP) and population of all developing countries and territories in 1995. The countries in the sample account for more than 95 per cent of the GDP and population of each of the geographical regions into which the developing countries are divided, with the exception of sub-Saharan Africa for which the countries included in the sample account for at least 90 per cent of GDP and population.

The *Survey* uses the following designations of geographical regions for developing countries: Africa; Latin America and the Caribbean; Western Asia; China; and Eastern and Southern Asia (including the Pacific islands).[b] Country classification by geographical region is specified in table C below.

The *Survey* also uses a geographical subgrouping entitled "Sub-Saharan Africa", which contains African countries south of the Sahara Desert, excluding Nigeria and South Africa. The intent in using this grouping is to give a picture

[b] Names and composition of geographical areas follow those of "Standard country or area codes for statistical use" (ST/ESA/STAT/SER.M/49/Rev.3), with the exception of Western Asia, in which the *Survey* includes the Islamic Republic of Iran (owing to the large role of the petroleum sector in its economy).

of the situation in the large number of smaller sub-Saharan economies by avoiding any distortion that may be introduced by including the two countries that dominate the region in terms of GDP, population and international trade.

For analytical purposes, developing countries are classified as **fuel exporters** or **fuel importers** inasmuch as the ability to export fuel or the need to import fuel has a large effect on a country's capacity to import other goods and services—and therefore on the growth of output, as growth in developing countries is often constrained by the availability of foreign exchange. Fuels, rather than energy sources more broadly, are considered because fuel prices are more directly linked to oil prices, and oil prices are particularly volatile and often have a considerable impact on countries' incomes and capacity to import.

A country is defined as a **fuel exporter** if, simultaneously: (a) its domestic production of primary commercial fuel (including oil, natural gas, coal and lignite, but excluding hydro- and nuclear electricity) exceeds domestic consumption by at least 20 per cent; (b) the value of its fuel exports amounts to at least 20 per cent of its total exports; and (c) it is not classified as a least developed country.

The **least developed countries** are a subgroup of the fuel-importing developing countries. The list of least developed countries is decided by the General Assembly, on the basis of recommendations by the Economic and Social Council emanating from proposals by the Committee for Development Policy. The Committee proposes criteria for identifying the least developed countries and assesses the eligibility of individual countries. The basic criteria for inclusion require being below specified thresholds with regard to per capita GDP, an economic vulnerability index and an augmented physical quality of life index.[c] As of May 2003, the following 49 countries were classified as least developed countries:

Afghanistan, Angola, Bangladesh, Benin, Bhutan, Burkina Faso, Burundi, Cambodia, Cape Verde, Central African Republic, Chad, Comoros, Democratic Republic of the Congo, Djibouti, Equatorial Guinea, Eritrea, Ethiopia, Gambia, Guinea, Guinea-Bissau, Haiti, Kiribati, Lao People's Democratic Republic, Lesotho, Liberia, Madagascar, Malawi, Maldives, Mali, Mauritania, Mozambique, Myanmar, Nepal, Niger, Rwanda, Samoa, Sao Tome and Principe, Senegal, Sierra Leone, Solomon Islands, Somalia, Sudan, Togo, Tuvalu, Uganda, United Republic of Tanzania, Vanuatu, Yemen, Zambia.

A classification of **net-creditor** and **net-debtor** countries is used in some tables. This is based on the net foreign asset position of each country at the end of 1995, as assessed by IMF in its *World Economic Outlook,* October 1996.[d] The **net-creditor** countries are indicated by footnote indicator [b] in table C.

The **heavily indebted poor countries** (HIPCs), are those considered by the World Bank and IMF for their debt-relief initiative (the enhanced HIPC Initiative). As of April 2003, the heavily indebted poor countries were: Angola, Benin, Bolivia, Burkina Faso, Burundi, Cameroon, Central African Republic, Chad, Comoros, Congo, Côte d'Ivoire, Democratic Republic of the Congo (formerly Zaire), Ethiopia, Gambia, Ghana, Guinea, Guinea-Bissau, Guyana, Honduras, Kenya, Lao People's Democratic Republic, Liberia, Madagascar, Malawi, Mali, Mauritania, Mozambique, Myanmar, Nicaragua, Niger, Rwanda, Sao Tome and Principe, Senegal, Sierra Leone, Somalia, Sudan, Togo, Uganda, United Republic of Tanzania, Viet Nam, Zambia.[e]

[c]   See report of the Committee for Development Policy on its second session (3-7 April 2000) *(Official Records of the Economic and Social Council, 2000, Supplement No. 13* (E/2000/33)), chap. IV.

[d]   Washington, D.C., IMF, 1996.

[e]   See IMF, "Debt relief under the Heavily Indebted Poor Countries (HIPC) Initiative: a factsheet", April 2003 (http: //www.imf.org/external/np/exr/facts/hipc.htm).

Table C.
DEVELOPING ECONOMIES BY REGION[a]

	Latin America and the Caribbean	Africa	Asia and the Pacific		
			East Asia	South Asia	Western Asia

Net fuel exporters	Bolivia
	Colombia
	Ecuador
	Mexico
	Trinidad and Tobago
	Venezuela
		Algeria
		Angola
		Cameroon
		Congo
		Egypt
		Gabon
		Libyan Arab
		  Jamahiriya[b]
		Nigeria
			Brunei Darussalam[b]
			Indonesia
			Viet Nam
					Bahrain
					Iran (Islamic
					  Republic of)
					Iraq
					Kuwait[b]
					Oman[b]
					Qatar[b]
					Saudi Arabia[b]
					Syrian Arab
					  Republic
					United Arab
					  Emirates[b]

Net fuel importers	Argentina
	Barbados
	Brazil
	Chile
	Costa Rica
	Cuba
	Dominican Republic
	El Salvador
	Guatemala
	Guyana
	Haiti
	Honduras
	Jamaica
	Nicaragua
	Panama
	Paraguay
	Peru
	Uruguay
		Benin
		Botswana
		Burkina Faso
		Burundi
		Central African
		  Republic
		Chad
		Côte d'Ivoire
		Democratic
		  Republic of
		  the Congo
		Ethiopia
		Ghana
		Guinea
		Kenya
		Madagascar
		Malawi
		Mali
		Mauritius
		Morocco
		Mozambique
		Namibia
		Niger
		Rwanda
		Senegal
		South Africa
		Sudan
		Togo
		Tunisia
		Uganda
		United Republic
		  of Tanzania
		Zambia
		Zimbabwe
			Hong Kong,
			  SAR[c]
			Malaysia
			Papua New Guinea
			Philippines
			Republic of Korea
			Singapore[b]
			Taiwan Province
			  of China[b]
			Thailand
			
			China
				Bangladesh
				India
				Myanmar
				Nepal
				Pakistan
				Sri Lanka
					Cyprus
					Israel
					Jordan
					Lebanon
					Turkey
					Yemen

[a]   Countries systematically monitored by the Economic Monitoring and Assessment Unit of the United Nations Secretariat
[b]   Net-creditor economy.
[c]   Special Administrative Region of China

DATA QUALITY

Statistical information that is consistent and comparable over time and across countries is of vital importance for monitoring economic developments, discussing social issues and poverty, and assessing environmental change. The multifaceted nature of these and other related issues calls for an integrated approach to national and international economic, social and environmental data.

The 1993 revision of the System of National Accounts (SNA)[f] and the 1993 *Balance of Payments Manual*(the IMF Manual)[g] provide a basis for an integrated and harmonized system of statistics that reflect economic and social change. The SNA embodies concepts, definitions and classifications that are interrelated at both the macro- and microlevels. Concepts in the IMF Manual have been harmonized, as closely as possible, with those of the SNA and with IMF methodologies pertaining to banking, government finance and money statistics. In addition, a system of satellite accounts, which are semi-integrated with the central framework of the SNA, provides linkages between national accounts data and other statistical data, such as social statistics, health statistics, social protection statistics and tourism statistics.

Governments are increasingly reporting their data on the basis of these standards and, where available, such data are used in the statistics in this annex. However, inconsistency of coverage, definitions and data-collection methods among reporting countries mars some of the national and international statistics that are perforce used in this *Survey* and other international publications. In the case of late, incomplete or unreported data, adjustments and estimations are made in selected cases.

One widespread source of inaccuracy is the use of out-of-date benchmark surveys and censuses or obsolete models and assumptions about behaviour and conditions. On the other hand, when statistical administrations seek to improve their estimates by using new sources of data and updated surveys, there can be discontinuities in the series. National income estimates are especially affected, sometimes being subject to revisions on the order of 10-30 per cent.

National accounts and related indicators record mainly market transactions conducted through monetary exchange. Barter, production by households, subsistence output and informal sector activities are not always recorded; yet such items can constitute a large share of total activity in some countries and their omission can lead to a considerable underestimation of national output. As the degree of underestimation varies across countries, comparisons may give faulty results. In addition, as the non-market sector is absorbed over time into the mainstream of production through increasing monetization, output growth will be overstated.

The extent of the economic activity not captured by national statistics and the evolution of such activity over time have become a concern in some countries, particularly economies in transition. In addition, new modes of production, transactions and organization have made parts of the previous institutional and methodological framework for statistics inadequate. A comprehensive reform of national statistical systems has thus been under way in many economies in transition. As a result, there have been revisions to several data series for these countries and further revisions of measures of past and current performance are expected.[h]

[f] Commission of the European Communities, IMF, OECD, United Nations and World Bank, *System of National Accounts, 1993* (United Nations publication, Sales No. E.94.XVII.4).

[g] IMF, *Balance of Payments Manual*, 5th ed. (Washington, D.C., IMF, 1993).

[h] See *World Economic and Social Survey, 1995* (United Nations publication, Sales No. E.95.II.C.1), statistical annex, sect. entitled "Data caveats and conventions".

Weaknesses at the national level handicap comparisons between countries or groupings of countries at a given time or over time. Missing, unreliable or incompatible country data necessitate estimation and substitution in order to retain a consistent country composition of aggregated data over time. In particular, the absence of reliable GDP estimates for many developing countries and economies in transition requires the use of estimates in preparing country aggregations for many data series, as GDP weights are often used for such aggregations.

The veracity of estimates of output and of other statistical data of developing countries is related to the stage of development of their statistical systems. In Africa in particular, there are wide divergences in the values of the economic aggregates provided by different national and international sources for many countries. In addition, data for countries in which there is civil strife or war often provide only rough orders of magnitude. Finally, in countries experiencing high rates of inflation and disequilibrium exchange rates, there can be substantial distortions in national accounts data.

There are also problems with other economic statistics, such as those on unemployment, consumer price inflation, and the volume of exports and imports. For example, cross-country comparisons of unemployment must be made with caution, owing to differences in definition among countries, hence table A.7 employs the standardized definitions of unemployment rates for those developed countries where data are available. In a number of cases, such data differ substantially from national definitions.

Consumer price indices are among the oldest of the economic data series collected by Governments, but they are still surrounded by controversy, even in countries with the most advanced statistical systems. This is attributable particularly to the introduction of new goods and to changes in the quality of goods and consumer behaviour that are often not captured because of, inter alia, infrequent consumer surveys and revisions to the sample baskets of commodities.

There are no clear-cut solutions to many of the problems noted above, and even when there are, inadequate resources allocated to the improvement of statistical systems and reporting can perpetuate statistical shortcomings. In this light, some of the economic and social indicators presented in this *Survey* should be recognized as approximations and estimations.

DATA DEFINITIONS AND CONVENTIONS

Aggregate data are either sums or weighted averages of individual country data. Unless otherwise indicated, multi-year averages of growth rates are expressed as compound annual percentage rates of change. The convention followed is to omit the base year in a multi-year growth rate; for example, the 10-year average growth rate of a variable in the 1980s would be identified as the average annual growth rate from 1981 to 1990.

Output

National practices are followed in defining real GDP for each country and these national data are aggregated to create regional and global output figures. The growth of output in each group of countries is calculated from the sum of

GDP of individual countries measured at 1995 prices and exchange rates. Data for GDP in 1995 in national currencies were converted into dollars (with adjustments in selected cases[i]) and extended forward and backward in time using changes in real GDP for each country. This method supplies a reasonable set of aggregate growth rates for a period of about 15 years, centred on 1995.

Alternative aggregation methodologies for calculating world output

The *World Economic and Social Survey* utilizes a weighting scheme derived from exchange-rate conversions of national data in order to aggregate rates of growth of output of individual countries into regional and global totals, as noted above. This is similar to the approach followed in some other international reports, such as those of the World Bank. However, the aggregations used by IMF in its *World Economic Outlook* and by OECD in its *Economic Outlook* rely on country weights derived from national GDP in "international dollars", as converted from local currency using purchasing power parities (PPPs). The different weights arising from these two approaches are given in table D. The question which approach to use is controversial.

The reason advanced for using PPP weights is that, when aggregating production in two countries, a common set of prices should be used to value the same activities in both countries. This is frequently not the case when market exchange rates are used to convert local currency values of GDP. The PPP approach revalues gross expenditure in different countries using a single set of prices, in most cases some average of the prices in the countries being compared. By construction, these revalued GDP magnitudes are then related to a numeraire country, usually the United States of America, by assuming that GDP at PPP values for that country is identical with its GDP at the market exchange rate. The PPP conversion factor is then, in principle, the number of units of national currency needed to buy the goods and services that can be bought with one unit of the currency of the numeraire country.

In principle as well as in practice, however, PPPs are difficult to calculate because goods and services are not always directly comparable across countries, making direct comparisons of their prices correspondingly difficult. It is particularly difficult to measure the output and prices of many services, such as health care and education.

One problem in employing PPP estimates for calculating the relative sizes of economies is that even the most recently completed set of PPP prices covers only a comparatively small group of countries. Initially, in 1985, there were PPP data for only 64 countries. Subsequent work under the auspices of the International Comparison Programme (ICP) has increased this number, but it remains far lower than the number of countries for which this *Survey* needs data.

However, certain regularities have been observed, on the one hand, between GDP and its major expenditure components when measured in market prices and, on the other, between GDP and its components measured in "international" prices as derived through ICP. On that basis (and using other partial data on consumer prices), a technique was devised to approximate PPP levels of GDP and its major expenditure components for countries that had not participated in ICP. The results are known as the Penn World Tables.[i]

Neither the PPP approach nor the exchange-rate approach to weighting country GDP data can be applied in a theoretically pure or fully consistent way.

[i] When individual exchange rates seemed unrealistic, alternative exchange rates were substituted, using averages of the exchange rates in relevant years or the exchange rate of a more normal year, adjusted using relative inflation rates since that time.

[i] See Robert Summers and Alan Heston, *The Penn World Table (Mark 5): An Expanded Set of International Comparisons, 1950-1988*, National Bureau of Economic Research (NBER) Working Paper, No. R1562 (Cambridge, Massachusetts, May 1991).

Table D.
OUTPUT AND PER CAPITA OUTPUT IN THE BASE YEAR

	GDP (billions of dollars)		GDP per capita (dollars)	
	Exchange-rate basis 1995	PPP basis 1995	Exchange-rate basis 1995	PPP basis 1995
World	28 767	34 716	5 157	6 230
Developed economies *of which:*	22 425	19 061	27 017	22 965
United States of America	7 401	7 401	27 537	27 537
European Union	8 427	7 345	22 615	19 711
Japan	5 134	2 879	40 920	22 948
Economies in transition	785	2 327	1 913	5 666
Developing countries	5 557	13 328	1 281	3 072
By region:				
Latin America	1 689	3 037	3 569	6 418
Africa	463	1 321	685	1 952
Western Asia	735	1 253	3 449	5 878
Eastern and Southern Asia	2 669	7 717	897	2 594
China	700	3 237	574	2 654
By analytical grouping:				
Net-creditor countries	574	791	10 695	14 734
Net-debtor countries	4 983	12 537	1 163	2 926
Net fuel exporter countries	4 856	3 184	1 660	4 042
Net fuel importer countries	1 308	10 144	1 197	2 857
Memorandum items:				
Sub-Saharan Africa	128	452	314	1 111
Least developed countries	140	528	247	931

Source: UN/DESA.

The data requirements for a global ICP are enormous, although coverage has grown in each round. Similarly, since a system of weights based on exchange rates presumes that those rates are determined solely by external transactions and services and that domestic economies operate under competitive and liberal conditions, its application has been constrained by exchange controls and price distortions in many countries. Moreover, there are a large number of non-traded goods and services in each country to which the "law of one price" does not apply. However, the global trend towards liberalization may make possible a more consistent application over time of the exchange-rate method. Even so, the methods are conceptually different and thus yield different measures of world output growth.

The differences for the periods 1981-1990 and 1991-2002 are shown in table A.1. The estimates employ the same countries and the same data for the growth rates of GDP of the individual countries in the two computations. The differences in the aggregate growth rates are purely the result of using the two different sets of weights shown in table D.

Even though the growth rates for the regions do not differ much when data are converted at PPP rather than at exchange rates, the measure of the growth of world GDP is larger when country GDPs are valued at PPP conversion factors rather than at exchange rates (see table A.1). This is because the developing countries, in the aggregate, grew more rapidly than the rest of the world in the 1990s and the share of GDP of these countries is larger under PPP measurements than under market exchange rates. The influence of China is particularly important, given its high growth rate for nearly two decades.

International trade and finance

Trade values in table A.13 are based largely on customs data for merchandise trade converted into dollars using average annual exchange rates and are mainly drawn from IMF, *International Financial Statistics*. These data are supplemented by balance-of-payments data in certain cases. Estimates of the dollar values of trade include estimates by the regional commissions and the Economic Monitoring and Assessment Unit, while forecasts for both the volume and value of imports and exports rely largely on Project LINK.

The unit values that are used to determine measures of the volume of exports and imports for groupings of developing countries are estimated in part from weighted averages of export prices of commodity groupings at a combination of three- and four-digit Standard International Trade Classification (SITC) levels, based on the United Nations External Trade Statistics Database (COMTRADE); the weights reflect the share of each commodity or commodity group in the value of the region's total exports or imports.

For developed economies and economies in transition, the growth of trade volumes are aggregated from national data, as collected by the Economic Commission for Europe (ECE), IMF and the Economic Monitoring and Assessment Unit. As of 1 January 1993, customs offices at the borders between States members of the European Union (EU), which used to collect and check customs declarations on national exports and imports, were abolished as the single European market went into effect and a new system of data collection for intra-EU trade, called INTRASTAT, was put in place. INTRASTAT relies on information collected directly from enterprises and is linked with the system of declarations of value-added tax (VAT) relating to intra-EU trade so as to allow for quality control of the data. There is therefore a discontinuity between 1992 and 1993 for these countries owing to the change in methodology.

Total primary commodities refer to SITC sections 0 to 4:
- *Food*s comprise SITC sections 0 and 1, namely, food and live animals chiefly for food; and beverages and tobacco.
- *Agricultural raw materials* include SITC section 2 (crude materials, inedible, except fuels), except for divisions 27 and 28 (crude fertilizers and crude minerals, and metalliferous ores and metal scrap, respectively) and section 4 (animal and vegetable oils, fats and waxes).
- *Fuels* refer to SITC section 3 (mineral fuels, lubricants and related materials).

Total manufactures comprise sections 5 to 8:
- *Textiles* include divisions 65 (textile yarn, fabrics, made-up articles, not elsewhere specified or included, and related products) and 84 (articles of apparel and clothing accessories).
- *Chemicals* are SITC section 5.
- *Machinery and transport equipment* refer to SITC division 7.
- *Metals* include divisions 67 (iron and steel) and 68 (non-ferrous metals).

Tables A.19 to A.22 are based on the IMF *Balance of Payments Statistics* and on the definitions and methodologies set out in the IMF *Balance of Payments Manual*. Data from the regional commissions, and official and private sources, as well as estimates by the Economic Monitoring and Assessment Unit, were used to complement the IMF data. Whenever necessary, data reported in national currency were converted into United States dollars at the average market exchange rate in the period. Regional and subregional aggregates are sums of individual country data so that the current-account balance for the euro zone countries reflects the aggregation of individual country positions and does not exclude intra euro-zone transactions.

Table A.18 is, with the exception of data for OPEC in 2003, based on the International Energy Agency (IEA) *Monthly Oil Market Report*. The estimate of supply from OPEC in 2003 is based on production data for the first quarter of 2003 and information about OPEC production quotas. The country groups and regions used in this *Survey* differ from those used by IEA, and adjustments were made to take account of these differences.

LIST OF TABLES

I. GLOBAL OUTPUT AND MACROECONOMIC INDICATORS

II. INTERNATIONAL TRADE

III. INTERNATIONAL FINANCE AND FINANCIAL MARKETS

I. GLOBAL OUTPUT AND MACROECONOMIC INDICATORS

Table A.1.
WORLD POPULATION, OUTPUT AND PER CAPITA GDP, 1980-2002

	Growth of GDP (annual percentage change)				Growth rate of population (annual percentage change)		Population (millions)		GDP per capita Exchange-rate basis (1995 dollars)	
	Exchange-rate basis (1995 dollars)		Purchasing power parity (PPP) basis							
	1981-1990	1991-2002	1981-1990	1991-2002	1981-1990	1991-2002	1980	2002	1980	2002
World	2.9	2.4	3.0	2.8	1.7	1.4	4 367	6 110	4 531	5 669
Developed economies	3.0	2.1	3.0	2.3	0.6	0.6	756	860	20 225	30 721
United States	3.2	2.9	3.2	2.9	1.0	1.0	230	289	20 851	32 081
European Union[a]	2.3	1.9	2.4	1.9	0.3	0.3	355	377	17 628	26 035
Japan	4.1	1.2	4.1	1.2	0.6	0.3	117	128	27 381	43 384
Economies in transition[b]	1.8	-1.4	2.0	-1.8	0.7	0.0	378	406	2 616	2 349
Developing countries	2.3	4.2	3.4	5.0	2.1	1.7	3 233	4 844	1 087	1 498
by region:										
Latin America	1.1	2.5	1.3	2.6	2.0	1.6	356	527	3 654	3 705
Africa	2.0	2.5	1.9	2.4	2.9	2.5	446	798	801	730
Western Asia	-2.8	2.3	-1.5	2.6	3.3	2.3	137	248	6 758	3 673
Eastern and Southern Asia	7.0	6.2	6.9	6.8	1.8	1.4	2 295	3 270	407	1 164
China	9.1	9.7	9.1	9.7	1.5	1.0	999	1 294	167	932
Region excluding China	6.6	5.0	5.9	4.8	2.1	1.8	1 296	1 976	592	1 316
East Asia	7.0	5.0	6.3	4.8	1.9	1.5	411	599	1 322	3 236
South Asia	5.3	4.9	5.2	4.9	2.2	1.9	885	1 377	252	480
by analytical grouping:										
Net-creditor countries	1.6	3.9	0.9	3.6	3.1	1.9	37	62	10 624	11 670
Net-debtor countries	2.4	4.3	3.6	5.1	2.1	1.7	3 197	4 782	977	1 365
Net fuel exporters	-1.1	2.6	0.7	2.9	2.6	2.0	552	897	2 403	1 795
Net fuel importers	4.0	4.8	4.6	5.6	2.0	1.6	2 682	3 947	816	1 430
Memo items:										
Sub-Saharan Africa	1.8	2.5	1.2	2.2	3.1	2.7	261	486	388	334
Least developed countries	2.2	3.5	1.9	3.3	2.7	2.6	381	675	270	286

Source: UN/DESA.

[a] Including the eastern *Länder* (States) of Germany from 1991.
[b] Including the former German Democratic Republic until 1990.

Table A.2.
DEVELOPED ECONOMIES: RATES OF GROWTH OF REAL GDP, 1994-2004

Annual percentage change[a]

	1994-2002	1994	1995	1996	1997	1998	1999	2000	2001	2002[b]	2003[c]	2004[c]
Developed economies	2.4	2.9	2.4	2.7	3.0	2.5	2.7	3.5	0.9	1.4	1¾	2½
United States	3.3	4.0	2.7	3.6	4.4	4.3	4.1	3.8	0.3	2.4	2½	4
Canada	3.4	4.7	2.8	1.7	3.9	3.6	4.5	4.8	1.5	3.4	2¾	3¾
Japan	1.2	1.0	1.9	3.4	1.8	-1.1	0.1	2.8	0.4	0.2	¾	¾
Australia	4.5	4.8	3.5	4.3	3.7	5.2	4.8	8.0	2.7	3.5	3	2½
New Zealand	3.1	5.1	3.7	3.1	2.6	-0.4	4.1	3.8	2.5	3.8	2¾	2½
EU-15	2.3	2.8	2.4	1.6	2.5	2.8	2.8	3.4	1.6	1.0	1¼	2½
Euro zone	2.2	2.4	2.3	1.4	2.3	2.8	2.8	3.4	1.5	0.8	1	2¼
Austria	2.2	2.4	1.7	2.0	1.3	3.3	3.7	3.0	1.0	1.5	1½	2½
Belgium	2.4	3.2	2.4	1.2	3.6	2.2	3.0	4.0	1.0	0.7	1¼	1¾
Finland	3.9	4.0	3.8	4.0	6.3	5.3	4.1	6.1	0.7	1.4	1¾	2¾
France	2.2	2.1	1.8	1.1	1.9	3.1	3.2	3.6	2.1	1.2	1¼	2½
Germany	1.5	2.3	1.7	0.8	1.4	2.0	2.0	2.9	0.6	0.2	½	2
Greece	3.1	1.5	1.9	2.4	3.6	3.4	3.6	3.9	4.0	3.6	3¼	4
Ireland	8.1	5.8	10.0	7.8	10.8	8.6	10.9	10.0	5.7	4.0	3½	4¼
Italy	1.9	2.2	2.9	1.1	2.0	1.8	1.6	2.8	1.8	0.5	1	2
Luxembourg	4.5	4.2	3.8	3.6	9.0	5.8	6.0	7.5	1.0	0.3	¾	3
Netherlands	2.8	3.2	2.3	3.1	3.6	4.3	4.0	3.3	1.3	0.5	¾	1¾
Portugal	3.3	2.4	5.5	3.5	4.0	4.6	3.8	3.5	1.7	0.5	¾	2½
Spain	3.0	2.3	2.7	2.4	3.5	3.8	3.7	4.1	2.8	1.9	2	2¾
Other EU	2.8	4.6	3.0	2.4	3.2	3.0	2.7	3.2	1.8	1.8	2¼	3
Denmark	2.7	5.5	2.8	2.5	3.0	2.5	2.3	3.0	0.9	1.8	2½	2
Sweden	2.8	3.3	3.7	1.1	2.1	3.6	4.5	3.6	1.2	1.9	1½	2¾
United Kingdom	2.9	4.7	2.9	2.6	3.4	2.9	2.4	3.1	2.1	1.8	2¼	3
Other Europe	1.8	2.2	1.6	1.9	2.8	2.3	1.4	2.9	1.1	0.3	¼	1¾
Iceland	3.5	4.0	0.1	5.2	5.3	5.1	3.9	5.5	2.9	-0.5	1¾	3¼
Malta	3.8	5.7	6.2	4.0	4.9	3.4	4.1	6.4	-1.2	1.0	1½	2
Norway	3.0	5.5	3.8	4.9	4.7	2.0	0.9	2.3	1.4	1.3	0	1¾
Switzerland	1.2	0.5	0.5	0.3	1.7	2.4	1.5	3.2	0.9	-0.2	½	1¾
Memo item:												
Major developed economies	2.3	2.8	2.3	2.7	3.0	2.3	2.6	3.3	0.7	1.4	1¾	2¾

Source: UN/DESA.

[a] Calculated as a weighted average of individual country growth rates of gross domestic product (GDP) where weights are based on GDP in 1995 prices and exchange rates. For methodology, see *World Economic and Social Survey, 1992* and corrigenda (United Nations publication, Sales No. E.92.II.C.1 and corr.1 and 2), annex, introductory text.
[b] Partly estimated.
[c] Forecast, based in part on Project LINK.

Table A.3.
ECONOMIES IN TRANSITION: RATES OF GROWTH OF REAL GDP, 1994-2004

Annual percentage change[a]												
	1994-2002	1994	1995	1996	1997	1998	1999	2000	2001	2002[b]	2003[c]	2004[c]
Economies in transition	1.3	-7.2	-0.6	-0.1	2.4	-0.8	3.4	6.7	4.4	3.8	4	4
Central and Eastern Europe and Baltic States	3.4	3.6	5.5	4.1	3.5	2.8	1.3	3.9	2.9	2.8	3½	4
Central and Eastern Europe	3.4	4.0	5.7	4.1	3.3	2.6	1.4	3.9	2.7	2.6	3¼	3¾
Albania	6.5	8.3	13.3	9.0	-7.0	8.0	7.3	7.8	6.5	6.0	6	6
Bulgaria	0.8	1.8	2.8	-10.2	-7.0	3.5	2.4	5.8	4.1	4.8	4	4½
Croatia	4.4	5.9	6.8	5.9	6.8	2.5	-0.4	3.7	3.8	5.2	3¾	4¼
Czech Republic	2.0	2.2	6.0	4.3	-0.8	-1.2	-0.4	2.9	3.1	2.0	3	4
Hungary	3.5	3.1	1.4	1.4	4.6	4.9	4.2	5.2	3.8	3.3	3¾	4
Poland	4.4	5.1	7.1	6.0	6.9	4.8	4.1	4.0	1.0	1.2	2½	3
Romania	1.3	3.9	7.1	4.0	-6.1	-5.4	-3.2	1.8	5.3	4.9	4¼	4¾
Serbia and Montenegro[d]	1.8	2.7	6.0	5.9	7.4	2.5	-19.3	5.0	6.2	3.0	4	4
Slovakia	4.5	4.8	7.0	6.5	6.5	4.1	1.9	2.2	3.3	4.4	4	4½
Slovenia	4.1	5.3	4.2	3.5	4.5	3.8	5.2	4.6	3.0	3.1	3½	4
The former Yugoslav Republic of Macedonia	0.6	-1.9	-1.2	0.7	1.5	2.9	2.7	5.1	-4.5	0.3	3	3½
Baltic States	3.7	-4.7	2.2	4.2	8.4	5.8	-0.2	5.5	6.7	6.3	5½	5¾
Estonia	4.2	-2.0	4.3	3.9	10.6	4.7	-1.1	6.4	5.4	5.8	5½	6
Latvia	4.4	0.6	-0.9	3.7	8.4	4.8	2.8	6.8	7.9	6.1	5	5½
Lithuania	3.0	-9.8	3.3	4.7	7.0	7.3	-1.8	4.0	6.5	6.7	6	6
Commonwealth of Independent States	-0.2	-13.7	-5.1	-3.6	1.4	-4.0	5.5	9.3	5.7	4.7	4½	4¼
Armenia	6.7	5.4	6.9	5.9	3.3	7.3	3.3	6.0	9.6	12.9	8	7
Azerbaijan	2.1	-19.7	-11.8	1.3	5.8	10.0	7.4	11.1	9.9	10.6	9	8
Belarus	1.7	-12.6	-10.4	2.8	11.4	8.4	3.4	5.8	4.1	4.7	3	2
Georgia	3.1	-11.4	2.4	10.5	10.8	2.9	2.9	1.8	4.5	5.4	6	7
Kazakhstan	1.2	-12.6	-8.2	0.5	1.7	-1.9	1.7	9.6	13.2	9.5	7	6½
Kyrgyzstan	-1.2	-20.1	-5.4	-7.1	9.9	2.1	3.6	5.0	5.3	-0.5	4	5
Republic of Moldova	-4.6	-31.2	-1.4	-7.8	1.3	-6.5	-4.4	1.9	6.1	7.2	6	5
Russian Federation	-0.1	-12.7	-4.1	-3.6	1.4	-5.3	6.4	10.0	5.0	4.3	4½	4
Tajikistan	-0.2	-18.9	-12.5	-4.4	1.7	5.3	3.7	8.3	10.2	9.1	7	7
Turkmenistan[e]	3.0	-17.3	-7.2	-6.7	-11.3	5.0	16.0	17.6	20.5	19.3	12	10
Ukraine	-3.9	-23.0	-12.2	-10.0	-3.0	-1.9	-0.4	5.8	9.0	4.8	4	4½
Uzbekistan	2.2	-4.2	-0.9	1.6	2.5	4.4	4.4	4.0	4.5	4.2	4	4

Source: UN/DESA, based on data of Economic Commission for Europe (ECE).

a   Calculated as a weighted average of individual country growth rates of gross domestic product (GDP), where weights are based on GDP in 1995 prices and exchange rates.
b   Partly estimated.
c   Forecast, based in part on Project LINK.
d   As of 4 February 2003, "Serbia and Montenegro" became the official name of the Federal Republic of Yugoslavia.
e   Reliability of figures is questionable owing to deflation procedures that are not well documented .

Table A.4.
DEVELOPING ECONOMIES: RATES OF GROWTH OF REAL GDP, 1994-2004

Annual percentage change[a]	1994-2002	1994	1995	1996	1997	1998	1999	2000	2001	2002[b]	2003[c]	2004[c]
Developing countries[d] _of which:_	4.2	5.6	5.0	5.7	5.4	1.6	3.5	5.8	2.1	3.2	3½	5
Africa	3.2	2.5	2.7	5.2	3.0	3.0	2.9	3.1	3.3	2.9	3¼	4
Net fuel exporters	3.2	0.5	3.9	4.2	3.3	3.6	3.7	3.4	2.9	3.0	3¼	3¾
Net fuel importers	3.2	3.7	1.9	5.8	2.8	2.7	2.5	2.9	3.5	2.8	3¼	4¼
Eastern and Southern Asia	5.9	8.4	8.1	7.3	6.0	0.5	6.3	7.1	3.7	5.7	5¼	6
East Asia	4.5	9.1	8.5	7.6	6.3	-0.5	6.3	7.6	3.5	5.8	5	6¼
East Asia (excluding China)	4.7	7.6	7.6	6.7	5.1	-4.6	5.9	7.4	1.4	4.5	3½	5
South Asia	5.3	5.2	6.3	6.0	4.8	5.3	5.9	5.0	4.6	4.8	5¾	6
Western Asia	2.8	-0.8	4.0	4.6	5.5	4.1	0.7	6.4	-1.2	2.0	1¼	3¾
Net fuel exporters	2.9	-0.5	1.7	3.9	5.9	4.7	2.6	6.4	1.0	0.7	1	4
Net fuel importers	2.6	-1.3	7.5	5.8	4.9	3.3	-2.1	6.3	-4.6	4.2	2	3¼
Latin America and the Caribbean	2.4	5.3	1.4	3.7	5.2	2.0	0.4	3.9	0.3	-0.8	2	3¾
Net fuel exporters	2.3	3.6	-2.4	3.7	5.7	3.2	1.5	5.5	0.6	-0.2	½	4½
Net fuel exporters	2.4	6.1	3.0	3.8	4.9	1.5	0.0	3.3	0.2	-1.0	2½	3¼
Memo items:												
Sub-Saharan Africa (excluding Nigeria and South Africa)	3.4	2.1	3.8	5.4	4.3	3.3	2.8	2.5	3.3	2.9	3½	4½
Least developed countries	4.4	2.0	4.4	5.0	5.5	4.3	4.6	4.7	4.7	4.0	4½	5
Major developing economies												
Argentina	0.0	5.8	-2.8	5.5	8.1	3.9	-3.4	-0.5	-4.5	-10.9	4	4½
Brazil	2.8	6.2	4.2	2.9	3.5	0.2	0.8	4.5	1.5	1.5	1¾	2¾
Chile	4.7	5.4	9.9	7.0	7.6	3.9	-1.1	5.4	2.8	2.1	3	4
China	8.8	12.6	10.5	9.6	8.8	7.8	7.1	8.0	7.3	8.0	7½	8
Colombia	2.0	6.3	5.4	2.1	2.8	0.5	-4.3	2.7	1.6	1.5	1¾	2¾
Egypt	4.3	2.3	4.7	5.0	5.5	5.6	6.0	3.2	3.5	3.0	1¾	3¼
Hong Kong SAR[e]	3.6	5.3	4.7	4.8	5.2	-5.1	3.0	12.1	0.6	2.3	2	3
India	5.7	5.4	6.7	6.4	5.3	5.6	6.4	5.1	5.1	5.0	6	6¼
Indonesia	2.8	7.5	8.1	8.0	4.7	-13.1	0.1	4.8	3.3	3.6	3½	4¼
Iran (Islamic Republic of)	3.9	1.8	4.2	5.0	2.5	2.2	2.5	6.1	5.0	5.7	5¾	4¼
Israel	3.1	6.6	7.1	4.5	2.1	2.2	2.2	6.0	-0.9	-1.2	0	3½
Korea, Republic of	5.8	8.6	8.9	7.1	5.5	-5.8	10.7	8.8	3.0	6.3	4	6
Malaysia	4.9	9.2	9.5	8.2	7.7	-7.5	5.6	8.3	0.4	4.2	4¼	6
Mexico	3.1	4.6	-6.2	5.5	6.8	4.8	5.2	6.9	-0.3	0.9	2½	4½
Nigeria	2.7	1.3	2.5	4.3	2.7	1.8	1.0	3.8	3.9	2.7	3	4½
Pakistan	3.9	4.2	4.9	5.2	1.3	3.7	4.1	3.9	3.1	4.6	5	5¼
Peru	4.4	12.8	8.6	2.5	6.7	-0.4	1.4	3.6	0.2	5.2	4½	5
Philippines	3.8	4.4	4.8	5.5	5.2	-0.5	3.4	4.0	3.3	4.6	4¼	5
Saudi Arabia	1.4	-2.7	-0.2	4.0	3.0	1.6	0.5	4.5	1.2	0.7	3	3
Singapore	5.5	10.1	8.9	7.0	7.8	0.3	5.9	10.3	-2.0	2.2	2½	4¾
South Africa	2.8	3.2	3.1	4.3	2.6	0.8	2.0	3.5	2.8	3.0	2¾	3½
Taiwan Province of China	4.7	6.5	6.1	5.6	6.8	4.6	5.4	5.9	-1.9	3.5	3¼	4½
Thailand	2.9	8.7	8.6	6.7	-1.3	-10.2	4.2	4.4	1.6	5.2	4¼	4½
Turkey	2.2	-6.1	8.0	7.0	6.8	3.8	-5.1	7.1	-8.0	7.8	2¾	3
Venezuela	-0.7	-3.0	3.1	-1.3	5.1	0.2	-6.1	3.2	2.7	-8.9	-12	8½

Source: United Nations.

a Calculated as a weighted average of individual country growth rates of gross domestic product (GDP), where weights are based on GDP in 1995 prices and exchange rates.
b Partly estimated.
c Forecast, in part based on Project LINK.
d Covering countries that account for 98 per cent of the population of all developing countries.
e Special Administrative Region of China.

Table A.5.
DEVELOPED ECONOMIES: INVESTMENT, SAVING AND NET TRANSFER, 1985-2001

Percentage of GDP		Gross domestic investment	Gross domestic saving	Net financial transfer
Total[a]	1985	21.8	21.4	0.4
	1990	22.9	22.7	0.1
	1995	21.5	22.2	-0.7
	2000	21.9	21.1	0.7
	2001	20.4	19.8	0.7
Major developed economies[a]	1985	21.7	21.1	0.5
	1990	22.6	22.4	0.2
	1995	21.5	22.0	-0.4
	2000	21.8	20.5	1.2
	2001 .	20.1	18.9	1.2
European Union (EU-15)	1985	14.9	15.5	-0.7
	1990	16.6	16.7	-0.1
	1995	14.7	15.9	-1.2
	2000	15.1	15.5	-0.5
	2001	14.4	15.2	-0.8
Germany[b]	1985	20.0	23.0	-3.0
	1990	22.7	26.0	-3.3
	1995	22.6	23.3	-0.6
	2000	21.9	22.3	-0.4
	2001	19.6	21.5	-1.9
Japan	1985	28.3	31.7	-3.4
	1990	32.8	33.7	-0.9
	1995	28.2	29.6	-1.4
	2000	25.9	27.4	-1.4
	2001	25.5	26.1	-0.6
United States of America	1985	20.2	17.4	2.7
	1990	17.6	16.4	1.2
	1995	18.1	17.0	1.1
	2000	20.7	17.0	3.7
	2001	18.7	15.2	3.5

Source: OECD, *National Accounts.*

[a] National data converted to dollars for aggregation at annual average exchange rates.
[b] Prior to 1991, data referring to Western Germany only.

Table A.6.
DEVELOPED ECONOMIES: UNEMPLOYMENT RATES[a], 1994-2004

Percentage	1994	1995	1996	1997	1998	1999	2000	2001	2002[b]	2003[c]	2004[c]
Developed economies[c]	7.9	7.5	7.6	7.3	6.9	6.3	5.9	6.1	6.7	7	6¾
United States	6.1	5.6	5.4	4.9	4.5	4.2	4.0	4.7	5.8	6	5½
Canada	10.4	9.5	9.7	9.1	8.3	7.6	6.8	7.2	7.7	7¼	6¾
Japan	2.9	3.2	3.4	3.4	4.1	4.7	4.7	5.0	5.4	5½	5½
Australia	9.7	8.5	8.5	8.5	7.7	7.0	6.3	6.7	6.3	6¼	6¾
New Zealand	8.2	6.3	6.1	6.6	7.5	6.8	6.0	5.3	5.2	5½	5½
EU-15	11.1	10.7	10.8	10.6	9.9	8.7	7.8	7.4	7.6	8	8
Euro zone	11.5	11.3	11.5	11.5	10.8	9.4	8.5	8.0	8.3	8¾	8¾
Austria	3.8	3.9	4.3	4.4	4.5	4.0	3.7	3.6	4.3	4½	4
Belgium	10.0	9.9	9.7	9.4	9.5	8.6	6.9	6.7	7.3	7¼	7
Finland	16.6	15.4	14.6	12.7	11.4	10.2	9.7	9.1	9.1	9¼	9¼
France	12.3	11.7	12.4	12.3	11.8	10.7	9.3	8.5	8.7	9	8¾
Germany	8.4	8.2	8.9	9.9	9.3	8.4	7.8	7.8	8.2	9	9¾
Greece	9.6	10.0	9.8	9.8	11.1	12.0	11.0	10.4	9.9	9½	8¾
Ireland	14.3	12.3	11.7	9.9	7.5	5.6	4.3	3.9	4.4	5¾	5½
Italy	11.1	11.6	11.7	11.7	11.8	11.3	10.4	9.4	9.0	9	8¾
Luxembourg	3.2	2.9	3.0	2.7	2.7	2.4	2.3	2.0	2.4	3¼	3
Netherlands	7.1	6.9	6.3	5.2	4.0	3.2	2.8	2.4	2.7	4	5
Portugal	6.9	7.3	7.3	6.8	5.2	4.5	4.1	4.1	5.1	6¼	5¾
Spain	24.2	22.9	22.2	20.8	18.8	12.8	11.3	10.6	11.4	11¼	10½
Other EU	9.5	8.6	8.3	7.2	6.4	5.9	5.3	4.9	5.0	5¼	5¼
Denmark	8.2	7.2	6.8	5.6	5.2	4.8	4.4	4.3	4.5	4¼	4¼
Sweden	9.4	8.8	9.6	9.9	8.3	7.1	5.6	4.9	4.9	5½	5¼
United Kingdom	9.6	8.7	8.2	7.0	6.3	5.8	5.4	5.0	5.1	5¼	5½
Other Europe	4.4	4.1	4.3	4.2	3.4	3.1	2.9	2.9	3.2	4	4¼
Iceland	5.4	4.9	3.8	3.9	2.7	2.0	2.3	2.3	3.1	3¼	3
Malta[d]	4.1	3.7	4.4	5.5	5.6	5.8	5.0	5.1	5.2	5¼	5¼
Norway	5.5	5.0	4.9	4.1	3.3	3.2	3.4	3.6	3.9	4¼	4¾
Switzerland	3.8	3.5	3.9	4.2	3.5	3.0	2.6	2.5	2.8	4	4
Memo item: Major developed economies	7.1	6.8	6.8	6.6	6.4	6.1	5.7	6.1	6.7	7	6¾

Source: UN/DESA, based on data of OECD.

[a] Unemployment data are standardized by OECD for comparability among countries and over time, in conformity with the definitions of the International Labour Office (see OECD, *Standardized Unemployment Rates: Sources and Methods* (Paris, 1985)).
[b] Partly estimated.
[c] Forecast, based partly on Project LINK.
[d] Not standardized.

Table A.7.
CENTRAL AND EASTERN EUROPE AND THE BALTIC STATES: UNEMPLOYMENT RATES[a], 1994-2004

Percentage	1994	1995	1996	1997	1998	1999	2000	2001	2002[b]	2003[c]	2004[c]
Central and Eastern Europe											
Albania	18.0	12.9	12.3	14.9	17.6	18.2	16.9	14.5	14.2	14¼	14
Bulgaria	12.8	11.1	12.5	13.7	12.2	16.0	17.9	18.1	17.7	16	15
Croatia	17.3	17.6	15.9	17.6	18.6	20.8	22.6	23.1	21.9	21¾	20
Czech Republic	3.2	2.9	3.5	5.2	7.5	9.4	8.8	8.6	9.2	9	8½
Hungary	10.9	10.4	10.5	10.4	9.1	9.6	8.9	8.4	8.1	8	7¾
Poland	16.0	14.9	13.2	10.3	10.4	13.1	15.1	16.2	17.8	17¾	17¾
Romania	10.9	9.5	6.6	8.8	10.3	11.5	10.5	8.6	8.4	9	8½
Serbia and Montenegro[d]	23.9	24.7	26.1	25.6	27.2	27.4	26.6	27.9	29.0	30	29
Slovakia	14.8	13.1	12.8	12.5	15.6	19.2	17.9	18.6	17.8	18	17½
Slovenia	14.2	14.5	14.4	14.8	14.6	13.0	12.0	11.6	11.6	11	11
The former Yugoslav Republic of Macedonia	30.0	36.6	38.8	41.7	41.4	44.0	45.0	45.0	43.0	40	40
Baltic States											
Estonia	5.1	5.0	5.6	4.6	5.1	6.7	7.7	7.7	7.7	7	6½
Latvia	6.5	6.6	7.2	7.0	9.2	9.1	7.8	7.7	8.5	7¾	7
Lithuania	4.5	7.3	6.2	6.7	6.9	10.0	12.6	12.5	11.3	10¼	9¾

Source: UN/DESA, based on data of Economic Commission for Europe (ECE).

[a] End-of-period registered unemployment data.
[b] Partly estimated.
[c] Forecast, based partly on Project LINK.
[d] As of 4 February 2003, "Serbia and Montenegro" became the official name of the Federal Republic of Yugoslavia.

Table A.8.
DEVELOPED ECONOMIES: CONSUMER PRICE INFLATION[a], 1994-2004

Average annual percentage change

	1994	1995	1996	1997	1998	1999	2000	2001	2002	2003[b]	2004[b]
Developed economies	2.2	2.1	2.0	2.0	1.3	1.2	2.0	1.8	1.2	1¼	1¼
United States	2.6	2.8	2.9	2.3	1.6	2.2	3.4	2.8	1.6	2¼	1½
Canada	0.2	2.2	1.6	1.6	1.0	1.7	2.7	2.5	2.2	2¼	2¼
Japan	0.7	-0.1	0.1	1.8	0.7	-0.3	-0.7	-0.7	-0.9	-1¼	-¼
Australia	1.9	4.6	2.6	0.3	0.9	1.5	4.5	4.4	3.0	2	2
New Zealand	1.7	3.8	2.6	0.9	1.3	1.4	2.7	2.7	2.3	2	2
EU-15	2.9	2.8	2.3	1.9	1.5	1.2	2.3	2.5	2.0	2	1¾
Euro zone	3.0	2.7	2.3	1.8	1.3	1.1	2.3	2.6	2.0	1¾	1½
Austria	3.0	2.3	1.8	1.3	0.9	0.6	2.4	2.7	1.8	1½	1¾
Belgium	2.4	1.5	2.1	1.6	1.0	1.1	2.5	2.5	1.6	1	1¼
Finland	1.1	1.0	0.6	1.2	1.4	1.2	3.4	2.6	1.8	1¾	1½
France	1.7	1.8	2.0	1.2	0.7	0.5	1.7	1.6	1.9	1¾	1½
Germany	2.8	1.7	1.4	1.9	0.9	0.6	1.9	2.5	1.3	1¼	1¼
Greece	10.9	8.9	8.2	5.5	4.8	2.6	3.1	3.4	3.6	3½	3¼
Ireland	2.4	2.5	1.7	1.4	2.4	1.6	5.6	4.9	4.7	3¾	3½
Italy	4.0	5.2	4.0	2.0	2.0	1.7	2.5	2.8	2.5	2¼	2
Luxembourg	2.2	1.9	1.4	1.4	1.0	1.0	3.1	2.7	2.1	2	1¾
Netherlands	2.8	1.9	2.0	2.2	2.0	2.2	2.5	4.5	3.5	2¼	1
Portugal	4.9	4.1	3.1	2.2	2.8	2.3	2.9	4.4	3.6	3	2½
Spain	4.7	4.7	3.6	2.0	1.8	2.3	3.4	2.8	3.1	2¼	2
Other EU	2.4	3.1	2.1	2.6	2.7	1.5	2.6	2.0	1.8	2½	2¾
Denmark	2.0	2.1	2.1	2.2	1.9	2.5	2.9	2.3	2.4	2¼	2
Sweden	2.2	2.5	0.5	0.5	-0.1	0.5	1.0	2.4	2.2	2	1½
United Kingdom	2.5	3.4	2.4	3.1	3.4	1.6	2.9	1.8	1.6	2½	3¼
Other Europe	1.1	2.0	1.0	1.2	0.8	1.3	2.1	1.7	0.9	1	½
Iceland	1.6	1.7	2.3	1.7	1.7	3.2	5.2	6.4	5.2	2½	2¾
Malta	4.1	4.0	2.5	3.1	2.4	2.1	2.4	2.9	2.2	1½	1½
Norway	1.4	2.5	1.3	2.6	2.3	2.3	3.1	3.0	1.3	3¼	1¼
Switzerland	0.9	1.8	0.8	0.5	0.1	0.7	1.6	1.0	0.6	0	0
Memo item:											
Major developed economies	2.0	1.9	1.9	2.1	1.3	1.1	1.9	1.6	1.0	1¼	1¼

Source: UN/DESA, based on data of IMF, *International Financial Statistics*.

a   Data for country groups are weighted averages, where weights for each year are 1995 GDP in United States dollars.
b   Forecast, partly based on Project LINK.

Table A.9.
ECONOMIES IN TRANSITION: CONSUMER PRICE INFLATION, 1994-2004

Average annual percentage change

	1994	1995	1996	1997	1998	1999	2000	2001	2002ᵃ	2003ᵇ	2004ᵇ
Economies in transitionᶜ	412.6	145.1	41.1	38.3	21.9	50.6	19.6	14.6	10.7	9	8½
Central and Eastern Europe and Baltic States	45.0ᶜ	25.8	25.2	66.9	16.6	11.7	12.2	9.0	5.0	4	4
Central and Eastern Europe	44.6ᶜ	25.5	25.4	69.4	17.0	12.1	12.7	9.3	5.2	4	4
Albania	21.5	8.0	12.7	33.1	20.3	-0.1	0.0	3.1	5.1	2½	2
Bulgaria	96.2	62.0	121.7	1 058.3	18.7	2.6	10.2	7.4	5.8	4	4
Croatia	97.5	2.0	3.6	3.7	5.9	4.3	6.2	5.2	2.3	2¼	3
Czech Republic	10.0	9.1	8.9	8.4	10.6	2.1	3.9	4.7	1.8	1	2½
Hungary	19.1	28.5	23.6	18.4	14.2	10.1	9.9	9.2	5.0	5	4¾
Poland	33.2	28.1	19.8	15.1	11.7	7.4	10.2	5.5	1.9	1½	2
Romania	137.1	32.2	38.8	154.9	59.3	45.9	45.7	34.5	22.5	15	12
Serbia and Montenegroᵈ	ᵉ	71.8	90.5	23.2	30.4	44.1	75.7	88.9	19.2	12	8
Slovakia	13.4	10.0	6.1	6.1	6.7	10.5	12.0	7.1	3.3	8	5
Slovenia	21.0	13.5	9.9	8.4	8.1	6.3	9.0	8.4	7.5	5	4
The former Yugoslav Republic of Macedonia	126.6	16.4	2.5	0.9	-1.4	-1.3	6.6	5.5	1.8	2½	2½
Baltics States	54.2	32.1	22.0	9.3	6.3	2.0	2.2	2.8	1.6	2	2¾
Estonia	47.9	28.9	23.1	11.1	10.6	3.5	3.9	5.8	3.6	3½	4
Latvia	35.7	25.0	17.6	8.4	4.7	2.4	2.6	2.5	1.9	2	2½
Lithuania	72.0	39.5	24.7	8.8	5.1	0.8	1.0	1.3	0.3	1	2
Commonwealth of Independent States	670.4	232.4	52.8	17.3	25.8	79.1	24.8	18.5	14.6	12¾	12
Armenia	4 964.0	175.5	18.7	13.8	8.7	0.7	-0.8	3.0	1.1	4	3
Azerbaijan	1 663.9	411.5	19.8	3.6	-0.8	-8.6	1.8	2.0	2.8	3	3½
Belarus	2 219.6	709.3	52.7	63.9	73.2	293.7	168.9	61.0	42.6	35	40
Georgia	22 286.1	261.4	39.4	7.1	3.5	19.3	4.2	5.0	5.6	6	6
Kazakhstan	1 880.1	176.3	39.2	17.5	7.3	8.4	13.4	8.0	5.9	6½	6
Kyrgyzstan	278.1	42.9	31.3	23.4	10.3	35.7	18.7	7.0	2.1	4	5
Republic of Moldova	486.4	29.9	23.5	11.8	7.7	39.3	31.3	10.0	5.2	7	8
Russian Federation	309.0	197.4	47.8	14.7	27.8	85.7	20.8	18.6	15.8	13	12
Tajikistan	350.3	682.1	422.4	85.4	43.1	27.5	32.9	37.0	10.2	10	12
Turkmenistan	2 719.5	1 105.3	714.0	83.7	16.8	23.5	7.0	8.2	15.0	18	15
Ukraine	891.2	376.7	80.2	15.9	10.6	22.7	28.2	12.0	0.8	6	5
Uzbekistan	1 910.2	304.6	54.0	58.8	17.7	29.0	24.9	26.6	24.2	25	20

Source: UN/DESA, based on data of Economic Commission for Europe (ECE).

ᵃ Partly estimated.
ᵇ Forecast.
ᶜ Excluding Serbia and Montenegro.
ᵈ As of 4 February 2003, "Serbia and Montenegro" became the official name of the Federal Republic of Yugoslavia.
ᵉ Annual rates of hyperinflation of over 1 trillion percentage points.

Table A.10.
DEVELOPING COUNTRIES: CONSUMER PRICE INFLATION,[a] 1994-2004

Average percentage change

	1994	1995	1996	1997	1998	1999	2000	2001	2002[b]	2003[c]	2004[c]
Developing countries by region:	139.5	23.2	14.2	9.7	10.7	6.5	5.6	5.6	6.9	8	6¼
Africa[d]	19.6	19.2	12.9	7.9	6.5	5.3	6.0	6.1	8.8	11	7¾
Eastern and Southern Asia	11.6	9.5	6.7	4.6	9.1	2.4	1.4	2.9	2.2	3	3
East Asia	12.0	9.3	6.3	4.0	8.6	1.9	0.9	2.7	1.8	2¾	2¾
South Asia	10.1	10.3	9.0	7.4	11.6	4.9	4.1	3.7	4.0	4½	4¾
East Asia excluding China	6.2	5.8	5.3	4.6	13.0	3.4	1.1	3.7	3.0	3½	3¼
Western Asia	39.7	37.8	31.2	28.9	27.8	22.3	18.3	16.8	16.3	14	10
Latin America and											
the Caribbean	408.5	40.8	20.1	11.3	8.1	7.5	7.4	5.8	10.5	13	9½
Memo items:											
Sub-Saharan Africa											
(excluding Democratic Republic of the											
Congo, Nigeria and South Africa)	32.7	22.0	20.8	12.0	8.7	9.8	10.3	11.0	14.4	12¼	12¼
Least developed countries[d]	25.3	21.4	20.0	11.8	14.4	11.9	6.0	5.6	10.7	8	8
Major developing economies											
Argentina	4.2	3.4	0.2	0.5	0.9	-1.2	-0.9	-1.1	25.9	19	12
Brazil	930.0	66.0	15.8	6.9	3.2	4.9	7.0	6.9	8.4	14	10
China	24.2	16.9	8.3	2.8	-0.8	-1.4	0.3	0.5	-0.7	1	1
Hong Kong SAR[e]	8.7	9.1	6.3	5.8	2.9	-4.0	-3.7	-1.6	-3.0	½	½
India	10.2	10.2	9.0	7.2	13.2	4.7	4.0	3.7	4.4	4	4½
Indonesia	8.5	9.4	8.0	6.7	57.6	20.5	3.7	12.6	12.6	9¼	9
Israel	12.3	10.0	11.3	9.0	5.4	5.2	1.1	-5.0	5.7	3	2½
Korea, Republic of	6.2	4.5	4.9	4.4	7.5	0.8	2.2	4.1	2.8	3¾	3
Malaysia	3.7	3.5	3.5	2.7	5.3	2.7	1.5	1.4	1.8	1½	2
Mexico	7.0	35.0	34.4	20.6	15.9	16.6	9.5	6.4	5.0	5	3¾
Saudi Arabia	0.6	4.9	1.2	0.1	-0.4	-1.6	-0.8	-0.5	-0.5	2	1½
South Africa	8.9	8.7	7.4	9.0	6.7	5.1	5.2	4.8	10.6	6¾	5
Taiwan Province of China	4.1	3.7	3.1	1.8	2.6	0.2	-1.9	0.6	-0.2	¼	½
Thailand	5.0	5.8	5.8	5.6	8.1	0.3	1.5	1.7	0.6	2	1½
Turkey	106.3	88.1	80.3	85.7	84.6	64.9	54.9	54.4	45.0	36¼	24

Source: UN/DESA, based on data of IMF, *International Financial Statistics*.

[a] Weights used are GDP in 1995 dollars.
[b] Partly estimated.
[c] Forecast, based in part on Project LINK.
[d] Excluding Democratic Republic of the Congo.
[e] Special Administrative Region of China.

Table A.11.
MAJOR DEVELOPED ECONOMIES: FINANCIAL INDICATORS, 1994-2002

Percentage	1994	1995	1996	1997	1998	1999	2000	2001	2002
Short-term interest rates[a]									
Canada	5.1	6.9	4.3	3.3	4.9	4.7	5.5	4.1	2.5
France[b]	5.7	6.4	3.7	3.2	3.4	2.7	4.2	4.3	4.0
Germany	5.3	4.5	3.3	3.2	3.4	2.7	4.1	4.4	3.3
Italy	8.5	10.5	8.8	6.9	5.0	3.0	4.4	4.3	3.3
Japan	2.2	1.2	0.5	0.5	0.4	0.1	0.1	0.1	0.0
United Kingdom	4.9	6.1	6.0	6.6	7.2	5.2	5.8	5.1	3.9
United States	4.2	5.8	5.3	5.5	5.4	5.0	6.2	3.9	1.7
Long-term interest rates[c]									
Canada	8.6	8.3	7.5	6.4	5.5	5.7	5.9	5.8	5.7
France	7.4	7.6	6.4	5.6	4.7	4.7	5.5	5.0	4.9
Germany	6.7	6.5	5.6	5.1	4.4	4.3	5.2	4.7	4.6
Italy	10.6	12.2	9.4	6.9	4.9	4.7	5.6	5.2	5.0
Japan	3.7	2.5	2.2	1.7	1.1	1.8	1.7	1.3	1.3
United Kingdom	8.0	8.3	8.1	7.1	5.4	4.7	4.7	4.8	4.8
United States	7.1	6.6	6.4	6.4	5.3	5.6	6.0	5.0	4.6
General government financial balances[d]									
Canada	-6.7	-5.3	-2.8	0.2	0.1	1.7	3.1	1.8	1.3
France	-5.6	-5.6	-4.1	-3.0	-2.7	-1.6	-1.3	-1.4	-3.1
Germany	-2.5	-3.2	-3.4	-2.7	-2.1	-1.4	1.5	-2.7	-3.6
Italy	-9.1	-7.6	-6.5	-2.7	-2.8	-1.9	-0.3	-1.4	-2.3
Japan[e]	-3.7	-4.7	-5.0	-3.8	-5.5	-7.2	-7.4	-6.8	-7.1
United Kingdom	-6.8	-5.8	-4.4	-2.0	0.4	1.3	4.3	0.9	-1.4
United States	-3.6	-3.1	-2.2	-0.9	0.3	0.7	1.4	-0.5	-3.4

Sources: UN/DESA, based on IMF, *International Financial Statistics*; OECD, *Economic Outlook*; and EUROPA (EU on line), *European Economy.*

[a]   Money market rates.
[b]   From January 1999 onward, representing the three-month Euro Interbank Offered Rate (EURIBOR), which is an Interbank deposit bid rate.
[c]   Yield on long-term government bonds.
[d]   Surplus (+) or deficit (-) as a percentage of nominal GNP or GDP.
[e]   The 1998 deficit does not take account of the assumption by the central Government of the debt of the Japan National Railway Settlement Corporation and the National Forest are Special Account, amounting to 5.2 percentage points of GDP. Deferred tax payments on postal savings accounts are included in 2000 and 2001.

Table A.12.
SELECTED COUNTRIES: REAL EFFECTIVE EXCHANGE RATES, BROAD MEASUREMENT,[a] 1994-2002

1990 = 100									
	1994	1995	1996	1997	1998	1999	2000	2001	2002
Developed economies									
Australia	89.7	87.5	96.2	97.8	90.0	92.5	86.9	83.2	88.5
Austria	109.6	112.4	110.7	107.6	108.5	107.0	103.9	105.8	107.9
Belgium	109.6	112.6	111.0	106.8	108.0	107.8	102.3	102.3	103.2
Canada	88.6	92.2	91.4	92.6	91.1	89.6	89.1	84.4	79.7
Denmark	104.5	107.6	107.8	105.7	108.7	109.3	104.4	87.6	86.6
Finland	79.4	85.2	84.0	81.7	80.6	78.4	72.7	128.2	123.7
France	102.9	103.7	103.7	98.9	100.9	98.0	91.2	110.2	106.9
Germany	99.9	105.0	101.8	95.9	96.9	94.6	90.8	106.9	109.9
Greece	106.4	108.1	113.2	114.8	111.5	114.3	112.7	144.7	164.2
Ireland	97.5	97.6	100.0	100.6	98.3	95.6	89.8	72.8	72.0
Italy	79.1	75.5	83.2	83.5	84.0	82.3	80.8	91.3	92.4
Japan	125.9	127.0	108.5	103.1	100.7	110.3	116.6	93.4	97.0
Netherlands	110.3	114.2	113.3	109.4	112.1	112.5	108.2	114.6	115.5
New Zealand	100.0	107.5	117.8	120.8	105.4	100.8	92.1	122.0	119.5
Norway	98.6	101.0	100.4	102.3	97.9	97.2	94.0	85.6	82.7
Portugal	104.2	104.1	105.4	112.6	112.6	112.5	108.7	68.3	81.8
Spain	79.8	83.1	83.2	79.5	79.9	78.2	76.5	91.3	93.2
Sweden	83.7	90.7	95.4	91.4	90.4	87.3	87.4	81.3	82.0
Switzerland	111.4	118.2	116.2	108.9	111.6	110.8	108.1	103.9	95.7
United Kingdom	92.2	89.3	91.8	105.5	109.7	108.2	109.7	73.9	77.3
United States	100.3	95.6	100.1	106.2	114.2	114.3	117.7	182.7	182.3
Developing economies									
Argentina	111.4	109.0	113.0	120.5	123.0	125.0	127.5	131.8	70.5
Brazil	94.2	100.5	98.8	105.0	103.9	77.2	93.3	84.4	79.7
Chile	113.9	120.3	126.6	135.1	128.9	125.1	135.0	128.2	123.7
Colombia	118.4	117.1	121.6	132.7	126.1	113.2	109.1	110.2	106.9
Ecuador	137.6	135.0	137.1	148.4	152.7	115.0	102.1	144.7	164.2
Hong Kong SAR[b]	113.9	112.4	120.7	130.9	137.4	125.3	121.0	122.0	119.5
India	77.7	75.6	74.0	80.9	77.8	77.2	82.6	85.6	82.7
Indonesia	99.8	98.3	103.0	96.3	47.6	72.3	70.8	68.3	81.8
Korea, Republic of	85.8	87.5	89.9	84.4	65.9	72.9	78.9	73.9	77.3
Kuwait	148.5	140.1	147.7	156.0	162.6	165.5	172.8	182.7	182.3
Malaysia	106.1	105.9	111.1	108.5	83.3	84.8	86.8	93.4	95.5
Mexico	112.2	78.9	89.8	102.8	102.4	112.7	126.2	133.1	133.4
Morocco	104.8	108.0	111.9	111.3	115.9	118.1	121.1	119.3	117.8
Nigeria	141.2	58.3	79.2	91.2	99.8	99.3	100.3	110.9	114.9
Pakistan	104.7	104.9	105.6	110.4	110.9	106.2	102.7	97.1	101.3
Peru	97.8	98.3	102.5	106.5	106.4	97.1	98.9	103.4	103.8
Philippines	104.3	103.4	114.7	107.4	83.0	88.2	86.9	92.5	95.6
Saudi Arabia	99.8	96.2	103.4	114.7	126.2	129.7	140.5	153.7	156.1
Singapore	108.8	110.0	114.8	116.8	113.4	109.0	108.9	110.1	109.5
South Africa	98.4	96.9	90.6	97.2	86.0	82.7	84.1	75.9	66.5
Taiwan Province of China	96.4	97.3	94.9	96.1	87.4	82.5	87.1	82.9	80.1
Thailand	99.2	96.2	99.8	93.8	81.9	85.7	86.3	83.8	85.7
Turkey	73.0	75.9	74.5	78.6	78.4	77.8	87.8	77.5	88.6
Venezuela	109.3	139.2	119.1	139.4	157.5	169.1	179.8	197.7	163.5

Source: Source: JPMorgan Chase.

[a] Indices based on a "broad-" measure currency basket of 22 OECD currencies and 23 developing-economy currencies (mostly Asian and Latin American). The real effective exchange rate, which adjusts the nominal index for relative price changes, gauges the effect on international price competitiveness of the country's manufactures due to currency changes and inflation differentials. A rise in the index implies a fall in competitiveness and vice versa. The relative price changes are based on indices most closely measuring the prices of domestically produced finished manufactured goods, excluding food and energy, at the first stage of manufacturing. The weights for currency indices are derived from 1990 bilateral trade patterns of the corresponding countries.

[b] Special Administrative Region of China.

II. INTERNATIONAL TRADE

Table A.13.
WORLD TRADE: CHANGES IN VALUE AND VOLUME OF EXPORTS AND IMPORTS, BY MAJOR COUNTRY GROUP, 1994-2003

Annual percentage change	1994	1995	1996	1997	1998	1999	2000	2001	2002[a]	2003[b]
Dollar value of exports										
World	13.5	19.4	4.3	3.5	-2.3	3.9	11.9	-3.8	4.1	10
Developed economies	12.5	18.9	2.6	2.3	0.3	2.2	6.4	-3.4	2.8	10½
North America	11.2	14.6	6.4	9.3	-0.7	5.0	13.0	-6.5	-2.8	6
Western Europe	13.7	22.5	3.0	-1.5	1.8	-0.3	2.3	0.6	0.5	13¾
Japan	9.6	11.6	-7.3	2.5	-7.9	8.6	10.0	-17.3	3.9	4
Economies in transition	17.5	29.1	8.0	2.2	-2.1	-1.0	27.0	5.2	7.9	9
Central and Eastern Europe and Baltic States	16.3	30.1	5.7	6.5	13.5	-1.2	14.0	11.3	10.0	9
Commonwealth of Independent States	19.0	27.9	10.9	-1.8	-17.0	-1.0	39.0	-1.4	5.6	9
Developing countries	15.5	19.5	7.6	6.4	-6.5	7.7	22.7	-5.9	6.3	8¼
Latin America and the Caribbean	16.4	20.9	10.2	10.4	-2.4	5.6	19.2	-3.6	0.7	4¾
Africa	2.7	12.5	19.7	2.5	-15.0	10.3	22.8	-5.9	2.7	8¼
Western Asia	6.6	12.3	13.6	-5.7	-24.1	25.1	43.4	-4.0	0.3	6
Eastern and Southern Asia	16.8	21.3	5.0	4.0	-6.9	6.5	18.7	-10.6	5.8	7¾
China	33.1	22.9	1.6	20.8	0.5	6.1	28.1	6.5	22.3	15
Memo items:										
Fuel exporters	5.9	15.9	19.5	0.5	-9.9	14.4	59.1	-5.9	-2.1	6¼
Non-fuel exporters	18.5	21.3	4.4	6.7	-4.7	4.7	13.1	1.2	6.4	4¾
Dollar value of imports										
World	13.3	19.4	4.8	2.8	-2.3	5.4	10.8	-4.0	3.3	10
Developed economies	13.4	18.0	3.6	2.6	1.9	5.2	9.7	-4.0	2.3	10½
North America	13.7	11.3	6.2	10.3	4.6	10.9	18.2	-6.3	1.8	7½
Western Europe	13.0	20.7	2.3	0.0	3.8	1.4	3.7	-1.9	3.5	14
Japan	13.9	22.0	4.0	-3.0	-17.2	11.2	21.4	-7.4	-5.7	2½
Economies in transition	13.0	33.4	13.9	9.0	0.5	-8.0	13.0	11.0	8.9	9¼
Central and Eastern Europe and Baltic States	14.1	37.0	16.5	6.7	13.0	-2.5	12.0	9.0	8.6	9
Commonwealth of Independent States	10.2	24.4	6.7	15.9	-19.0	-24.0	16.0	15.8	9.6	10
Developing countries	13.0	21.0	6.3	4.3	-10.2	4.4	19.9	-4.9	5.4	8
Latin America and the Caribbean	18.6	11.6	9.7	16.2	5.2	-3.7	15.8	-3.0	-6.3	5¼
Africa	5.8	21.2	2.0	6.0	-1.0	1.0	10.9	-4.2	5.1	8¾
Western Asia	-7.9	23.1	9.3	0.6	-6.4	-0.3	3.2	3.3	8.4	-2½
Eastern and Southern Asia	18.4	24.8	5.3	2.0	-20.0	7.6	23.7	-10.8	5.1	8¾
China	12.2	11.6	7.6	2.5	-1.5	18.2	35.8	8.2	21.2	16
Memo items:										
Fuel exporters	3.9	9.5	7.8	7.1	-5.7	7.3	7.4	2.7	2.6	4¼
Non-fuel exporters	15.4	23.8	5.8	3.7	-12.0	2.8	-0.8	4.0	14.4	-8¾

Table A.13 (continued)

	1994	1995	1996	1997	1998	1999	2000	2001	2002[a]	2003[b]
Volume of exports										
World	10.5	9.4	4.8	9.3	3.6	5.1	10.8	-0.9	2.0	3¾
Developed economies	9.5	7.3	4.2	9.2	4.0	4.4	9.2	-1.2	0.1	2¾
North America	9.0	9.1	6.2	10.9	3.7	6.4	10.6	-5.3	-2.5	2¾
Western Europe	11.4	7.6	3.8	7.7	5.4	3.9	10.0	2.1	0.0	3¼
Japan	1.7	3.3	0.6	9.6	-3.7	2.7	5.1	-11.8	7.0	¼
Economies in transition	2.7	13.7	6.0	-0.9	6.9	4.0	13.0	8.7	7.8	6¾
Central and Eastern Europe and Baltic States	0.2	16.7	4.5	0.8	15.0	7.0	20.0	11.6	6.0	6¾
Commonwealth of Independent States	5.8	10.0	7.9	-2.9	0.2	2.0	7.0	5.5	9.9	6¾
Developing countries	14.1	13.7	6.5	9.9	1.9	7.2	13.9	-1.5	5.8	5½
Latin America and the Caribbean	9.2	9.9	9.3	12.8	7.8	6.6	9.7	-0.1	0.7	2
Africa	11.7	7.3	8.2	5.2	-0.9	2.1	2.6	2.3	2.6	½
Western Asia	8.1	6.0	9.0	-0.7	-1.5	0.6	9.7	3.2	-1.9	-¼
Eastern and Southern Asia	14.5	16.6	5.8	9.3	0.1	10.0	15.4	-5.4	4.8	5¾
China	31.0	18.9	2.4	26.3	4.1	7.4	25.8	7.6	23.6	14¾
Memo items:										
Fuel exporters	5.7	9.0	15.1	4.9	1.2	7.5	7.7	5.1	-4.4	-1½
Non-fuel exporters	15.0	16.5	5.9	11.3	2.9	7.1	13.5	-0.3	2.8	2
Volume of imports										
World	10.5	7.8	6.1	9.0	3.0	5.3	10.2	-1.0	1.6	4¼
Developed economies	11.1	7.0	4.9	8.7	5.9	6.1	6.4	-1.6	0.0	4½
North America	12.0	7.2	5.6	13.3	10.3	10.4	15.1	-3.5	1.1	3
Western Europe	10.0	5.9	4.4	7.6	6.1	3.4	2.4	0.0	0.0	6½
Japan	13.6	12.5	3.5	2.7	-10.0	9.5	0.3	-4.3	-7.1	-2¼
Economies in transition	9.6	9.9	13.8	9.0	2.0	-6.0	15.0	12.7	9.3	8½
Central and Eastern Europe and Baltic States	13.0	11.4	17.9	7.6	10.0	5.0	15.0	9.0	6.8	8
Commonwealth of Independent States	1.3	6.0	2.4	13.6	-15.0	-28.0	14.0	21.7	15.4	10
Developing countries	9.5	9.7	8.5	10.2	-4.7	4.0	19.6	-1.1	4.4	3¾
Latin America and the Caribbean	14.4	4.2	8.4	23.1	7.2	-6.9	4.1	2.7	-8.3	½
Africa	2.0	10.8	3.8	6.3	2.0	1.5	18.2	-2.2	2.6	2¼
Western Asia	-11.1	11.3	11.8	6.4	-2.6	2.3	14.4	4.6	4.8	-7¾
Eastern and Southern Asia	14.8	12.5	8.2	8.4	-12.7	6.9	19.4	-7.4	4.0	4¾
China	9.1	0.1	11.4	9.4	6.0	18.6	52.6	12.3	20.1	12¼
Memo items:										
Fuel exporters	-0.2	-1.0	11.2	13.8	-0.2	-0.4	17.0	4.2	0.1	-½
Non-fuel exporters	11.9	11.6	8.7	10.1	-6.7	10.3	11.8	5.0	9.7	-14¼

Source: United Nations, based on data of United Nations Statistics Division, ECE, ECLAC and IMF.

[a] Partly estimated.
[b] Forecast.

Table A.14.
DIRECTION OF TRADE: EXPORTS (F.O.B.), 1990-2002

							Destination[a]						
		World[b]	Devd.	EU	US	Japan	EIT	Devg.	LAC	Africa	SSA	WA	ESA
		bn. $						Percentage					
World[b]	1990	3 381.7	72.1	43.7	14.5	6.1	..	22.8	3.8	2.8	1.1	3.5	12.8
	1995	5 077.9	65.1	37.5	14.7	5.8	4.3	29.0	5.0	2.3	0.8	3.2	18.5
	2000	6 369.2	66.6	35.7	18.5	5.3	4.1	28.5	5.7	2.0	0.7	3.3	17.5
	2002	6 389.2	65.9	36.2	17.9	4.8	4.8	28.3	5.3	2.2	0.7	3.4	17.5
Developed	1990	2 444.4	76.4	50.3	12.4	4.2	..	19.9	3.9	2.8	1.0	3.3	9.9
economies	1995	3 427.8	70.6	45.4	12.4	3.9	3.5	24.9	5.1	2.4	0.7	3.1	14.3
(Devd.)	2000	4 027.6	71.9	44.1	15.4	3.2	3.8	23.8	6.2	2.0	0.5	3.2	12.4
	2002	3 994.5	71.4	44.9	14.8	2.9	4.8	23.1	5.6	2.1	0.6	3.3	12.0
European Union	1990	1 488.4	81.8	65.9	7.0	2.1	..	13.2	1.8	3.5	1.2	3.4	4.4
(EU)	1995	2 018.3	77.4	62.4	6.7	2.1	5.3	15.7	2.5	3.0	0.9	3.5	6.8
	2000	2 284.0	78.9	62.1	9.3	1.8	6.1	14.3	2.4	2.6	0.7	3.8	5.5
	2002	2 409.0	77.6	61.0	9.4	1.7	7.3	14.1	2.2	2.7	0.7	3.7	5.5
United States	1990	393.1	63.9	26.3	-	12.4	..	34.6	13.7	2.0	0.5	3.4	15.5
(US)	1995	583.5	57.3	21.2	-	11.0	1.1	41.5	16.5	1.7	0.3	3.5	19.8
	2000	772.0	55.6	21.3	-	8.4	0.9	43.4	21.7	1.4	0.3	3.1	17.3
	2002	693.1	54.9	20.8	-	7.4	1.0	44.0	21.5	1.5	0.3	3.2	17.8
Japan	1990	287.7	58.6	20.4	31.7	-	..	40.1	3.4	1.9	0.9	3.5	31.3
	1995	443.0	47.7	15.9	27.5	-	0.5	51.7	4.2	1.7	0.7	2.2	43.7
	2000	478.2	50.9	16.4	30.1	-	0.6	48.5	3.9	1.0	0.3	2.3	41.3
	2002	412.8	48.8	14.7	29.2	-	0.7	50.5	3.6	1.1	0.4	3.1	42.7
Economies in	1995	205.7	50.6	41.6	3.9	1.8	35.6	13.0	1.6	1.3	0.2	3.9	6.2
transition	2000	284.4	58.2	49.1	4.9	1.2	28.2	13.2	1.8	1.3	0.3	4.9	5.3
(EIT)	2002	309.0	59.7	51.1	4.6	1.0	26.4	13.1	1.4	1.4	0.3	4.7	5.6

Table A.14 (continued)

							Destination[a]						
		World[b]	Devd.	EU	US	Japan	EIT	Devg.	LAC	Africa	SSA	WA	ESA
		bn. $						Percentage					
Developing	1990	831.3	61.3	23.4	22.2	12.2	..	32.5	4.0	2.5	1.4	4.0	21.9
countries	1995	1 442.0	54.1	18.1	21.9	10.9	1.6	41.2	5.2	2.4	1.2	3.4	30.2
(Devg.)	2000	2 054.5	57.4	17.5	26.5	10.0	1.1	39.6	5.1	2.1	1.0	3.3	29.1
	2002	2 083.1	56.2	17.3	25.9	9.0	1.4	40.5	5.1	2.3	1.1	3.4	29.6
Latin America	1990	128.0	71.9	24.5	38.9	5.6	..	24.7	16.5	1.5	0.4	2.1	4.6
and the Caribbean	1995	228.5	68.0	16.7	44.4	3.9	0.9	29.1	20.7	1.3	0.4	1.3	5.9
(LAC)	2000	366.6	73.9	11.3	57.8	2.2	0.7	22.7	17.7	0.8	0.2	1.0	3.4
	2002	355.9	72.2	12.3	53.3	2.1	1.0	24.9	18.1	1.1	0.2	1.2	4.5
Africa	1990	98.7	71.0	50.6	14.8	3.0	..	14.2	1.1	7.1	5.2	2.3	3.7
	1995	102.3	65.9	47.1	13.2	3.0	1.4	23.9	1.9	10.5	7.8	3.0	8.5
	2000	140.5	70.2	47.8	16.6	2.1	1.1	26.1	3.5	9.0	6.8	3.5	10.2
	2002	143.5	70.5	48.6	14.5	3.4	1.2	25.9	3.5	9.2	7.0	3.6	9.6
Sub-Saharan	1990	28.1	74.9	49.8	16.9	3.4	..	21.2	1.7	11.9	9.2	1.3	6.4
Africa	1995	29.8	69.6	46.6	17.6	3.7	1.7	26.8	1.2	13.5	9.5	2.2	9.9
(SSA)	2000	43.8	59.7	36.3	17.5	2.1	1.6	33.8	2.2	11.0	8.1	1.4	19.2
	2002	47.4	63.9	41.2	15.3	2.8	1.7	29.6	2.3	10.6	8.2	1.3	15.4
Western Asia	1990	149.4	59.7	25.4	13.7	17.7	..	31.0	3.0	2.9	0.9	10.6	14.6
(WA)	1995	169.6	50.3	22.8	10.3	15.1	3.4	34.4	1.6	3.0	0.8	9.9	19.8
	2000	278.4	52.7	20.5	14.0	16.1	1.7	38.8	1.0	3.3	0.8	7.8	26.7
	2002	264.2	49.8	20.4	13.6	13.7	2.2	40.0	1.2	3.8	1.0	8.6	26.4
Eastern and	1990	455.2	56.8	16.5	21.9	14.3	..	39.1	1.5	1.7	1.0	2.8	33.1
Southern Asia	1995	941.6	50.2	14.5	19.5	12.7	1.4	47.2	2.4	1.7	0.8	2.7	40.4
(including China)	2000	1 269.1	52.2	15.3	21.3	11.8	1.2	46.2	2.6	1.5	0.6	2.9	39.1
(ESA)	2002	1 319.5	51.6	14.7	22.1	10.6	1.5	46.4	2.6	1.6	0.7	2.9	39.2

Source: UN/DESA, based on IMF, *Direction of Trade Statistics.*

a   Owing to incomplete specification of destinations in underlying data, shares of trade to destinations do not add up to 100 per cent.
b   Including data for economies in transition; before 1994, data for economies in transition are highly incomplete.

Table A.15.
COMPOSITION OF WORLD MERCHANDISE TRADE: EXPORTS, 1990-2001

Billions of dollars and percentage

Exporting country group	Total exports (billions of dollars)			Primary commodities											
				Total			Food			Agricultural raw materials			Fuels		
	1990	1995	2001	1990	1995	2001	1990	1995	2001	1990	1995	2001	1990	1995	2001
World (billions of dollars)	2 848.5	4 906.4	5 814.4	797.5	990.1	1 119.0	268.8	413.9	395.8	119.2	176.0	142.6	372.7	331.4	515.1
World (percentage share)	-	-	-	100.0	100.0	100.0	100.0	100.0	100.0	100.0	100.0	100.0	100.0	100.0	100.0
Developed economies	1 865.1	3 338.6	3 696.0	45.1	51.6	47.6	63.0	65.8	66.0	62.2	60.3	62.0	23.0	31.3	31.0
Economies in transition[a]	124.6	194.7	254.1	6.1	6.5	7.3	3.5	3.7	2.9	5.3	6.8	5.5	8.2	9.1	11.0
Developing countries	858.9	1 973.0	1 864.3	48.8	41.9	45.2	33.5	30.5	31.1	32.5	32.9	32.5	68.8	59.6	58.0
Africa	92.5	111.4	103.4	8.5	7.1	7.0	4.1	4.0	2.8	5.1	4.1	3.3	13.7	12.1	11.1
Latin America	154.3	237.6	351.2	11.0	10.7	11.6	14.5	12.6	14.1	7.3	8.5	11.4	9.3	8.5	9.1
Eastern and Southern Asia	459.1	862.6	1 170.5	13.4	13.1	11.9	13.1	12.2	12.4	19.0	19.1	16.5	12.3	11.1	10.1
Western Asia	153.0	163.9	244.6	16.0	11.1	14.6	1.9	1.8	1.9	1.1	1.1	1.3	33.6	27.9	27.7
Memo items: Sub-Saharan Africa	29.7	33.5	36.4	2.6	2.4	2.5	2.6	2.6	2.1	3.1	2.7	2.8	2.3	2.1	2.7
Least developed countries	58.4	24.2	33.7	2.9	1.5	1.7	2.0	1.3	0.9	3.0	1.7	1.5	3.9	1.5	2.3

Table A.15 (continued)

Exporting country group				Manufactures														
				of which:														
	Total			Textiles			Chemicals			Machinery and transport			Metals		
	1990	1995	2001	1990	1995	2001	1990	1995	2001	1990	1995	2001	1990	1995	2001
World (billions of dollars)	1 992.0	3 797.8	4 577.2	178.2	325.9	359.5	236.4	455.4	562.9	953.1	1 890.6	2 418.9	152.7	267.0	223.3
World (percentage share)	100.0	100.0	100.0	100.0	100.0	100.0	100.0	100.0	100.0	100.0	100.0	100.0	100.0	100.0	100.0
Developed economies	73.3	72.0	67.0	42.1	42.2	36.2	81.0	80.2	80.4	79.7	77.7	69.7	65.2	63.0	66.5
Economies in transition[a]	3.7	3.3	3.5	2.1	4.1	4.2	3.6	4.3	2.8	3.7	1.4	2.8	8.5	14.4	9.8
Developing countries	23.0	24.7	29.5	55.7	53.7	59.6	15.4	15.5	16.8	16.5	20.9	27.5	26.3	22.5	23.8
Africa	1.1	0.9	0.5	2.5	2.5	2.4	1.4	1.0	0.4	0.3	0.2	0.2	6.2	3.2	1.0
Latin America	3.3	3.3	4.7	3.4	4.3	6.8	2.9	2.8	2.9	2.6	2.8	4.8	9.4	7.9	8.1
Eastern and Southern Asia	17.3	19.2	22.8	47.3	43.4	46.1	8.2	9.5	11.1	13.2	17.3	21.8	8.7	9.6	12.4
Western Asia	1.3	1.3	1.5	2.5	3.4	4.2	2.9	2.2	2.4	0.4	0.5	0.7	2.0	1.9	2.2
Memo items: Sub-Saharan Africa	0.5	0.2	0.2	0.5	0.5	0.5	0.3	0.1	0.1	0.2	0.0	0.1	2.2	0.8	0.7
Least developed countries	1.6	0.2	0.3	1.6	1.3	2.6	1.6	0.1	0.1	1.6	0.0	0.1	2.6	0.2	0.4

Source: UN/DESA, based on COMTRADE.

[a]   Data for 1995 onward including trade flows between the States of the former Union of Soviet Socialist Republics (USSR). Prior to 1992, these flows were considered internal.

Table A.16.
COMPOSITION OF WORLD MERCHANDISE TRADE: IMPORTS, 1990-2001

Billions of dollars and percentage

Importing country group	Total imports (billions of dollars)			Primary commodities											
				Total			of which:								
							Food			Agricultural raw materials			Fuels		
	1990	1995	2001	1990	1995	2001	1990	1995	2001	1990	1995	2001	1990	1995	2001
World (billions of dollars)	2 848.5	4 906.4	5 814.4	797.5	990.1	1 119.0	268.8	413.9	395.8	119.2	176.0	142.6	372.7	331.4	515.1
World (percentage share)	-	-	-	100.0	100.0	100.0	100.0	100.0	100.0	100.0	100.0	100.0	100.0	100.0	100.0
Developed economies	1 941.6	3 381.7	4 144.2	68.6	72.3	74.8	66.2	71.3	72.7	66.0	67.9	65.6	69.0	75.3	79.5
Economies in transition[a]	128.9	193.4	240.7	5.5	5.3	4.6	8.2	6.0	5.1	3.9	2.6	3.9	4.2	6.2	4.4
Developing countries	778.0	1 331.3	1 429.5	25.9	22.4	20.6	25.6	22.7	22.2	30.1	29.5	30.4	26.8	18.5	16.1
Africa	98.8	112.7	87.4	3.0	2.6	1.7	4.9	3.6	3.3	3.7	3.1	2.0	1.4	1.4	0.5
Latin America	110.7	233.9	314.5	4.4	4.5	4.7	4.7	4.6	5.9	3.9	4.5	5.1	4.5	4.8	3.9
Eastern and Southern Asia	467.3	834.7	856.2	15.2	12.4	11.7	10.9	10.5	9.2	19.8	19.4	20.5	18.3	10.8	10.3
Western Asia	101.2	150	171.4	3.3	2.8	2.5	5.2	4.0	3.9	2.8	2.6	2.7	2.7	1.5	1.3
Memo items:															
Sub-Saharan Africa	29.6	39.6	37.5	1.0	1.0	0.6	1.5	1.3	1.2	0.8	1.0	0.6	0.7	0.7	0.8
Least developed countries	27.4	35.7	34	1.0	1.0	0.7	1.6	1.4	1.1	1.7	1.0	1.0	2.7	0.5	0.3

Table A.16 (continued)

Importing country group		Total				Manufactures										
										of which:						
				Textiles			Chemicals			Machinery and transport			Metals		
	1990	1995	2001	1990	1995	2001	1990	1995	2001	1990	1995	2001	1990	1995	2001
World (billions of dollars)	1 992.0	3 773.2	4 504.9	178.2	321.3	346.1	236.4	468.0	576.5	953.1	1 881.2	2 364.1	152.7	258.7	235.2
World (percentage share)	100.0	100.0	100.0	100.0	100.0	100.0	100.0	100.0	100.0	100.0	100.0	100.0	100.0	100.0	100.0
Developed economies	68.0	68.1	70.4	69.5	68.1	71.0	61.6	67.3	69.7	66.8	66.5	68.9	63.9	66.8	67.6
Economies in transition[a]	4.2	3.6	4.0	2.6	4.9	4.1	4.4	4.1	4.6	5.1	3.1	3.7	4.4	3.2	5.3
Developing countries	27.9	28.4	25.6	27.9	27.0	24.9	34.0	28.6	25.6	28.1	30.4	27.4	31.7	30.0	27.2
Africa	3.6	2.2	1.5	2.5	2.4	2.1	4.5	2.5	1.5	4.0	2.3	1.5	3.2	2.0	1.5
Latin America	3.8	4.9	5.6	2.1	4.0	5.5	5.9	5.7	6.6	4.0	5.4	5.8	3.4	3.2	4.3
Eastern and Southern Asia	16.9	18.2	15.5	19.8	16.9	14.2	19.4	17.5	14.6	16.9	19.9	17.2	20.0	21.4	17.7
Western Asia	3.6	3.1	3.0	3.5	3.6	3.1	4.1	3.0	2.9	3.2	2.8	3.0	5.0	3.4	3.7
Memo items: Sub-Saharan Africa	1.1	0.8	0.5	0.8	0.7	0.6	1.1	0.8	0.5	1.3	0.8	0.6	0.7	0.6	0.4
Least developed countries	1.0	0.7	0.6	1.2	3.7	3.7	0.9	3.1	3.1	1.1	0.7	0.5	2.2	0.5	0.5

Source: UN/DESA, based on COMTRADE.

[a]   Data for 1995 onward, including trade flows between the States of the former Union of Soviet Socialist Republics (USSR). Prior to 1992, these flows were considered internal.

Table A.17.
INDICES OF PRICES OF PRIMARY COMMODITIES, 1994-2003

		Non-fuel commodities[a]							Manufac-tured export prices[b]	Real prices of non-fuel commodities[c]	*Memo item:* Crude petroleum[d]
		Food	Tropical beverages	Vegetable oilseeds and oils	Agricultural raw materials	Minerals and metals	Combined index				
							Dollar	SDR			
1994		152	91	107	140	124	130	92	99	83	57.5
1995		160	92	118	161	149	143	96	110	82	62.4
1996		170	78	113	145	131	137	96	106	81	75.1
1997		162	104	112	130	131	136	100	99	87	69.2
1998		140	86	120	116	110	118	89	95	78	45.5
1999		114	68	92	104	108	102	76	91	71	64.7
2000		120	59	71	106	121	104	80	87	75	102.2
2001		126	46	65	104	109	101	80	84	76	85.6
2002		121	50	82	97	107	99	78	86	73	90.2
2000	I	114	66	79	101	123	104	77	89	74	95.0
	II	117	61	76	105	119	103	79	88	74	99.3
	III	122	56	67	111	122	105	82	86	77	109.4
	IV	128	52	63	108	119	105	83	84	79	104.9
2001	I	133	50	61	110	118	107	84	87	77	88.7
	II	127	48	60	106	114	102	82	84	77	96.5
	III	127	44	73	106	105	101	80	84	76	90.5
	IV	119	42	70	95	101	94	75	83	72	67.2
2002	I	119	47	71	93	107	96	78	82	74	72.2
	II	120	48	78	96	109	98	78	84	74	92.3
	III	120	51	86	100	105	100	76	87	72	97.9
	IV	126	55	92	99	107	103	78	89	73	98.0
2003	I	129	56	93	107	112	107	79	..	..	177.9

Sources: UNCTAD, *Monthly Commodity Price Bulletin*; United Nations, *Monthly Bulletin of Statistics* and *OPEC Bulletin.*

a   All non-fuel commodity indices are based on 1985.
b   Index of prices of manufactures exported by developed countries (1990 base year).
c   Combined index of non-fuel commodity prices in dollars deflated by manufactured export price index.
d   Composite price of the OPEC basket of seven crudes.

Table A.18.
WORLD OIL SUPPLY, DEMAND AND PRICES, 1994-2003

	1994	1995	1996	1997	1998	1999	2000	2001	2002	2003
World oil supply[a, b] (millions of barrels per day)	68.4	70.1	72.0	74.3	75.5	74.1	76.8	76.8	76.6	79.4
Developed economies	17.6	18.0	18.4	18.6	18.4	18.1	18.5	18.3	18.3	18.6
Economies in transition	7.5	7.3	7.3	7.4	7.5	7.7	8.1	8.7	9.6	10.2
Developing countries	41.9	43.3	44.8	46.7	48.0	46.7	48.5	48.0	46.9	48.8
OPEC[c]	27.3	27.7	28.4	29.9	30.8	29.4	30.7	30.1	28.5	30.0
Non-OPEC[d]	14.6	15.7	16.4	16.8	17.1	17.3	17.8	17.9	18.4	18.8
Processing gains[e]	1.4	1.5	1.5	1.6	1.6	1.7	1.7	1.7	1.8	1.8
World total demand[f]	68.9	69.9	71.6	73.1	73.5	75.3	76.2	76.5	76.9	78.0
Oil prices (dollars per barrel)										
OPEC basket	15.53	16.86	20.29	18.68	12.28	17.47	27.60	23.13	24.36	26.00
Brent oil	15.83	17.06	20.45	19.12	12.72	17.81	28.27	24.42	24.97	28.00

Sources: United Nations; International Energy Agency, *Monthly Oil Market Report*, various issues; and Middle East Economic Survey; http://www.mees.com/Energy_Tables/basket.htm (accessed on 30 April 2003).

a   Including crude oil, condensates, natural gas liquids (NGLs), oil from non-conventional sources and other sources of supply.
b   Totals may not add up because of rounding.
c   Energy Information Administration (United States Department of Energy) for 2003.
d   Including Ecuador starting in 1993, including neutral zone, and excluding Gabon starting in 1995.
e   Net volume gains and losses in refining process (excluding net gain/loss in the economies in transition and China) and marine transportation losses.
f   Including deliveries from refineries/primary stocks and marine bunkers, and refinery fuel and non-conventional oils.

III. INTERNATIONAL FINANCE AND FINANCIAL MARKETS

Table A.19.

WORLD BALANCE OF PAYMENTS ON CURRENT ACCOUNT, BY COUNTRY GROUP, 1994-2002

Billions of dollars									
	1994	1995	1996	1997	1998	1999	2000	2001[a]	2002[b]
Developed countries	15.0	54.1	39.3	86.2	-28.6	-164.1	-274.1	-244.6	-275.0
Euro area	20.5	56.3	80.7	100.8	63.8	24.9	-21.8	10.6	64.7
Japan	130.3	111.0	65.8	96.8	118.7	114.6	119.7	87.8	112.9
United States	-118.2	-105.8	-117.8	-128.4	-203.9	-292.9	-410.3	-393.4	-503.5
Developing countries[c]	-71.9	-97.0	-70.6	-43.8	-11.3	66.4	122.6	99.8	163.4
Net fuel exporters	-45.5	-16.2	18.6	1.7	-51.5	16.3	99.4	50.5	50.1
Net fuel importers	-26.4	-80.8	-89.2	-45.5	40.2	50.1	23.3	49.3	113.3
Net-creditor countries	9.8	20.3	37.5	38.6	8.6	37.9	85.8	81.1	89.2
Net-debtor countries	-81.7	-117.3	-108.1	-82.4	-19.9	28.5	36.8	18.7	74.2
Economies in transition	1.3	-4.4	-12.9	-27.7	-29.0	-2.1	27.2	14.5	10.2
Central and Eastern Europe	-3.3	-7.4	-16.7	-19.3	-19.4	-23.8	-19.6	-17.4	-21.4
Commonwealth of Independent States	4.6	3.8	5.2	-6.5	-7.2	23.8	48.2	33.5	33.8
World residual[d]	55.6	47.3	44.2	-14.7	68.9	99.9	124.3	130.3	101.5
Trade residual	-96.5	-114.4	-101.9	-117.4	-80.3	-52.2	-29.0	-12.2	-59.6

Source: United Nations, based on data of IMF and other national and international sources.

Note: Aggregates for major country groupings may not add up due to rounding.

[a] Partially estimated.
[b] Preliminary estimate.
[c] Ninety-five economies.
[d] Unreported trade, services, income and transfers, as well as errors and timing asymmetries in reported data.

Table A.20.
CURRENT-ACCOUNT TRANSACTIONS: DEVELOPED ECONOMIES, 1994-2002

Billions of dollars

	1994	1995	1996	1997	1998	1999	2000	2001	2002[a]
All developed economies[b]									
Goods: exports (f.o.b.)	2 871.1	3 434.8	3 528.8	3 616.5	3 644.6	3 711.6	3 970.8	3 824.2	3 901.7
Goods: imports (f.o.b.)	-2 777.1	-3 312.1	-3 436.1	-3 520.6	-3 617.8	-3 821.2	-4 207.3	-4 024.8	-4 098.0
Trade balance	94.0	122.8	92.6	95.9	26.8	-109.6	-236.5	-200.7	-196.3
Net services, income and current transfers	-78.9	-68.7	-53.3	-9.7	-55.4	-54.6	-37.6	-44.0	-78.7
Net investment income	0.4	11.7	17.5	38.2	21.6	29.3	53.3	45.8	23.7
Current-account balance	15.0	54.1	39.3	86.2	-28.6	-164.1	-274.1	-244.6	-275.0
Major industrialized countries									
Goods: exports (f.o.b.)	2 117.6	2 477.7	2 537.5	2 626.7	2 626.9	2 684.7	2 890.9	2 750.7	2 781.7
Goods: imports (f.o.b.)	-2 049.5	-2 396.5	-2 494.7	-2 586.0	-2 632.0	-2 810.9	-3 159.9	-3 004.3	-3 044.9
Trade balance	68.1	81.1	42.8	40.7	-5.1	-126.1	-269.0	-253.6	-263.3
Net services, income and current transfers	-79.6	-77.6	-52.3	-15.9	-44.2	-58.5	-37.5	-26.8	-58.6
Net investment income	30.8	30.3	44.8	56.0	49.7	48.9	76.0	83.3	57.7
Current-account balance	-11.5	3.6	-9.5	24.7	-49.3	-184.6	-306.5	-280.4	-321.9
Euro area									
Goods: exports (f.o.b.)	1 324.0	1 653.1	1 688.3	1 668.0	1 766.2	1 757.2	1 790.4	1 813.5	1 895.9
Goods: imports (f.o.b.)	-1 234.0	-1 527.3	-1 540.2	-1 515.7	-1 616.0	-1 651.9	-1 734.6	-1 704.2	-1 739.9
Trade balance	90.0	125.8	148.1	152.3	150.2	105.3	55.8	109.3	156.0
Net services, income and current transfers	-69.5	-69.5	-67.5	-51.5	-86.4	-80.4	-77.6	-98.7	-91.3
Net investment income	-31.9	-32.5	-31.1	-23.7	-45.5	-38.5	-35.9	-49.0	-63.6
Current-account balance	20.5	56.3	80.7	100.8	63.8	24.9	-21.8	10.6	64.7
Japan									
Goods: exports (f.o.b.)	385.7	428.7	400.3	409.2	374.0	403.7	459.5	383.6	394.9
Goods: imports (f.o.b.)	-241.5	-296.9	-316.7	-307.6	-251.7	-280.4	-342.8	-313.4	-301.3
Trade balance	144.2	131.8	83.6	101.6	122.4	123.3	116.7	70.2	93.6
Net services, income and current transfers	-13.9	-20.7	-17.8	-4.8	-3.6	-8.7	2.9	17.6	19.2
Net investment income	40.9	45.0	53.5	58.2	54.6	57.5	60.4	69.3	66.0
Current-account balance	130.3	111.0	65.8	96.8	118.7	114.6	119.7	87.8	112.9
United States									
Goods: exports (f.o.b.)	504.9	577.1	614.0	680.3	672.4	686.3	774.6	721.8	685.4
Goods: imports (f.o.b.)	-668.7	-749.4	-803.1	-876.5	-917.1	-1 030.0	-1 224.4	-1 146.0	-1 167.0
Trade balance	-163.8	-172.3	-189.1	-196.2	-244.7	-343.7	-449.8	-424.2	-481.6
Net services, income and current transfers	45.6	66.5	71.3	67.8	40.9	50.8	39.5	30.8	-21.9
Net investment income	21.1	29.1	28.6	25.1	12.7	23.9	27.7	20.5	-1.2
Current-account balance	-118.2	-105.8	-117.8	-128.4	-203.9	-292.9	-410.3	-393.4	-503.5

Source: United Nations, based on data of IMF and national sources.

[a] Preliminary estimate.
[b] Figures may not add up owing to rounding.

Table A.21.
CURRENT-ACCOUNT TRANSACTIONS: ECONOMIES IN TRANSITION, 1994-2002

Billions of dollars									
	1994	1995	1996	1997	1998	1999	2000	2001[a]	2002[b]
Economies in transition[c]									
Goods: exports (f.o.b.)	172.0	218.4	234.6	245.1	236.5	232.9	291.5	306.4	339.0
Goods: imports (f.o.b.)	-168.9	-220.5	-252.4	-272.8	-266.2	-234.9	-263.1	-292.4	-326.1
Trade balance	3.1	-2.2	-17.7	-27.7	-29.7	-1.9	28.4	14.1	12.9
Net services, income and current transfers	-1.8	-2.2	4.8	0.0	0.6	-0.2	-1.2	0.5	-2.7
Net investment income	-6.5	-7.8	-9.8	-13.8	-18.4	-15.1	-15.8	-12.7	-14.7
Current-account balance	1.3	-4.4	-12.9	-27.7	-29.0	-2.1	27.2	14.5	10.2
Commonwealth of Independent States									
Goods: exports (f.o.b.)	95.0	115.6	126.0	124.3	106.7	107.6	146.3	145.0	154.7
Goods: imports (f.o.b.)	-81.7	-99.8	-112.6	-117.9	-98.5	-73.3	-83.9	-96.4	-106.4
Trade balance	13.3	15.8	13.4	6.4	8.1	34.3	62.4	48.7	48.3
Net services, income and current transfers	-8.7	-12.0	-8.2	-12.9	-15.3	-10.6	-14.2	-15.1	-14.5
Net investment income	-1.8	-3.3	-5.9	-9.4	-13.0	-9.4	-9.5	-6.4	-6.4
Current-account balance	4.6	3.8	5.2	-6.5	-7.2	23.8	48.2	33.5	33.8
Russian Federation									
Goods: exports (f.o.b.)	67.4	82.4	89.7	86.9	74.4	75.5	105.0	101.9	107.2
Goods: imports (f.o.b.)	-50.5	-62.6	-68.1	-72.0	-58.0	-39.5	-44.9	-53.8	-61.0
Trade balance	16.9	19.8	21.6	14.9	16.4	36.0	60.2	48.1	46.3
Net services, income and current transfers	-9.1	-12.9	-10.7	-15.0	-16.2	-11.4	-13.3	-13.2	-13.5
Net investment income	-1.7	-3.1	-5.0	-8.4	-11.6	-7.9	-7.0	-4.1	-4.3
Current-account balance	7.8	7.0	10.8	-0.1	0.2	24.6	46.8	35.0	32.8
Baltic States									
Goods: exports (f.o.b.)	4.3	5.8	6.7	8.3	8.7	7.5	9.4	10.4	12.1
Goods imports (f.o.b.)	-5.1	-7.7	-9.4	-11.4	-12.4	-10.8	-12.3	-13.7	-16.0
Trade balance	-0.9	-1.9	-2.7	-3.1	-3.8	-3.3	-2.9	-3.2	-3.9
Net services, income and current transfers	0.8	1.2	1.3	1.2	1.3	1.2	1.5	1.6	1.7
Net investment income	-	-	-0.1	-0.3	-0.3	-0.4	-0.5	-0.6	-0.6
Current-account balance	-0.1	-0.8	-1.4	-1.9	-2.4	-2.1	-1.5	-1.6	-2.2

Table 21 (continued)

	1994	1995	1996	1997	1998	1999	2000	2001[a]	2002[b]
Central and Eastern Europe[c]									
Goods: exports (f.o.b.)	72.8	97.0	102.0	112.5	121.2	117.9	135.8	151.0	172.2
Goods: imports (f.o.b.)	-82.1	-113.1	-130.4	-143.4	-155.2	-150.8	-166.8	-182.3	-203.7
Trade balance	-9.4	-16.0	-28.4	-30.9	-34.0	-33.0	-31.0	-31.4	-31.5
Net services, income and current transfers	6.1	8.7	11.7	11.6	14.6	9.2	11.5	14.0	10.1
Net investment income	-4.7	-4.5	-3.8	-4.0	-5.1	-5.3	-5.8	-5.8	-7.6
Current-account balance	-3.3	-7.4	-16.7	-19.3	-19.4	-23.8	-19.6	-17.4	-21.4
Central Europe									
Goods: exports (f.o.b.)	55.5	76.3	80.9	90.7	98.9	97.0	111.4	125.1	142.8
Goods: imports (f.o.b.)	-61.5	-85.3	-99.6	-110.3	-119.9	-118.5	-130.6	-140.6	-155.6
Trade balance	-6.0	-8.9	-18.8	-19.6	-21.0	-21.5	-19.2	-15.5	-12.8
Net services, income and current transfers	3.3	6.2	7.6	7.3	8.2	3.6	3.9	4.7	-0.1
Net investment income	-4.2	-3.8	-3.0	-3.2	-4.0	-4.1	-4.6	-4.4	-5.8
Current-account balance	-2.7	-2.7	-11.1	-12.3	-12.8	-17.9	-15.3	-10.8	-12.9
Southern and Eastern Europe									
Goods: exports (f.o.b.)	17.3	20.7	21.1	21.8	22.3	20.9	24.4	25.9	29.4
Goods: imports (f.o.b.)	-20.7	-27.8	-30.8	-33.1	-35.3	-32.3	-36.3	-41.7	-48.2
Trade balance	-3.4	-7.1	-9.7	-11.3	-13.0	-11.5	-11.8	-15.8	-18.8
Net services, income and current transfers	2.8	2.5	4.7	4.1	6.4	5.6	7.5	9.4	10.3
Net investment income	-0.6	-0.7	-0.9	-0.8	-1.1	-1.2	-1.2	-1.4	-1.5
Current-account balance	-0.6	-4.6	-5.0	-7.3	-6.7	-5.8	-4.4	-6.4	-8.5

Source: UN/DESA, based on data of IMF and ECE.

[a]   Partially estimated.
[b]   Preliminary estimate.
[c]   Figures may not add up owing to rounding.

Table A.22.
CURRENT-ACCOUNT TRANSACTIONS: DEVELOPING ECONOMIES, 1994-2002

Billions of dollars

	1994	1995	1996	1997	1998	1999	2000	2001[a]	2002[b]
Developing countries[c]									
Goods: exports (f.o.b.)	1 189.5	1 430.9	1 576.4	1 684.7	1 557.4	1 687.1	2 085.3	1 950.0	2 073.0
Goods: imports (f.o.b.)	-1 190.0	-1 437.0	-1 549.4	-1 635.5	-1 474.3	-1 523.3	-1 848.2	-1 751.2	-1 829.9
Trade balance	-0.5	-6.1	27.0	49.2	83.1	163.8	237.1	198.7	243.1
Net services, income and current transfers	-71.4	-90.8	-97.6	-93.0	-94.4	-97.4	-114.5	-98.9	-79.7
Net investment income	-68.2	-83.5	-90.3	-88.8	-97.7	-99.4	-105.9	-104.4	-107.4
Current-account balance	-71.9	-97.0	-70.6	-43.8	-11.3	66.4	122.6	99.8	163.4
Net fuel exporters									
Goods: exports (f.o.b.)	293.9	345.9	413.5	438.3	374.4	446.4	616.8	561.6	564.4
Goods: imports (f.o.b.)	-260.6	-284.4	-309.0	-347.5	-349.7	-353.2	-418.7	-420.6	-423.9
Trade balance	33.4	61.5	104.5	90.7	24.7	93.2	198.1	141.0	140.6
Net services, income and current transfers	-78.8	-77.7	-85.9	-89.0	-76.2	-76.8	-98.7	-90.5	-90.5
Net investment income	-25.6	-24.3	-26.2	-23.1	-24.1	-25.8	-30.2	-30.1	-31.2
Current-account balance	-45.5	-16.2	18.6	1.7	-51.5	16.3	99.4	50.5	50.1
Net fuel importers									
Goods: exports (f.o.b.)	895.6	1 084.9	1 162.9	1 246.4	1 183.0	1 240.7	1 468.6	1 388.4	1 508.5
Goods: imports (f.o.b.)	-929.5	-1 152.6	-1 240.4	-1288.0	-1 124.6	-1 170.1	-1 429.5	-1 330.6	-1 406.0
Trade balance	-33.9	-67.6	-77.5	-41.6	58.4	70.6	39.0	57.7	102.5
Net services, income and current transfers	7.5	-13.2	-11.7	-4.0	-18.2	-20.5	-15.8	-8.5	10.8
Net investment income	-42.6	-59.2	-64.1	-65.7	-73.5	-73.6	-75.7	-74.3	-76.2
Current-account balance	-26.4	-80.8	-89.2	-45.5	40.2	50.1	23.3	49.3	113.3
Net-creditor countries									
Goods: exports (f.o.b.)	290.2	342.4	380.3	386.6	320.9	360.4	474.1	417.8	429.3
Goods: imports (f.o.b.)	-243.5	-289.2	-298.1	-314.1	-275.7	-283.5	-339.7	-294.0	-299.6
Trade balance	46.7	53.2	82.1	72.5	45.2	76.9	134.4	123.7	129.7
Net services, income and current transfers	-36.9	-32.9	-44.6	-33.9	-36.6	-39.0	-48.6	-42.7	-40.6
Net investment income	9.8	14.2	12.8	18.5	15.6	17.0	17.2	15.4	1.1
Current-account balance	9.8	20.3	37.5	38.6	8.6	37.9	85.8	81.1	89.2
Net-debtor countries									
Goods: exports (f.o.b.)	899.3	1 088.4	1 196.1	1 298.1	1 236.5	1 326.7	1 611.2	1 532.2	1 643.7
Goods: imports (f.o.b.)	-946.5	-1 147.8	-1 251.3	-1 321.5	-1 198.6	-1239.8	-1 508.6	-1 457.2	-1 530.3
Trade balance	-47.2	-59.4	-55.1	-23.3	37.9	86.9	102.7	75.0	113.3
Net services, income and current transfers	-34.5	-57.9	-53.0	-59.1	-57.8	-58.3	-65.9	-56.3	-39.1
Net investment income	-78.0	-97.7	-103.0	-107.2	-113.3	-116.4	-123.1	-119.8	-108.5
Current-account balance	-81.7	-117.3	-108.1	-82.4	-19.9	28.5	36.8	18.7	74.2

Table 22 (continued)

	1994	1995	1996	1997	1998	1999	2000	2001ᵃ	2002ᵇ
Totals by region:									
Latin America									
Goods: exports (f.o.b.)	193.8	236.0	264.1	293.2	289.3	305.6	366.1	352.0	353.6
Goods: imports (f.o.b.)	-207.8	-234.9	-261.8	-309.7	-328.2	-316.2	-366.7	-359.2	-334.4
Trade balance	-14.0	1.0	2.3	-16.5	-38.9	-10.6	-0.6	-7.2	19.2
Net services, income and current transfers	-37.4	-39.2	-41.0	-49.5	-49.8	-44.2	-46.8	-45.4	-34.4
Net investment income	-37.9	-42.6	-44.6	-49.4	-52.9	-52.6	-54.3	-55.9	-53.4
Current-account balance	-51.3	-38.1	-38.7	-66.0	-88.7	-54.8	-47.4	-52.6	-15.2
Africa									
Goods: exports (f.o.b.)	95.0	110.6	122.8	124.9	106.3	115.1	150.4	139.6	142.4
Goods: imports (f.o.b.)	-95.5	-111.6	-111.7	-118.3	-118.3	-116.0	-120.5	-122.0	-125.1
Trade balance	-0.5	-1.0	11.0	6.6	-12.0	-0.9	29.9	17.6	17.3
Net services, income and current transfers	-9.5	-11.8	-8.4	-10.9	-8.8	-7.8	-12.1	-9.2	-11.8
Net investment income	-12.0	-12.8	-13.6	-11.8	-10.2	-11.8	-13.3	-13.4	-12.8
Current-account balance	-10.0	-12.7	2.6	-4.3	-20.8	-8.7	17.8	8.4	5.5
Western Asia									
Goods: exports (f.o.b.)	156.9	176.9	216.0	219.7	178.5	216.3	299.4	277.9	281.9
Goods: imports (f.o.b.)	-137.8	-165.8	-179.9	-188.4	-184.6	-178.7	-210.7	-202.0	-214.7
Trade balance	19.0	11.1	36.2	31.3	-6.1	37.6	88.7	75.9	67.2
Net services, income and current transfers	-27.9	-20.9	-31.1	-26.7	-13.5	-24.6	-32.7	-32.5	-32.4
Net investment income	-3.2	0.2	0.4	1.8	2.3	-1.1	-4.5	-4.8	-3.8
Current-account balance	-8.9	-9.8	5.0	4.6	-19.6	13.0	56.0	43.4	34.8
Eastern and Southern Asia									
Goods: exports (f.o.b.)	743.8	907.4	973.5	1 046.9	983.3	1 050.1	1 269.5	1 180.5	1 295.1
Goods: imports (f.o.b.)	-748.9	-924.7	-996.0	-1 019.1	-843.1	-912.4	-1 150.4	-1 068.1	-1 155.7
Trade balance	-5.1	-17.3	-22.5	27.7	140.1	137.6	119.1	112.4	139.4
Net services, income and current transfers	3.4	-19.0	-17.1	-5.9	-22.3	-20.7	-22.9	-11.8	-1.1
Net investment income	-15.1	-28.4	-32.4	-29.3	-36.8	-33.8	-33.8	-30.4	-37.4
Current-account balance	-1.7	-36.3	-39.6	21.8	117.8	117.0	96.2	100.6	138.3

Source: UN/DESA, based on data of IMF and official national and other sources.

ᵃ Partially estimated.
ᵇ Preliminary estimate.
ᶜ Ninety-five economies. Figures may not add up owing to rounding.

Table A.23.
NET IMF LENDING TO DEVELOPING COUNTRIES, BY FACILITY, 1993-2002

Billions of dollars

	1993	1994	1995	1996	1997	1998	1999	2000	2001	2002
Regular facilities	-0.2	-0.8	12.5	-2.6	13.0	14.1	-9.8	-6.5	17.6	15.3
Repayment terms:										
3¼-5 years (credit tranche)[a]	-0.2	0.1	12.4	-1.4	13.6	11.2	-9.6	-5.8	18.5	15.2
3½-7 years (SFF/EAP)[b]	-1.5	-1.4	-1.6	-1.3	-0.7	-0.1	0.0	0.0	0.0	-0.1
4½-10 years (Extended Fund Facility (EFF))	1.5	0.5	1.8	0.1	0.2	3.1	-0.2	-0.7	-0.9	0.2
Concessional facilities	0.2	0.9	1.5	0.2	-0.1	0.2	0.1	-0.2	0.0	-0.1
Trust Fund[c]	-0.1	0.0	0.0	0.0	0.0	0.0	0.0	0.0	0.0	0.0
SAF[d]	-0.1	-0.2	-0.1	-0.4	-0.3	-0.2	-0.2	-0.1	-0.1	-0.3
ESAF/PRGF[d]	0.4	1.1	1.6	0.5	0.2	0.4	0.2	-0.1	0.1	0.2
Additional facilities[e]	-0.2	-0.9	-1.6	-0.7	-0.9	-0.7	0.7	0.0	0.0	-0.3
Compensatory financing[f]	-0.2	-0.9	-1.6	-0.7	-0.9	-0.7	0.7	0.0	0.0	-0.3
STF[f]	0.0	0.0	0.0	0.0	0.0	0.0	0.0	0.0	0.0	0.0
Total	-0.2	-0.7	12.5	-3.1	12.0	13.7	-9.0	-6.7	17.6	15.0
Memo items:										
Selected characteristics of lending agreements										
Number initiated during year	13	26	18	20	14	15	16	18	12	15
Average length (months)	24	25	23	29	33	29	32	28	22	29
Total amount committed ($bn)	3.0	6.6	23.2	5.2	38.4	29.5	13.0	22.1	24.2	50.8

Source: IMF, *International Financial Statistics* and *IMF Survey.*

a   Primarily standby arrangements, including Supplemental Reserve Facility (SRF) (created December 1997) for use when a sudden and disruptive loss of market confidence causes pressure on the capital account and on reserves, creating a large short-term financing need (higher-cost and shorter-term than regular drawings), and adding to commitments under standby or extended arrangements for up to one year, with drawings in two or more tranches. Also includes emergency assistance for natural disasters and, since 1995, for post-conflict situations.

b   Supplementary Financing Facility (SFF) (1979-1981) and Enhanced Access Policy (EAP) (1981-1992) provided resources from funds borrowed by IMF from member States on which the Fund paid a higher interest rate than the remuneration paid to countries that had a net-creditor position with the Fund. Thus, users of SFF and EAP resources paid a higher interest rate than on drawings from ordinary resources, which are at below-market interest rates. (However, interest payments under SFF were partly subsidized for countries eligible to borrow from the World Bank's International Development Association (IDA); there was no subsidy on EAP drawings).

c   Mainly using resources from IMF gold sales, the Trust Fund lent during 1977-1981 under 1-year adjustment programmes; eligibility was based on maximum per capita income criteria; loans had 10-year maturities, with repayments beginning in the sixth year; the interest rate was 0.5 per cent per year.

d   Structural Adjustment Facility (SAF) and Enhanced Structural Adjustment Facility (ESAF) (the first financed mainly from Trust Fund reflows and the second from loans and grants) made loans to IDA-eligible countries with protracted balance-of-payments problems; funds were disbursed over 3 years (under Policy Framework Paper arrangements), with repayments beginning in 5.5 years and ending in 10 years; the interest rate was 0.5 per cent. On 22 November 1999, the facility was renamed the Poverty Reduction and Growth Facility (PRGF) and now supports policy reforms contained in Poverty Reduction Strategy Papers (PRSPs).

e   Compensatory Financing Facility (CFF) from 1963 to 1988; Compensatory and Contingency Financing Facility (CCFF) from August 1988; CFF again from February 2000 (same terms as credit tranche).

f   See description in table A.24 below.

Table A.24.

NET IMF LENDING TO ECONOMIES IN TRANSITION , BY FACILITY, 1993-2002

Billions of dollars	1993	1994	1995	1996	1997	1998	1999	2000	2001	2002
Regular facilities	0.1	0.2	4.4	3.7	2.1	3.0	-3.0	-3.1	-0.7	-0.9
Repayment terms:										
3¼-5 years (credit tranche)	0.1	0.5	4.9	1.2	0.0	-0.8	-3.1	-3.2	-0.6	-0.1
3½-7 years (SFF/EAP)	0.0	-0.3	0.0	0.0	0.0	0.0	0.0	0.0	0.0	0.0
4½-10 years (Extended Fund Facility) (EFF)	0.0	0.0	-0.5	2.6	2.2	3.9	0.1	0.2	0.0	-0.8
Concessional facilities (ESAF)	0.0	0.0	0.1	0.2	0.2	0.2	0.1	0.1	0.1	0.0
Additional facilities										
Compensatory financing	0.0	-0.7	-0.6	-0.2	0.1	2.9	0.1	0.0	-2.8	-0.1
STF[a]	2.0	2.8	0.9	0.0	0.0	-0.5	-0.8	-1.1	-0.8	-1.0
Total	2.1	2.3	4.8	3.7	2.4	5.6	-3.6	-4.1	-4.1	-1.8
Memo items:										
Selected characteristics of lending agreements										
Number initiated during year	9	8	12	12	7	6	4	5	9	5
Average length (months)	18	18	13	28	21	32	19	28	25	27
Total amount committed ($bn)	1.6	2.1	9.2	13.2	2.1	3.4	5.6	0.3	1.5	1.4

Source: IMF, *International Financial Statistics.*

a   The Systemic Transformation Facility (STF), created in April 1993 and closed to new drawings in December 1995, assisted economies in transition with severe balance-of-payments problems arising from discontinuance of former trade arrangements. For members that had not yet had a standby arrangement, drawings could be made in two tranches in support of a written statement of policy reform intentions, the second 6-18 months after the first, assuming satisfactory progress towards an upper credit tranche arrangement (repayment terms were the same as for the Extended Fund Facility (EFF)). See table A.23 above for description of other facilities.

Table A.25.
NET ODA FROM MAJOR SOURCES, BY TYPE, 1982-2001

Donor group or country	Growth rate of ODA[a] (2000 prices and exchange rates)		ODA as percentage of GNP	Total ODA (millions of dollars)	Percentage distribution of ODA by type, 2001					
					Bilateral			Multilateral		
	1982-1991	1992-2001	2001	2001	Grants[b]	Technical cooperation	Loans	United Nations	IDA	Other
Total DAC countries	2.84	-0.50	0.22	52 336	63.8	26.0	3.1	10.0	6.8	16.3
Total EU	3.34	-0.33	0.33	26 290	61.7	19.9	-1.8	8.8	6.4	24.9
Austria	3.03	1.03	0.29	533	62.7	16.7	1.3	3.4	4.7	27.8
Belgium	0.04	0.56	0.37	867	58.5	24.7	..	4.2	5.7	32.3
Denmark	4.49	3.81	1.03	1 634	64.1	8.4	-0.9	16.6	3.1	17.1
Finland	14.17	-5.16	0.32	389	58.9	18.3	-1.0	17.2	8.0	17.2
France[c]	5.04	-4.34	0.32	4 198	69.6	31.8	-7.7	2.6	5.5	30.0
Germany	1.85	-1.85	0.27	4 990	57.3	31.8	-0.1	9.2	7.0	26.6
Greece	..	..	0.17	202	40.1	7.9	0.5	3.0	2.5	53.5
Ireland	3.08	14.83	0.33	287	64.1	..	..	8.7	2.8	24.0
Italy	8.99	-5.88	0.15	1 627	33.6	5.7	-6.4	11.2	14.8	46.9
Luxembourg	16.41	15.31	0.82	141	75.2	3.5	..	5.7	2.8	16.3
Netherlands	1.03	2.77	0.82	3 172	75.4	20.0	-5.3	14.3	3.6	12.0
Portugal	..	3.63	0.25	268	118.1	33.2	-52.0	3.0	0.0	28.7
Spain	..	4.73	0.30	1 737	50.5	9.0	9.8	2.9	5.6	25.3
Sweden	3.21	1.16	0.81	1 666	67.9	3.9	1.1	16.4	0.0	11.3
United Kingdom	-0.34	3.51	0.32	4 579	56.9	15.2	3.2	7.6	10.2	25.0
Australia	1.02	1.08	0.25	873	75.6	45.9	..	5.8	7.6	10.9
Canada	3.29	-3.17	0.22	1 533	79.7	22.6	-1.4	8.1	0.0	13.6
Japan	4.66	-0.37	0.23	9 847	48.2	19.7	27.6	8.6	8.8	6.9
New Zealand	-0.77	2.74	0.25	112	75.9	36.6	..	8.9	3.6	11.6
Norway	5.60	0.86	0.83	1 346	73.2	8.6	0.7	18.2	5.9	6.0
Switzerland	5.92	1.52	0.34	908	68.3	11.2	2.2	9.0	9.1	10.8
United States	1.68	-2.61	0.11	11 429	81.3	43.4	-6.9	13.7	6.8	7.1
Arab countries[d]										
Saudi Arabia	..	..	..	490	———	80.6	———	———	19.4	———
Kuwait	..	..	..	73	———	100.0	———	———	0.0	———
Other developing economies[d]										
Korea, Republic of	..	..	..	265	———	64.9	———	———	35.1	———
Taiwan Province of China			..	..	———	..	———	———	100.0	———

Source: UN/DESA, based on OECD, *Development Co-operation: 2002 Report* (Paris, 2003).

a   Average annual rates of growth, calculated from average levels in 1980-1981, 1990-1991 and 2000-2001.
b   Including technical cooperation.
c   Excluding flows from France to the Overseas Departments, namely, Guadeloupe, French Guiana, Martinique and Réunion.
d   Bilateral ODA includes all grants and loans; multilateral ODA includes United Nations, IDA and "other", including technical cooperation.

Table A.26.
REGGIONAL DISTRIBUTION OF ODA FROM MAJOR SOURCES, 1990-2001

Millions of dollars, two-year average										
	All developing countries		of which:							
			Latin America		Africa		Western Asia		Eastern and Southern Asia[a]	
Donor group or country	1990-1991	2000-2001	1990-1991	2000-2001	1990-1991	2000-2001	1990-1991	2000-2001	1990-1991	2000-2001
Total ODA[b] (net)	59 819.4	51 004.4	5 614.7	5 471.3	25 307.5	16 020.4	5 642.8	1 777.6	15 117.6	15 429.7
DAC countries										
Bilateral	40 967.1	35 538.6	4 522.5	4 148.4	16 322.5	10 190.2	3 604.8	9 15.9	9 985.0	10 631.8
Australia	738.7	709.2	0.6	0.7	71.9	36.1	2.3	0.2	616.8	590.3
Austria	367.7	299.2	19.5	46.4	84.5	78.4	52.1	16.1	151.3	63.6
Belgium	521.3	490.1	40.6	41.9	293.5	231.7	8.0	0.4	41.5	61.0
Canada	1 731.1	1 179.8	179.9	124.8	511.9	217.4	27.9	6.9	369.1	190.6
Denmark	690.7	1 029.0	30.9	76.3	329.6	441.0	12.9	4.3	139.3	210.9
Finland	541.7	220.7	35.5	15.5	281.0	72.9	16.7	4.6	110.5	54.1
France[c]	5 691.9	2 712.3	258.8	110.6	3 662.6	1 670.7	144.0	74.9	1 092.6	281.7
Germany	4 592.9	2 772.9	525.4	340.2	1 752.8	848.9	746.8	232.1	920.3	622.0
Greece	0.0	90.7	0.0	0.4	0.0	2.8	0.0	3.5	0.0	6.5
Ireland	26.3	169.6	0.2	6.2	17.4	114.7	0.8	0.5	0.5	11.8
Italy	2 178.5	409.5	406.6	-5.8	1 108.8	218.7	56.4	6.2	93.0	22.9
Japan	7 823.4	8 613.0	704.1	768.9	1 354.0	1 158.4	756.0	216.3	4 070.1	5 006.2
Luxembourg	20.3	102.2	2.6	15.8	10.0	44.6	1.2	0.6	5.0	18.8
Netherlands	1 794.4	2 233.6	315.6	206.2	581.5	727.1	50.4	48.4	486.8	414.6
New Zealand	81.2	84.8	0.4	2.3	1.1	5.2	0.0	0.1	58.5	74.4
Norway	744.9	937.1	64.9	73.3	412.7	331.6	4.8	27.2	150.0	196.8
Portugal	130.8	181.0	0.0	1.3	129.0	112.2	0.0	0.0	0.0	56.8
Spain	697.1	934.9	243.7	506.6	231.3	125.4	4.5	22.7	135.5	110.9
Sweden	1 427.5	1 223.2	134.7	152.1	740.5	375.2	31.1	11.7	252.4	233.9
Switzerland	638.9	636.0	78.7	63.0	269.7	158.5	16.5	12.5	146.8	126.8
United Kingdom	1 646.4	2 665.6	110.1	193.4	679.2	1 177.7	52.1	28.8	434.3	586.0
United States	8 881.5	7 844.4	1 370.0	1 408.3	3 799.5	2 041.0	1 620.5	189.5	710.5	1 699.7
Multilateral	14 598.5	14 619.6	1 071.1	1 275.3	6 844.2	5 541.4	576.7	639.3	4 974.3	4 406.9
Total DAC	55 565.6	50 158.3	5 593.6	5 423.6	23 166.7	15 731.5	4 181.5	1 555.2	14 959.3	15 038.6
Arab countries										
Bilateral[d]	652.9	519.0	..	..	..	..	..	..	..	..
Multilateral	113.9	131.0	..	..	..	..	..	..	..	..

Source: UN/DESA, with calculations based on OECD, *Geographical Distribution of Financial Flows to Aid Recipients.*

[a]   Including Central Asian transition economies.

[b]   Excluding assistance provided by centrally planned and transition economies, owing to measurement difficulties. Donor total includes amounts to certain European countries and unallocated amounts and hence is larger than the sum of the amounts per region.

[c]   Excluding flows from France to the Overseas Departments, namely, Guadeloupe, French Guiana, Martinique and Réunion.

[d]   Approximately 35-40 per cent of Arab bilateral aid being geographically unallocated.

Table A.27.

RESOURCE COMMITMENTS OF MULTILATERAL DEVELOPMENT INSTITUTIONS,[a] 1994-2002

Millions of dollars

	1994	1995	1996	1997	1998	1999	2000	2001	2002
Financial institutions	40 656	43 516	44 701	45 760	57 928	42 770	36 882	41 787	38 523
African Development Bank	1 655	802	823	1 880	1 742	1 765	1 984	2 373	2 039
Asian Development Bank	3 864	5 759	5 878	9 648	6 208	5 158	5 830	5 513	5 700
Caribbean Development Bank	56	110	99	54	122	153	184	120	129
European Bank for Reconstruction and Development	2 232	2 616	2 774	2 625	2 658	2 784	2 901	3 276	4 130
Inter-American Development Bank	5 298	7 454	6 951	6 224	10 403	9 577	5 336	8 067	4 753
Inter-American Investment Corporation	43	36	72	67	223	190	143	128	123
International Fund for Agricultural Development	364	414	447	430	443	434	409	434	390
World Bank Group	27 187	26 361	27 729	24 899	36 352	22 899	20 238	22 004	21 382
International Bank for Reconstruction and Development	16 427	15 950	15 325	15 098	24 687	13 789	10 699	11 709	10 176
International Development Association	7 282	5 973	6 490	5 345	7 325	5 691	5 861	6 859	8 040
International Finance Corporation	3 478	4 438	5 914	4 456	4 340	3 419	3 678	3 436	3 166
Operational agencies of the United Nations system	3 537	3 931	3 726	3 453	4 290	4 198	3 803	4 690	4 569
United Nations Development Programme[b]	1 036	1 014	1 231	1 529	1 764	1 632	1 458	1 526	1 493
United Nations Population Fund	278	340	285	322	326	245	171	236	296
United Nations Children's Fund	810	1 481	1 133	521	962	891	1 016	1 152	1 188
World Food Programme	1 413	1 096	1 077	1 081	1 238	1 430	1 158	1 776	1 592
Total commitments	44 193	47 447	48 427	49 213	62 218	46 968	40 685	46 477	43 092
Memo item:									
Commitments in units of 1990 purchasing power[c]	44 639	43 134	45 686	49 710	65 493	51 613	46 764	55 330	50 107

Sources: Annual reports and information supplied by individual institutions.

[a] Loans, grants, technical assistance and equity participation, as appropriate; all data are on a calendar-year basis.
[b] Including United Nations Development Programme (UNDP)-administered funds.
[c] Total commitments deflated by the United Nations index of manufactured export prices in dollars of developed economies: 1990=100.

Litho in United Nations, New York
39966—August 2003—4,870
ISBN 92-1-109143-8

United Nations publication
Sales No. E.03.II.C.1
E/2003/70/Rev.1
ST/ESA/283